BERLIN
POTSDAM

www.marco-polo.com

Sightseeing Highlights

There is more to Berlin than the old glories of Prussia and the sorry tale of the Wall. Although these two aspects are inseparable from the city, many other sights await discovery. Here is a summary of what you should not miss.

❶ ✷✷ Brandenburg Gate • Pariser Platz
The emblem of the city on a recreated showcase square
page 168

❷ ✷✷ Charlottenburg Palace and Park
Testimony to the Prussian kings' desire to build beautiful palaces
page 180

❸ ✷✷ Dahlem Museums
All the peoples of the world, assembled in a single place
page 186

❹ ✷✷ Gemäldegalerie
The picture gallery at Kemperplatz has old masters – eight works by Dürer and the »Man with the Golden Helmet« – even if it was not painted by Rembrandt
page 228

❺ ✷✷ Berlin Wall Memorial
Nowhere else is the absurdity of the Wall so tangible
page 201

❻ ✷✷ Gendarmenmarkt
The loveliest square in the city, with the Deutscher Dom, Französischer Dom and theatre
page 208

❼ ✷✷ Kunstgewerbemuseum
Germany's oldest museum of arts and crafts, in two locations
pages 166 and 231

⑫ ✷✷ Potsdamer Platz
Berlin's new centre, with exciting architecture, a film museum, shopping and dining **page 284**

⑧ ✷✷ Neues Museum
Nefertiti is back in her old place in this wonderfully restored museum **page 258**

⑨ ✷✷ Alte Nationalgalerie
Exquisite German painting **page 260**

⑩ ✷✷ Pergamonmuseum
Three collections under one roof, with the Pergamon Altar (unfortunately closed for years!) and the Ishtar Gate as unique highlights **page 260**

⑪ ✷✷ Parliament and Government Quarter
New architecture is combined with the old Reichstag in the district from which Germany is governed **page 273**

⑬ ✷✷ Unter den Linden
Berlin's fine boulevard is lined with buildings celebrating the glory of the Prussian kings **page 329**

⑭ ✷✷ Zoo
Berlin's oldest zoo – in the middle of the city **page 341**

Do You Feel Like ...

... seeing works by the greatest Prussian architect, exploring Jewish heritage or modern art, learning about technology or Berlin in films? Explore the city according to your own personal interests.

KARL FRIEDRICH SCHINKEL

- **Neuer Pavillon**
  Exhibition, including designs for cast-iron structures and furniture
  page 183
- **Schinkel's Tomb**
  In the Dorotheenstädtischer Friedhof
  page 172
- **Altes Museum**   ▶
  His masterpiece
  page 255
- **Neue Wache**
  His first work in Berlin
  page 333

JEWISH BERLIN

- **Monument to the Murdered European Jews**
  In memory of the victims of the Holocaust
  page 171
- **Weissensee Cemetery**
  The biggest Jewish cemetery in Europe
  page 179
- **Jewish Museum**
  A living centre of Jewish history
  page 218
◀ **New Synagogue**
  Once the largest synagogue in Germany
  page 303

MODERN ART

- **Boros Collection**
  Art in a Bunker
  page 47
- ◄ **Street art**
  The whole city is a gallery
  page 112
- **Hamburger Bahnhof and Neue Nationalgalerie**
  Leading addresses for modern art
  pages 217 and 234

TECHNOLOGY

- **GDR Motorbike Museum**
  Long-gone brands from East Germany
  page 127
- **Deutsches Technikmuseum**
  El Dorado for the curious
  page 188
- **Luftwaffenmuseum** ►
  More than 100 military aircraft from around the world
  page 298

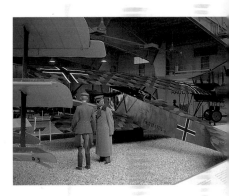

FILM LOCATIONS

- **Karl-Marx-Allee**
  The East German apartment in »Goodbye Lenin« **page 194**
- ◄ **Stasimuseum**
  HQ of the East German secret police in »The Lives of Others« (2006).
  page 242
- **Bohemian village in Neukölln**
  The house where Oskar Matzerath was born in »The Tin Drum« stood in Uthmannstrasse **page 265**
- **Siegessäule**
  Where angels landed in »Wings of Desire« (1987) **page 311**

BACKGROUND

12 Facts
13 Population · Politics · Economy
16 ■ *Facts and Figures*
18 *Welcome to Everyday Life!*

22 History of the City
32 ■ *Special: No-one Intends to Build a Wall ...*

40 Art and Culture
41 Art History
47 Cultural Life in Berlin

50 Famous People

ENJOY BERLIN

64 Accommodation
65 Something for Every Taste

PRICE CATEGORIES
Restaurants
(main dish without drinks)
€€€€	more than €35
€€€	€25 – €35
€€	€15 – €25
€	up to €15

Hotels
(double room with breakfast)
€€€€	more than €300
€€€	€200 – €300
€€	€120 – €200
€	up to €120

Note
Billable service telephone numbers are marked with an asterisk: *0180…

72 Children in Berlin
76 No Reason to be Bored

76 Entertainment
77 Going out in Berlin

88 Festivals and Events
89 Highlights of the Year

92 Food and Drink
93 Pork Knuckle, Curry Sausage and ...?
96 ■ *Special: Registered Trade Mark 721 319*
98 ■ *Typical Berlin Dishes*

116 Museums and Galleries
117 Berlin, Museum Capital
120 ■ *Special: All of Berlin is an Open-Air Gallery*

132 Shopping
133 Almost as Good as London
130 ■ *Special: Fashion made in Berlin*

140 Tours and Guides
141 Explore Berlin
142 ■ *Special:Themes are in Demand*

TOURS

146 Getting Around in Berlin
146 Tour 1: What a History!
150 Tour 2: All kinds of art
152 Tour 3: The Old West
153 Tour 4: A Park, Art and Politics
156 Tour 5: Dark Ways
158 Contrasts

BERLIN FROM A TO Z

162 Alexanderplatz
163 Alliierten-Museum
164 Alt-Köpenick
166 Berliner Dom
168 Brandenburger Tor ·
     Pariser Platz
172 Cemeteries
180 Schloss Charlottenburg
     and Park
184 Dahlem
188 Deutsches Technikmuseum
189 Exhibition Grounds
190 Fernsehturm
191 Friedrichshain
192 🔲 *Infographic: Berlin from
     Above and Below*
196 Friedrichstrasse
201 Gedenkstätte Berliner
     Mauer

202 🔲 *Infographic: The Wall
     Has Gone!*
204 🔲 *3D: A Perfidious
     Construction*
206 Gedenkstätte Deutscher
     Widerstand
207 Gedenkstätte Plötzensee
208 Gendarmenmarkt
211 Schloss Glienicke and Park
214 Grunewald
217 Hamburger Bahnhof ·
     Museum für Gegenwart
218 Jüdisches Museum
220 KaDeWe
220 Kreuzberg
222 🔲 *Infographic: Multi-
     cultural Berlin*
227 Kulturforum
235 Kurfürstendamm
240 Leipziger Strasse
242 Lichtenberg
243 Marienkirche

An old structure where a cool scene meets: the Oberbaumbrücke

244   Märkisches Ufer ·
      Märkisches Museum
247   Marzahn
249   Müggelsee
251   Museum Berggruen
252   Museum für Naturkunde
254   Museumsinsel
256   ◪ *3D: A Home for Art and
      Antiquities*
264   Neukölln
266   Nikolaiviertel
271   Olympiagelände
273   Parlaments- und
      Regierungsviertel
276   ◪ *Infographic: More
      Deputies = More
      Democracy?*
278   ◪ *3D: Seat of German
      Parliaments*
282   Pfaueninsel
284   Potsdamer Platz
289   Prenzlauer Berg
292   Rathäuser
294   Schlossplatz
297   Schloss Schönhausen
297   Spandau
301   Spandauer Vorstadt ·
      Scheunenviertel
307   Tegel
308   Tempelhof
310   Tiergarten
312   ◪ *Infographic: Green
      Berlin*
316   Tierpark Friedrichsfelde
317   ◪ *Special: More Bold Than
      Diplomatic*
322   Topography of Terror
323   ◪ *Special: A Stage for
      German History*
327   Treptower Park
329   Unter den Linden
339   Wannsee
341   Zoologischer Garten

POTSDAM FROM A TO Z

347   City Centre
354   Neuer Garten
355   Sanssouci
360   ◪ *3D: Sanssouci Park
      and Palace*
364   Suburbs

PRACTICAL INFORMATION

370   Arrival · Before the Journey
373   Electricity
373   Emergency
374   Etiquette and Customs
375   Health
375   Information
377   Language
384   Literature
386   Lost Property
386   Media
387   Money
388   Post and Communications
388   Prices and Discounts
389   Time
389   Transport
392   Travellers with Disabilities
393   Weights and Measures
393   When to Go

394   Index
402   List of Maps and
      Illustrations
403   Photo Credits
404   Publisher's Information
406   ◪ *Berlin Curiosities*

The magnificent Baroque
architecture of the Zeughaus

BACKGROUND

Everything you need to know about Berlin: its economy, its architecture, its history and its people

Population · Politics · Economy

Capital city and seat of government, more multicultural than any other German city, still with traces of East and West in people's habits of mnd, a magnet for party people from all over Europe – Berlin truly has many faces.

Berlin and the march of Brandenburg (Mark Brandenburg) were colonized in the 13th century by people from the lowlands around the Harz mountains and from the Lower Rhine. At the end of the Middle Ages it is estimated that there were 6000 people living in the town. The demographic structure was greatly influenced by the arrival of some 20,000 **Huguenot** refugees from France, who came to Brandenburg after the Edict of Potsdam (1685). About 6000 of these »Réfugiés« were settled in Berlin itself and made up around a third of the population at the time. With the expansion of industry after 1800, more and more people flooded into the city. The influx increased even more after Berlin was declared the capital of the German Empire in 1871. By 1943 the population had peaked at around 4.3 million people. Political developments after the Second World War, economic troubles and the building of the Berlin Wall in 1961 all led to a complete upheaval of the demographic and the flow of people. Although the return of evacuees and the arrival of refugees from East Germany initially led to the population of West Berlin steadily rising until 1957, all such growth was dramatically arrested after 13 August 1961. In East Berlin numbers had declined continuously until then, due to defectors fleeing to the West. After 1961, though, the population increased slowly but steadily. Since the fall of the Wall more than 1.3 million Berliners have left the city but this exodus has been more than compensated by a simultaneous influx of newcomers. More than 466,000 Berliners are from immigrant families (▶MARCO POLO Insight p. 222)..

Immigrants

CAPITAL, FEDERAL STATE, COMMUNITY

A vote in the German parliament, the Bundestag, on 20 June 1991 established Berlin as the seat of government and parliament in the new united Germany. However, it was not until eight years later that the government and the Bundestag itself departed Bonn. Only then could Berlin start to regard itself once again as a fully fledged capital

Seat of government and parliament

The restrained architecture of this parliament building is not intended to suggest aloofness from citizens: the Paul-Löbe-Bau on the Spreeufer

city. To minimize the consequences to the former West German capital of Bonn, each of the national ministries has a primary and a secondary headquarters, one in each of the two cities. Most of the primary headquarters, though, are on the Spree rather than the Rhine (►MARCO POLO Insight p.276).

Berlin state The metropolitan district of Berlin also makes up one of Germany's federal states in its own right. The government of the city and of the eponymous state is a senate voted by the elected councillors of the Abgeordetenhaus (House of Representatives) and led by a mayor whose rank is equivalent to that of a prime minister of a state of the federation. This model is the same as that employed in West Berlin from 1950 to 1990. The traditional model involving a municipal government led by a mayor had been retained in East Berlin until that time. The Berlin state legislature, the House of Representatives, is elected every four years and meets in the former Prussian parliament building.

Districts At the end of 2000/start of 2001 the number of boroughs (»Bezirke«) in Berlin was reduced from 23 to 12. These districts are administered by borough officials led by a local mayor. Two of the newly formed districts (Friedrichshain-Kreuzberg and Mitte = Mitte / Tiergarten / Wedding) cross the former east/west boundaries.

THE SHIFT FROM INDUSTRY TO SERVICES

Great indust- Before the Second World War, Berlin was one of the major centres of
rial tradition the German economy. It was home to the country's most important banks, insurers and syndicates. Companies like Borsig, Siemens & Halske and AEG (Allgemeine Elektrizitätsgesellschaft) also gave Berlin its reputation as Germany's most important centre of industry. After the end of the war, the economy suffered due to the destruction wrought by war, the dismantling of industrial concerns by the Soviets and the blockade of the city: Berlin lost 77% of its pre-war industrial capacity. Nevertheless both sectors of the city developed, in spite of their contrasting economic policies, into important centres of trade and industry. In spite of its forced isolation, West Berlin became one of the key industrial contributors to the economy of the German Federal Republic. East Berlin took on a similar role in the east and grew to become its primary economic and planning nexus as well as the most important industrial base of the German Democratic Republic.

The merging After the collapse of the Wall, the head-on collision of two such ut-
of the terly polarized economic systems caused serious problems. Most of
economies the factories in the eastern sector were totally out of date and there

A meeting of cultures in Kreuzberg

was practically no chance that their products would find a market. Many of them were forced to close or to drastically cut staff levels. In the west too, however, the sudden combination of two economic regions had negative effects. The loss of subsidies that had been supporting the isolated city meant that many of its businesses were no longer profitable either. Many companies relocated their business to other regions, especially to parts of the former East Germany but sometimes to what had been East Berlin. The city's status as federal capital, though, meant that many large companies decided to move their headquarters to the new united Berlin. These included Deutsche Bahn AG, Coca Cola, IBM, Daimler-debis and the European arm of Sony.

Over 800 industrial enterprises are based in Berlin. The city's leading sector is the electrical industry (the former AEG, Siemens, DeTeWe, Bosch, Osram), followed by mechanical engineering (Rotaprint, ABB, Otis) and motor vehicles (BMW motorcycles, Mercedes Benz, Ford). Further important branches are the paper and printing industry, including the Axel-Springer Verlag, textiles, food (bakeries) and tobacco (Philip Morris). The chemical industry primarily produces consumer goods (Bayer Pharma, Gillette).

Industry

Commerce and service companies have become the driving force behind the Berlin economy. The areas of software, telecommunications, media, music and film are the main engines of growth and there are more than 8000 companies active in these fields. The International Congress Centre (ICC) with its accompanying exhibition and convention grounds has made Berlin an outstanding location for

Commerce and services

Location
North German Plain
**Altitude 31–115m/100–380ft
above sea level**
Founded in the 13th century
at the crossing of major
trade routes on the Spree

**Area
892 sq km/344 sq mi**
Length: 38 km/24mi
Breadth: 45 km/28mi

Population: **3.48 Mio.**
By comparison:
Paris: 2.1 Mio.
London: 7.83 Mio.
New York: 8.1 Mio.

Population density:
**3880 inhabitants per sq km/
10,060 per sq mi**

13° 25' east

▶ 12 districts

52°
nor

Reinickendorf · Pankow · Lichten-berg
Spandau · Mitte · Marzahn Hellersdorf
Charlottenburg Wilmersdorf · Tempelhof-Schöne-berg · **Friedrichshain-Kreuzberg**
Steglitz Zehlendorf · Neukölln · Treptow Köpenick

©BAEDEKER

▶ **Political status**

State of the Federal Republic
Head of state: Ruling Mayor

▶ **Population growth**

from 2001 to 2013

3.5 million
3.4
3.3

▶ **Districts**

Most populous:
Pankow with **373,000** residents
Most densely populated:
Friedrichshain-Kreuzberg
with **12,500** per sq km/
32,400 per sq mi
Berliners from **immigrant
families: 14.1 %**

▶ **Tourism**

11.32 million visitors in 2013
(1st place in Germany, 3rd in Europe)

Overnight stays from 2009 to 2013

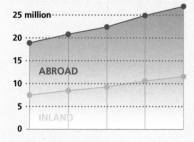

25 million
20
15
ABROAD
10
5
INLAND
0

▶ **Transport**

Air passengers (2013): 26 million
15 S-Bahn (local train) lines,
length 331.5km/206mi
10 U-Bahn (subway) lines,
length 146.2km/90.8mi
23 tram lines, length 189.4km/117.6mi
130 bus lines
6 ferries
1.28 million vehicles
77km/48mi of autobahn in the city

▶ Economy

Gross domestic product 2013:
109.2 billion €

Employment

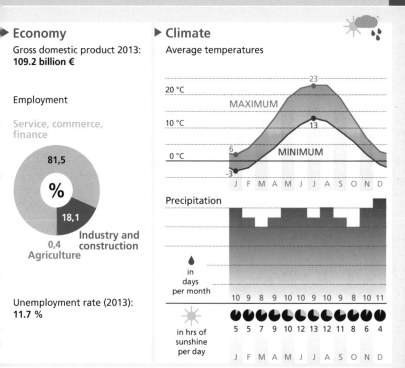

Service, commerce,
finance

81,5

%

18,1

Industry and
construction

0,4
Agriculture

Unemployment rate (2013):
11.7 %

▶ Climate

Average temperatures

MAXIMUM

20 °C

10 °C

0 °C

23

13

6

-3

MINIMUM

J F M A M J J A S O N D

Precipitation

in
days
per month

10 9 8 8 10 10 9 10 9 8 10 11

in hrs of
sunshine
per day

5 5 7 9 10 12 13 12 11 8 6 4

J F M A M J J A S O N D

▶ West Berlin under observation

In December 1988, 399 West Berliners were spying for the Stasi (East German secret police). The Stasi intelligence headquarters was thus running the densest network of unofficial employees (IMs) and contact persons (KPs) in the Federal Republic, including:

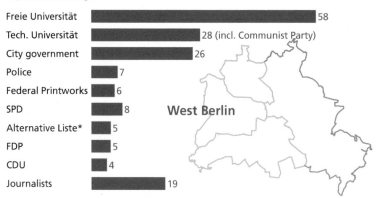

Freie Universität	58
Tech. Universität	28 (incl. Communist Party)
City government	26
Police	7
Federal Printworks	6
SPD	8
Alternative Liste*	5
FDP	5
CDU	4
Journalists	19

West Berlin

* Predecessor of Green Party/Source: Rosenholz-Dateien

Welcome to Everyday Life

Get to know Berlin off the tourist track and meet some »completely normal« people. Here are a few tips:

THEATRE CANTEEN

It is a long time since the dramatist and director Heiner Müller smoked his daily cigar here, but guests who come for down-to-earth food, a salad, Italian coffee or cake in the canteen of the Berliner Ensemble theatre might recognize someone at a neighbouring table from the stage yesterday or a recent TV production. Huge photos of BE performance decorate the walls, and some shots show what it looks like behind the scenes. In summer there is a beer garden.

Mitte, Bertolt-Brecht-Platz 1
Canteen through the courtyard
Mon–Sat 9am–midnight,
Sun 4pm–midnight

A TOUR WITH LOCALS

At the place where Prenzlauer Berg, now an upscale district, meets the problem-ridden area called Wedding, you can explore a part of Berlin on foot or bicycle with local people to guide you. The tours go in search of »God in Wedding«, for example, visiting churches, mosques, temples and other places of worship, or visit small shops under the heading »Frau Goldfisch and her shop«.

www.ausfahrtwedding.de

A SUCCESSFUL PROJECT

The wasteland on the roundabout now produces flowers, radishes, potatoes, carrots and herbs. This exemplary urban gardening project is known as the »Prinzessinnengarten«. The founding princesses are a film maker and a historian, who welcome every helping hand.

Moritzplatz, exit to Oranienstrasse/
Prinzessinnenstrasse
www.prinzessinnengarten.net

FARMYARD FOR CHILDREN

In the presence of trained supervisors at the Pinke-Panke farmyard, children can help feed the animals, do gardening work, play football and table tennis, listen to stories ...

Pankow, Am Bürgerpark 15–18, S-Bahn Wollankstrasse

April–Oct Tue–Fri 12 noon–6.30pm; Sat, Sun, holidays 10am–6.30pm; Nov–March Tue–Fri 12 noon–5.30pm, Sat, Sun, holidays 10am–5.30pm

ROUTE 44

Guided tours to a typical Berlin area start at Richardplatz, where genuine residents of Neukölln – women and girls from immigrant families – show their multicultural district as few know it.

www.route44-neukoelln.de

ROUTE 1

What are Berliners like? A trip on U-Bahn (subway) line 1 from Warschauer Strasse in Friedrichshain to Wittenbergplatz in Wilmersdorf shows you in 18 minutes. At first the colourful mix of passengers is mainly young, then clearly more international at Kottbusser Tor, where Turkish kids speak their urban dialect, and from Hallesches Tor the passengers are older and better-off.

congresses and trade fairs. The most important events include the International Radio Exhibition (Internationale Funkausstellung; IFA), the International Tourism Exchange (Internationale Tourismusbörse, ITB), the International Agricultural Products Exhibition (Grüne Woche) and the International Aerospace Exhibition (Internationale Luft- und Raumfahrt-Ausstellung, Berlin-Brandenburg; ILA).

Tourism   Berlin is **Germany's leading destination for city breaks**. 782 hotels and other sites make 125,400 beds available for visitors and accommodated 21 million overnight stays in 2011. 40% of the tourists come from abroad, mainly from the United Kingdom, Italy, the Netherlands and Spain. Budget flights have brought the city its very own tourist boom the so-called **Easyjetset**, mostly young or very young, who come in their thousands every weekend. From Thursday to Sunday they hang out in the techno scene at about half a dozen clubs between Alexanderplatz, Oberbaumbrücke and Ostbahnhof. They have created a subculture that is remarkable in terms of numbers but is hardly noticed by normal Berliners but contributes to Berlin's reputation as the cheap, hip party capital of Europe.

Six S-Bahn (local train) lines pass through Friedrichstrasse station

Before the war Berlin was a transport hub to equal any in Europe. In   Transport
terms of rail traffic in particular, it was a hub between western and
eastern Europe with 500 trains a day entering its stations. After the
war the city lost some of that earlier importance. Only very few land
routes, road or rail, were left open for
traffic to West Berlin and only companies of the western allies offered
flights to the city. After the Wall was
built, East Berlin was initially closed
entirely to westerners and only became accessible to those with passes
to visit relatives, then later by means
of a one-day visa. Access to the non-
urban areas surrounding the city always required a visa. Berlin has its
own circular motorway ring road,
the »**Berliner Ring**«. Motorways
within the inner city include the

> ? | MARCO ◉ POLO INSIGHT
>
> **»Built out of the barge«**
>
> The material for Berlin's building
> sites, including that of the huge
> new Mediaspree district at the Os-
> tbahnhof, was and still is mainly
> transported by water. Thus the
> contours of the great pit in
> Rüdersdorf to the east of the city,
> from which material was extract-
> ed, became a »negative cast« of
> Berlin in the 800 years up to 1990.

Avus (»Automobil-Verkehrs- und Übungsstrasse«), which was
opened as early as 1921 and was the first »dual carriageway with no
crossroads, solely for motor vehicles«, i.e. the world's first motorway.
Its two parallel straights are both 8.5km/5.3mi long and lead through
the Grunewald to the Nikolassee. Nowadays it is designated the A
115. The Avus was even used for the first ever German Grand Prix in
1926. In 1937 Bernd Rosemeyer set a lap record of 276.4kmh /
171.7mph driving an Auto Union car. Rudolf Caracciola set the speed
record on the straight, reaching 400kmh / 248.5mph in his Mercedes.
It is planned that Berlin's sole airport will be the new **Berlin Brandenburg Willy Brandt Airport**, but there have been repeated delays in
opening; in the meantime, Berlin-Tegel Airport continues to operate.
With the new central station, Berlin **Hauptbahnhof**, Europe's largest
and most modern rail interchange, Berlin is seeking to regain some
of its earlier status as a key transport hub in Europe. The two previous
main stations (Bahnhof Zoo in the west, Ostbahnhof in the east) have
thus lost their importance for long-distance traffic.
Berlin is linked via the Oder-Spree canal, the Teltow canal and the
Oder-Havel canal to the **European river and canal system**. A large
proportion of the freight traffic to and from Berlin, especially for
building materials, travels via these canals using the Westhafen docks
at Wedding/Tiergarten in the west and the Osthafen docks at Friedrichshain in the east.

From Russian to German Capital

From a trading centre at a ford on the Spree to the capital of the Prussian and finally of the German state. After the defeat of Germany, the city almost faced ruin but since its forced division has been ended, Berlin has begun to sparkle once again.

GERMANS, SLAVS AND THE HOUSE OF ASCANIA

600	Migration of the West Slavs
1134	Albrecht the Bear becomes first margrave of the northern march of Brandenburg
1237	First documentary evidence of Cölln: official founding of the city, but finds made in 2008 have been dated to 1170 and 1192

At the time of the Roman empire a German tribe called the Semnoni settled alongside the Havel. Locations where villages and homesteads have been found include modern-day Buch (Pankow), Lichterfelde (Steglitz) and what is now the parkland around Schloss Bellevue. — **Germans**

In around AD 600 West Slavic tribes entered the region and founded settlements including **Spandau** and **Köpenick**. They maintained independence until 928 when King Heinrich I conquered their Brandenburg fortress. King Otto the Great established the bishoprics of Havelberg and Brandenburg in 948. — **Slavs**

Under Holy Roman Emperor Lothar I the settlements in the northeast began. In 1134 the Ascanian Albrecht the Bear became margrave of the northern march. This encouraged some Ascanian settlers to move to the shores of the Spree from their homelands in the Harz region. People also immigrated from the Rhine and Frankish territories. A trading post was established on the site of what is now Mühlendamm. This became the core of the twin settlements, Berlin and Cölln. The towns must have been granted charters in around 1230 by the margraves Johann I and Otto III. However, no documentary mention of Cölln exists until 1237 (and there is no mention of it as a town until 1251). Evidence naming the town of Berlin only exists as of 1244. Nevertheless, 1237 is usually regarded as the official date — **Ascanians**

Will the Cold War get hot? Soviet and US tanks confronting each other at Checkpoint Charlie in late October 1961

for the founding of the city. The twin towns profited from the merchants passing through and they were soon able to afford city walls and churches such as the Marienkirche (Church of St Mary) and the Nikolaikirche (Church of St Nicholas). In 1280 a mint was established that was the first in the march east of the Elbe. The two towns combined to build a joint town hall in 1307 but with the death of Margrave Waldemar, the last of the Ascanians, that period of peace and prosperity came to an end. Berlin was admitted to the Hanseatic League in 1359 but the twin towns were already caught up in a power struggle between the houses of Luxemburg and Wittelsbach for control of the march. Two major fires in 1376 and 1380 also hindered the growth of the town.

RESIDENCE OF THE ELECTORS

1415	Friedrich VI of Hohenzollern becomes elector of Brandenburg
1432	Merging of Berlin and Cölln
1447 / 1448	The Berlin Indignation
1640 – 1688	The Great Elector

Elevation to electors' residence
The struggle for power in the march finally ended when emperor Sigismund appointed the burgrave of Nuremberg, Friedrich VI of Hohenzollern, to take control of the march of Brandenburg in 1411. Friedrich won back both goods and regions that had been stolen by maverick nobles such as the brothers Johann and Dietrich von Quitzow and was rewarded with the title Elector of Brandenburg by the Council of Constance in 1415. Berlin and Cölln were formally amalgamated into a single municipality in 1432. In 1440 Friedrich's son **Friedrich II, »Eisenzahn«** (»Irontooth«), became elector. He initiated the building of a castle in Cölln in 1443 but separated the two towns and withdrew their privileges. The citizens of Cölln and Berlin rose in revolt unsuccessfully in 1447 and 1448 in a rebellion called the »Berlin Indignation«. Berlin was developed as the electors' residence with the castle at »Cölln on the Spree« becoming the permanent home of the ruler as of 1470. In 1539 **Elector Joachim II** converted to Protestantism. He invited artists to the city, and among the buildings he built was the Spandau Citadel. Upon his death, however, in 1571 the economy of the march collapsed and Berlin was plunged into serious poverty. In 1600 Berlin still had around 12,000 inhabitants but the Thirty Years' War had a particularly drastic effect on the march of Brandenburg and Berlin's suburbs dwindled.

The Great Elector
In 1640 the electorship passed to **Friedrich Wilhelm**. During his reign the suburbs of Friedrichswerder and Dorotheenstadt came into

being, Schloss Köpenick was built, the Lustgarten park was laid out and Berlin was fortified. Construction of the Oder-Spree Canal (Friedrich-Wilhelm Canal) between 1662 and 1668 meant that Berlin became a major transit port between Hamburg and Breslau (Wroclaw). In 1671 the elector authorized the establishment of a Jewish community and his Edict of Potsdam proclaimed in 1685 made it possible for Huguenots being persecuted in France to settle in the march. It is not without reason that Friedrich Wilhelm has gone down in history as »The Great Elector«. His son Friedrich III continued in the same tradition, founding the Akademie der Künste (Academy of Arts) in 1696. A corresponding academy for science was instituted in 1700 by **Gottfried Wilhelm Leibniz**.

CAPITAL OF THE KINGDOM OF PRUSSIA

1701–1713	King Friedrich I
1713–1740	King Friedrich Wilhelm I
1740–1786	King Friedrich II (Frederick the Great)
1806–1808	French occupation
1810	Founding of the Friedrich Wilhelm University
1848	March Revolution

Prussia becomes a kingdom

Friedrich's own ambitions had a quite different objective, however. In 1701 he made a proclamation in Königsberg declaring himself to be Friedrich I, the first king of Prussia. During his rule the suburb of Friedrichstadt was created and major edifices such as the Zeughaus (arsenal) and Schloss Charlottenburg were built. He also founded the Charité University in 1710. At this point Berlin had 56,000 inhabitants, 6000 of whom were French.

The Soldier King

Friedrich I's son, Friedrich Wilhelm I, the »Soldier King«, was the very opposite of his father. He had little time for grandeur. His father had left the state coffers empty and he was forced to make savings. This did not prevent him expanding the army and improving city defences, however, and money was also found for roads, commercial buildings and housing, as well as for the advancement of education. Life was strict and spartan, though, and the Lustgarten park was transformed into a parade ground.

Germany's »Capital of the Enlightenment«

During the reign of Friedrich II, known as Frederick the Great or even »Old Fritz«, Berlin developed into one of the major cities of Europe. The king managed to persuade **Voltaire**, one of the great thinkers of the age, to join his court and take his place at the head of an illustrious group of artists and philosophers. They and others such as **Friedrich Nicolai** and **Moses Mendelssohn** made Berlin into Germany's »Capital of Enlightenment«. Frederick ordered the planting of the Unter den Linden boulevard, the construction of Schloss Bellevue and a new wing for Schloss Charlottenburg. Cotton and silk manufacturing also took off, making Berlin the major textile manufacturing centre in Germany. In 1761 the Königliche Porzellan-Manufaktur (Royal Porcelain Factory) was established. By that time, though, Berlin had also seen the flip side of the monarch's politics. The city had come under bombardment from Austrian and Russian forces in 1760 in the course of the Seven Years' War and was occupied for four days. Nevertheless, in the year that Frederick the Great died, Berlin's population was as high as 150,000.

The rise of modern Berlin

Upon the death of »Old Fritz«, Prussia withdrew from European politics. But by 1800 Berlin had 200,000 inhabitants and was the third-largest city on the continent after London and Paris. It remained the spiritual centre of Prussia and it was a major centre of **German Romanticism**, as epitomized by Schlegel, Tieck, Chamisso and E.T.A. Hoffmann. Even two years of occupation by the French after Napoleon marched into the city on 27 October 1806 was unable to dent this trend. Subsequently Berlin developed into a modern city, which by the end of the 19th century was one of the greatest metropolises in the world. The Friedrich-Wilhelm University was established in 1810 by Wilhelm von Humboldt, in 1816 the Princess Charlotte, Germany's first steamship, was launched on the Spree, in 1826 the city's first gas works started supplying fuel, the Borsig machine factory opened in 1837, with the first railway line starting operation between Berlin and Potsdam in 1838 followed by the inaugural horse-drawn tram between Alexanderplatz and Potsdamer Platz in 1839. There was a wave of construction, with which the name of Karl **Friedrich Schinkel** is closely associated. This produced such buildings as the Neue Wache, the Schauspielhaus and the Altes Museum. Industrialization had its price, though, with a swathe of social problems arising from the grinding poverty of the working classes.

March Revolution 1848

Demands for free speech and freedom of the press had been growing throughout Europe, and Berlin was no exception. This meant putting an end to an oppressive law called the Karlsbad Resolution. On 18 March 1848 troops opened fire on a crowd gathered before the palace in Berlin. Prince Wilhelm of Prussia, brother of the king, was said to have given the order and was thereafter known as the »Kartätschenprinz« (prince of canister shot). The subsequent riots led to 250 deaths (»**March Martyrs**«). On 19 March the garrison abandoned the city and the king granted freedom of the press, freedom of congregation, coalition and the right to vote. Friedrich Wilhelm IV saw himself as »a romantic on the throne of Prussia« and on 21 March he delivered a proclamation to the German people, declaring that he would seek to lead Germany to the »salvation of the fatherland«. Nevertheless he refused to accept the title of emperor when it was offered to him by the parliament in Frankfurt on 3 April 1849. In 1861 the aforesaid »Kartätschenprinz« succeeded him as Wilhelm I, and a year later Otto von Bismarck was appointed prime minister of Prussia. Berlin became the capital of the North German Confederation and its seat of parliament in 1866.

At the same time, though, Berlin was just as much the centre of Germany's labour movement. The town had hosted the country's first workers' congress as early as August and September of 1848. In April 1862 **Ferdinand Lasalle** published his »programme for workers« and a general labour congress took place in 1868 that resulted in the founding of Germany's first trades unions.

Capital of the German labour movement

CAPITAL OF »DEUTSCHES REICH«

1871	18 January: proclamation of the German Empire
1878	Berlin Congress
1918	Proclamation of the republic
1919	Spartacus revolt
1920	Kapp Putsch; formation of Greater Berlin
1933	30 January: Hitler becomes chancellor
	27 February: burning of the Reichstag
1936	XI Olympic Games
1943	18 February: Goebbels declares »total war« in the Sportpalast
1945	8 May: surrender of German forces in Berlin-Karlshorst

On 18 January 1871 in the Hall of Mirrors at Versailles, a German empire (»Deutsches Reich«) was declared with the Prussian Wilhelm I as emperor or »Kaiser«. Berlin was appointed capital and imperial residence. By this time, the city had become home to some 823,000 people. Politics pushed Berlin to the forefront with the Berlin Congress of 1878 and the **Year of the Three Emperors** in 1888 when Wilhelm I's successor, Friedrich III, died after reigning for just 99 days to be followed by Wilhelm II. The **resignation of Otto von Bismarck** was soon to follow. In terms of daily life in Berlin, though, it was the technical developments that were of greater importance. In 1879 came the first electric lights and the **world's first electric railway** ran at the World's Fair in Moabit, in 1881 a telephone service was instituted and electric trams ran for the first time in Lichterfelde, with the tram system opening to the public the following year. In 1902 elevated and underground railways (Zoo – Warschauer Tor) were opened, and 1905 saw the debut of motorized buses on the city

Imperial Berlin

streets. The city grew apace. 1.9 million people were resident in Berlin by 1900. Rapid industrialization led to the building of masses of typical barrack-like houses, where working people lived in miserable conditions.

First World War and revolution

Berlin suffered no direct attacks during the First World War, but suffered the deprivations of the conflict in the form of rationing and hunger. Disillusionment with the war was widespread and finally led to revolution. On 9 November 1918, Social Democratic Party leader **Philipp Scheidemann** declared Germany a republic from the window of the Reichstag, the parliament building in Berlin. The intention was to form a socialist republic, as announced by **Karl Liebknecht** from the balcony of the imperial palace on the same day. Kaiser Wilhelm II went straight from the German headquarters at Spa in Belgium into exile in Holland. However wrangles between the government, under the leadership of the social democrats, and the communist party led to the outbreak of the Spartacus Revolt in January 1919. In Berlin, particularly around the newspaper publishing district, there was major street fighting. On 15 January **Rosa Luxemburg** and Karl Liebknecht, the leaders of the German communist party, the KPD, were murdered by soldiers of the Freikorps. No sooner was the extreme left dealt with than the right-wing also made a play. During the Kapp Putsch of March 1920, Freikorps militiamen occupied government offices in Berlin and the government itself fled to Stuttgart, but a general strike put an end to the putsch. Berlin itself underwent a boundary reform in the very year that the crisis emerged, its suburbs being divided into 20 boroughs to create a Greater Berlin area that made it the second-biggest city in Europe after London.

Perfectly turned out. Wilhelm II put his stamp on an era

During the period of the Weimar Republic, Berlin developed into an economic, political, cultural and social cynosure for all of Europe and **Germany's centre for film, theatre and news publishing**. It was a heady time for the city when names such as Erwin Piscator, Max Reinhardt, Fritz Lang, Elisabeth Bergner, Josephine Baker, Kurt Tucholsky and Bertolt Brecht all came to the fore. In 1923 Germany's first radio broadcast was made from the Vox Haus. Nevertheless, all the glamour could not obscure the political tension beneath. As the National Socialist party gained strength enough for **Joseph Goebbels** to become »Gauleiter« (regional party leader) of Berlin, conflict between left and right grew in intensity. Fights in public places and on the streets were practically daily occurrences as Berlin suffered badly from the depression that had gripped the world.

The »Golden Twenties«

On 30 January 1933 **Adolf Hitler** was appointed chancellor of the German Reich. Nazi stormtroopers celebrated with a torchlight parade through the Brandenburg Gate to the Reichskanzlei (Chancellery). In the midst of it Berlin itself became the headquarters for a reign of terror. A fire that tore through the Reichstag building on 28 February gave the Nazis the chance they needed to eliminate their opponents. By 1 April a boycott of Jewish businesses had begun. On 10 May books by left-wing, democratic and Jewish authors were burned at Opernplatz. In 1936 forced emigration of Jews was instituted. That same year the Olympic games were held in Berlin but the Nazis perverted the event to serve their own propaganda. During the event, a façade of goodwill was presented in which all traces of anti-Semitism were removed from the streets and Jewish athletes were even named in the German Olympic team, while the expulsions continued in the background. In 1937 Hitler appointed Albert Speer to the post of general inspector with the task of redesigning Berlin so that it could be transformed into a pan-Germanic capital to be named »Germania«. Clearly such a design would exclude any Jewish presence and on the night of the 9 and 10 November 1938, **Pogrom Night** (perhaps better known by the Nazis' own euphemism for the event, »Kristallnacht« or »the night of broken glass«), some 80 synagogues in Berlin were destroyed or severely damaged and more than 400 lives are thought to have been lost.

Berlin under the Nazis

When World War II broke out, Berlin had a population of 4.3 million people including 82,000 Jews (that number had been 160,000 in 1933). The city experienced its first air raid on 25 August 1940; however, such raids were minor in comparison to the first really major attack on 1 March 1943. That is when the »total war« that Goebbels had professed in a notorious speech at the Sportpalast just two weeks earlier on 18 February really hit home. On 20 July 1944 the city also saw the leading officers of a failed conspiracy to assassinate Hitler

Berlin during the Second World War

executed by firing squad in the courtyard of the army high command headquarters on Bendlerstrasse. By April 1945 the Red Army was able to start its assault on Berlin. Hitler committed suicide on 30 April and by 2 May Soviet troops occupied the city. Less than a week later on 8 May, the leaders of Germany's army, the Wehrmacht, signed an unconditional surrender in Berlin-Karlshorst. The population of Berlin at the end of the war was down to 2.8 million and just 7247 Jewish citizens had survived the persecution. 75 million cubic metres/98 million cubic yards of rubble lay in the streets and a fifth of all buildings had been irreparably destroyed, with **75% of the city centre obliterated**.

THE DIVIDED CITY

1946	Forced amalgamation of the KPD (communist party) and SPD (social democrats) to form the SED (Socialist Unity Party)
1948–1949	Blockade of Berlin
1949	23 May: establishment of a West German state, the Bundesrepublik Deutschland (Federal Republic of Germany) 7 October: East German state, the Deutsche Demokratische Republik (German Democratic Republic; DDR / GDR) established
1953	17 June: riots in the GDR
1961	13 August: erection of the Berlin Wall
1971	Quadripartite (Four Power) Agreement
1972	Berlin Agreement
1989	9 November: opening of the borders

City of four sectors

In June 1945 Berlin became the base for the **Allied Control Council**. British and US troops occupied their sectors on 4 July and on 12 August the French took control of theirs. Berlin was now split into four sectors. It did not take long for cracks in the alliance to become apparent; soon they would lead to the division of the city. Berlin was now the »front« in the Cold War. The Soviet military administration had already permitted the reformation of political parties in their sector in June of 1945. On 21 April 1946 the SPD and KPD were now compelled to amalgamate to form the SED (Sozialistische Einheitspartei Deutchlands) or Socialist Unity Party. Elections to the city council were held on 20 October 1946 under allied supervision. They were the first free elections for 13 years but they would be the last to be held in a united Berlin for another 44. The SPD were the clear victors. On 20 March 1948, the Soviet Union cited the intention of the western allies to create a constitution for their sectors as a reason to leave the Allied Control Council. Three months later on 24 June, the

Berlin's lowest point: a Soviet tank in May 1945 in front of the remains of the Brandenburg Gate

crisis over electoral reform came to a head with the Soviets instituting a **Blockade of Berlin** blockade of all routes to West Berlin. The blockade was not lifted until 12 May 1949, during which time supplies were only maintained to the West Berlin populace by means of the famous **Berlin Airlift**. On 13 October 1948 the properly elected magistracy was forced to move headquarters from East to West Berlin. From then on politics on either side of the city were totally divorced, even though free movement between sectors remained.

On 23 May 1949 the »Grundgesetz« or fundamental legal structure for the western Federal Republic of Germany (Bundesrepublik Deutschland) was announced. On 7 October, an independent eastern state called the German Democratic Republic was declared in East Berlin. Berlin's new constitution came into force on 1 October, declaring Berlin to be a federal state of the Bundesrepublik Deutschland and claiming to apply to the city as a whole. The intervening years before the building of the Berlin Wall were marked by an uprising in the east on **17 June 1953**. It was triggered by a **strike of construction workers in Stalinallee** against the excessive raising of work quotas. The revolt was put down with the help of Soviet troops and was utilized for symbolic and propaganda purposes by both sides. In the West this included holding some sessions of the federal parliament in the Reichstag after October 1955. In the east, Soviet leader **Nikita Khrushchev** delivered his »Berlin Ultimatum«, whereby Berlin would lose its status of occupation by the four powers to become a »free«, demilitarized city. A summit of foreign ministers in Geneva the following year was unable to agree on a solution. The two halves of the town were also drifting apart in economic terms. Whereas

Two German states

No-one Intends to Build a Wall ...

»As I understand your question, there are people in West Germany who want us to mobilize building workers in the capital of the GDR to construct a wall. I am not aware that there is any such intention. The building workers of our capital are mainly occupied constructing housing. (...) No-one intends to build a wall.«

On 15 June 1961 **Walter Ulbricht**, chairman of the State Council of the GDR and secretary general of the SED (Party of Socialist Unity), gave a heated and outraged answer to a journalist who hoped for clarity on rumours that had been circulating for some time. Just under two months later, at about 2am on the night of 12 to 13 August, the police, works units and the National People's Army closed off the eastern part of Berlin for the purpose of »reliable guarding and effective control of the state border« along the boundary of the Soviet sector, and started to erect road blocks and barbed-wire fences. Hours later a report was made to the responsible official, **Erich Honecker**, that the work had been completed.

Escape Through Berlin

For years the steady stream of persons crossing the sector boundaries had been a thorn in the flesh of the GDR regime. Since the closure of the border to the Federal Republic of Germany in 1952, Berlin had been the only hole in the Iron Curtain, as the four Allied powers guaranteed freedom of movement in the city. From 1952 until the building of the Wall, approximately 2.7 million people grasped this opportunity. The GDR was faced with the threat of losing its people, and for the SED the last resort was to enclose them. This was, of course, never officially admitted. Instead construction of the Wall was described as a measure to preserve peace and as protection against »constant provocation from West Berlin« – in propaganda terminology an **»anti-fascist protective wall«**.

Berlin is Walled in

At the same time as the first road blocks, the number of transit points was reduced from 81 to twelve and a short time later to seven. Train and underground train traffic, with the exception of Friedrichstrasse station, was completely cut off, which meant that the two subway lines U 6 and U 8, which passed beneath East Berlin, and the train lines S 1 und S 2 from then onwards had to pass through ghost stations watched by East German police. On 15 August a start was made on replacing the road blocks and barbed wire with a first wall of masonry and concrete slabs. Houses that were right on the boundary, for example in **Bernauer Strasse**, were evacuated from 19 August, and west-facing entrances and windows were walled up. Many escaped by jumping out of windows on the West

Berlin city boundary
Boundary between east and west sectors
Sector boundaries in West Berlin
Borough boundaries

Berlin side, where passers-by, policemen and the fire brigade tried to catch hold of them. On 24 August the first escaper was shot while swimming through the Humboldthafen docks. All of a sudden, Berlin was divided. The wall within the city separated the western districts of Reinickendorf, Wedding, Tiergarten, Kreuzberg and Neukölln from Pankow, Prenzlauer Berg, Mitte, Friedrichshain and Treptow in the east. Over the years the Wall, which had been built in haste, was brought to a state of technical perfection and made into an almost insuperable obstacle (▶MARCO POLO Insight p.204 ff.).

Attempts to Flee

In all 136 people died attempting to escape. They are remembered with memorial crosses and stones in many places, for example at Bernauer Strasse, the Reichstag building and Zimmerstrasse. Well over 100 people were shot at and injured by border guards of the GDR, and more than 3000 arrests were observed from the West Berlin side. However, many people succeeded in fleeing; the lengths to which desperation drove them are apparent in their imaginative, inventive and brave means of escape, as shown by the photos, documents and original items in the museum **Haus am Checkpoint Charlie** (corner of Zimmerstrasse and Friedrichstrasse; ▶p.200).

Where Two Systems Met

Checkpoint Charlie (»Allied Checkpoint Charlie«, according to the word for »C« in the NATO alphabet; for Alpha »A« was the border

Building the Wall under watchful eyes

crossing in Helmstedt, Bravo for »B« the checkpoint at Dreilinden) was the world-famous crossing point for foreigners, certain citizens of the GDR, diplomats, and the place where agents and military personnel were exchanged across the border of the US and Soviet sectors in the heart of Berlin. Nowhere was the atmosphere of the Cold War more palpable than here, when West Berlin police and French, British and US soldiers on one side, and GDR border guards and Soviet soldiers on the other side, watched each other suspiciously. The security arrangements on the eastern side were elaborate: several barriers, chicanes to make vehicles follow a curved path and armed guards in watchtowers were installed to thwart any attempt to break out. At the climax of the **Berlin crisis** between 25 and 28 October 1961, American and Soviet tanks faced each other with engines running when the Americans enforced their right to uncontrolled access to the eastern sector of the city. Today almost nothing of this can be seen. A left-over watchtower is overshadowed by the American Business Center, the course of the border is marked on the road, and a checkpoint hut has been reconstructed.

The Wall has Disappeared

The opening of the borders of the GDR to West Berlin and the Federal Republic of German on **9 Novem-**

ber 1989 meant the end of the Wall. From 10pm and on the following days, East Berliners flooded across to the West. On 11 November the order to shoot border crossers was revoked; by 14 November nine new crossing points had been opened, and on 22 December the opening of the Brandenburg Gate after 28 years put a symbolic end to the partition of Berlin. In the night of 9 to 10 November 1989 the so-called »Wall-peckers« started to chip away at the concrete monstrosity with hammers and chisels. Later it was pulled down with heavy machinery and made into concrete granulate. By December 1990 one million tons of concrete had been disposed of! Many large pieces – especially those that had been painted by well-known artists – were sold and sent all over the world.

Traces

Today it is not easy to find traces of the Wall in Berlin. In many places, its course can only be guessed at. However, the explanatory panels of the Geschichtsmeile Berliner Mauer (Berlin Wall History Mile) and a double row of cobblestones mark the site of the Wall. It is possible to walk or cycle along the inner or outer side of the Berlin Wall on the 14 sections of the Berliner Mauerweg. The first place to go for comprehensive information is the Gedenkstätte Berliner Mauer (Berlin Wall Memorial Site) on Bernauer Strasse (►p.201), where parts of the border installations, including the rear and the front wall, the path for

troops and the floodlit strip have been preserved. Further remains are on the site of the Topographie des Terrors at Niederkirchnerstrasse, at the Invalidenfriedhof, in the Mauerpark in Prenzlauer Berg and at the 1300m/1450yd-long East Side Gallery, now a visitor attraction where well-known artists have painted on the Wall. Most people are not aware that this is only a stretch of the rear wall. For further remains of the Wall, see MARCO POLO Insight p.202).

Taking souvenirs of the Wall in Zimmerstrasse

West Berlin quickly became one of the key industrial centres of the Federal Republic, development in the east was stagnant. The GDR was also struggling with serious difficulties, not least the number of people fleeing to the west across the still open sector borders.

In the shadow of the Wall
In order to stem the exodus, the East Germans began construction of a wall on 13 August 1961. East Berlin was initially separated from the western sectors by a barbed wire fence and later by a heavily guarded concrete wall. Local rail traffic and underground railways were cut off at the frontier (▶MARCO POLO Insight p.32). Berlin was now completely divided. On 26 July 1963, however, there was an unforgettable visit by the American president, **John F. Kennedy**. In a speech in front of the Rathaus in Schöneberg he declared: »All free men, wherever they may live, are citizens of Berlin, and, therefore, as a free man, I take pride in the words ›**Ich bin ein Berliner!**‹«

»Change through rapprochement«
Quiet diplomacy did lead to some improvement in the situation – Egon Bahr coined the phrase »Wandel durch Annäherung« (»change through rapprochement«). Thus in December 1963 an initial transit permit agreement was formalized whereby West Berliners were able to visit relatives in the east for the first time in 28 months. In 1971 telephone services that had been broken off in 1952 were reinstituted between the two sectors. On 3 September 1971 the quadripartite or »four power« agreement over Berlin was signed. It was a milestone in post-war history. The key points were the acknowledgement of the status quo in Berlin, a declaration repudiating violence and the agreement by the Soviet Union to allow traffic to pass between West Berlin and the Federal Republic and not to hinder communications between West Berlin and neighbouring districts, indeed to improve them. For their part, the western allies acknowledged the special status of West Berlin. In 1972 the Berlin Agreement once again allowed West Berliners to enter East Germany; and transit between West Germany and Berlin was made much easier. In 1974 West Germany established a permanent mission in East Berlin. However, throughout the period of existence of the Berlin Wall many continued to be killed in the attempt to cross it.

> **!** MARCO ● POLO TIP
>
> *Recalling the Wall* Insider Tip
>
> Considering the enormity of the events of 13 August 1961 in the history of the city, it is astonishing how little is left after 15 years to recall the Wall. The documentation centre in the Berlin Wall Memorial at Bernauer Strasse 11 is the place to look for detailed information on the era when West Berlin was »walled in« (Bernauer Str. 111; S1, S2 to Nordbahnhof, U8 to Bernauer Strasse; open: April – Oct 9.30am – 7pm, Nov – Mar until 6pm; www.berlinger-mauer-gedenkstaette.de; see p.202).

At the end of the 1960s West Berlin and Frankfurt am Main were the hotbeds of the New Left movement and non-parliamentary opposition in West Germany. On 2 June 1967 during a demonstration against a state visit by the shah of Iran, a student called Benno Ohnesorg was shot by a policeman. The non-parliamentary opposition grouping or APO (Ausserparlamentarische Opposition) organized numerous demonstrations during 1968, primarily against the Vietnam war and the Springer publishers. On 11 April, one of the group's leaders, Rudi Dutschke, was seriously injured when he was attacked on the Kurfürstendamm.

Developments in West Berlin

After 1953 there was little in the way of demonstrations in East Berlin. The city was in the grip of the Stasi (Staatssicherheit / State Security Police). East German leaders made efforts to give the city back some of its lustre as an international capital. Thus the Palace of the Republic was built on the site of the imperial palace, which had been blown up in 1950. Unter den Linden, the Nikolai Quarter and Gendarmenmarkt (Platz der Akademie) were restored in exemplary fashion and the Fernsehturm (TV Tower) became a striking new landmark. Nevertheless, by the end of the 1980s, as the Soviet Union opened its doors to **perestroika and glasnost**, discontent with the economic and political crisis could no longer be quelled. Major celebrations to mark the 40th anniversary of the GDR did take place on 7 October 1989, but the mood of the country remained unsettled. Soviet communist party leader and head of state **Mikhail Gorbachev** said of the situation in East Germany: »**He who acts too late will be punished by life.**« The reaction of the Politburo was to remove Erich Honecker from his position as party leader and head of state on 18 October 1989, replacing him with Egon Krenz. Unimpressed by this cosmetic action, close to a million people joined a demonstration for democratic reform on 4 November. On 7 November the entire East German government resigned. The government and Politburo reformed the following day with new personnel.

Developments in East Berlin

On the evening of 9 November 1989, Politburo member Günter Schabowski prematurely announced the new government's decision to open the borders to West Berlin and the Federal Republic, without being fully informed of the details and without foreseeing the consequences. Spontaneously, tens of thousands of East German citizens stormed across the border into the west of the city. Over that weekend from 10 to 12 November more than a million people from East Berlin and other parts of the GDR flooded into West Berlin. The opening of the Wall at the Brandenburg Gate The fall of the Berlin Wall on 22 December symbolized the ending of 28 years of division in Berlin. From 24 December there was freedom of passage between the two German states with no need for visas or exchange permits.

The opening of the borders

BERLIN REUNIFIED

1990	31 August: reunification agreement
	3 October: German reunification
1991	20 June: the German parliament, the Bundestag, agrees to re-establish Berlin as the seat of parliament and government in Germany
1999	Bundestag and government complete the move to Berlin
2008	Closure of Tempelhof Airport. Berlin's Modernist housing estates are declared World Heritage sites.
2010	Reopening of the Neues Museum
2012	Repeated postponements in opening Berlin Brandenburg Airport and associated corruption scandals dominate newspaper headlines in the city.

The path to reunification
Council elections in East Germany on 6 May 1990 led to an SPD-led grand coalition succeeding the former magistracy of East Berlin. The senate and magistracy of Berlin met in common session for the first time on 12 June. As of 20 June elected officials from Berlin received full voting rights in the German parliament. On 1 July an economic, social and currency union between the two German states came into force. A formal **reunification agreement** was signed by heads of both states at the Palais Unter den Linden on 31 August 1991. On 12 September a final agreement was signed in Moscow by foreign ministers from the Federal Republic of Germany, the German Demo-

10 November 1989 at the Brandenburg Gate:
the Wall is no longer a barrier

cratic Republic, France, Britain, the Soviet Union and the United States of America at the end of the so-called **Two Plus Four Summit**. The agreement declared that the victorious powers of the Second World War would immediately suspend their special rights in Berlin and in Germany as a whole. Overnight between 2 and 3 October the **reunification of Germany** was accompanied by massive popular celebrations around the Brandenburg Gate, Unter den Linden and Alexanderplatz. The following day a **combined parliament** comprising all the members of the East German Volkskammer and the West German Bundestag met for the first time in the Reichstag building. On 2 December the first free elections in a united Germany and a united Berlin since 1946 were held. During 1990 and 1991 the Berlin Wall was almost completely dismantled.

The first parliamentary session of the newly elected Bundestag for all Germany took place on 17 January 1991 in the Reichstag building with the aim of ratifying a new constitution. On 20 June a decision was made to move the seat of parliament and government permanently to Berlin. The troops of the western allies held a parade on Strasse des 17. Juni to mark their departure. Russian troops held a similar parade in Köpenick.

Berlin – capital of Germany

17 October 1992 saw a state ceremony at the Reichstag in honour of **Willy Brandt**, who had been mayor of Berlin at the time the Wall was being constructed. During the summer of 1995 the project of Christo and Jeanne-Claude attracted art lovers from all over the world to Berlin. On 19 April 1999 the Bundestag completed its move from Bonn to Berlin and Chancellor Schröder's move into the former Staatsratsgebäude (privy council building) on 23 August marked the **official transfer of government itself to the new capital**.

The opening of the Sony Center at the beginning of 2000 marked the virtual **completion of building work at Potsdamer Platz**. At the turn of the year from 2000 to 2001 the 23 boroughs of Berlin were reorganized into just twelve new districts. The final newly constructed section of railway between Westhafen and Gesundbrunnen was opened in June 2002 to close the local railway loop (S-Bahn ring) for the first time since 1961. The Bundestag voted on 4 July to restore the façade of the historic Stadtschloss palace. In February 2006 work began on the demolition of the Palace of the Republic and in May that year the new central station in the Spreebogen was officially opened. **Tempelhof Airport was closed** in October 2008. At the same time began the expansion of Schönefeld to become BBI (Berlin Brandenburg International). Technical problems have led to repeated delays, and the airport is now not expected to open before 2017. In 2009 the restored **Neues Museum** opened on Museum Island, which has now been returned to its pre-war condition.

21st century

Art and Culture

Art History

What was »Prussian Rococo«? Are there still traces of Third Reich architecture in Berlin? Where are the city's finest sculptures? Who has been responsible for the building of the »New Berlin«?

FROM THE MIDDLE AGES TO THE 19TH CENTURY

There are very few examples of buildings from the Middle Ages in Berlin. The **Nikolaikirche** (Church of St Nicholas), the oldest parish church in the city (from around 1230), has been restored. The **Klosterkirche** (Franciscan monastery church), which also dates from the 13th century, has been in ruins since the Second World War. Churches that are relatively well preserved include the 13th/14th-century Marienkirche (St Mary's) and the former **Heiliggeist-Kapelle** (Chapel of the Holy Spirit, Spandauer Str. 1, open at midday). The Nikolaikirche in Spandau from the early 15th century is worth mentioning as an example of the late Gothic style. Many of the 20 or so former village churches, e.g. in Marienfelde and Mariendorf (▶p.310), date back to the 13th century. The earliest examples of medieval painting are the murals in the Church of St Anne in Dahlem (14th century) along with the frescoes on the vaults of the village church in Buckow (15th century). The now faded but still famous Dance of Death in the Marienkirche (1485) is important mainly for its iconography.

Few traces of the Middle Ages

During the Renaissance, artists from outside Berlin were favoured. Joachim I had the headstone for Elector Johann Cicero (1532, in the Berliner Dom) made by Peter Vischer in Nuremberg. The construction of the new palace starting in 1538 was contracted to Caspar Theyss of Saxony, the Italian Count Rochus Guerini of Lynar and Peter Kummer the Elder from Dresden. In addition to the Stadtschloss or city palace, a hunting palace in Grunewald (as of 1542), the Spandauer Citadel (from 1560) and private buildings were erected, although of the latter only the **Ribbeckhaus** on Breite Strasse remains. The conversion of the ruling house to Calvinism (1613) and the Thirty Years' War led to a hiatus in artistic endeavour that only ended in the time of the Great Elector. This ruler brought Dutch-schooled architects (Johann Arnold Nering), painters (Willem van Honthorst) and the sculptors (Artus Quellinus) to his court. One important relic of this era is the palace **Schloss Köpenick** with its chapel.

Imported Renaissance

A small piece of »New Berlin«: Frank O. Gehry's DZ Bank at Pariser Platz – plain outside, stunning inside

Baroque | Initially Johann Arnold Nering and Martin Grünberg (1655 – 1706) continued in the Dutch tradition, but the genius of **Andreas Schlüter** (1659 – 1714) adopted a vigorous new direction in the form of Italian Baroque. Schlüter was not only the most important artist in northern Germany at the time, he was also a sculptor and architect (having worked on the remodelling of the palace and the Zeughaus). He joined the Berlin court in 1694 and inspired the blossoming of art all over the town. His best-known works are the **equestrian statue of the Great Elector** that is now on view outside Schloss Charlottenburg, the first such statue to be erected out of doors in Germany, and the 21 heads of dying warriors in the atrium of the Zeughaus. Men working in the same vein were the Swede Johann Friedrich Eosander von Göthe and the Frenchman Jean de Bodt. The church in Dorotheenstadt (1687), which was destroyed during the Second World War, was the first new Protestant church to be built. It was followed by several more around 1700, including the French and German churches (Französischer Dom and Deutscher Dom) on Gendarmenmarkt, which are noteworthy as examples of buildings with a central ground plan. Under the »the Soldier King« Friedrich Wilhelm I the three large squares Quarré (Pariser Platz), Oktogon (Leipziger Platz) and Rondell (Belle-Alliance-Platz, now called Mehringplatz) were all built, completing his expansion of the suburbs Dorotheenstadt and Friedrichstadt. During his reign the Lustgarten was converted into a parade ground and the palace was completed. The leading architects on the project were Philipp Gerlach and Schlüter's pupil Martin Böhme. The king also brought in Johann Boumann from Holland.

»Frederician« (Prussian) Rococo | Frederick the Great put his stamp on the French-influenced Friderician Rococo style, which took on Classical aspects in Prussia and remained alive in Prussia longer than elsewhere in Europe. When he was still crown prince, had already unearthed one of the most talented architects of the age in **Georg Wenzeslaus von Knobelsdorff** (1699 – 1753) brilliantly realized Frederick's ideas as Schloss Rheinsberg, Schloss Charlottenburg, in Sanssouci and Potsdam and in particular at the opera house (his masterpiece). As of 1763 he was succeeded by Karl von Gontard, who designed the towers of the Französischer Dom and the Deutscher Dom, then by Georg Friedrich Boumann, who designed the Alte Bibliothek (old library). Frederick the Great's also brought French artists to Berlin. The only painter to respond to this call was Charles Amédée van Loo, who joined **Antoine Pesne** (1683 – 1757) and Pesne's most important pupil from the Berlin school, Christian Bernhard Rode (1725 – 97), best known for his ceiling paintings in the royal palaces. The sculpture studio that the king set up was more successful, attracting such artists as François-Gaspard Adam, Sigisbert-François Michel and Jean Pierre Antoine Tassaert. The motifs of painter and engraver

Daniel Chodowiecki (1726 – 1801) also introduced a bourgeois element into art.

At the end of the 18th century the burgeoning movement towards Classicism produced some of Berlin's most important monuments. In addition to **Carl Gotthard Langhans** (1732 – 1808), the director of the court department of works, who created the Brandenburg Gate, Friedrich Wilhelm von Erdmannsdorff (1736 – 1800) worked in Berlin, as did David Gilly (1748 – 1808), who founded what would become the Bauakademie or Academy of Architecture. The outstanding talent of **Karl Friedrich Schinkel** (1781 – 1841) from Neuruppin united the Classical and Romantic styles (his legacy includes the Neue Wache, Schauspielhaus, Altes Museum, Schlossbrücke, Friedrichswerdersche Kirche and the Nikolaikirche in Potsdam). His influence endured into the second half of the 19th century. The most important sculptors in those first half of the 19th century included **Gottfried Schadow** (1764 – 1850; responsible for the four-horsed chariot on the Brandenburg Gate, the marble Prinzessinnengruppe of the later Queen Luise and her sister) and his even more influential pupil **Christian Daniel Rauch** (1777 – 1857), who sculpted the equestrian statue of Frederick the Great and the sarcophagus of Queen Luise. One of the trailblazers for the Romantic movement was the landscape painter Carl Blechen (1798 – 1840).

Classicism and Romanticism

Towards the middle of the 19th century the historicist movement sought to instigate a new renaissance in art by harking back to historical art forms. Schinkel's concepts were initially propagated by his pupils Ludwig Persius, Friedrich August Stüler (designer of the Neues Museum) and Johann Heinrich Strack (Siegessäule and Nationalgalerie). With the scholarly and archaeological study of building forms, a variety of styles emerged that found expression in the major public buildings designed by Hermann Friedrich Waesemann (Rotes Rathaus), **Paul Wallot** (Reichstag) and Ernst von Ihne (Neuer Marstall, Staatsbibliothek, Bodemuseum). After the mid-19th century, the Berlin school of sculpture lacked an outstanding figure. Artists such as Christian Friedrich Tieck, August Kiss, Friedrich Drake and Gustav Bläser remained locked in the tradition of Rauch. Reinhold Begas, though, moved away from Classicism to create a new Baroque

Historicism

style. One of his major works is the monument to Bismarck (now at Grosser Stern). In the world of painting, the pathos of Anton von Werner's historical depictions dominated art in Berlin for decades. The one towering figure was **Adolph Menzel** (1815 – 1905), who not only chronicled his own age but also evoked the era of Frederick the Great. Fate was not kind to him, however: his extremely small stature and large bald head earned him the nickname »Little Excellency«, and he reacted with a misanthropic attitude to his contemporaries.

20TH CENTURY

Architecture before 1939 — Ludwig Hoffmann (1852 – 1932), head of the city planning office, was a guiding figure of the architectural scene of »**Wilhelmine Berlin**« for many years with his works harking back to the Renaissance and Baroque periods. The Wertheim building (1896 – 1906) created by Alfred Messel instigated a new, practical style for department stores. Peter Behrens similarly opened up a new direction for industrial structures with his AEG turbine hall (1909). In the 1920s **Walter Gropius**, **Ludwig Mies van der Rohe**, Erich Mendelssohn, Hans Poelzig, Bruno and Max Taut, and **Hans Scharoun** were the men who defined the architectural visage of the city, particularly its housing estates, such as in four major projects including the Hufeisensied-

Scharoun's Philharmonie opened for concerts in 1963

lung (Horseshoe Estate) in Britz (Taut and Wagner), Onkel Toms Hütte (Uncle Tom's Cabin) in Zehlendorf (Taut, Häring and Otto Rudolf Salvisberg) and Siemensstadt (Scharoun, Gropius and others). Other important buildings include the trade fair and exhibition grounds around the Funkturm (radio tower) by Richard Ermisch and Tempelhof Airport by Ernst Sagebiel. The Olympic Stadium and Waldbühne by Werner March already provide a foretaste of the spirit of the Nazi era. The gargantuan plans of Albert Speer, appointed as inspector general of buildings by Hitler in 1937 and given the task of redesigning Berlin and making it a new capital for the Third Reich under the name Germania, were barely begun. Central to the new concept was construction of a new boulevard 120m/130yd wide leading from Tempelhof to the Spreebogen (bend in the river Spree), where a gigantic building called the »Volkshalle« 290m/950ft in height was to be built. What is interesting about this is that the flattening of the Spreebogen area and the district south of it was not caused solely by enemy bombs, but was actually begun by Speer's bulldozers.

Architects from all over the world were involved in creating major landmarks in Berlin after the war. The outstanding edifices in the west include the **Kongresshalle** (1957) by the American Hugh A. Stubbins, the Unité d'Habitation (1957) by Le Corbusier, the new **Kaiser-Wilhelm-Gedächtniskirche** (memorial church, 1960/61) by Egon Eiermann, the Philharmonie (1963) by Hans Scharoun, the Neue Nationalgalerie (New National Gallery; 1968) by Ludwig Mies van der Rohe, Tegel Airport (1975) by von Gerkan, Marg and Nickels, the Staatsbibliothek (State Library for Prussian Cultural Heritage, 1979) by Scharoun, the Bauhaus-Archiv (1979) by Walter Gropius and the **Kulturforum at Kemperplatz**, which followed a concept by Hans Scharoun and was only finished after the fall of the Berlin Wall. In East Berlin, too, there was plenty of construction going on, as witnessed by Hermann Henselmann's Stalinallee, the now-demolished Palast der Republik by Heinz Graffunder (1973–76) and the reconstruction of Friedrichstrasse, although the last-named has since been replaced. Rising above it all is the internationally hailed **Fernsehturm** (TV Tower, 1965–69) by Dieter and Franke. An amalgamation of many modern ideas can be found in the **Hansaviertel** (International Building Exhibition 1957), with contributions from 48 architects from 13 countries, including Alvar Aalto, Walter Gropius and Oscar Niemeyer. Housing estates at **Gropiusstadt** (1973) in Berlin-Buckow and the Märkisches Viertel (1974) in northern Berlin exemplify the kind of architecture that was thought to be trailblazing in its day, but has engendered social problems. The prefabricated, late-seventies tower blocks of Marzahn, Hellersdorf and Hohenschönhausen are typical of the communist era.

Post-war architecture

Chapel of Reconciliation Insider Tip

Helmut Jahn, Renzo Piano, I.M. Pei, Sony Center, Daimler City: the new Berlin is replete with great names and great buildings. Rudolf Reitermann and Peter Sassenroth are known to only a few insiders but their fine creations are attracting fans of architecture from all over the world. Their Kapelle der Versöhnung (Chapel of Reconciliation) on Bernauer Strasse is a wonderfully airy building made of rammed clay sandwiched in wooden laminate walls that replaces the Church of Reconciliation that was blown up by East German border troops in 1985 (S1, S2 to Nordbahnhof, U8 to Bernauer Strasse).

Reunified Berlin has experienced an unparalleled construction boom. Some massive building projects were begun, especially the **Potsdamer Platz** development, the rebuilding of Pariser Platz, and the construction of a new central station on the site of the former Lehrter station, the Kanzleramt (Chancellery) and the parliament precinct, not to mention the renovation of existing buildings, in particular the refurbishment of the Museumsinsel (Museum Island). Smaller projects that may be overshadowed by all these major efforts include the Jüdisches Museum (Jewish Museum) by Daniel Libeskind, Frank O. Gehry's DZ-Bank on Pariser Platz and the Mosse centre on Zimmerstrasse in Mitte district. Even on Berlin's outskirts, in Treptow, there were new creations in the form of the 125m / 410ft-tall Treptowers and the even more distinctive Twin Towers, and in Dahlem the Philological Faculty Library (»The Brain«) by Norman Foster.

Painting
In 1898 Berlin-born **Max Liebermann** (1847 – 1935), a major figure in German Impressionism, and Walter Leistikow, painter of the Brandenburg landscape, founded the Secession grouping, which set out entirely new artistic objectives. They were joined by Lovis Corinth, Max Slevogt and Lesser Ury, who were among the most important names in German Impressionism. Käthe Kollwitz (1867 – 1945) and **Heinrich Zille** (1858 – 1929), who popularly depicted Berlin's working-class milieu, took a stance that was critical of the prevalent society. Expressionism had important pioneers and champions such as the art dealer Herwarth Walden (publisher of the periodical Der Sturm), Paul Cassirer and Alfred Flechtheim. Max Beckmann, Ernst Ludwig Kirchner, Emil Nolde, Max Pechstein, Erich Heckel, Karl Schmidt-Rottluff and Oskar Kokoschka all developed their own style in Berlin. The city's own Dadaist movement was primarily led by Hannah Höch (1889 – 1978) and George Grosz (1893 – 1959), while the Berlin Realism school was dominated by painters like Otto Dix (1891 – 1969) and Rudolf Schlichter (1890 – 1955). Artists such as Georg Baselitz and Markus Lüpertz carried on Berlin's international reputation as a hotbed for art, in which they were succeeded in the 1980s by the »Junge Wilde« (Young

Wild Ones) including Salome and Rainer Fetting, among whose works is the sculpture of Willy Brandt at the SPD headquarters (▶ill. p.57).

630 galleries, more than in London or New York, present the latest trends to art lovers. Alongside Auguststrasse and Linienstrasse in Mitte more and more new centres of art are springing up: in Potsdamer Strasse, on Rosa-Luxemburg-Platz, in Rudi-Dutschke-Strasse and Lindenstrasse in Kreuzberg, Holzmarkt in Friedrichshain and in Heidestrasse behind the Hamburger Bahnhof. The Berlin Biennale (2016, 2018) and Art Forum give impulses to the art market. In 1987 a »sculpture boulevard« was opened on Kurfürstendamm (▶p.249). This unleashed a flurry of sculpture projects that continue to this day. New buildings and squares have been adorned with sculptures by prominent artists, including Rauschenberg's *Riding Bikes* on Potsdamer Platz and Claes Oldenbourg's *Houseball* on Mauerstrasse. Most prominent of them all,

Galleries

MARCO⊕POLO TIP   **The Boros Collection**   Insider Tip

With his Kunstbunker at Reinhardtstr. 20, Christian Boros has created Berlin's most unusual art collection. He converted an above-ground war bunker next to the Deutsches Theater, where the Red Army held war criminals and the GDR stored tropical fruit, into a fascinating space where works by such artists as Anselm Reyles, Santiago Sierra and Tobias Rehberger can be admired against a backdrop of raw concrete and surviving graffiti (visits by appointment, www.sammlungboros.de, admission 10 €).

though, is Jonathan Borofsky's aluminium *Molecule Men*, which soars 30m / 100ft over the banks of the Spree in Treptow.

Cultural Life in Berlin

In the Golden Twenties Berlin was the cultural heart of Germany and set the standards for theatre, film and literature. Today there is a trend in the same direction, but competition with other German cities remains keen.

Elector Friedrich III and his wife Sophie Charlotte had the ambition of creating in Berlin an »excellently appointed academy or school of art, but no ordinary painting or sculpture academy of the kind that is already ubiquitous«. Thus in 1696 the Prussian Akademie der Künste (Academy of Arts) was established. Its directors have included Andreas Schlüter, Daniel Chodowiecki and Gottfried Schadow. The heyday of the academy was in the 1920s under its then president Max

Akademie der Künste

Liebermann, when the school was supplemented by a section for the literary arts (1926). Its nadir came not long afterwards during the Nazi era, when the academy meekly »cleansed« itself of all those members who were anathema to the National Socialists, including Heinrich Mann, Alfred Döblin and Käthe Kollwitz. The academy's premises on Pariser Platz were destroyed during the war, so that during the Cold War era, two successor establishments were founded. In 1950 the Deutsche Akademie der Künste was founded in East Berlin, claiming to be the true inheritor of the Prussian academy's mantle before being renamed the Akademie der Künste der DDR in 1972. The West Berliners reacted to this by opening their own institution, the West Berlin Akademie der Künste in 1954. The two academies were amalgamated in 1992 (information at www.adk.de).

Festivals Among the most interesting events are the Berlin Festival, a cross section of international art, the International Film Festival, the Berlin Theatre Festival, the Festival of World Culture, the International Summer Festival and the Berlin JazzFest.

Theatre Berlin has been the backdrop for much of the theatrical history of Germany. It is where Gerhart Hauptmann, Henrik Ibsen, August Strindberg and Bertolt Brecht made their breakthroughs and directors such as Max Reinhardt, Erwin Piscator and Gustaf Gründgens also left their legacy. Among 100 theatres regularly showing plays, the most important are the Deutsches Theater, the Schaubühne on Lehniner Platz, the Berliner Ensemble and the Volksbühne on Rosa-Luxemburg Platz. In addition there are a large number of independent theatre groups with no regular venue. This makes Berlin the number one theatre destination in German-speaking countries, purely on numbers alone.

Music 90 music publishers, more than 130 record labels, 50 recording studios and several hundred groups make the city the hub of the German music scene. For classical music aficionados there are no less than four opera houses: the Staatsoper Unter den Linden, the Deutsche Oper Berlin, the Komische Oper and the Neuköllner Oper. There are also numerous orchestras, most prominent of which are the world-famous Berlin Philharmonic Orchestra, founded in 1882 and based in the Philharmonie at the Kulturforum, and the Berlin Symphony Orchestra, who play in the Konzerthaus on Gendarmenmarkt.

Film and television Before the Second World War, Berlin was the centre of filmmaking in Germany. Max Skladanowsky showed the earliest films here in 1895 and Oskar Messter, the early master of the cinema who made the first cinema projector for normal film in 1896, was born in Berlin.

The world's very first sound picture was shown here in 1922 by Vogt, Engl and Masolle. The city presently lies in third place for film and television production in Germany after Munich and Cologne. The most important sites are Media City in Adlershof, the Berliner Union film studio in Tempelhof and UFA in Potsdam-Babelsberg. The Deutsche Kinemathek and Museum für Film und Fernsehen (TV and film museum) in the Sony Center on Potsdamer Platz, the venue for the Berlin Film Festival, highlight how the public authorities are also supporting the city's claim to be a film centre. These establishments also provide. Berlin has appeared as a film location in more and more movies. The best-known examples include *Goodbye, Lenin*, *The Lives of Others* and *Run, Lola, Run*.

Berlin's tradition as a source of literature is well founded, with names such as Friedrich Nicolai, Gotthold Ephraim Lessing, Moses Mendelssohn, E.T.A. Hoffmann, Theodor Fontane, Georg Heym, Gerhart Hauptmann, Kurt Tucholsky, Bertolt Brecht, Alfred Döblin, Heinrich Mann and Anna Seghers. Berlin still has more living and working authors than any other German city. The recently deceased Jurek Becker, Christa Wolf and Stefan Heym join Thomas Brasch, Yaak Karsunke, Christoph Meckel, Hertha Müller, Elisabeth Plessen, Botho Strauss and Jürgen Theobaldy among the best-known at present. Berlin also has more than 400 publishers, making it second only to Munich in terms of modern German publishing.

Literature

> **!** MARCO POLO TIP *Reviving tradition* **Insider Tip**
>
> There are literary salons in Berlin again like that of Britta Gansebohm at changing venues a dozen readings daily in the Grüner Salon of the Volksbühne, in bookshops and pubs (www.salonkultur.de). And there are reading events where the protagonists – almost all male – read short new texts about everyday life and meet on Saturdays for readings at the KulturBrauerei in Prenzlauer Berg.

The reconstitution of **Berlin's museums** is one of the key objectives for the city's cultural policy. As a result of the Second World War, world-famous collections were fragmented in the two halves of the city. A large part of the original inventory was returned to East Berlin from the Soviet Union in 1958. Those parts of the state museums' collections that had been stored in the west were entrusted to the Prussian Cultural Heritage Foundation. The treasures are gathered under the official name »**Staatliche Museen zu Berlin – Preussischer Kulturbesitz**« (Berlin State Museums – Prussian Cultural Heritage) in Germany's largest complex of cultural institutes. A large number of other museums dotted around the city provide a fitting supplement to the official (▶Enjoying Berlin, Museums and Galleries, p.109).

Famous People

WILLY BRANDT (1913 – 92)

In Berlin's darkest hour since the war, 13 August 1961, the day the building of the Wall began, the serving mayor Willy Brandt gave a spontaneous speech to an agitated crowd, in which he eloquently expressed his bitterness over the events, yet still managed to calm the explosive mood of his listeners. His ability to see the reality yet continue in hope was one of his outstanding attributes. Willy Brandt was born on 18 December 1913 in Lübeck under the name Herbert Frahm. His membership of Germany's socialist workers' party meant that he was forced to flee to Norway in 1933, where he adopted the

 Chancellor

name »Willy Brandt« to conceal his identity from the Nazis. In 1938 he became a citizen of Norway. He arrived in Berlin after the war as the Norwegian press attaché, but soon readopted German nationality and joined the SPD in 1947. By 1949 he was a member of the first Bundestag. In 1957 he was elected mayor of Berlin, a post he was to keep until 1966. Throughout this period, he was already displaying the guiding focus of his politics, a recognition of and a pragmatic interaction with reality. He became leader of the SPD in 1964 and in 1966 he accepted the posts of foreign minister and deputy chancellor in a grand coalition of the parties. In 1969

Sculpture of Willy Brandt by Rainer Fetting in the party headquarters of the SPD in Kreuzberg

he accomplished an historic »shift of power«, becoming federal Germany's first social democratic chancellor in a coalition with the FDP (Free Democratic Party). With his slogan »mehr Demokratie wagen« (»risk greater democracy«) he sought to incorporate the political underswell of the 1968 generation into mainstream society. His policies towards the east were his greatest historical triumph as he succeeded in reconciling with the countries of eastern Europe that had been invaded by Hitler's Germany. His most unforgettable gesture was when he got to his knees before the monument to the victims of the Warsaw Ghetto in 1971. Only in Germany itself was he disparaged as a »denial politician« or »betrayer of the Fatherland«. He had already become the first West German chancellor to visit the GDR in 1970 and in 1973 he was a signatory to the new »basis agreement« between the two German states. The exposure of the Guillaume spy affair

A global star from Berlin: Marlene Dietrich

caused Brandt to resign in 1974. In 1976 he took on the leadership of the Socialist International grouping. For Willy Brandt, Berlin was a symbol for the division of Europe and it was only right and proper that, although he was no longer in any political office, he should make a speech to the people in front of the Schöneberg Rathaus in November 1989. He died in Unkel near Bonn on 8 October 1992 and was given a state funeral in Berlin.

BERTOLT BRECHT (1898 – 1956)

Dramatist Brecht was born in Augsburg but lived in Berlin from 1924 onwards, occasionally directing for Max Reinhardt at the Deutsches Theater. In 1933 he took flight from the Nazis via Denmark and Moscow, then moving on to the USA in 1941. He returned from there in 1947 and settled in Zurich. A year later he founded the Berliner Ensemble in East Berlin, which was then managed by his wife, the actress Helene Weigel. Both their names are inextricably associated with the building in Schiffbauerdamm. Brecht's dramas are often structured as parables and polemics. He developed a method that he described with the term »epic theatre«, in which he sought not to divert and entertain the public, but to tell a story that would make a clear statement. His best known works include the *Threepenny Opera* written in conjunction with Kurt Weill as well as *Mother Courage and Her Children*, *The Good Person of Szechwan* and *The Caucasian Chalk Circle*.

MARLENE DIETRICH (1901 – 92)

Actress and singer The daughter of an officer from Schöneberg had already played in 17 silent films before she made her breakthrough in 1930 as the seedy Lola opposite Emil Jannings as Professor Unrat in *The Blue Angel*. This cemented her reputation as the eternal femme fatale. That same year she followed Josef von Sternberg, the director of *The Blue Angel*, to Hollywood. She made six more films with him there, including *Morocco* with Gary Cooper. But though Sternberg's career thereafter faded away, hers was only beginning to take off. The most renowned directors – Lubitsch, Hitchcock, Orson Welles – used her in films alongside some of Hollywood's greatest stars. After the Second World War – during which she maintained committed opposition to Hitler and did much work entertaining US troops – she gradually retired from film work, although roles in *Judgement at Nuremberg* and *Witness for the Prosecution* brought her further successes. She retained a high profile even outside the film world, and performed as a singer on the world's premier stages, further cementing her image as a diva and a vamp. She had numerous affairs, of which the one with Jean

Gabin was probably the most intense. Nevertheless she never divorced from her husband Rudolf Sieber, whom she had married in 1924. In 1974 a fall on stage caused her to give up her singing career. She lived the rest of her life as a total recluse in Paris.

RUDI DUTSCHKE (1940 – 79)

In the late sixties, German students responded to the call to »shake the dust of a thousand years from the caps and gowns of your peers« and conceived a new kind of non-parliamentary opposition under the charismatic leadership of Rudi Dutschke. Dutschke was born in Schönefeld near Luckenwalde on 7 March 1940. He arrived in West Berlin shortly before the building of the Wall to study sociology at the Free University. He became an active member of the SDS, the Sozialistische Deutsche Studentenbund (Socialist Union of German Students), and he was soon to be seen leading protests against the war in Vietnam. His political objective was the non-violent refashioning of what he believed to be the repressive society of West Germany. He summed this up in his credo of »the long march through the institutions«. Rudi Dutschke was the symbol of the APO (non-parliamentary) movement and its era. Some saw him as a visionary of clear-minded sociological analysis while others regarded him as the embodiment of

Student leader

A call to change the established order

a violent enemy of society. On 11 April 1968 he was shot in broad daylight by a 23-year-old worker on Kurfürstendamm and suffered serious head injuries. After his recovery he left the country and died of an epileptic fit related to the attack on Christmas Eve in 1979. Even long after his death Rudi Dutschke once again caused a furore in Berlin: in 2008, and only after a plebiscite on the subject, the section of Kochstrasse between Friedrichstrasse and Axel-Springer-Strasse was named after him – the street that passes right by the office building of the Springer-Verlag.

THEODOR FONTANE (1819 – 98)

Theodor Fontane was born on 30 December 1819. He initially worked as an apprentice apothecary before taking up writing full time, chronicling 19th-century Berlin and its environs. Country

Writer

landscapes and cityscapes play a major role in his greatest novels. In his *Travels Through the March of Brandenburg* (1862 – 82) he wrote in loving detail and with dutiful attention to historical truth about the founding and the significance of Havelland, Oderland, Spreeland and their interactions with Berlin. His most important works include the novels *A Man of Honour* (1883) and *Effi Briest* (1895).

FRIEDRICH II, FREDERICK THE GREAT (1712 – 86)

King of Prussia Friedrich Wilhelm I (1688 – 1740), the »Soldier King« and father of the third king of Prussia, had been a strict and pragmatic individual with a liking for military matters. As crown prince, his son Frederick was more inclined towards music and was open to the new ideas of the Enlightenment. He corresponded with Voltaire, whom he later invited to join his court. The antagonism with his father apparently got so bad that in 1730 he unsuccessfully tried to flee to England with his friend Lieutenant von Katte and was put on trial for treason by his father. Katte was condemned to death and executed at the castle of Küstrin before the eyes of the prince. Only when Frederick was engaged to Elisabeth Christine of Brunswick-Beveren in 1732 was there reconciliation between him and his father. Frederick lived at the Rheinsberg Palace, where he wrote down his concept of the king as »prime servant of the state« in his treatise Anti-Machiavell. In 1740 he ascended to the throne. His achievements as monarch are characterized by the expansion of Prussian lands in the Silesian Wars (1740 – 42 and 1744) and the Seven Years' War (1756 – 63), by the end of which Prussia had become a major European power. He also continued the internal stabilization of Prussia that had been begun by his father, organizing the state along strictly corporate lines. The latter years of the king's reign were characterized by personal isolation and mistrust. His nickname »Old Fritz« typifies the ambivalence of his personality, reflecting both the many anecdotes of his fatherly rule as well as what he finally became, a reclusive and cynical Prussian king with no issue.

E.T.A. HOFFMANN (1776 – 1822)

Writer Ernst Theodor Amadeus Hoffmann, born in Königsberg, was one of the most idiosyncratic and bizarre poets of the German Romantic era. He studied law in his home town from 1792 to 1795 before heading for Berlin in 1798 to take up a post as clerk to the Court of Justice. Two years later he became an assessor in Posen. He spent time in various other towns in Prussia before returning to Berlin to earn his living as a musician, draughtsman, man of letters and newspaper editor. In

1808 he took up a post as a music teacher, producer, decorative painter and orchestra director in Bamberg. From 1813 to 1814 he directed
orchestras in Leipzig and Dresden and then in 1816 he was appointed
councillor to Berlin's Court of Justice. He set up a round table of the
Serapion Fraternity at the famous Lutter & Wegner wine lodge on
Gendarmenmarkt and counted many actors and poets among his
friends, including Ludwig Devrient, the Brentanos, Adelbert von
Chamisso and Friedrich de la Motte-Fouqué. Hoffmann was considered among the most amusing and witty of individuals in the Berlin
salon scene, but was also one of its thirstiest. His often rather peculiar
behaviour caused some alarm but he nevertheless gained both esteem
and popularity, particularly thanks to his artistic fairy tales.

THE HUMBOLDT BROTHERS

Brothers Alexander and Wilhelm von Humboldt were widely travelled and entertaining wits who were very popular figures in Berlin's
society and literary circles as well as at the Prussian court.

Berlin-born Alexander von Humboldt is considered the originator of
agricultural economics, meteorology, marine geography and plant geography. He initially studied law along with his brother Wilhelm in
Frankfurt an der Oder, but later went to the mountaineering academy
in Freiberg, Saxony. In 1790 he travelled throughout Europe, then from
1792 to 1797 he was a mountain asses-
sor and expert in Franconia. Along
with French botanist A. Bonpland he
spent the years from 1799 to 1804 on
an extensive expedition to South and
Central America. After his return he
was based for most of the period between 1807 and 1827 in Paris, where
he assimilated the results of his South
American studies. He returned to Berlin in 1827 and gave lectures at the
Friedrich-Wilhelm University before
undertaking another expedition in
1829, this time to the Asian regions of
Russia. His principal work Cosmos
was published in four volumes be-
tween 1845 and 1858 (with a fragment of a fifth appearing posthumous-
ly in 1862). He died on 6 May 1859.

Alexander von Hum-boldt (1769 – 1859), scientist

> **?** | *Did you know*
>
> **MARCO POLO INSIGHT**
>
> ... that Alexander von Humboldt
> was a world record mountaineer?
> On 23 June 1802 he climbed
> Mount Chimborazo in Ecuador, at
> 6310m / 20,700ft the highest
> known peak in the world at the
> time, to a height of 5878m /
> 19,285ft equipped with no warm-
> er clothing than a frock coat, pon-
> cho and jackboots. It was the
> highest that anyone would reach
> for another thirty years.

Wilhelm Freiherr von Humboldt was born in Potsdam. He studied
law in Frankfurt an der Oder and in Göttingen. Between 1802 and
1808 he was the diplomatic representative of Prussia in Rome until
he was named as head of the Prussian culture and education board

Wilhelm von Humboldt (1767 – 1835) Prussian civil servant

in Berlin in 1809. It was in this role that he founded and built the Berlin University (now the Friedrich-Wilhelm University) with the sponsorship of Friedrich Wilhelm III. In 1819 he became a member of the state ministry. Upon retiring from state service later that year he undertook linguistic studies in his mansion next to Lake Tegel. He died there on 8 April 1835.

FRIEDRICH LUDWIG JAHN (1778 – 1852)

»Father of gymnastics«

Jahn, born in Freyburg an der Unstrut, was to become famous as the father of gymnastics. In 1811 he set up his first gymnasium at the Hasenheide fields in Berlin and sought to toughen up young people by means of spartan living and exercise. His patriotism was initially directed in its entirety against Napoleon and during the wars of liberation he commanded one of the Lützow battalions. With the restoration of the Prussian state though, his outspokenness brought him into conflict with the authorities. In 1819, his gymnastic facilities were closed down and he was put on trial. He received a pardon, however, in 1825, although he remained under police observation until 1840. During the German national assembly of 1848, his ideas on the monarchy were rejected and he sullenly retired from public life. There is a memorial to him at the north-eastern corner of Hasenheide park.

HILDEGARD KNEF (1925 – 2002)

The Sinner

Berlin, dein Gesicht hat Sommersprossen (Berlin, you have freckles) or *Ich hab' noch einen Koffer in Berlin* (I still have a suitcase in Berlin) were among the chansons sung in the breathy tones of Hildegard Knef that gave musical expression to a way of life in the isolated West Berlin of the 1960s and made her the very epitome of Berlin itself. She was born in Ulm but grew up in Berlin, taking acting lessons in 1942. Her first leading role was in the first film to be made in post-war Germany, *Die Mörder sind unter uns* (The Murderers Are Among Us) directed by Wolfgang Staudte in 1946. In 1948 she received the Best Actress award at the Locarno Film Festival for her role in *Film ohne Titel* (Film Without A Title). There was, however, absolute furore at her brief nude appearance in *Die Sün-*

derin (The Sinner; 1951). She made her ultimate breakthrough in the USA, where she appeared on Broadway 675 times as Ninotchka in the Cole Porter musical *Silk Stockings*. It was not until 1963 that she started her new career as a singer of chansons. Her unusual style led Ella Fitzgerald to dub her »the best singer without a voice«. In 1970 her autobiography *Der geschenkte Gaul* (The Gift Horse) brought her huge success as a writer. The last three decades of her life were scarred by illness, against which she struggled indomitably.

KÄTHE KOLLWITZ (1867 – 1945)

The graphic artist and painter was born Käthe Schmidt on 8 July 1867   Artist
in Königsberg. She studied in Berlin, Königsberg and Munich, marrying the doctor Karl Kollwitz from Berlin in 1891. She lived in the capital until her studio was destroyed in 1943. In 1919 she was appointed as a professor at the Berlin Akademie der Künste, but was forced to give up the distinction in 1933. Käthe Kollwitz completely dedicated her work to the impoverished sufferings of the capital's proletariat. At times her creations – particularly her wood cuts – were akin to expressionism. She died on 22 April 1945 in Moritzburg near Dresden.

MAX LIEBERMANN (1847 – 1935)

Painter and graphic artist Max Liebermann, one of the great masters of   Painter
impressionism in Germany, came from a wealthy family of Berlin merchants and joined the Berliner Akademie in 1898. In 1899 he combined with Walter Leistikow and Max Slevogt to found the Berlin Secession group. From 1920 to 1932 he served as president of the Akademie der Künste but in 1933 he was prohibited from exhibiting as a dedicated opponent of National Socialism. His response to the stormtroopers' march to the Kanzleramt through the Brandenburg Gate on 30 January 1933 has become famous: »I can't eat enough to be as sick as I want to be.« Many of his works are on display in the Nationalgalerie

PAUL LINCKE (1866 – 1946)

The most famous operetta by Paul Lincke, *Frau Luna*, describes a bal-   Composer
loon ride to the moon by a handful of Berliners and includes the march *Das ist die Berliner Luft, Luft, Luft* (That's the Berlin air), which has become the anthem of Berlin. Born 7 November 1866 in Berlin he led his first orchestra at just 18, mostly conducting for the popular stage. After a while he left for Paris before returning to make his career in Berlin.

ADOLPH MENZEL (1815 – 1905)

Painter

Among the most important painters and graphic artists of the German realism movement, Adolph Menzel was born on 8 December 1815 in Breslau and was trained by his own father in lithography. He inherited his parent's workshop in 1832 and in 1842 he produced his first major work, the illustrations for *The Life of Frederick the Great* by Franz Kugler. During the 1840s and 1850s he mainly produced paintings, many of which anticipated the later impressionist movement. One of the most famous of these pictures, *Frederick the Great with Friends at Table in Sanssouci* was probably destroyed during the Second World War. Adolph Menzel was soon highly in demand – for portraits too – and was given all kinds of public awards. He was even elevated to the aristocracy, became a member of the Akademie and was invested with several orders. His diligence was famous. Wherever he went, wherever he stood, he would sketch the scene around him. Although he was unusually small with an impressive bald pate, he was a veritable institution in both Berlin's cafés and its mansions. However, his own personal fate was to be quite tragic. Due to his short stature, he was playfully dubbed the »Little Excellency«, which rendered him mistrustful and brusque with people. He died on 9 February 1905. An excellent collection of his works can be seen at the Alte Nationalgalerie (►Museumsinsel).

WOLFGANG NEUSS (1923 – 89)

Cabaret
performer

Wolfgang Neuss, born in Breslau, was called the »Mann mit der Pauke« (man with the drum) and made sharp commentaries on the politics of the early 1960s. After his matriculation examination, he spent five years as a soldier until he deliberately shot off his own left index finger and thus avoided service at the front. After the war ended he started his new career in cabaret in Düsseldorf, appearing in popular films, mostly in comic but subtle roles. His key sphere however was film and stage satire, working as author, producer and leading actor along with his congenial friend Wolfgang Müller in shows such as *Wir Kellerkinder* (We Children of the Cellar) and *Genosse Münchhausen* (Comrade Münchhausen) and exhibiting a decidedly contrary way of thinking laterally. In 1962 he even went as far as giving away in the *Bild* newspaper the carefully guarded name of the murderer in *Das Halstuch*, a serialized German television version of Francis Durbridge's mystery, *The Scarf*. His greatest successes came in West Berlin in the years following 1963 where he had his own cabaret revue *Das jüngste Gerücht* (The Latest Rumour). He was a sympathizer of left-wing political groups and was one of the founder members of the Republican Club. As of the early 1970s, Wolfgang

Neuss faded from public view, in the news for little else than his increasing drug consumption.

ERNST REUTER (1889 – 1953)

Ernst Reuter was born in Apenrade, Denmark. He joined the SPD in Germany in 1912 and was elected to the Berlin Magistracy in 1926. He was also appointed to organize the Berlin transport company (BVG), became mayor of Magdeburg in 1931 and was elected to the Reichstag in 1932. 1933, though, saw him emigrate from Germany and he was not to return until after the war, when he re-entered politics and was elected mayor of Berlin in 1947, although a Soviet veto prevented him from taking office in 1948. He was returned as mayor of West Berlin from 1950 until he died on 29 September 1953 and his incumbency saw the events of the Berlin blockade and airlift. His fame was cemented with the appeal he made before the Reichstag during a demonstration against the blockade on 9 September 1948: »If we call the world to this city today, then we shall do so because we know that the strength of our people is in the very earth where we grew up and shall continue to grow until the powers of darkness are broken and smashed. We shall experience this day in front of our old Reichstag with its proud inscription ›for the German people‹; and we will celebrate with assurance that in our trouble and need, our cares and misery, we have brought this about with steadfastness and stamina… You peoples of the world! You peoples in America, in England, France and Italy! Look upon this city and see that you must not betray this city and its people, you cannot betray it. There is only one chance for all of us: to hold together every one of us until this struggle has been won, until the struggle has finally been crowned with victory over the enemy, victory over the powers of darkness. The people of Berlin have spoken. We have done our duty and we will continue to do our duty. Peoples of the world, look upon Berlin and the people of Berlin and be assured of them that this fight, this fight they are seeking, this fight we shall win!«

Elected mayor

HANS ROSENTHAL (1925 – 87)

Hans Rosenthal, a dyed in the wool Berliner, became one of the most popular comperes of German radio and television. He was the son of a Jewish bank clerk, killed in 1937. His mother and his brother were both murdered at a concentration camp in Riga in 1941. Between 1940 and 1943 he was compelled to perform forced labour, including as a gravedigger, until he succeeded in escaping. For two years he managed to remain concealed in an allotment with the aid of two

Compère

Berlin women. After the war he started as a cub reporter at Berliner Rundfunk, swapping to the broadcaster RIAS in 1948. There his career took off and he became an editor, director, ideas man and most memorably a quizmaster. His best known shows included Allein gegen alle (Alone Against the World). In 1967 he took his first steps in the world of television, where he took control of the ZDF quiz Dalli-Dalli from 1971. This assured him of his greatest success. Behind the smiling face of the TV star, though, there was a man of substance. Until 1980 he was a member of the directorate of Germany's central council of Jews and as chairman at the conference of representatives for the Jewish community in Berlin, he actively worked for reconciliation between Germans and Jews.

KURT TUCHOLSKY (1890 – 1935)

Writer

Born on 9 January 1890, the writer initially studied law but between 1924 and 1929 worked as a journalist and foreign correspondent (primarily in Paris, later in Sweden). In 1926 he briefly acted as publisher of the *Weltbühne* magazine, for which he had been working since 1913. Tucholsky also published under pseudonyms such as Theobald Tiger, Peter Panter, Ignaz Wrobel and Kaspar Hauser. A satirist and critic of his times, he created, along with Erich Kästner and Walter Mehring, the modern urban chansons and made many imaginative contributions to the Berliner Kabarett. He also produced tales such as *Rheinsberg* and *Schloss Gripsholm*. He fled from the Nazis in 1933 and, in despair at the political regime in Germany, he took his own life in Hindås in Sweden on 21 December 1935.

WILHELM VOIGT (1849 – 1922)

»Captain of Köpenick«

Wilhelm Voigt was born on 13 February 1849 at Tilsit in East Prussia. He got into trouble with the authorities at a very early age and was sentenced to 12 years' imprisonment for counterfeiting deeds at the age of 18. After his release he spent some years leading a more respectable existence as a cobbler, but he fell into unemployment and began to pursue one crime after another. He sought to leave Prussia but was denied a passport. This was an object lesson to him in how intransigent civil servants could be, but it also enlightened him as to how much they were in thrall to anyone in uniform. This fact and his own criminal modus operandi, favouring money stored in legal and council institutions, may have led him to devise his slick caper. On 16 October 1906, Wilhelm Voigt apprehended the mayor of the then independent Köpenick dressed in a captain's uniform that he had assembled from flea markets and junk shops and »confiscated« the city funds. When the mayor asked the reason for the arrest, Voigt simply pointed to the fixed bayonets of the soldiers behind him (who he had gathered from a public street simply by ordering them to accompany him in a suitably commanding tone) and declared that resistance would be useless, stating: »Orders are orders. You can make your complaints afterwards.« The heist was greeted with amusement throughout Germany. Wilhelm Voigt was soon caught and sentenced to four years in prison, although he was released after just two. He moved to Luxemburg in May 1909, although he actually planned to emigrate to Canada. In 1910 he did indeed travel overseas, although it was only a short trip to the USA, where he appeared in Barnum & Bailey's circus as the »Captain of Köpenick«. He returned to Luxemburg that same year, and he died there on 3 January 1922.

CLAIRE WALDOFF (1884 – 1957)

Claire Waldoff was born on 21 October 1884 and worked as an actress, but she became better known for her cabaret appearances and her »Schnauze« (big mouth), epitomizing the Berlin version of the »chanson« musical form with lines like »Wer schmeißt denn da mit Lehm? Der sollte sich was schäm'« (Who's chucking mud? Shame on them!). Her cheeky but thoughtful couplets told of the city, its »Zillemilljöh« (Zille's milieu), and the joys and troubles of ordinary people. Her perky voice was recorded on plenty of discs, and her red hair and chubby little frame were trademarks of Berlin's poster painters. When she died on 22 January 1957, Germany lost a true character. At her own wish she was buried in Stuttgart in the family grave of her life companion Olga von Roeder.

Actress

HEINRICH ZILLE (1858 – 1929)

Heinrich Zille was born in Radeburg, Saxony on 10 January 1858. Famous as the chronicler of Berlin's backstreet milieu, he himself came from humble beginnings. He was a pupil of the popular painter Theodor Hosemann and started out as a lithographer. He worked for the periodicals *Simplicissimus, Jugend* and *Lustige Blätter* before joining the Prussian Academy Of Arts. Zille made his name with drawings laced with social critique depicting the poverty of Berlin's backstreets and yards. Zille's humour, based on caricature, his brilliant hand and sharp eye for funny situations often led people astray from the artist's own view of himself as a critic of social deprivation, seeking not to cheer people with joviality but to challenge those seeing his work, to evoke pity, and to recognize the reality of poverty and need.

Draughtsman

ENJOY
BERLIN

Does a Berlin cuisine exist, and if so, which restaurant serves it? How about a guided tour with a difference? And what's on in the evening in the city's legendary nightlife?

Something for Every Taste

In 2011 visitors to Berlin could choose between 782 places to stay with a total of 125,400 beds. All the major international hotel chains are represented in the city.

This applies to the luxury brand Waldorf Astoria, whose first newly built hotel in Europe stands opposite the Gedächtniskirche, close to the Kurfürstendamm: 31 storeys, 242 luxurious rooms, a conference area of 1100 m² and a spacious spa.

Hotel prices in Berlin are below the level that is usual in a capital city, and furthermore keen competition in the business gives visitors the opportunity to look out for discounts: it is well worth asking and bargaining. Some partners of the tourist office, Berlin Tourismus und Kongress GmbH, are willing to offer discounts.

The hotel information line of the tourist information offices is tel. 030 25 00 25; for online bookings go to www.visitBerlin. Holiday apartments and private rooms can be found on www.ferienwohnung-berlin.de and a host of similar websites.

Not included among the almost 21 million annual overnight stays (2011) in guesthouses, hotels and hostels are the users of private apartments that Berliners – often to the annoyance of their neighbours – let as holiday homes from as little as €25 per night. It is estimated that some 10,000 apartments have been taken off the housing market for this purpose.

Hotels

Service numbers subject to charges are marked *: Tel. *01805 .

Holiday flats

Recommended hotels

PRICE CATEGORIES

For a double room, usually with breakfast, though more and more often an extra charge is made for the breakfast buffet.

€ € € € over €300
€ € € €200 – €300
€ € €120 – €200
€ €80 – €120

❶ See maps on pages 104 – 107
No number: not in the area covered by the maps

⓫ Adlon Kempinski Berlin
€ € € €
Unter den Linden 77 (Mitte)
Tel. 030 22 61-0
www.kempinski.com
S/U-Bahn: Brandenburger Tor
(S 1, S 2, S 25, U 55
382 rooms and 78 suites, wellness studio. Legendary hotel where Enrico Caruso, Tsar Nicholas, Albert Einstein and Thomas Alva Edison all stayed. Restaurant/bistro, Club Bar, American

A room with a sea view in the Radisson Blu thanks to the Aquadom

There is a wonderful view of the city from the terrace of the Hotel de Rome

Bar, smoker's lounge and lifestyle shop.

23 Alma Berlin Schlosshotel im Grunewald € € € €
Brahmsstr. 10 (Grunewald)
Tel. 030 89 58 40
www.schlosshotelberlin.com
53 rooms, restaurant, bars, gym
Top location in Grunewald, rooms by Karl Lagerfeld with plush decor and stucco.

20 Brandenburger Hof € € € €
Eislebener Str. 14 (Wilmersdorf
Tel. 030 21 40 50
www.brandenburger-hof.com
U-Bahn: Augsburger Str. (U 3)
68 rooms. Luxury hotel of the Relais & Châteaux group in a Wilhelmine city mansion. Piano bar, lovely winter garden and gourmet restaurant.

16 Grand Hyatt Berlin € € € €
Marlene-Dietrich-Platz 2 (Tiergarten)
Tel. 030 25 53 12 34
http://berlin.grand.hyatt.com
S-Bahn/U-Bahn: Potsdamer Platz (S 1, S 2, S 25, U 2)
342 rooms. Super-modern luxury hotel on the new Potsdamer Platz with every conceivable luxury; spa and swimming pool with a view on the top floor.

12 Hotel de Rome € € € €
Behrenstr. 37 (Mitte)
Tel. 030 4 60 60 90
www.hotelderome.com
U-Bahn: Französische Str. (U 6)
146 rooms for luxury travellers in what was once the Dresdner Bank. Packing and unpacking service, spa, Bebel-Bar and a good Italian restaurant: On the terrace

above Bebelplatz, Museum Island seems close enough to touch.

⑯ The Ritz-Carlton € € € €
Potsdamer Platz 3 (Tiergarten)
Tel. 030 33 77 77
www.ritzcarlton.com
S-/U-Bahn: Potsdamer Platz (S 1, S 2, S 25, U 2)
302 rooms Modern outside, historic charm inside. With a bath butler who perfumes the bathwater, antiques and tea lounge.

③ Ackselhaus € € €   **Insider Tip**
Belforter Str. 21 (Prenzlauer Berg) Charlottenburg.) D-10719 Berlin
Tel. 030 44 33 76 33
www.ackselhaus.de
U-Bahn: Senefelderplatz (U 2)
35 rooms. Possible the finest hotel in Prenzlauer Berg, situated on Kollwitzplatz. Each room has a different theme, and guests who come back exhausted from walking around the city can relax in a well-tended garden.

⑥ Casa Camper € € €
Weinmeisterstr. 1 (Mitte)
Tel. 030 20 00 34 10
www.casacamper.com
U-Bahn: Weinmeisterstr. (U 8)
51 rooms. Design hotel, as quirky as the fashionable footwear of the group it belongs to. A few paces from Hackescher Markt, with luxuriously fitted rooms. Fresh meals and drinks 24 hours a day. Asian food is served in the open restaurant.

㉑ Ellington € € €
Nürnberger Str. 50 – 55 (Schöneberg)
Tel. 030 68 31 50

www.ellington-hotel.com
U-Bahn: Wittenbergplatz (U 1)
285 rooms. A house with a history near Kudamm: behind the striking façade of this modern hotel lay the public office for regulating liquor sales in 1931, later a ballroom and a stage for Duke Ellington.

⑨ Radisson Blu € € €
Karl-Liebknecht-Str. 3 (Mitte)
Tel. 030 23 82 80
www.radissonblu.com/hotel-berlin
S/U-Bahn: Alexanderplatz (S 5, S 7, S 75, U 2, U 5, U 8)
427 rooms. A sea view? Almost, as in the atrium is a 25 m/80ft-high circular aquarium with tropical fish. The panorama lift in the Aquadom is only for visitors to the Sea Life Center, however.

⑮ Scandic Berlin € € €
Gabriele-Tergit-Promenade 19 (Mitte)
Tel. 030 7 00 77 90
www.scandichotels.com/berlin
S/U-Bahn: Potsdamer Platz (S 1, S 2, S 25, U 2)
563 rooms. Elks guard the foyer. This hotel, pleasant despite its size, opened in 2010 and has Scandinavian ecological certification: parquet flooring instead of carpeting, resource-saving operations, and kitchens that work to the specifications of Jamie Oliver, even for the children's menu.

⑦ Soho House € € €
Torstr. 1 (Mitte)
Tel. 030 4 05 04 40
www.sohohouseberlin.com
U-Bahn: Rosa-Luxemburg-Platz (U 2)

40 rooms. Once a department store for the poor, then a headquarters for the Party of Socialist Unity, since 2010 a club (for members only) and a hotel for everybody. This enormous, heritage-listed Bauhaus building has large rooms, all in vintage design, which extends to vinyl for the record player, as well as a small pool on the roof terrace, a spa and private cinema.

⑩ Alexander Plaza € €
Rosenstr. 1 (Mitte)
Tel. 030 24 00 10
www.alexander-plaza.com
S-Bahn: Hackescher Markt (S 5, S 7, S 75)
94 rooms. The Alexander was built from 1897 to 1900 for fur trader Siegfried Abrahamson as a commercial building. Unbeatable location opposite the Hackesche Höfe near the new Hackesches Quartier.

⑬ Bleibtreu
Bleibtreustr. 31 (Charlottenbg.),
Tel. 030 8 84 74-0, www.bleibtreu.com
60 rooms, restaurant, spa
S-Bahn: Savignyplatz (S 5, S 7, S 75)
In one of the loveliest side streets of Kurfürstendamm, a hotel in a large town house that seeks to be environmentally friendly in terms of both fittings and cuisine.

㉒ Estrel Hotel Berlin € €
Sonnenallee 225 (Neukölln)
Tel. 030 6 83 12 25 22, www.estrel.com,
S-Bahn: Sonnenallee (S 41, S 42)

Europe's biggest hotel (1125 rooms) is a bit off the beaten track. It is an ultra-modern building with all facilities for congresses, fitness and health, five restaurants, a bar – and a live show, »Stars in Concert«.

⑭ Hotel Gates € €
Knesebeckstr. 8 – 9 (Charlottenburg)
Tel. 030 31 10 60
www.hotel-gates.com
S-Bahn: Savignyplatz (S 5, S 7, S 75)
104 rooms. Internet connection to the inhouse computer in every room, action and sports TV channels in the evening. Guests can use a red city-bike to explore Berlin.

❹ Honigmond Garden € € Insider Tip
Tieckstr. 11 (Mitte)
Tel. 030 28 44 55 77 www.honigmond.de
U-Bahn: Naturkundemuseum (U 6)
25 rooms. To pass through the door of this lovingly restored building dating from 1845 is to enter an unexpected paradise in the middle of the city with a Mediterranean garden where birds twitter, frogs croak and a fountain splashes. Beautiful paintings decorate the walls, and the furniture is antique. Café and restaurant a few paces away in the Honigmond Hotel at Tieckstr. 11.

❺ mitArt € €
Linienstr. 139 –140(Mitte)
Tel. 030 28 39 04 30
www.mitart.de
U-Bahn: Oranienburger Tor (U 6)
30 rooms. Berlin's first certified green and organic hotel lies at the

heart of the old Scheunenviertel in a quiet cycling street, and has been converted from a GDR army printworks. The unpretentious rooms, decorated with works by international artists in changing exhibitions and without radio or TV, are a haven of peace in the hubbub of the city. The organic food in the courtyard café is available to everyone.

❾ Myer's Hotel € € *Insider Tip*
Metzstr. 26 (Prenzlauer Berg)
Tel. 030 4 40 14-0
www.myershotel.de
U-Bahn: Senefelder Platz (U 2)
56 rooms. Stylish accommodation in an excellent place for going out in the evening.

⓲ Bogotà €
Schlüterstr.45 (Charlottenbg.)
Tel. 030 8 81 50 01
www.hotelbogotaberlin.com
S-Bahn: Savignyplatz (S 5, S 7, S 75)
123 rooms Comfy but slightly aged-ooking hotel, which is well priced given its location around the corner from Ku'damm.

⓭ Dittberner €
Wielandstr. 26 (Charlottenbg.)
Tel. 030 884695-0
U-Bahn: Adenauerplatz (U 7
www.hotel-dittberner.de
20 rooms Budget guesthouse in a large and convoluted town house, very friendly service.

⓭ Hansablick €
Flotowstr. 6 (Tiergarten)
Tel. 030 3 90 48 00
www.hansablick.de
U-Bahn: Hansaplatz (U 9)

23 rooms. Comfortable and stylish small hotel on the banks of the Spree. A few rooms have a balcony. Big breakfast buffet and gym.

❷ Kastanienhof €
Kastanienallee 65
(Prenzlauer Berg)
Tel. 030 44 30 50
www.kastanienhof.biz
U-Bahn: Senefelder Platz (U 2)
35 rooms. Family atmosphere in an old residential building a few paces from the pub scene, Oderberger Str. and the Kulturbrauerei.

❽ Platte Mitte €
Rochstr. 9 (Mitte)
Tel. 030 01 77 2 83 26 02
www.plattemitte.de
S-Bahn: Hackescher Markt (S 5, S 7, S 75)
4 rooms. Those who appreciate a wonderful view of the city centre and TV tower by night from the

Myer's Hotel is an inviting place to stay

21st storey more than a rooms with a well-designed interior, and who don't baulk at kitsch and pastel colours, will feel at home in the rooms in this Socialist-style prefabricated block.

IN POTSDAM
(SEE PLAN PP. 348/349)
❶ Am Jägertor € €
Hegelallee 11
Tel. 0331 2 01 11 00
www.hotel am-jaegertor.de
62 rooms. Centrally located romantic hotel with a garden terrace and the excellent Fiore restaurant.

❷ Filmhotel Lili Marleen €
Grossbeerenstr. 75 (Babelsberg)
Tel. (03 31) 74 32 00
www.filmhotel.potsdam.de
65 rooms; ideal place for film fans because its neighbour is the Filmstadt Babelsberg.

HOSTELS €
East Seven
Schwedter Str. 7 (Prenzlauer Berg)
Tel. 030 93 62 22 40
www.eastseven.de
U-Bahn: Senefelderplatz (U 2)
60 beds. Small, cosy, popular hostel in retro design, guests can barbecue in the garden and cook for themselves. Busy Kastanienallee is not far away.

Eastern Comfort
Mühlenstr. 73 – 77
(Friedrichshain)
Tel. 030 66 76 38 06
www.eastern-comfort.com
U-Bahn: Warschauer Str. (U 1)
25 cabins, This hostel ship bobs at anchor behind the East Side Gal-

lery next to the Oberbaumbrücke in the party scene between Kreuzberg and Friedrichshain. Cabins from 1st to 3rd class, and space on deck for tents.

Generator
Storkower Str. 160
(Prenzlauer Berg)
Tel. 030 4 17 24 00
www.generatorhostels.com
S-Bahn: Landsberger Allee
(S 41, S 42)
902 rooms. One of Germany's biggest hostels, also used by school groups, situated between Prenzlauzer Berg and Friedrichshain. Unbeatable prices, evening meal available

❺ Mitte's Baxpax Hostel
Chausseestr. 102 (Mitte)
Tel. 030 28 39 09 65
www.baxpax.de;
U-Bahn: Naturkundemuseum (U 6)
100 beds. One of Berlin's first hostels, started up in the 1990s when only old-style youth hostels catered for backpackers. The name and fittings have been brought up to date, the café and internet access remain.

ASSOCIATION YOUTH HOSTELS
Deutsches Jugendherbergswerk Berlin-Brandenburg
Tempelhofer Ufer 32
Tel. 030 26 49 52-0
www.djh-Berlin-Brandenburg.de

Jugendherberge Berlin International
Kluckstr. 3 (Tiergarten)
Tel. 030 7 47 68 79 10
U-Bahn: Kurfüstenstraße (U 1)

Jugendherberge Ernst Reuter
Hermsdorfer Damm 48–50
(Tegel/Hermsdorf)
Tel. 030 4 04 16 10
Bus 125 from U-Bahn station
Alt-Tegel (U 6)

Jugendgästehaus Am Wannsee
Badeweg 1
(Zehlendorf)
Tel. 030 803 20 34
S-Bahn: Wannsee (S 1, S 7)

CAMPING
Deutscher Camping Club (DCC)
Kladower Damm 113 – 117
Tel. 030 2 18 60 71
www.dcc-berlin.de

Bürgerablage (BCC)
Niederneuendorfer Alle 63
(Spandau)
Tel. 030 3 35 45 84
www.berlin-campingclub.com
April – Sep. With beach and pier
for swimming on the river Havel.

DCC-Campingplatz Gatow
Kladower Damm 113 – 117
(Spandau)
Tel. 3654340 F
Open all year round.

DCC-Campingplatz Kladow
Krampnitzer Weg 111 – 117
(Spandau)
Tel. 030 3652797
www.dcc-berlin.de
Open all year round. 150 spaces,
restaurant. Near Glienicker See.

Campingplatz Am Krossinsee
Wernsdorfer Str. 38
(Treptow-Köpenick)
Tel. 030 6758687
www.campingplatz-krossinsee.de
Open all year round. Restaurant,
terrace on the lake, playground,
holiday homes, boat moorings.

Campingplatz Am Krossinsee
An der Pirschheide 41, Potsdam
Tel. 03 31 9 51 09 88
www.campingpark-sanssouci-
potsdam.de
Open April – Oct

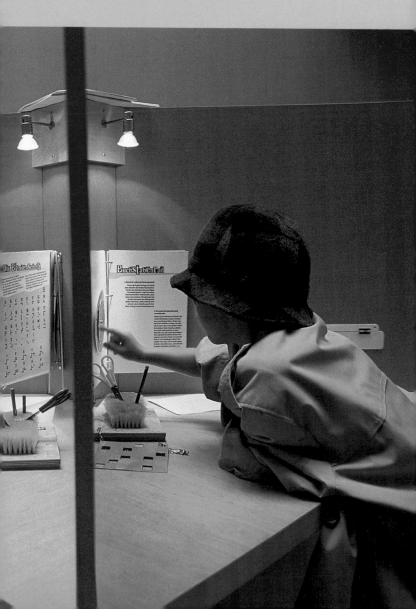

No Reason to be Bored

It should be impossible for children to get bored in Berlin. Many districts of Berlin have special leisure facilities for children so that fun and excitement are always available.

Using public transport to get there is free for any child of six and under and there is a discount for any children who have not yet reached their 15th birthday (▶Transport). In the state museums (Staatliche Museen Berlin), children up to 16 years of age pay no admission. Many museums offer guided tours and courses for children as part of the »Jugend im Museum« programme. Theatrical performances for children and youngsters include a varied programme of plays and a trip on the Spree is fun for young and old alike. Those who love water are well catered for in Berlin anyway since the range of lakes and swimming pools is huge. Two zoos have an exciting selection of exotic animals for kids from one to ninety-one (▶Tierpark Friedrichsfelde, ▶Zoologischer Garten). One very special attraction – even for grown-ups – is the **sweet factory** at Oranienburger Str. 32. Most hotels will also help out with babysitters.

Berlin for children

SWIMMING POOLS

Kinderbad Monbijou (children's swimming pool)
Oranienburger Str. 78
(Mitte)
www.berlinerbaederbetriebe.de
S-Bahn: Hackescher Markt
(S 5, S 7, S 75)
May – July Mon – Fri 11am – 7pm,
Sat, Sun 10am – 7pm; Aug daily
10am – 7pm
Admission: €4/€2.50

Strandbad Wannsee
Wannseebadweg 25
(Zehlendorf)
www.berlinerbaederbetriebe.de
S-Bahn: Nikolassee (S1, S 7), then
10 min. walk

Mon – Fri 10am – 7pm, Sat, Sun
8am – 8pm
Admission: €4 / €2.50

LEISURE CENTRES

Britzer Garten
Sangerhauser Weg 1 (Neukölln)
Tel. 70 09 09-0 Fax 70 09 06-70
www.britzer-garten.de
Admission: €2
▶Neukölln, Britz

FEZ Wuhlheide
An der Wuhlheide 197 (Köpenick)
Tel. 030 53 07 12 81
www.fez-berlin.de
S-Bahn: Wuhlheide (S 3)
School term: Tue – Fri 9am – 10pm,
Sat 1pm – 7pm, Sun 12

Creative play in the Labyrinth children's museum

noon – 6pm; holidays Tue – Fri
11am – 6pm, Sat 1pm to 7pm,
Sun 12 noon – 6pm
20 minutes from the city centre:
creative activities (including puppet shows, pottery, model making, computer courses), theatricals,
concerts, ceinema, swimming and
sports hall, open-air plays, lakes to
bathe in, sports facilities and playing fields plus park railway.

Ökowerk
Teufelsseechaussee 22 – 24
(Wilmersdorf)
Tel. 030 3 00 00 50
www.oekowerk.de
S-Bahn: Grunewald (S 7), then 20
min. walk along Schildhornweg
Summer Tue – Fri 9am – 6pm, Sat,
Sun 12 noon – 6pm; winter
Tue – Fri 10am – 4pm, Sat, Sun
11am – 4pm
Admission: adults €2.50 / children
over 5, €1
Nature activities on the site of an
old waterworks

MUSEUMS FOR CHILDREN
Jugendmuseum Schöneberg (Museum of Youth)
Hauptstr. 40/42 (Schöneberg)
Tel. 030 78 76 21 76
www.jugendmuseum.de
U-Bahn: Rathaus Schöneberg (U 4)
Wed and Thu 3pm to 6pm, Sun
from 2pm
History museum for the young
with exhibitions and workshops.

Labyrinth Kindermuseum
Osloer Str. 12 (Wedding)
Tel. 030 93 11 50
www.kindermuseum-labyrinth.de
U-Bahn: Pankstrasse (U 8), then 5
min. walk

Fri, Sat 1pm – 6pm, Sun
11am – 6pm, longer hours in
school holidays; admission: €4.50
Interactive exhibitions.

Machmit! Museum für Kinder
Senefelder Str. 5 (Prenzlauer Berg)
Tel. 030 74778200
www.machmitmuseum.de
U-Bahn: Eberswalder Straße (U 2)
Tue – Sun 10am – 6pm; admission:
€4.50 (adults) / €3 (children)
Play for six to twelve year olds in a
former church

Puppentheater-Museum Berlin (Puppetry Museum)
Karl-Marx-Str. 135 (Neukölln)
Tel. 030 6 87 81 32
www.puppentheater-museum.de
U-Bahn: Karl-Marx-Straße (U 7)
 Mon – Fri 9am – 3.30pm, Sun
11am – 4pm
Admission: €3 / €2.50
Story of puppetry in theatres with
puppets to touch and play with
and puppet show performances.

Science Center Spectrum
in the Deutsches Technikmuseum
Scientific phenomena demonstrated specially for children, (►p.188)

Waldmuseum mit Waldschule (Forestry Museum and School)
Jagdschloss Grunewald
(Zehlendorf)
Königsweg 04 / Jagen 57
Tel. 030 8 13 34 42
www.waldmuseum-waldschule.de
S-Bahn: Grunewald (S 7), then 6
min. walk
Tue – Fri 10am – 3pm, Sun
1pm – 6pm, admission: free

Everything about life in the woods, with many dioramas, guessing games and the chance of a look through a microscope.

THEATRE FOR CHILDREN
Berliner Kindertheater
Summer: open-air stage at Zitadelle Spandau; winter: Fontane-Haus in the Märkisches Viertel, Wilhelmsruher Damm 142c
Tel. 030 62 70 59 26
www.berliner-kindertheater.de

Theater an der Parkaue
Parkaue 29 (Lichtenberg)
Tel. 030 55 77 52 52
www.parkaue.de
S/U-Bahn: Frankfurter Allee (S 41, S 42, U 5)
Germany's largest children's theatre, founded in the GDR in 1950, for children aged 5 and over

Fliegendes Theater
Urbanstr. 100 (Kreuzberg)
Tel. 030 6 92 21 00
www.fliegendes-theater.de
U-Bahn: Hermannplatz (U 7, U 8)
From 3 years; plays for adults, too

Figurentheater Grashüpfer
(puppet theatre)
Puschkinallee 16a
(Treptower Park))
Tel. 030 53 69 51 50
www.theater-grashuepfer.de
S-Bahn: Treptower Park (S 41, S 42, S 8, S 9)
Plays and fairy-tale readings, for children aged 3 or older

Grips Theater
Altonaer Str. 22 (Tiergarten) and Klosterstr. 68 (Mitte)
Tel. 030 39 74 74 77
www.grips-theater.de
U-Bahn: Hansaplatz (U 9) or Klosterstrasse (U 2)
Berlin's legendary theatre for children and young people.

Zaubertheater Igor Jedlin
(magic theatre)
Roscherstr. 7
(Charlottenburg)
Tel. 030 3 23 37 77
www.zaubertheater.de
Thu – Sun 3.30pm: magic for kids
U-Bahn: Adenauerplatz (U 7)

Going Out in Berlin

Those who prefer to see the glass half-empty say that there are more opportunities to have a disappointing evening in Berlin than anywhere else: with some 300 events every day, entertainment of high or low quality is on offer.

This figure does not include going to a bar (130 options) or cinema (230), watching an unknown number of spectacular sunsets, or sitting, talking, singing and laughing together on bridges, or joining the crowds of hundreds who come to the parks to beat drums. Bear in mind here that the popular practice of partying on bridges in residential areas is now prohibited from 10pm. So what else is there to do?

Three large and one small opera houses (the most-performed opera is *The Magic Flute*), 31 theatres, 29 venues for small-scale shows, 18 children's theatres and 15 cabarets, a huge number of clubs for music and dancing, small stages for concerts and large venues such as the Olympic Stadium in Charlottenburg, the O2 arena in Friedrichshain and the C-Halle (previously Columbia-Halle), the American sports arena in Kreuzberg. In summer the open-air Waldbühne in Charlottenburg, Zitadelle Spandau and the Kindl-Bühne in Wuhlheide add to the number of approximately 250 event venues, not to mention a dozen open-air cinemas.

What's on offer?

It is almost impossible to be incorrectly dressed. Even at high-class cultural events, nobody minds when visitors from all over the world leave rucksacks in the theatre cloakroom. At some clubs the doormen react badly when visitors turn up with trainers on their feet, but others take a look at the sneakers and recognize whose outfit and outlook suit the place. Although music clubs often open at 8pm, 9pm or 10pm, most people who arrive at midnight are still too early, and they can never be too late, especially at weekends and in the so-called Bermuda Triangle between Alexanderplatz, the Ostbahnhof and the Oberbaumbrücke, including the banks of the Spree – i.e. in the Mitte, Friedrichshain and Kreuzberg districts.

Etiquette

Smokers can indulge their habit. 650 pubs are registered as smoking establishments, meeting the conditions that the room has to be smaller than 75 m², that no meals are served and that under-18s are not admitted. Smokers' lounges in the high-class hotels cater for those who don't object to cigar smoke.

Smokers?

The Chamäleon Varieté

Cinema, dancing, music

⑪ etc.: see maps on pages 74–77. No number means it is off the map.

⑯ Arena and Badeschiff
Eichenstr. 4 (Treptow)
030 5 33 73 33
www.arena-berlin.de
S-Bahn: Treptower Park
(S 41, S 42, S 8)
Theatre, concerts, dance and cin-ema in a former bus depot; space for 800 bathers in summer from 8am on the Badeschiff (swim ship).

⑪ Berghain
Am Wriezener Bahnhof (Frie-drichshain)
S-Bahn: Ostbahnhof
(S 5, S 7, S 75, U 1)
Legendary techno club with live acts by top DJs.

⑤ Clärchens Ballhaus
Auguststr. 24 (Mitte)
Tel. 030 2 82 92 95   Insider Tip
www.ballhaus.de
S-Bahn: Hackescher Markt
(S 5, S 7, S 75)
Classic Berlin ballroom from the good old days, no longer just a place for senior citizens: now it has been refurbished, afternoons

can be spent in its beer garden until the youngsters start dancing in the evening.

⑤ Cookies
in the Westin Grand Hotel
Friedrichstr./Unter den Linden
(Mitte)
Tel. 030 2 80 88 06
www.cookies-berlin.de
U-Bahn: Französische Str. (U 6)
An institution in Berlin's nighlife, only Tue und Thu

⑦ Grüner Salon at the Volksbühne
Rosa-Luxemburg-Platz
(Mitte)
Tel. 030 28 59 89 38
U-Bahn: Rosa-Luxemburg-Platz
(U 2)
Live music, chansons, also swing, tango and salsa evenings

❹ Kaffee Burger
Torstr. 60 (Mitte)
Tel. 030 28 04 64 96
www.kaffeeburger.de
U-Bahn: Rosenthaler Pl. (U 2)
Gipsy jazz, grooves, electro, Rus-sian disco and readings

❻ Kulturbrauerei
Sredzkistr. 15
(Prenzlauer Berg)
Tel. 030 4 43 15-100
www.kulturbrauerei.de
U-Bahn: Eberswalder Str. (U 2)
A leading venue for music, read-ings, exhibitions and theatre

⑰ Lido
Cuvrystr. 7 (Kreuzberg)
Tel. 030 78 95 84 10

The Kulturbrauerei

www.lido-berlin.de
U-Bahn: Schlesisches Tor (U 1)
Rock, indie, electro and pop

⑭ Tresor
Köpenicker Str. 70 (Kreuzberg)
Tel. 030 69 53 77-0
www.tresorberlin.de
U-Bahn: Heinrich-Heine-Str. (U 8)
The new home of this famous
techno club is a decommissioned
power station in Mitte district.

Watergate
Falckensteinstr. 49
(Kreuzberg) No tel.
www.water-gate.de
S-Bahn: Ostbahnhof
(S 5, S 7, S 75, U 1)
Berlin's nicest club in a warehouse
by the river bank with views of
the Spree and the Oberbaum-
brücke, with terrace

JAZZ AND BLUES
⑳ A Trane Jazzclub
Bleibtreustr. 1
(Charlottenburg)
Tel. 030 3 13 25 50
wwww.a-trane.de
S-Bahn: Savignyplatz
(S 5, S 7, S 75)
Modern jazz, late-night jam ses-
sions for connoisseurs

❻ b-flat Jazzclub
Rosenthaler Str. 13 (Mitte)
Tel. 030 2 83 31 23
S-Bahn: Hackescher Markt
(S 5, S 7, S 75)
Small jazz bar that hosts concerts
by major acts

㉓ Quasimodo
Kantstr. 12a (Charlottenburg)
Tel. 030 3 12 80 86
www.quasimodo.de

Harry's New York Bar, a Berlin institution

S/U-Bahn: Zoologischer Garten
(S 5, S 7, S 75, U 2, U 9)
The classic place in the west for
jazz, blues, folk, funk and soul.

TRENDY BARS, PUBS
⑮ Ankerklause

Insider Tip

Kottbusser Damm 104/
Maybachufer (Kreuzberg)
Tel. 030 6 93 56 49
www.ankerklause.de
U-Bahn: Kottbusser Tor (U 1, U 8)
Terrace on the Landwehr canal
with a view of the restaurants op-
posite

⑫ CSA-Bar
Karl-Marx-Allee 96 (Friedrichshain)
Tel. 030 29 04 47 41
U-Bahn: Weberwiese (U 5)
www.csa-bar.de
Pure nostalgia for the East in the
former head office of the Czech
airline, Ceskoslovensko Aeroline

㉖ Green Door
Winterfeldtstr. 50 (Schöneberg)

Tel. 030 2 15 25 15
U-Bahn: Nollendorfplatz (U 1, U 4)
Everything is green and the cock-
tail menu is endless.

㉔ Harry's New York Bar
Lützowufer 15, in Grand Hotel Es-
planade (Tiergarten)
Tel. 030 2 54 78-0
U-Bahn: Nollendorfplatz (U 1, U 4)
Live piano music and excellent
cocktails from a long bar made of
black granite

⑨ King Size Bar
Friedrichstr. (Mitte)
U-Bahn: Oranienburger Tor (U 6)
www.kingsizebar.de
The opposite of what the name
promises, but for some, this is the
ultimate bar: a counter and an
over-30 or over-40 crowd. Dancing sometimes.

㉕ Kumpelnest
Lützowstr. 23 (Schöneberg)
Tel. 030 2 61 69 18

www.kumpelnest3000.com
U-Bahn: Kurfürstenstr. (U 1, U 2)
Trash-art venue and rendezvous
for the new gallery scene

㉒ La Casa del Habano
Fasanenstr. 9
Hotel Savoy (Charlottenburg)
Tel. 030 3 11 03-0
www.hotel-savoy.com
U-Bahn: Kurfüstendamm (U 1)
Havannas in the humidor and in-
tellectual guests

❷ Metzer Eck
Metzer Str. 33 (Prenzlauer Berg)
Tel. 030 4 42 76 56
U-Bahn: Senefelderplatz (U 2)
This makes a change in Prenzlauer
Berg: an original Berlin pub with
food to match, established in
1913

❸ Saphire Bar
Bötzowstr. 31 (Prenzlauer Berg)
Tel. 030 25 56 21 58
www.saphirebar.de
S-Bahn: Greifswalder Str.
(S 41, S 42)
The 1970s, brought back to life
elegantly

❾ Tausend Bar
Schiffbauerdamm 11 (Mitte)
www.tausendberlin.com
S-/U-Bahn: Friedrichstr. (S 1, S 2,
S 5, S 7, S 75, U 6)
No admission for those wearing
trainers. Guests are 30+, the light-
ing trendy, the cocktails superb.

❿ Windhorst
Dorotheenstr. 65 (Mitte)
Tel. 030 20 45 00 70
S/U-Bahn: Friedrichstr. (S 1, S 2,
S 5, S 7, S 75, U 6)

Classic bar with outstanding cocktails and delicious snacks

⓳ Würgeengel
Dresdener Str. 122 (Kreuzberg)
Tel. 030 6 15 55 60
www.wuergeengel.de
U-Bahn: Kottbusser Tor (U 1, U 15,
U 12, U 8)
Stylish cocktail bar with jazz

㉗ Yorckschlösschen
Yorckstr. 15 (Kreuzberg)
Tel. 030 2 15 80 70
S/U-Bahn: Yorckstr./Grossgör-
schenstrasse (S 1, U 7)
A Kreuzberg institution with a
beer garden, regular jazz and
blues on Sundays

㉑ Zwiebelfisch
Savignyplatz 7 (Charlottenburg)
Tel. 030 3 12 73 63
www.zwiebelfisch-berlin.de
S-Bahn: Savignyplatz
Keeps its 1968 revolutionary tradi-
tion alive, but the air is no longer
thick with smoke

CINEMAS
Most of the cinemas are located
in Mitte or in Friedrichshain-
Kreuzberg, and there are art-
house cinemas in every district.

Films are increasingly screened in the original language with subtitles. Every February the Berlin International Film Festival (Berlinale) takes place with movies competing for the Golden Bear awards, a children's film festival and Perspektive Deutsches Kino, a forum for new German film productions. The films are mostly shown in the cinemas at Potsdamer Platz or the Filmzentrum Zoo-Palast.

Programme information
Tel. *01 90 11 50 30
www.kino-berlin.de
www.kinokompendium.de

Astor Film Lounge
Kurfürstendamm 225 (Charlottenburg)
Tel. 030 883 55 51
www.astor-filmlounge.de
U-Bahn: Kurfürstendamm (U 1, U 9)
Luxurious cinema for those who are prepared to pay more for a doorman and valet parking, comfortable seats and waiter service for food and drinks.

Babylon
Rosa-Luxemburg-Str. 30 (Mitte)
Tel. 030 2 42 59 69
www.babylonberlin.de
U-Bahn: Rosa-Luxemburg-Platz (U 2)

The only cinema that has remained in its original condition since silent-movie days. Built in 1928 to a design by Expressionist architect Hans Poelzig. Retrospectives include examples from the former East German film archive.

Moviemento
Kottbusser Damm 22 (Kreuzberg)
Tel. 030 6 92 47 85
www.moviemento.de
U-Bahn: Hermannplatz (U 7, U 8)
Opened in 1907 and thus Berlin's oldest cinema. Today art-house movies, classics and premieres are presented here.

IMAX
Potsdamer Str. 4, Sony Center (Tiergarten)
Tel. 030 26 06 64 00
www.cinestar.de
U/S-Bahn: Potsdamer Platz (S 1, S 2, S 25, U 2)
The world's largest screen for 3D films, 25,000 watt sound system

Open-air cinema
www.freiluftkino-berlin.de
Kulturforum Potsdamer Platz, www.yorck.de
Open-air Charlottenburg www.openaircharlottenburg.de
Freiluftkino Hasenheide, www.freiluftkino-hasenheide.de

Theatre, Music, Concerts

TICKETS IN ADVANCE
Berliner Theater und Konzertkasse BTK
Spreeufer 6, Nikolaiviertel
Tel. 030 2 41 46 87
www.btk-berlin.de

Theaterkasse Alexanderplatz Galeria Kaufhof
in Galeria Kaufhof
Tel. 030 24 74 33 27
www.ctm-theaterkassen.de

Hekticket am Zoo/ am Alex
Hardenbergstr. 29d
(in the Foyer of the Deutsche Bank)
Tel. 030 2 30 99 30
Karl-Liebknecht-Str. 13
(Kulturkiosk at Berlin Carré)
Tel. 030 24 31 24 31
www.hekticket.de
Sometimes half-price tickets for shows the same day are available at 2pm.

Showtime GmbH
Tel. 030 80 60 29 29
www.showtimetickets.de
Branches in department stores, including KaDeWe, Karstadt on Hermannplatz, Karstadt in Spandau, Karstadt on Tempelhofer Damm

Theater- und Konzertkasse
S-Bahnhof Alexanderplatz
Tel. 030 24 72 16

BERLIN THEATRES
Berliner Ensemble
Theater am Schiffbauerdamm
Bertolt-Brecht-Platz 1 (Mitte)
Tel. 030 2 84 08-1 55 (tickets)
Tel. -1 53 (information, tours)
www.berliner-ensemble.de
S-Bahn/U-Bahn: Friedrichstrasse
(S 1, S 2, S 25, S 5, S 7, S 75, U 6)
Modern plays, contemporary and historical theatre pieces and works by Brecht

Deutsches Theater und Kammerspiele
Schumannstr. 13a (Mitte)

Tchaikovsky's »Eugene Onegin« at the Staatsoper

Tel. 030 2 84 41-2 25
www.deutschestheater.de
U-Bahn: Oranienburger Tor (U 6)
Classical and modern plays

F40-English Theatre Berlin
Fidicinstr. 40 (Kreuzberg)
Tel. 030 6 91 12 11
www.thefriends.de
U-Bahn: Platz der Luftbrücke (U 6)
English-speaking theatre

HAU 1 (Hebbel am Ufer)
Stresemannstr. 29 (Kreuzberg)
Tel. 25 90 04 27
www.hebbel-theater.de
U-Bahn: Hallesches Tor (U 1, U 6)
Theatre, dance, music

HAU 2
Hallesches Ufer 32 (Kreuzberg)
Tel. see above
U-Bahn: Möckernbrücke (U 1, U 7)

HAU 3
Tempelhofer Ufer 10
(Kreuzberg)
Tel. see above
U-Bahn: Möckernbrücke (U 1, U 7)

Maxim-Gorki-Theater and Gorki-Studio
Am Festungsgraben 2 and behind
Giesshaus (Mitte)
Tel. 030 20 22 11 15
www.gorki.de
S-Bahn: Hackescher Markt
Contemporary drama.

Renaissance-Theater
Knesebeckstr. 100
(Charlottenburg)
Tel. 030 3 12 42 02
www.renaissance-theater.de
S-Bahn: Savignyplatz
Plays and comedy

Schaubühne am Lehniner Platz
Kurfürstendamm 153
(Charlottenburg)
Tel. 030 89 00 23
www.schaubuehne.de
U-Bahn: Adenauerplatz (U 7)
Modern plays and classical drama

Schlossparktheater
Schlossstr. 48 (Steglitz)
Tel. 030 78 95 66 71 00
www.schlossparktheater.de
U-Bahn: Rathaus Steglitz (U 9)
After years of neglect the theatre
has come to life again under the
direction of a popular German co-
median, Dieter Hallervorden – serious drama is staged with renowned actors in addition to
comedy.

Sophiensäle
Sophienstr. 18 (Mitte)
Tel. 030 2835266
S-Bahn: Hackescher Markt (S 5,
S 7, S 75)
www.sophiensaele.com
Venue for avant garde theatre
performances

Theater 89
Torstr. 216 (Mitte)
Tel. 030 2 82 46 56
www.theater89.de
U-Bahn: Rosa-Luxemburg-Platz
(U 2)
Independent theatre founded in
1989

Volksbühne am Rosa-Luxemburg-Platz
Rosa-Luxemburg-Platz
(Mitte)
Tel. 030 2 40 65-777
www.volksbuehne-berlin.de

U-Bahn: Rosa-Luxemburg-Platz
(U 2)
Provocative works

OPERA/OPERETTA/BALLET
Deutsche Oper Berlin
Bismarckstr. 35 (Charlottenburg)
Tel. 030 34 38 43 43
www.deutscheoperberlin.de
U-Bahn: Deutsche Oper (U 2)

Staatsoper Unter den Linden
Unter den Linden 5-7 (Mitte)
Tel. 030 2 03 54-5 55
S-Bahn: Hackescher Markt (S 5,
S 7, S 75)
www.staatsoper-berlin.de

Komische Oper Berlin
Behrenstr. 55 – 57 (Mitte)
Tel. 030 47997400
www.komische-oper-berlin.de
U-Bahn: Französische Str. (U 6)

Neuköllner Oper
Insider Tip
Karl-Marx-Str. 131 – 133
(Neukölln)
Tel. 030 68 89 07-77
U-Bahn: Karl-Marx-Str. (U 7)
▶MARCO POLO Tip p.266

CONCERTS (VENUES)
C-Hall
Columbiadamm 9-11 (Tempelhof)
Tel. 030 69 81 28 14
www.c-halle.com
U-Bahn: Platz der Luftbrücke (U 6)

Huxleys Neue Welt
Hasenheide 107 – 113 (Kreuzberg)
Tel. 030 78 09 98 10
www.huxleysneuewelt.com
U-Bahn: Hermannplatz (U7, U 8)

Konzerthaus Berlin
Gendarmenmarkt (Mitte)

Tel. 030 2 03 09-21 01
www.konzerthaus.de
U-Bahn: Französische Str. (U 6)

O2 World
Am Ostbahnhof (Friedrichshain)
Tel. *01803 20 60 70
www.o2world.de
S/U-Bahn: Warschauer Str. (S 3,
S 5, S 7, S 75 ,U 1)

Philharmonie
Herbert-von-Karajan-Str. 1
(Tiergarten)
Tel. 030 2 54 88-999
www.berliner-philharmoniker.de
S / U-Bahn: Potsdamer Platz (S 1,
S 2, S 25, U 2)

Radialsystem Vt
Holzmarktstr. 33 (Friedrichshain)
Tel. 030 2 88 78 85 88
www.radialsystem.de
S-Bahn: Ostbahnhof (S 5, S 7,
S 75, U 1)
Contemporary dance, early music,
classics and pop in an old pump-
ing works

Tempodrom
Möckernstr. 10 (Kreuzberg)
Tel. 030 69 53 3885
www.tempodrom.de
S-Bahn: Anhalter Bahnhof (S 1,
S 2, S 25)
Legendary venue that has been
resurrected at Anhalter Bahnhof.
Classical and rock concerts, musi-
cals and circus performances.l

Waldbühne
Glockenturmstr. 1 (Charlotten-
burg)
Tel. 030 23 08 82 30
www.waldbuehne-berlin.de
S-Bahn: Pichelsberg (S 5)

PUPPET THEATRE
Die Schaubude
Greifswalder Str. 81–84
(Prenzlauer Berg)
Tel. 030 4 23 43 14
www.schaubude-berlin.de
S-Bahn: Greifswalder Straße (S 41,
S 42)

SHOWS
FriedrichstadtPalast
Friedrichstr. 107 (Mitte)
Tel. 030 23 26 23 26
www.show-palace.eu
S/U-Bahn: Friedrichstraße (S 1, S 2,
S 25, S 5, S 7, S 75, U 6)
Europe's largest revue theatre still
puts on big shows with men in
top hats and long-legged dancers.

Bluemax Theater
Marlene-Dietrich-Platz 4

(Tiergarten)
Tel. *01805 44 44
www.bluemangroup.de
S/U-Bahn: Potsdamer Platz (S 1,
S 2, S 25, U 2)

Stars in Concert
Sonnenallee 225 (Estrel Festival
Center, Neukölln)
Tel. 030 68 31 68 31
www.stars-in-concert.de
S-Bahn: Sonnenallee (S 41, S 42)
Live show with doubles of mega-
stars

CABARET, COMEDY
Admiralspalast
Friedrichstr. 101 (Mitte)
Tel. 030 47 99 74 99
www. admiralspalast.de
S/U-Bahn: Friedrichstraße (S 1,
S 2, S 25, S 5, S 7, S 75, U 6)

The »loveliest legs in Berlin« are on show at the Friedrichstadtpalast

BKA – Berliner Kabarett Anstalt

Mehringdamm 34 (Kreuzberg) U-Bahn: Mehringdamm and Luftschloss, Schlossplatz (Mitte) S-Bahn: Hackescher Markt (U 6, U 7)
Tel. 030 2 02 20 07
www.bka-theater.de
Cabaret, chansons, tango

Distel

Friedrichstr. 101 (Mitte)
Tel. 030 2 04 47 04
www.distel-berlin.de
S/U-Bahn: Friedrichstrasse (S 1, S 2, S 25, S 5, S 7, S 75, U 6)
The oldest cabaret surviving from East Berlin performs political and social satire in the Admiralspalast.

Quatsch Comedy Club

Friedrichstr. 107, (Mitte)
Tel. *01805 25 55 65
www.quatschcomedyclub.de
S/U-Bahn: Friedrichstr. (S 1, S 2, S 25, S 5, S 7, S 75, U 6)
Light entertainment in the Friedrichstadtpalast building (entrance on the right)

Die Stachelschweine

Tauentzienstr. (Charlottenburg)
Tel. 030 2 61 47 95
www.die-stachelschweine.de
S/U-Bahn: Zoolog. Garten (S 5, S 7, S75, U 2, U 9)
West Berlin's longest-standing satirical cabaret in the Europa-Center

UFA-Fabrik

Viktoriastr. 10 – 18 (Tempelhof)
Tel. 030 75 50 30
www.ufafabrik.de
U-Bahn: Ullsteinstraße (U 6)
Varieté, cabaret, music, circus

Festivals and Events

Highlights of the Year

Special festivals and events seem to take back seat in view of the great number of daily happenings. Nevertheless there are highlights in the calendar that attract not only Berliners, who are always on the move in their home town, but also visitors from other regions and countries.

When the Berlinale film festival brings glamour to the city in the grey, dark days of February, cinema fans from all over the world queue before daybreak at the box office on Potsdamer Platz in the hope of getting a seat. Some 200,000 tickets are sold for screenings of approximately 400 international films.

The Internationale Tourismusbörse, a leading trade fair for the tourist business in March, attracts about 180,000 visitors. For three days the halls of the trade fair grounds are filled with professionals, and at the weekend the general public is admitted. When this is over, it is already time to register for the Berlin Marathon in September. Each year 40,000 runners, as many as the inner city can handle, compete in the biggest one-day sports event in Germany. They are joined by 7500 inline skaters. There is also a breakfast run and a children's run, and a million spectators can be relied upon to come to the event. Superb cultural events are numerous in Berlin. The avant-garde of the international dance scene, world-famous orchestras, conductors and soloists come to the city. The Potsdamer Schlössernacht, a festival in the palaces at Potsdam, is sold out almost a year in advance. The international art fair, art forum, seems to take place all over the city. The chances of catching a special event on a visit to Berlin are therefore good at all times of the year. And for many people the only imaginable way to let in the New Year is to go to the Brandenburg Gate.

Calendar of Events

JANUARY
Internationale Grüne Woche
www.messe-berlin.de
Trade fair for the food industry and agriculture – with no end of stalls for tasting by the public

Sechs-Tage-Rennen
www.sechstagerennen-berlin.de
Cycle racing in the velodrome on Landsberger Allee

**A fixture in Berlin's calendar of events:
Christopher Street Day**

FEBRUARY
Internationale Filmfestspiele
www.berlinale.de
Glamour comes to Berlin for this festival, when the Golden Bear is awarded for the best film.

MARCH
Internationale Tourismus-Börse
www.messe-berlin.de
The world's biggest trade-fair for tourism

APRIL
Festtage
www.staatsoper-berlin.de
Opera and concerts in the German State Opera on Unter den Linden

MAY
Gallery Weekend
www.gallery-weekend-berlin.de
Exhibition openings in many galleries.

Karneval der Kulturen
www.karneval-berlin.de
A colourful multicultural spectacle in Kreuzberg

Theatertreffen
www.berlinerfestspiele.de
A festival of selected productions from German theatres in the Olympic stadium

JUNE
Christopher Street Day
www.csd-berlin.de
An uninhibited parade for the gay and lesbian community

Musikfestspiele Potsdam
www.musikfestspiele- potsdam.de
Classical music in palaces and gardens

JULY
Classic Open Air
www.classicopenair.de
Classical music on Gendarmenmarkt

AUGUST
Tanz im August
www.tanzfest.de
International dance festival

Historiale
www.historiale.de
History festival, cultural programme, guided tours of the city and in museums

Lange Nacht der Museen
www.lange-nacht-der-museen.de
More than 50 Berlin museums stay open into the early hours. This event is also held in late January or early February.

Potsdamer Schlössernacht
www.spsg.de
Music, dance, theatre, eating and drinking in the illuminated parks and palaces of Potsdam.

SEPTEMBER
Internationale Funkausstellung Berlin
www.ifa-berlin.de
Fair for media and media technology

Popkomm
www.popkomm.com
Music fair for the trade, with concerts for the public

Internationale Luft- und Raumfahrtausstellung ILA
www.ila-berlin.de
At Berlin Brandenburg International Airport

Internationales Literaturfestival
www.literaturfestival.com
Readings, dialogue with authors, discussions

Berlin-Marathon
www.berlin-marathon.de

abc (art berlin contemporary)
www.artberlincontemporary.com
Fair for contemporary art

OCTOBER
Festival of Lights
www.festival-of-lights.de
For ten days approximately 50 buildings and landmarks are used to create art with light after dark.

NOVEMBER
JazzFest Berlin
www.berlinerfestspiele.de
International bands, well-known and newly discovered

DECEMBER
Christmas Markets
In all districts of Berlin; the markets around the Gedächtniskirche and the Opernpalais on Unter den Linden are particularly enchanting.

New Year's Eve
www.silvester-in-berlin.de.

SPECTATOR SPORT

BASKETBALL
ALBA Berlin
O2-World (Friedrichshain)
S-Bahn: Ostbahnhof (S 5, S 7, S 75)
Tickets: tel. *01805 57 00 11
www.albaberlin.de

ICE HOCKEY
EHC Eisbären
O2-World, see above
Tickets: tel. 030 97 18 40 40
www.eisbaeren.de

FOOTBALL
Hertha BSC Berlin
Olympiastadion (Charlottenburg)
S / U-Bahn: Olympiastadion (S 5, S 75, U 2)
Tickets: tel. *01805 43 78 42,
www.herthabsc.de

1. FC Union
Stadion Alte Försterei (Köpenick)
S-Bahn: Köpenick (S 3)
Tickets: tel. 030 65 66 88-0
www.fc-union-berlin.de

Pork Knuckle, Curry Sausage and ...?

As far as the culinary arts are concerned, Berlin undoubtedly meets the standards of a capital city, as can be seen from the number of acclaimed top restaurants. For a normal budget, too, there is a wide range of good restaurants, and those who want more than the favourite local snacks, meat balls and curry sausage, can choose from all the cuisines of the world.

Restaurant critics are glad to come hungry to Berlin, where they are generous in awarding stars and other symbols of merit. When it comes to Michelin stars, the capital is Germany's leading gourmet destination, just ahead of Hamburg and Munich.

Berlin's young chefs are rediscovering regional products. They love to be purists, but are evolving their own authentic style, imaginative and cosmopolitan. A few years ago the top chefs in the city were to be found in the five-star hotels, but now they are gaining their independence. Tim Raue, taking inspiration from Asia, moved out of the Adlon Hotel to Rudi-Dutschke-Strasse in Kreuzberg, while Stefan Hartmann, who likes to gather mushrooms personally for his autumn dishes, has found attractive basement premises in Fichtestrasse, also in Kreuzberg. In Mitte district, hidden away in the Edison-Höfe, Daniel Achilles has opened his restaurant Reinstoff. Michael Hoffmann, who sources some of the vegetables for his highly praised »creative green cooking« from his own garden, even serves up dishes such as chickweed ice-cream in his restaurant Margaux. With the very best ingredients, for example lobster, but without fancy effects, Christian Lohse gained two Michelin stars at Fischers Fritz in the Regent Hotel. First-class chefs are at work in the kitchens of countless other restaurants. They often attract customers with more than their menus, by creating an individual ambience with the help of international architects and designers.

Top restaurants

Competition is keen. It is no longer enough to have white serviettes, coloured walls and a bit of decorative kitsch. The fishing nets have disappeared from Italian restaurants, as have the sirtaki ribbons from Greek and red lanterns from Chinese eateries. Even the numerous small ethnic restaurants in streets where the hungry can eat their way

Excellent alternatives

A high-class Italian restaurant,
Bocca di Bacco in Friedrichstrasse

around the world draw attention to themselves with a reasonably priced midday menu and fast service rather than eye-catching decoration. Those who still think that pork knuckle (Eisbein) with pureed peas is a typical Berlin meal will be able to find it – not in many places, but with the traditional surroundings to match the food.

Old Berlin style   The dishes that have long been regarded as Berlin food are not particularly old. The diet was as meagre as the crops that grew on the sandy soil between the rivers Oder and Elbe, until immigrants changed the food and the culinary identity of the city from the 17th century. It is thought to have been the Huguenots who brought meat balls and the kind of beer known as Weissbier. The Dutch drained the marshland of Brandenburg and cultivated cauliflower, spinach, cucumbers and asparagus. The emergence of Berlin food as it is seen today, with cabbage roulade, pork knuckle, potato cakes, calf's liver, ham and rollmop herring, took place only in the 19th century.

Breakfast   Breakfast until 4pm and Sunday brunch are now established habits in the city. There is, however, a gastronomic gap for those who need a hearty breakfast at dawn after partying for hours. For many years Das Schwarze Café in Kantstrasse in Charlottenburg was the only option for night owls, but today it is too far from the parallel universe of the clubbers. However, between Mitte and Prenzlauer Berg there are now a few places that open 24 hours a day.

Snacking   For a fast snack, no-one need look far. On Alexanderplatz and Friedrichstrasse the aroma of bratwurst (fried sausage) wafts from Grillwalker, while snack bars sell excellent soup, risotto, halloumi in bread, burgers, quiches, falafel, bagels, ciabatta, crêpes, fish & chips, pizza and hot dogs. Of course there is also currywurst (curry sausage) – with and without sausage-skin from intestines, also available made from certified organic meat served with hand-cut French fries (►MARCO POLO Insight, p.96) – and döner kebab, and on Mehringdamm the daily queues in front of Curry 36 are matched by the rapidly growing numbers waiting for at vegetable döner the neighbouring stall. If you have no time to eat before going out in the evening, you can rely on a pretzel vendor appearing in front of the theatre.

Berlin beer   In 1860 about 340,000 hectolitres of Weissbier and 150,000 hectolitres of bottom-fermented beer were brewed in Berlin. Then the Bavarians came along with a bottom-fermented beer that tasted better to Weissbier drinkers than the local products and could not be produced at the same level of quality by most of the Berlin breweries. Berliner Weisse, a low-alcohol wheat beer served in two ways – red with raspberry syrup or more commonly green with syrup from the woodruff herb – is mainly drunk by tourists, to whom it is marketed as a typical Berlin drink. Czech brews (Pilsener Urquell, Budweiser, Krusovice) are often on tap. Many pubs that serve no food are certified for smoking.

The two big Berlin breweries, Schultheiss and Berliner Kindl, are now part of the Radeberger group, but this does not mean that the citizens have all become wine drinkers. A change has happened in recent years. New, small private breweries – 14 of them – in Spandau and Kreuzberg, in Mitte, Köpenick and Neukölln are producing delicious beer. Friedrichshainer and Weddinator, Rollberger, Rixdorfer, Heller Stern and Bellevue-Pils are names that indicate to insiders where they were brewed and also where they can be drunk. Almost every district has its own brewer who swears that his products are natural, unfiltered and free from substances that stabilize or conserve them. These beers are not sold in bottles but are on tap in brew-pubs, some with a beer garden, and other local taverns. Some of them run courses in brewing.

A popular place to hang out in Kastanienallee, from breakfast time until the afternoon: Café Schwarz Sauer

Registered Trade Mark 721 319

Currywurst (curry sausage) polarizes opinion (with or without sausage skin from the gut?), and the snack bars seem to encourage their customers to make comparisons, which are shared on internet forums. Such huge quantities of them are consumed in Berlin that producers were forced to sell ecologically sound versions with organic French fries in order to steal a march on their competitors.

Currywurst (curry sausage) polarizes opinion (with or without sausage skin from the gut?), and the snack bars seem to encourage their customers to make comparisons, which are shared on internet forums. Such huge quantities of them are consumed in Berlin that producers were forced to sell ecologically sound versions with organic French fries in order to steal a march on their competitors.

Currywurst came into existence and on 4 September 1949 at a sausage stall, sadly no longer in existence, on Stuttgarter Platz. The inventor was Hertha Heuwer, who died in 1999. Her husband had been a prisoner of war under the Americans and had fallen in love with spare ribs with ketchup during that time. He was constantly sounding off about them to his wife. In post-war Berlin, though, there was no way under the sun that anyone was going to come by spare ribs; there were plenty of Brühwurst sausages, though. Hertha start experimenting. She mixed up various trial versions of a gooey tomato sauce containing all kinds of spices until she and her husband were happy with the taste. When they poured it over a sausage, the currywurst was born. The couple even registered the name as trade mark no. 721 319 as the dish took

Germany by storm. At the peak of the boom Hertha Heuwer was selling up to 10,000 of them per week and coined the slogan »often copied but never surpassed«. They soon left behind such traditional recipes as fried herring, rissoles, pickled eggs, pickled gherkins and bockwurst. To investigate the history of the cult sausage in more depth, go to the Deutsches Currywurst-Museum (▶p.130).

With or Without?

It may seem hard to believe that the currywurst has its secrets. Ideally the sausage is sliced lovingly by hand and served with a tasty sauce. In the worst cases it is pre-sliced and the ketchup is bought in. Be wary of establishments that simply pour a tasteless, ready-made product over the sausages. A true currywurst chef will make the sauce according to a house recipe. Non-Berliners are astonished at the »with or without?« debate, which is about whether real gut should be used for the sausage skin. Nobody asks this in Berlin's oldest snack bar, the legendary Konnopke in Prenzlauer Berg, where the answer is »without« – in GDR days, it was said, because there was a shortage. The finest snack food has been sold here since 1930 and the founder's daughter Waltraud Ziervogel still remains to ensure the reputation is maintained. Even the East German government was unable to harness the Konnopke family to its communist yoke. The shop remained private and nowadays, apart from selling what is said to be the finest currywurst in Berlin, it also offers such traditional Berlin specialities as bockwurst with potato salad and solyanka. Curry 195 in Charlottenburg has more class. Here the sausage is served on porcelain, and champage can be ordered to wash it down. The quality or popularity of an outlet can be measured by the queues outside, which is striking at Curry 36 in Kreuzberg.

Sauce?

Currywurst has a competitor, however, and ist name is döner kebab. Industrially produced cylinders of döner meat, each weighing 40 to 50 kg, led to the passing of regulations in 1989 that specified the use of only veal, beef and lamb, and up to 60 per cent minced meat. The last scandal about bad meat in Berlin in 2006, which started in a döner kebab bar, caused Turkish newspapers to speculate that this was deliberate libel with the aim of saving the meat ball and currywurst. However, Berlin's kebab king was sentenced to pay a fine as hefty as one of his lumps of döner meat. Since then chicken and vegetable kebabs have been gaining ground. With some 1300 döner bars, Berlin is the undisputed snack capital in this field. The search for a cheap meal has led to street-food wars, which quickly resulted in a fall in prices and quality. The best

policy is to eat döner in places where Turks ard queuing up, and where it is not too cheap. Lettuce, tomato, cucumber, onions and cabbage should always be included. Then comes the question: »Sosse?« If you nod, then yoghurt sauce is added.

Curry 36
Kreuzberg
Mehringdamm 36
Mon–Fri 9am–4am, Sat 10am–4am, Sun 11am–3am

Konnopke
Prenzlauer Berg
U-Bahnhof Eberswalder Straße
Mon–Fri 6am–8pm, Sat 12 noon–7pm

Curry 195
Charlottenburg
Kurfürstendamm 195
Mon–Sat 11am–5am, Sun 12 noon until 5am

Typical Berlin Dishes

... which, as a result of the globalization of eating habits (and more healthy eating), have been in retreat in restaurants for years, with the exception of the classic snacks.

Buletten: Meat balls, called Frikadellen in other German regions. The basic recipe is always the same: mixed pork and beef mince, an egg, an onion, salt and pepper and an old bread roll – the last ingredient being the most difficult, as it has to be a proper roll (see Schrippe above). The obligatory accompaniment to meat balls is potato salad.

Zander: Fillet of pike-perch, a dish that almost no restaurant of quality serving typical Berlin food will fail to include on the menu. There are countless versions and adornments of pike-perch from the river Havel. A classic way to serve it is fried with the skin. Kohlrabi, leeks and lettuce go well with this fish.

Schrippe: This is the local word for a bread roll. In other parts of Germany it is called a »brötchen«, a term that used to be greeted in Berlin with an unfriendly »None of those here!« In at least half of the bakeries in the city, the staff behind the counter are from immigrant families, and anyway, outsiders can simply point to what they want if they don't know the right terminology. The problem is not to get an ordinary Schrippe (made of white flour, to be broken open in the middle), but to find out where the authentic rolls are sold. The ones that are delivered in the night, so that the dough only has to be baked on the spot, are full of air and not especially crispy. They are derided as a »Westschrippe« in some areas, as opposed to the more compact »Ostschrippe« from a traditional bakery in the east of the city.

Leber Berliner Art: (Berlin-style liver) Innards do not normally feature on Berlin menus, but this is an exception. Calf or beef liver, tossed in flour, is fried in hot fat along with onion rings and slices of apples. Mashed potato is usually served with this dish.

Königsberger Klopse: Berlin is not Königsberg (now Kaliningrad, in Russian territory), but has adopted a famous dish from East Prussian immigrants. Königsberger Klopse are often included on the menu in fashionable eateries. What's special about these meat balls is the mixture of minced meat and anchovy fillets, with capers and a sauce.

Currywurst: The principle is simple: a fried sausage with a spicy sauce based on ketchup. The questions that remain are: What kind of sausage? Whole or slices? Ready-made sauce or the house recipe? With rolls (costs more) or French fries (also costs more, of course)? With sausage skin made from gut? Or perhaps covered with gold leaf?

Döner Kebap: What needs to be said here? Perhaps that döner was reportedly first sold in 1971 in Kreuzberg by Mehmet Aygün, though some say he copied the idea of putting the meat in flatbread from Kadir Nurman's snack bar in Hardenbergstrasse ...

Eisbein: Knuckle of pork. This is not difficult to prepare – just boil it in salty water for two hours – but there are ways to make it more complicated, for example by adding onions and cloves to the meat, putting spices in the water, and deciding whether to make the sauerkraut and pureed peas, yourself or to buy them – both being absolutely essential for a perfect Eisbein.

Recommended Restaurants

Don't worry – if you can't afford a top restaurant, the tips be-low will help. Why not dine in the canteen of the Ministry of Defence?

❶ etc. see maps on pages 104 – 107
No number: not in the area cov-ered by the maps

Price categories
For a main course
€ € € € over €35
€ € € €25 – €35
€ € €15 – €25
€ below €15

TOP RESTAURANTS
㉗ First Floor € € € €
Hotel Palace, Budapester Str. 45 (Charlottenburg)
Tel. 030 25 02 10 20
www.firstfloor.palace.de
S/U-Bahn: Zoolog. Garten (S 5, S 7, S 75, U 9)
This top-class restaurant has had its star since 1997. Just reading the wine list can take up a full evening (22 successive vintages of Mouton Rothschild), and the list of mineral waters contains 40 kinds from 18 countries. The food is largely French haute cuisine.

⓮ Fischers Fritz € € € €
In the Regent Hotel
Charlottenstr. 49 (Mitte)
Tel. 030 20 33 63 63
www.fischersfritzberlin.com
U-Bahn: Französische Straße (U 6)
Berlin's only two-star chef, Chris-tian Lohse, learned his trade in

France. Fish and seafood are his speciality. Delicate lobster foam is conjured from a silver lobster press, something boasted by no other restaurant in Germany.

❾ Margaux € € €
Unter den Linden 78 (Mitte), Entrance on Wilhelmstr.
Closed Sun
Tel. 030 22 65 26 11
www.margaux-berlin.de
S/U-Bahn: Brandenburger Tor (S 1, S 2, S 25, U 55)
Michael Hoffmann makes vegeta-bles the centre of attention on the plate, and his vegetable menu re-ceives high accolades. Gelée of braised and smoked paprika tastes as mysterious as it sounds. Rare and precious items such as Grabu-din roots and Black Prince toma-toes put in appearances.

❶ Reinstoff € € € €
Edisonhöfe, Schlegelstr. 26c (Mitte); closed Sun, Mon
Tel. 030 30 88 12 14
www.reinstoff.eu
U-Bahn: Naturkundemuseum (U 6)
Daniel Achilles employs regional products and molecular methods, cooks langoustines in vanilla milk and serves vinaigrette granité an. His ideas about »extending the senses« earned his first star in 2009..

Vau is ready for its diners

⑯ Restaurant Tim Raue
€ € € €
Rudi-Dutschke-Str. 26
(Kreuzberg)
Closed Sun, Mon
Tel. 030 25 93 79 90
www.tim-raue.com
U-Bahn: Kochstr. (U 6)
Aiming for his second Michelin
star, Raue describes his cuisine as
»a combination of Japanese prod-
uct perfection, Thai aromas and
Chinese cooking philosophy«..

㉚ Die Quadriga € € € €
In the Hotel Brandenburger Hof,
Eislebener Str. 14 (Wilmersd.)
Closed Sun, Mon
Tel. 030 21 40 56 51

www.brandenburger-hof.com
U-Bahn: Kurfürstendamm (U 1)
Cloudberries, burbot fish and fir
shoots reveal that the Finnish chef
Sauli Kemppainen is at work here.
Scandinavian treats of this kind
are something special in Berlin.
The wine list has 12,550 items.

⑮ Vau € € € €
Jägerstr. 54 – 55 (Mitte)
Closed Sun
Tel. 030 2 02 97 30
www.vau-berlin.de
U-Bahn: Französische Strasse (U 6)
TV chef Kolja Kleeberg guarantees
utmost quality. His success formu-
la sounds simple: never more than
three products on one plate.

INTERNATIONAL CUISINE

❷ Alpenstück € €

Gartenstr. 9 (Mitte))
Tel. 030 21 75 16 46
www.alpenstueck.de
S-Bahn: Nordbahnhof (S 1)
South German food, but almost all the fresh products are from the Berlin region, even the fish. The lunch menu is popular with employees from nearby offices.

㉑ Ana e Bruno € € € €

Sophie-Charlotten-Str. 1
(Charlottenburg)
Closed Sun, Mon
Tel. 030 3 25 71 10
www.ana-e-bruno.de
U-Bahn: Sophie-Charlotte-Pl. (U 2)
On the elegantly laid tables of one of the best restaurants in the city, treats such as marinated tuna, Calabrian wild basil crostino, risina beans, giant prawns, fried goose liver, glazed rhubarb, lavender panna cotta and Bengal long pepper are served.

⑫ Bocca di Bacco € € €

Friedrichstr. 167
Tel. 030 20 67 28 28
www.boccadibacco.de
U-Bahn: Französische Straße (U 6)
The chef is a devotee of classic Italian food. That means dishes like cotoletto alla Milanese and spaghetti alle vongole... at their very best!

❾ Borchardt € €

Französische Str. 45 (Mitte)
Tel. 030 20 38 71 10
U-Bahn: Französische Str. (U 6)
For 20 years the famous clientele has been perhaps better known than the cuisine at this elegant bistro on Gendarmenmarkt.

? *Spirits and Liqueurs*

MARCO ⊕ POLO INSIGHT

In 1874 a factory was founded in Wedding to distill alcohol using the surfeit of potatoes. The factory manager Max Delbrück made it into a training school for distillers and a liqueur factory, producing spirits under the brand name Adler. Since 2005 Gerald Schroff from the Black Forest in collaboration with Ulf Stahl, a professor at the Technical University, has been upholding Delbrück's tradition: Adler gin is on sale again, and 35 further products such as vodka and a digestif called Kurfürstlicher Magenbitter (factory visits and sales: Mon–Fri 9am–5pm; Seestr. 13, U-Bahn: Amrumer Strasse / U 9, tel. 030 45 02 85 37, www.likoerfabrik-berlin.de)

❺ Dos Palillos € €

Rosenthalerstr. 53 (Mitte)
Tel. 030 20 00 34 13
www.dospalillos.com
U-Bahn: Weinmeisterstr. (U 8)
The original version of this small restaurant is in Barcelona, and the dishes are similar to tapas, but the menu has signs of Iberian-Asian cross-over: monkfish liver marinaded in sake, onsen egg (cooked at 63°C), candied walnuts in Chinese spices.

㉕ Engelbecken € – € €   *Insider Tip*

Witzlebenstr. 31
(Charlottenburg)
Tel. 030 6 15 28 10
www.engelbecken.de
U-Bahn: Sophie-Charlotte-Pl. (U 2)
A certified organic restaurant serving Alpine dishes: Tafelspitz beef and Vienna schnitzel, white sausage and Bavarian beer.

Hotels, Restaurants, Cafés & Entertainment in Berlin East

Hotels

1. Honigmond
2. Kastanienhof
3. Ackselhaus
4. Myer's Hotel
5. mit Art
6. Casa Camper
7. Soho House
8. Platte Mitte
9. Radisson Blu
10. Alexander Plaza
11. Adlon
12. de Rome

Entertainment

1. Kulturbrauerei
2. Metzer Eck
3. Saphire Bar
4. Kaffe Burger
5. Clärchens Ballhaus
6. b-flat
7. Grüner Salon
8. King Size Bar
9. Tausend Bar
10. Windhorst
11. Cookies
12. CSA-Bar
13. Berghain
14. Tresor
15. Ankerklause

16. Arena
17. Lido
18. Watergate
19. Würgeengel

Restaurants

1. Reinstoff
2. Alpenstück
3. Zander
4. Neu
5. Dos Palillos
6. Grill Royal
7. Ganymed
8. Domklause
9. Margaux
10. Zur letzten Instanz
11. Sanâdhi
12. Bocca di Bacco
13. Borchardt
14. Fischers Fritz
15. Vau
16. Tim Raue
17. Sale e Tabbacchi
18. 3-Schwestern
19. Freischwimmer
20. Mamo Falafel

Cafés

1. Barcomi's
2. Café Einstein

—— Former route of the Berlin Wall

Hotels, Restaurants, Cafés & Entertainment in Berlin West

Former route of
the Berlin Wall

Hotels
13 Hansablick
14 Gates
15 Scandic
16 Grand Hyatt
16 Ritz Carlton
17 Dittberner
18 Bogota
19 Bleibtreu
20 Brandenburger Hof
21 Ellington
22 Estrel
23 Alma

Entertainment
20 A Trane
21 Zwiebelfisch
22 Casa del Habano
23 Quasimodo
24 Harry's New York Bar
25 Kumpelnest
26 Green Door
27 Yorck-Schlösschen

Restaurants
21 Ana e Bruno
22 Zollpackhof
23 Le Piaf
24 Café am Neuen See
25 Engelbecken
26 Good Friends
27 First Floor
28 Kantine Bundes verteidigungs- ministerium
29 Solar
30 Quadriga
31 Shabuki
32 Horvath
33 Hartmanns
34 Noi quattro
35 Brauhaus Süd- stern

Cafes
3 Kleine Orangerie
4 Buchwald
5 Wintergarten
6 Kranzler
7 Café Einstein

❼ Ganymed Brasserie € € – € € €

Schiffbauerdamm 5 (Mitte)
Tel. 030 28 59 90 46
www.ganymed-brasserie.de
S/U-Bahn: Friedrichstrasse (S 1, S 2, S 5, S 7, S 75, U 6)
Once the haunt of stars from the neighbouring Berliner Ensemble, now equally popular with theatre audiences. Oysters and shellfish, choucroute (sauerkraut) and Alsatian Flammkuchen are among its specialities.

❷❻ Good Friends € € € *Insider Tip*

Kantstr. 30 (Charlottenburg)
Tel. 030 3 13 26 59
www.goodfriends-berlin.de
S-Bahn: Savignyplatz (S 5, S 7, S 75)
This place is sometimes as noisy as a sports venue and it's obvious that no-one comes for the interior design, but it is always packed with lovers of authentic Cantonese food! Book a table.

❻ Grill Royal € € – € € € €

Friedrichstr. 105b (Mitte)
Tel. 030 28 87 92 88
www.grillroyal.com
S/U-Bahn: Friedrichstrasse (S 1, S 2, S 5, S 7, S 75, U 6)
Steakhouse de luxe on the banks of the Spree with excellent meat, crispy salads, grilled fish and the clientele to match. Following the initial hype, there is now space for normal diners.

❸❸ Hartmanns € € – € € €

Fichtestr. 31 (Kreuzberg)
Closed Sun
Tel. 030 61 20 10 03
www.hartmanns-restaurant.de
U-Bahn: Südstern (U 7)
Bus: M 41
The tasting menu has between three and six courses. If that is too much, choose from the German and Mediterranean menu: halibut in a bread crust, duo of chickpea and olive tapenade, forest berry tarts with sorbet and zabaione…

❸❷ Horvath € € €

Paul-Lincke-Ufer 44a (Kreuzberg)
Closed Mon
Tel. 030 61 28 99 92
www.restaurant-horvath.de
U-Bahn: Kottbusser Tor (U 1, U 8)
One of the classiest restaurants on the Landwehrkanal, with wood-panelled walls, stucco and flowers. The amuse-bouche menus have five, seven or ten courses and all deserve the name. The less adventurous can look forward to an evening of excellent Austrian food..

Lavanderia Vecchia € – € €

Flughafenstr. 46, 2. Hof (Neukölln)
Closed Sun
Tel. 030 62 72 21 52
www.lavanderiavecchia.de
U-Bahn: Boddinstr. (U 8)
Evening diners should not be in a hurry and should arrive on time at 7.30pm so that the ten courses of antipasti in the style of high-class rustic Italian food can be served in leisurely succession. Reservations are advisable.

❷❸ Le Piaf € €

Schlossstr. 60 (Charlottenburg)
Tel. 030 3 42 20 40
www.le-piaf.de
Bus: M 45 from U-Bahn Richard-Wagner-Platz (U 7)

Boule players enjoy themselves on the grass, and other guests are treated to the cuisine of Alsace and France in the garden in summer.

❹ Neu € €
Heckmannhöfe
Oranienburger Str. 32 (Mitte)
Closed Mon
Tel. 030 66 40 84 27,
www.restaurant-neu.de
U-Bahn: Oranienburger Tor (U 6)
At the heart of the city but far from roaring traffic, with tables outside in summer. German food with international influences.

❸❹ Noi quattro € € – € € €
Südstern 14 (Kreuzberg)
Closed Sun
Tel. 030 32 53 45 83
www.noiquattro.de
U-Bahn: Südstern (U 7)
Creative, surprising Italian cuisine at the Südstern: tagliatelle with chanterelles, rabbit with thyme pearl-barley.

❶❼ Sale e Tabacchi € € – € € €
Rudi-Dutschke-Str. 23 (Kreuzberg)
Tel. 030 25 29 50 03
www.sale-e-tabacchi.de
U-Bahn: Kochstr. (U 6)
Osteria, wine bar and café depending on the time of day, but like a trip to Tuscany at any time.

❸❶ Shabuki € – € €
Olivaer Platz 9 (Wilmersdorf)
Tel. 030 88 62 81 37;
www.mrhai.de
U-Bahn: Adenauerplatz (U 7)
For the traditional Japanese shabu shabu, diners sit in a circle around a pot in which raw ingredients are cooked. Here diners have their own pots, while vegetable, meat and tofu roll past on a conveyor belt to be selected.

❷❾ Solar € €
Stresemannstr. 76 (Kreuzberg),
cross the car park to the lift
Tel. 0163 65 27 00
www.solarberlin.com
S-Bahn: Anhalter Bahnhof (S 1, S 2, S 25)
The wonderful view across the city from a height of 70m/325ft might distract romantics from their meal - which would be a pity, as the cooking is both classical and given to experiments. Spiral steps lead up to a lounge and smoking room.

BERLIN CUISINE
❽ Domklause €
Karl-Liebknecht-Str. 1 (Mitte)
Tel. 030 84 71 23 73
www.ddr-restaurant.de
S/U-Bahn: Alexanderplatz (S 5, S 7, S 75, U 2, U 5, U 8)
Typical GDR dishes such as Goldbroiler (fried chicken), Ketwurst (hot dog) und Würzfleisch (pork ragout fin) are on the menu in this restaurant next to the GDR Museum, to the delight of the curious and the ostalgics (those with nostalgia for the East)..

❶❽ 3-Schwestern € – € €
Bethanien, Mariannenplatz 2 (Kreuzberg)
Closed Mon
Tel. 030 60 03 18 60 10
www.3schwestern-berlin.de
U-Bahn: Görlitzer Bahnhof (U 1)
Fresh regional cuisine in the atmosphere of a chapel.

❸ Zander € – € €
Kollwitzstr. 50 (Prenzlauer Berg)
Closed Mon
Tel. 030 44 05 76 78
www.zander-restaurant.de
U-Bahn: Senefelderplatz (U 2)
The char comes from the river Müritz, the venison from the Schorfheide woods north-east of Berlin, and the Sunday roasts are truly famous. New residents of Berlin like to take visitors from their old home towns here.

❿ Zur letzten Instanz € €
Waisenstr. 14 – 16 (Mitte)
Tel. 030 2 42 55 48
Closed Sun
Tel. 030 2 42 55 28,
www.zurletzteninstanz.de
U-Bahn: Klosterstr. (U 2)
Sit by the maiolica tiled stove as Napoleon and Charlie Chaplin once did in what is probably Berlin's oldest inn, next to some remains of the city wall. The name of the restaurant (»final court of appeal«) and its dishes refer to the nearby law courts: »repentance« and »cross-questioning« were never as nice as they are here, as most of the fare consists of hearty meat dishes..

The names of the restaurant and its dishes are taken from legal terminology at Die letzte Instanz

CANTEEN

Insider Tip

㉘ Bundesministerium der Verteidigung €
Stauffenbergstr. 18 (Tiergarten)
For guests from outside Mon–Fri 12.30–2pm, bus M 29
On the 5th floor of the Ministry of Defence (with a view of the Sony Center and Siegessäule) hearty meals are served, with an emphasis on potatoes in every from and plenty of meat.

VEGETARIAN

Hans Wurst €
Dunckerstr. 2a (Prenzlauer Berg)
Tel. 030 41 71 78 22
www.hanswurstcafe.com
S-Bahn: Prenzlauer Allee (S 42)
The name is misleading: there is no wurst (sausage) here, and the dishes are all meat-free, from a seitan steak with sweet potatoes to tarragon cream ragout..

La Mano Verde € €
Scharnhorststr. 28 – 29 (Mitte)
Closed Sun, Tue
Tel. 030 82 70 31 20,
www.lamanoverde.com
S-Bahn: Hauptbahnhof (S 5, S 7, S 75)
Vegans get a choice of delicious dishes, e.g. ravioli from swedes, with a tomato cashew cream filling.

㉗ Mamo Falafel €
Warschauer Str. 47 (Friedrichshain)
www.mamo-falafel.com
U-Bahn: Warschauer Str. (U 1)
Vegetarian fast food is gaining in popularity, with more and more snack bars opening in Friedrichshain. Here is a unique choice between three vegetarian

falafel options: classic, paprika and herbs..

⑪ Samâdhi € €
Wilhelmstr. 77 (Mitte)
Tel. 030 22 48 88 50
www.samadhi-vegetarian.de
U-Bahn: Mohrenstr. (U 2)
Excellent Vietnamese and Chinese food close to Pariser Platz.

BEER GARDENS AND OUTDOORS

Blockhaus Nikolskoe € – € €
Nikolskoer Weg (Zehlendorf)
Tel. 030 8 05 29 14
www.blockhaus-nikolskoe.de
S-Bahn: Wannsee (S 1),dann Bus 316
The best tables are at the edge of the beer garden with a view of the river Havel and even Pfaueninsel. The food is down-to-earth German.

㉔ Café am Neuen See €
Lichtenstein Allee (Tiergarten)
Tel. 030 2 54 49 30
www.café-am-neuen-see.de
S-Bahn: Tiergarten (S 5, S 7, S 75)

? Smiley

A practice that began in Prenzlauer Berg is spreading around the city: a smiley at the entrance reveals the verdict of the official kitchen inspectors. The smiling symbol of hygiene means all is well – no mould or mouse droppings in the kitchen. However, there are various gradings, indicating that there is room for improvement in kitchen hygiene.

The restaurant ship »Klipper« was brought from Holland to Berlin

For Berliners, tourists and staff from the nearby embassies in their lunch break. Huge, aromatic pizzas, as well as excellent Italian food in the restaurant (brunch only on Sunday morning). Boats can be hired too.

⑲ Freischwimmer €
Vor dem Schlesischen Tor 2 (Kreuzberg
Tel. 030 61 07 43 09)
www.freischwimmer-berlin.de
U-Bahn: Schlesisches Tor (U 1)
The planks of what used to be a boat pier on a canal leading to the Spree rock up and down, the kitchen is in the old boathouse and store, and across the water guests at the Club der Visionäre party hard.

Klipper € – € €
Bulgarische Str. (Treptow)
Tel. 030 53 21 64 90
www.klipper-berlin.de
S-Bahn: Treptower Park (S 41, S 42, S 8, S 9)
Following years plying the Ijsselmeer, the clipper finally rests at anchor in the Spree between Plänterwald and Treptower Park. Breakfast, freshly smoked fish and cake in the afternoon are its attractions.

Mauersegler €
Bernauer Str. 63 (Wedding)
Tel. 030 97 88 09 04
www.mauersegler-berlin.de
U-Bahn: Bernauer Str. (U 8)
At the end of the Mauerpark, sausage and steak sizzle on the grill.

When the Sunday flea market is held, football and karaoke make for a noisy atmosphere.

Schoenbrunn € – € €
Am Friedrichshain, by the lake in Volkspark Friedrichshain
Tel. 030 4 53 05 65 25
www.schoenbrunn.net
Bus 200: Bötzowstr.
All kinds of people with time to spare come to Volkspark Friedrichshain for coffee, wine or beer, for Italian food or a hearty Austrian dish.

㉒ZOLLPACKHOF €
Alt-Moabit 143 – 145 (Mitte)
Tel. 030 33 09 97 20
www.zollpackhof.de
S-Bahn: Hauptbahnhof
(S 5, S 7, S 75)
On the Spree beneath spreading old trees, with a view of the Reichstag, you can choose between self-service or service on the terrace of the neighbouring restaurant

MICRO-BREWERIES
Insider Tip
㉟Brauhaus Südstern
Hasenheide 69 (Kreuzberg)
Tel. 030 69 00 16 24
www.brauhaus-suedstern.de
U-Bahn: Südstern (U 7)

Hops & Barley
Wühlischstr. 22 (Friedrichshain)
Tel. 030 29 36 75 34, www.hopsandbarley-berlin.de
S-Bahn: Warschauer Str. (S 5, S 7, S 75)

Eschenbräu
Triftstr. 67 (Wedding)
Tel. 030 4 62 68 37

www.eschenbraeu.de
U-Bahn: Leopoldplatz (U 8, U 9)

CAFÉS
❶Barcomi's
Sophienstr. 21, 2nd courtyard (Mitte)
Tel. 030 28 59 83 63
www.barcomis.de
U-Bahn: Weinmeisterstr. (U 8)
New York cheese cake or a pastrami sandwich for breakfast. An American has realized her dream - twice, as there is another branch in Kreuzberg at Bergmannstr. 21. In the Sophie-Gips-Höfe some customers stay a long time for the all-day breakfast, international newspapers and WiFi.

❹Café Buchwald
Bartningallee. 29 (Tiergarten)
Tel. 030 3 91 59 31
www.konditorei-buchwald.de
S-Bahn: Bellevue (S 5, S 7, S 75)
A tradition since 1852, and the ultimate place to go for Baumkuchen, with a pretty garden for good weather.

Insider Tip

❷Café Einstein
Unter den Linden 42 (Mitte)
Tel. 030 2 04 36 32
www.einsteinudl.com
S/U-Bahn: Brandenburger Tor (S 1, S 2, U 55)
There is lots to watch here, with all kinds celebrities from the worlds of art and politics who dine at the tables at the back with white tablecloths, where many politicians have their regular place. Normal mortals crowd at the smaller tables, on the terrace and at the seats in the middle of

Unter den Linden for a view of the Brandenburg Gate.

❼ Café Einstein

Kurfürstenstr. 58 (Schöneberg)
Tel. 030 2 61 50 96
www.cafeeinstein.com
U-Bahn: Nollendorfplatz (U 1, U 2, U 3)
The villa that once belonged to the actress Henny Porten has become a Vienna-style café with Viennese coffee specialities and schnitzel. The tables are small, but that is a small inconvenience in this long-established institution, a veritable oasis..

❻ Kranzler

Kurfürstendamm 18 (Charlottenburg)
Tel. 030 8 87 13 90
www.cafekranzler.de
U-Bahn: Kurfürstendamm (U 1)
The red and white awning is still there, and on the 2nd floor a room remaining from the famous old café.

❸ Kleine Orangerie

Schloss Charlottenburg, Soandauer Damm 20
Tel. 030 3 22 20 21
www.kleineorangerie.de
U-Bahn: Richard-Wagner-Platz (U 7)
Historic premises with reminders of old Prussia inside; in summer there is seating in a shady garden, and music to match the surroundings on Sunday afternoons.

Kuchenkaiser   Insider Tip

Am Oranienplatz 11–13 (Kreuzberg)
Tel. 030 61 40 26 97
www.kuchenkaiser.blogspot.com
U-Bahn: Kottbusser Tor (U 1, U 8)
Extremely popular with cake-lovers and people from the Kreuzberg scene

La Femme

Kottbusser Damm 77 (Neukölln)
Tel. 030 46 06 39 79
U-Bahn: Schönleinstr. (U 8)
Brunch as if on the Bosphorus with simit (sesame rings) and garlic sausage with eggs (sucuklu yumurta) in a Turkish breakfast café. The German guests drink coffee, the Turks and Arabs prefer tea.

❺ Wintergarten

Fasanenstr. 23, im Literaturhaus (Charlottenburg)
Tel. 030 8 82 54 14
www.literaturhaus-berlin.de
U-Bahn: Uhlandstr. (U 1)
A good breakfast, lots of newspapers and a wonderfully quiet garden, only a few paces from Kudamm. For lunch and dinner, the kitchen turns out excellent dishes using certified organic meat and fresh ingredients.

RESTAURANTS AND CAFÉS IN POTSDAM

❶ Drachenhaus (cat. II)

Maulbeerallee 4a in Sanssouci Park
Tel. 0331 5 05 38 08
www.drachenhaus.de
Regional and international dishes in the »Dragon House«, built in 1770

❷ Café Heider

Friedrich-Ebert-Str. 29
Tel. 0331 2 70 55 96
www.cafeheider.de

Supplier of the royal court in imperial days, a trendy rendezvous in GDR days, now a coffee house and restaurant

❸ Zum Fliegenden Holländer (cat. III)
Benkertstr. 5
Tel. 0331 27 50 30
www.zum-fliegenden-hollaender.de
Traditional tavern in the Dutch quarter dating from 1869 where the food comes from Brandenburg rather than Holland.

❹ Waage € €
Am Neuen Markt 12

Closed Mon.
Tel. 0331 8 17 06 74
www.restaurant-waage.de
Good Mediterranean food in lovely surroundings in the only remaining Baroque ensemble in Potsdam.

❺ Kleines Schloss € – € €
Park Babelsberg 9
Closed Mon, in winter Wed too
Tel. 0331 70 51 54
www.kleinesschloss.de
Swiss cuisine and Franconian hospitality, right on the waterfront with a view of the Glienicker Brücke.

Museums and Galleries

Berlin, Museum Capital

With the Pergamonmuseum, Gemäldegalerie, Neues Museum, Alte Nationalgalerie and more, Berlin has no shortage of world-class museums. But that is by no means all: What about a visit to a watersports museum? Or a museum of tranquillity?

The Museumspass allows visitors to Berlin to explore the city's museum scene on three consecutive days without paying admission fees beyond the price of the pass. It is valid for about 60 Berlin museums, including all of the state museums (though not for special exhibitions). It costs €19 (concessions €9.50) and can be purchased in the participating museums, tourist information offices and online (▶Information).

For the Museumsinsel, Kulturforum, Charlottenburg and the museums in Dahlem, reasonably priced tickets giving admission to all museums on the site can be bought as an alternative to individual tickets. Tickets to the state museums (Staatliche Museen) can also be bought online at ww.smb.spk-berlin.de and printed at home. This is recommended for the Museumsinsel, as it saves time thanks to admission through a special entrance.

The right ticket

In all museums of the Federal State of Berlin (Landesmuseen), the Staatliche Museen zu Berlin and in the Akademie der Künste and the Deutsches Historisches Museum, admission is free for under-18s, and special exhibitions in the Martin-Gropius-Bau are free for under-17s. In all other Berlin museums schoolchildren and young people in professional training pay a reduced price.

Free admission?

Several of the Staatliche Museen stay open on Thursdays until 10pm: on the Museumsinsel all collections except the Neues Museum, and at the Kulturforum the Gemäldegalerie, Neue Nationalgalerie and Musikinstrumenten-Museum, in Charlottenburg the Museum für Fotografie. Guided tours and other events are on offer almost everywhere. In the Gemäldegalerie, Bode-Museum and Museum für Islamische Kunst, students answer questions about the exhibits on the »Junge Nächte« (Young Nights). Anyone who wants to kick off their Saturday night in a museum can do so in the Hamburger Bahnhof, which is open until 8pm. At the end of January and August many museums admit visitors until midnight and put on special events for the Lange Nacht (Long Museum Night).

Evenings in a museum

**Modern museum architecture:
the extension to the Zeughaus**

INFORMATION
www.museumsportal-berlin.de

ARCHITECTURE/DESIGN
Bauhaus Archive Berlin
(Museum für Gestaltung – Design Museum)
Klingelhöferstr. 14 (Tiergarten)
www.bauhaus.de
U-Bahn: Nollendorfplatz (U 2)
Wed – Mon 10am – 5pm, admission: Wed – Fri €6, Sat – Mon €7

**Museum der Dinge
(Museum of Objects)**
(Werkbund Archive)
Oranienstr. 25 (Kreuzberg)
U-Bahn: Kottbusser Tor (U 1, U 8)
www.museumderdinge.de
Fri – Mon noon – 7pm
Admission: €4

GALLERIES
Aedes Berlin
Christinenstr. 18 – 19
(Prenzlauer Berg) and
Savignyplatz,
Else-Ury-Bogen 600 – 601
(Charlottenburg)
www.aedes-arc.de
U-Bahn: Senefelderplatz (U 2) or S-Bahn: Savignyplatz (S 5, S 7, S 75)

Exhibitions on contemporary architecture and urban developments

Akademie der Künste
Pariser Platz 4 (Mitte)
www.adk.de
U-Bahn: Brandenburger Tor (U 55)
Tue – Sun 11am – 8pm

Boros Bunker
Reinhardstr. 20 (Mitte)
www.sammlung-boros.de
S / U-Bahn: Friedrichstr. (S 1, S 2, S 25, S5, S 7, S75, U 6)
Sat, Sun, pre-booking required
Admission: €10
Private museum in a bunker with a spectacular art collection

C / O Berlin
In the former studio building of Weissensee Art School in Monbijoupark
www.co-berlin.info
Renowned photographic gallery, seat of the International Forum for Visual Dialogues

Contemporary Fine Arts
Am Kupfergraben 10 (Mitte)
www.cfa-berlin.com
S / U-Bahn: Friedrichstr. (S 1, S 2, S 25, S 5, S 7, S75, U 6)
Tue – Sat 10am – 6pm
The excellent reputation of this gallery began with Daniel Richter, Jonathan Meese and Damien Hirst

Eigen + Art
Auguststr. 26 (Mitte)
Tel. 030 280 66 05
www.eigen-art.com
U-Bahn: Weinmeisterstr. (U 8)
Gerd Harry Lybke is famous for his ability to spot new talent. His gal-

lery represents stars from Leipzig such as Neo Rauch, Tim Eitel and David Schnell.

Galerie Max Hetzler
Oudenaarder Str. 16–20 (Wedding)
Tel. 229 24 37
U-Bahn: Nauener Platz (U 9)
Big names such as Jeff Coons and Ernesto Neto

Kunstwerke Berlin
Auguststr. 69 (Mitte)
www.kw-berlin.de
S-Bahn: Oranienburger Str. (S 1, S 2)
Tue – Sun 12 noon – 7pm, Thu until 9pm , admission: €6
Epicentre of Berlin's contemporary art scene, showing extraordinary exhibitions. Organiser of the Berlin-Biennale.

Neuer Berliner Kunstverein
Chausseestr. 128/129
www.nbk.org
U-Bahn: Oranienburger Tor (U 6)
Tue – Sun 12 noon – 6pm, Thu until 8pm
Changing exhibitions of contemporary art, films, videos, photography

HISTORY/HISTORY OF CIVILIZATION
Alliierten-Museum (Allies' Museum)
▶p.163

Anne Frank Zentrum
Rosenthaler Str. 39 (Mitte)
www.annefrank.de
S-Bahn: Hackescher Markt (S 5, S 7, S 9, S 75)
May – Sept Tue – Sun 10am – 8pm, Oct – April until 6pm

Admission: €5
Exhibition about the diary and life of Anne Frank

Anti-Kriegs-Museum (Anti-War Museum)
Brüsseler Str. 21 (Mitte)
www.anti-kriegs-museum.de
U-Bahn: Amrumer Str. (U 9)
4pm – 8pm daily, free admission
Documents and photographs from both world wars.

Schloss Cecilienhof
▶Potsdam, Neuer Garten

Deutsches Historisches Museum (German History Museum)
▶Unter den Linden, Zeughaus

DDR-Museum (Museum of the East German Republic)
▶Berliner Dom

Erinnerungsstätte Notaufnahmelager Marienfelde (memorial at the former refugee camp in Marienfelde)
Marienfelder Allee 66 – 80 (Tempelhof)
www.notaufnahmelager-berlin.de
S-Bahn: Marienfelde (S 2)
Tue – Sun 10am – 6pm Tours: Wed and Sun only at 3pm
Admission: free
About the arrival of refugees from East Germany at the former refugee camp.

Forschungs- und Gedenkstätte Normannenstrasse (Stasi research centre and memorial)
▶Lichtenberg

All of Berlin is an Open-Air Gallery

Who needs a museum for viewing art? A walk with your eyes open is just as good.

Subversive inhabitants of the death strip on the Berlin Wall surprise strollers at the corner of Chausseestrasse and Liesenstrasse: Karla Sachse's Kaninchenfeld (Rabbit Field) on the site of a former border crossing. At the Sonnenallee crossing between Treptow and Neukölln, two telescopes in Heike Ponwitz' sculpture Übergang (Transit) symbolize closeness and distance. On Koppenplatz in Mitte district you notice only at second glance that any attempt to put the toppled chair upright is in vain, as it is part of Klaus Biedermann's Der verlassene Raum (The Deserted Room): a table and empty chairs tell of the flight of Jews from Berlin. Art is everywhere in the city. It occupies public space, but is not always perceived as art, as in the case of the double row of cobblestones in the asphalt that marks the course of the Wall.

Pleasing or disturbing?

Art in public space and on buildings is sometimes the occasion for heated discussions. In 1987 Wolf Vostell provoked both enthusiasm and outrage with a car cast in concrete on Rathenauplatz in Halensee: many saw his statement about car-crazy society merely as defilement of the urban environment. The Boxers by Keith Haring, a proponent of Pop Art, and Riding Bikes by Robert Rauschenberg are pleasing adornments to Potsdamer Platz – like Eduardo Chillida's Berlin-Skulptur on the Federal Chancellery? Chillida's work has more intent: here Basque metalworkers produced a symbol of German reunification. Works that are easier to understand are the lightboxes bearing portraits of an American and a Soviet soldier by Frank Thiel at Checkpoint Charlie, where the two systems confronted each other, often threateningly, during the Cold War. Traditional monuments, public commissions such as the equestrian statue of Frederick the Great on Unter den Linden, based on a model by Christian Daniel Rauch and unveiled in 1851, are prominent. On Schlossplatz in Köpenick horses have come down from their pedestal, no longer carry rulers on their backs and move freely between cars and the trams. The creators of this work, the artists' collective called inges idee, do not reveal where the horses are going. It is obvious, however, that art has moved into a new era.

Art in the streets

Without receiving payment or entering competitions, a growing number of street artists is taking possession of public space and turning house walls and other surfaces into images, often pregnant with messages – for example in Kreuzberg on the banks of the Spree, where the golden wristwatches of a huge, white, headless man are bound with chains. The Italian artist BLU, who painted these large-format motifs in 2007 and 2008 in days of work, long ago achieved recognition. This fact sets him apart from the countless sprayers who place their work on public and private walls, signing it with their tags. The artistic sprayers among them usually produce writings, images formed from letters and numbers in conspicuous places, and sometimes slogans. They use lines of sight; they create connections or destroy them. What the skilled and unskilled sprayers have in common, according to a study by the Institute of Psychology at Potsdam University, is the intoxicating kick, the thrill of doing something forbidden, self-exploration and the hope of becoming famous.

Graffiti sprayers were the precursors of street artists. Even though they are no longer truly part of an underground movement, they have to work anonymously because their work, which they prefer to call urban art, is illegal. It is nevertheless regarded as the biggest movement in art of all time, and to come across work by XooooX, Blek le Rat or Banksy is seen as a stroke of luck.

Tours of street art in Berlin go through Kreuzberg and Friedrichshain, for example to the comic girl Little Lucy by El Bocho in Prenzlauer Berg. Yet urban art can be found in Mitte district too and in Neukölln, where a little dragon runs through the streets. So far the works have not been protected by Plexiglas, as some in London are, nor are they carefully removed from walls and auctioned, as at Christie's in London. In Circleculture Gallery in Gipsstrasse it is possible to buy urban art that has not been set free on the street.

Street Art happens on façades

Forum Willy Brandt
Unter den Linden 62 – 68
www.willy-brandt.de
U-Bahn: Brandenburger Tor (U 55)
Tue – Sun 10am – 6pm
Admission: free
About the life of the West German chancellor, and changing exhibitions

Gedenkstätte Berliner Mauer (Berlin Wall Memorial)
▶MARCO POLO Insight p.201

At the Berlin Wall Memorial

Gedenkstätte Berlin- Hohenschönhausen (Hohenschönhausen memorial)
Genslerstr. 66 (Lichtenberg)
www.stiftung-hsh.de
Tram/Metro: M 6, 7, 17
Tours: Mon – Fri 11am, 1pm and 3pm, Sat and Sun hourly
10am – 4pm
Admission: €5
Former Stasi interrogation cells where many political prisoners were held; the tour guides have relevant personal experience.

Gedenkstätte Deutscher Widerstand (Memorial to German Resistance)
▶p.206

Gedenkstätte Haus der Wannsee-Konferenz (Wannsee Conference Memorial)
▶Wannsee

Gedenkstätte Köpenicker Blutwoche Juni 1933
Puchanstr. 12 (Köpenick)
www.heimatmuseum- koepenick. de
S-Bahn: Köpenick (S 3)
Thu 10am – 6pm
Admission: free
Memorial to the victims of Nazi stormtroopers in a week of bloodshed that took place in June 1933 in Köpenick.

Gedenkstätte Plötzensee
▶p.207

Gotisches Haus
▶Spandau

Hauptmann von Köpenick (Captain of Köpenick)
▶Alt-Köpenick

Haus der brandenburgisch-preussischen Geschichte (House of Brandenburg and Prussian History)
▶Potsdam, city centre

Hugenottenmuseum
▶Gendarmenmarkt

Stasi – The Exhibition
Zimmerstr. 90/91 (Mitte)
www.bstu.de
U-Bahn: Kochstr. (U 6)

Mon – Sat 10am – 6pm ,
Admission: free
How the East German secret police (Stasi) ran its network of spies

Jüdisches Museum (Jewish Museum)
▶p.218

Knoblauchhaus
▶Nikolaiviertel

Märkisches Museum
▶Märkisches Ufer

Mauermuseum (Haus am Checkpoint Charlie – Museum for the Berlin Wall)
▶Friedrichstrasse

Mendelssohn-Remise
Jägerstr. 51 (Mitte)
www.jaegerstr.de
U-Bahn: Stadtmitte (U 6)
Daily 12 noon – 6pm
Admission: free
About the Jewish philosopher Moses Mendelssohn and the history of his family in Berlin.

Museum für Kommunikation (Museum for Communication)
▶Leipziger Strasse

Museum Berlin-Karlshorst
▶Lichtenberg

Museum für Vor- und Frühgeschichte (Museum of Early History and Prehistory)
▶Museumsinsel: Neues Museum

Museum im Gutshaus Dahlem
▶Dahlem

Museum gegen politische Gewalt (Museum against Political Violence)
▶Potsdam, city centre

Museumsdorf Düppel (museum village)
Clauertstr. 11 (Zehlendorf)
www.dueppel.de
S-Bahn: Mexikoplatz (S 1), then by 115, 118, 269 bus April – mid-Oct Thu 3pm – 7pm, Sun and holidays 10am – 5pm
Admission: €2
Open-air museum village on the site of an original archaeological dig at Machnow Fen. A reconstruction of how the village must have looked at the beginning of the 13th century with smithy, cobbler, potter, beekeeper. Regular demonstrations by craftsmen.

Polizeihistorische Sammlung (Police History Collection)
Platz der Luftbrücke 6 (Tempelhof)
www.phs-berlin.de
U-Bahn: Platz der Luftbrücke (U 6); bus: 104, 119, 184, 341
Mon – Wed 9am – 3pm
Admission: 2 €
The history of Berlin's police force from the 19th century to the present day.

Potsdam Museum
▶Potsdam, town centre

Preussenmuseum (Prussian Museum)
▶Potsdam, town centre

Rotkreuz-Museum Berlin (Red Cross Museum)
11Görresstraße 12 – 14 (Steglitz)
www.rotkreuzmuseum-berlin.de

S-Bahn: Bundesplatz (S 45, S 46)
U-Bahn: Friedrich-Wilhelm-Platz
(U 9)
Wed 5pm – 8pm
The Red Cross and its history in
Berlin.

Spandovia Sacra
▶Spandau

Stadtgeschichtliches Museum Spandau (history of the
town of Spandau)
▶Spandau

The Kennedys
Pariser Platz 4a (Mitte)
www.thekennedys.de
S / U-Bahn: Brandenburger Tor
(S 1, S 2, S 25, U 55),
Daily 10am – 6pm
Admission: €7
300 photographs, documents and
JFK's briefcase

The Story of Berlin
▶Kurfürstendamm

Topografie des Terrors
▶p.322

Wege – Irrwege – Umwege
(ways, lost ways and
diversions)
▶Gendarmenmarkt

ART AND ANTIQUITIES
Abgusssammlung antiker
Plastik (casts of ancient
statues)
Schlossstr. 69 b (Charlottenburg)
www.abguss-sammlung-berlin.de
S-Bahn: Westend (S 41, S 42)
Bus: M 45, 109, 309
Thu – Sun 2pm – 5pm
Admission: free

Copies of ancient masterpieces at
Schloss Charlottenburg.

Ägyptisches Museum und
Papyrussammlung (Egyptian
Museum and Papyrus
Collection)
▶Museumsinsel, Neues Museum

Alte Nationalgalerie
▶Museumsinsel

Altes Museum
▶Museumsinsel

Antikensammlung (Collec-
tion of Antiquities)
▶Museumsinsel: Altes Museum,
Pergamonmuseum

Berlinische Galerie
▶Jüdisches Museum
(Jewish Museum)

Bildergalerie (Picture
Gallery)
▶Potsdam, Sanssouci

Bodemuseum
▶Museumsinsel

Bröhan Museum
▶ Museum Berggruen

Brücke Museum
▶Dahlem

Daimler Contemporary
▶Potsdamer Platz

Dalí – The Exhibition
▶Leipziger Strasse

Ephraim Palais
▶Nikolaiviertel

Friedrichswerdersche Kirche
►Unter den Linden

Helmut Newton Trust
►Kurfürstendamm

Gemäldegalerie (Picture Gallery)
►Kulturforum

Georg Kolbe Museum
Sensburger Allee 25 (Charlottenburg)
www.georg-kolbe-museum.de
S-Bahn: Heerstr. (S 5, S 75) Bus: M 45 Tue – Sun 10am – 6pm
Admission: €5
Works by sculptor Georg Kolbe exhibited in his studio

Gutshaus Steglitz
(Wrangelschlösschen)
Schlossstr. 48 (Steglitz-Zehlendorf)
www.berlin.de/ba-steglitz-zehlendorf
S/U-Bahn: Rathaus Steglitz (S 1, U 9)
Tue – Sun 2pm – 7pm
Admission: free
Built in 1800 according to plans by David Gilly; rotating exhibitions

Haus am Waldsee
Argentinische Allee 30
www.hausamwaldsee.de
U-Bahn: Mexikoplatz (U 3)
Tue – Sun 11am – 6pm
Admission: €7
International contemporary art

Käthe Kollwitz Museum Berlin
►Kurfürstendamm

Keramik-Museum Berlin (Pottery Museum)
Schustehrusstr. 13 (Charlottenburg)
www.keramik-museum-berlin.de
U-Bahn: Richard-Wagner-Platz (U7), then bus M 45
Fri – Mon 1pm – 5pm
Admission: €2

Kunstbibliothek (Art Library)
►Kulturforum

Kupferstichkabinett (Engraving Museum)
►Kulturforum

Kunstgewerbemuseum (Museum of Applied Art)
►Alt-Köpenick ►Kulturforum

Kunstsammlung Süd-, Süd-ost- und Zentralasiens (Art of South, South-East and Central Asia)
►Dahlem, Dahlem museums

Martin-Gropius-Bau
►Topographie des Terrors

Museum für Fotografie (Photography Museum)
►Kurfürstendamm

museum Fluxus +
► Potsdam, p.352

Museum Berggruen
►p.251

Museum für Asiatische Kunst (Museum of Asian Art)
►Dahlem: Dahlem museums

Museum für Gegenwart (Museum of the Present Day)
►Hamburger Bahnhof

Museum für Islamische Kunst (Museum of Islamic Art)
►Museumsinsel, Pergamon- museum

Museum für Ostasiatische Kunst (Museum of Far Eastern Art)
►Dahlem, Dahlem museums

Museum für Spätantike und Byzantinische Kunst (Museum of Late Antiquity and Byzantine Art)
►Museumsinsel, Bodemuseum

Neue Nationalgalerie (New National Gallery)
Kulturforum

Neues Museum (New Museum)
►Museumsinsel

Nolde Stiftung Seebüll
Jägerstr. 55 (Mitte)
www.nolde-stiftung.de
U-Bahn: Hausvogteiplatz (U 2)
Daily 10am – 7pm, admission: €8
The work of the Expressionist painter Emil Nolde

Porcelain collection at the Belvedere
►Schloss Charlottenburg

Porcelain collection in the Chinese House
►Potsdam, Sanssouci

Pergamonmuseum
►Museumsinsel

Roman Baths
►Potsdam, Sanssouci

Sammlung Hoffmann
►Spandauer Vorstadt

Sammlung Scharf/ Gerstenberg
►Museum Berggruen

Schinkel Pavilion
►Schloss Charlottenburg

Skulpturensammlung
►Museumsinsel, Bodemuseum

Das Stille Museum (The Silent Museum)
Linienstr. 154a (Mitte)
www.das-stille-museum.de
S-Bahn: Oranienburger Strasse (S 1, S 2) U-Bahn: Oranienburger Tor (U 6)
Wed – Sun 1pm – 5pm
Admission: free
Meditative art experience

Das Verborgene Museum (The Hidden Museum)
Schlüterstr. 70 (Charlottenburg)
www.dasverborgenemuseum.de
S-Bahn: Savignyplatz (S 5, S 7, S 75)
Thu, Fri 3pm – 7pm, Sat, Sun noon – 4pm
Admission: €2
Art by women

Vorderasiatisches Museum (Museum of the Near East)
►Museumsinsel, Pergamonmuseum

LITERATURE, THEATRE AND FILM
Anna-Seghers-Gedenkstätte / Memorial
Anna-Seghers-Str. 81 (Treptow)
www.anna-seghers.de

Gaudy neon illuminations on the way to the Sammlung Hoffmann in the Sophie-Gips-Höfe

S-Bahn: Adlershof (S 6, S 8, S 9, S 45, S 46); Tue, Thu 10am – 4pm
Admission: free
The home of the writer

Brecht-Weigel-Gedenkstätte / Memorial
Chausseestr. 125 (Mitte)
www.adk.de
U-Bahn: Zinnowitzer Str. (U 6)
Tours: Tue, Sat 10am – 3pm, Wed and Fri 11.30am, Thu 10am – 6.30pm, Sun 11am – 6pm
Admission: €5
Home of Bertolt Brecht and Helene Weigel

Filmmuseum Potsdam
▶Potsdam, town centre

Museum für Film und Fernsehen/Deutsche Kinemathek (Museum of Film and TV)
▶Potsdamer Platz

Mori-Ogai-Gedenkstätte (Mori Ogai memorial)
Luisenstr. 39 (Mitte)
www2.hu-berlin.de/japanologie
S/U-Bahn: Friedrichstrasse (S 1, S 2, S 25, S 5, S 7, S 75, U 6)
Mon – Fri 10am – 2pm
Admission: €3
Memorial room for the Japanese poet and physician Mori Ogai

NATURE AND TECHNOLOGY
DDR-Motorradmuseum (GDR Motorbike Museum)
Rochstr. 14 C (Mitte, S-Bahnbögen)
www.erstesberliner-ddr-motorrad museum.de
S-Bahn: Hackescher Markt (S 5, S 7, S 75)
Daily 10am – 8pm , admission: €5.50
140 bikes from 40 years of the GDR

Arboretum at the Humboldt University in Berlin
Späthstr. 80/81 (Treptow)
www2.hu-berlin.de/biologie/arboretum
S-Bahn: Baumschulenweg (S 8, S 9, S 45, S 46), then by 260 or 170 bus
U-Bahn: Blaschkoallee (U 7), then by 270 bus
Early April – late Oct Wed, Thu, Sat, Sun and holidays 10am – 6pm
Admission: free
1200 types of trees and herbs

Archenhold-Sternwarte and Himmelskundliches Museum (Observatory and Museum of the Night Sky)
►Treptow

Berliner Medizinhistorisches Museum (History of Medicine Museum)
►Friedrichstrasse, Charité

Berliner S-Bahn Museum
Rudolf-Breitscheid-Str. 203 (S-Bahn depot Griebnitzsee)
Potsdam
www.s-bahn-museum.de
S-Bahn: Griebnitzsee (S 7)
April – Nov every other weekend 11am – 5pm
Admission: €2
Museum of Berlin's local train service.

Berliner U-Bahn Museum
Rossitterplatz 1 (Charlottenburg)
www.ag-berliner-u-bahn.de
U-Bahn: Olympiastadion (U 2)
Second Sat in each month 10.30am – 4pm, admission: 2€
A century of the underground railway. Includes the Olympiastadion

signal and control centre, commissioned in 1931

Computerspielemuseum (Computer Games Museum)
Karl-Marx-Allee 93 a (Friedrichshain)
www.computerspielemuseum.de
U-Bahn: Weberwiese (U 5)
Wed – Mon 10am – 8pm
Admission: €8
All about digital interactive entertainment – with attractions for games players

Botanisches Museum (Botanical Museum)
►Dahlem

Deutsches Technikmuseum (German Museum of Technology)
►p.188

Dampfmaschinenhaus (mosque)
Steam engine house, now the mosque in ►Potsdam city centre

Feuerwehrmuseum (Fire Brigade Museum)
Berliner Str. 16, (Tegel fire station)
U-Bahn: Alt-Tegel (U 6), Bus: 133
Tue – Thu 9am – 4pm, Wed 4pm – 7pm; admission: €3
Historical fire equipment demonstrating the development of fire fighting

Historischer Hafen (Historic docks)
►Märkisches Ufer

Jagdmuseum (Hunting Musuem)
►Grunewald

Luftwaffenmuseum der Bundeswehr (Air Force Musuem)
▶Spandau

Medizinhistorisches Museum (Museum of Medical History)
▶Friedrichstrasse, Charité

Museum für Kommunikation (Museum of Communication)
▶Leipziger Strasse

Museum für Naturkunde (Natural History Museum)
▶S. 252

Ökowerk Berlin
in the waterworks on Teufelssee, Teufelsseechausee 22 – 24 (Charlottenburg-Wilmersdorf)
Programme: www.oekowerk.de
S-Bahn: Heerstraße (S 7), then 20 minutes on foot
Admission: €2.50
All about water

Scheringianum
Fennstr. 10 (Wedding)
U-Bahn: Wedding, Reinickendorfer Strasse (U 6)
Mon – Fri 10am – noon
Museum of the Schering pharmaceutical company

Wasserwerk Friedrichshagen (water works)
▶Müggelsee

Wilhelm-Foerster-Sternwarte (Observatory)
Munsterdamm 90 (Steglitz)
See www.planetarium-berlin.de for programme
S-Bahn: Priesterweg (S 2)
Admission: €7

Zucker-Museum im Institut für Lebensmitteltechnologie (Museum of Sugar
Amrumer Str. 32 (Wedding)
www.sdtb.de/Zucker-Museum
U-Bahn: Amrumer Strasse (U 9), Seestrasse (U 6); Tram: M 13, 50; Bus: 106, 221
Mon – Thu 9am – 4.30pm, Sun 11am – 6pm; tours: Sun 11.30am and 2.30pm; admission: free
Everything about sugar crops and the production of sugar

LOCAL MUSEUMS
Almost every borough of the city has its own local museum. The following are of particular interest for the history of Berlin.

Museum Charlottenburg- Wilmersdorf
Schlossstr. 55
www.villa-oppenheim-berlin.de
U-Bahn: Sophie-Charlotte-Platz (U 2)
Tue – Fri 10am – 5pm, Sun 11am – 5pm
With an exhibition about the Oppenheim and Mendelssohn families, who occupied the villa until 1909

In the Air Force Mmuseum

Mitte Museum am Gesundbrunnen
Pankstr. 47 (Mitte)
www.mittemuseum.de
U-Bahn: Pankstraße (U 8)
Sun – Wed 10am – 5pm, Thu until 8pm; admission: free

FOLK CULTURE AND CRAFTS

Ethnologisches Museum (Ethnological Museum)
▶Dahlem, Dahlem museums

Gründerzeitmuseum (Museum of the Early Imperial Period)
▶Marzahn

Museum Europäischer Kulturen (Museum of European Cultures)
▶Dahlem

Underground Berlin in the Unterwelten-Museum

Museum der unerhörten Dinge (Museum of Unheard-of Things)
Crellestr. 5-6 (Schöneberg)
www.museumderunerhoerten dinge.de
S-Bahn: Julius-Leber-Brücke (S 1)
Wed – Fri 3pm – 7pm
Admission: free
Fantastical, »unheard-of« finds

OTHER MUSEUMS

Berliner Unterwelten-Museum (Berlin Underground Museum)
Brunnenstr. 108a (Mitte)
www.berliner-unterwelten.de
U-Bahn: Gesundbrunnen (U 8)
Tours Thu – Mon 11am – 4pm 12 noon, 2pm,4pm; admission: €9
The history and development of Berlin as seen from underground in a former air raid bunker

Blindenmuseum (Museum of the Blind)
Rothenburgstr. 14 (Steglitz)
www.blindenmuseum-berlin.de
U-Bahn: Rathaus Steglitz (U 9)
Wed 3pm – 6pm, admission: free

Buchstabenmuseum (Museum of Letters)
Karl-Liebknecht-Str. 13, Berlin-Carré, 1st floor (Mitte)
www.buchstabenmuseum.de
S/U-Bahn: Alexanderplatz (S 5, S 7, S 75, U 2, U 5, U 8)
Thu – Sat 1pm – 3pm
Admission: €2.50
About typographical fashions of recent decades, including neon signs and advertising typography

Deutsches Currywurst-Museum
▶Friedrichstrasse

Deutsches Fußballmuseum
Anton-Saefkow-Platz 13
(Lichtenberg)
www.dfm-berlin.de
S-Bahn: Storkower Str. (S 41, S 42)
Tue – Thu 10am – 4pm, Fri – Sun
10am – 6pm, admission: €4

Erotik-Museum Beate Uhse
Kantstrasse corner Joachimstaler
Strasse (Charlottenburg)
www.erotikmuseum.de
S-/U-Bahn: Zool. Garten (S 5, S 7,
S 75, U 1, U 2, U 9)
Mon – Sat 11am – midnight, from
18 years of age, admission: €14
Everything you need to know
about »eroticism« in a museum
run by the Beate Uhse company.

Grünauer Wassersport-museum (Museum of Water Sports)
Regattastr. 141 (Köpenick)
www.wassersportmuseum-gru-
enau.de
S-Bahn: Grünau (S 8, S 9, S 46),
then by 68 tram
April – Oct Wed 10am – 16.30, Sat
2pm to 4.30pm; admission: free

Hanfmuseum (Hemp Museum)
►Nikolaiviertel

Hofgärtnermuseum (Court Gardening Museum)
►Glienicke

Gaslaternen-Freilichtmuseum (Open-air Museum of Gas Lamps)
►MARCO POLO Tip p.311

Jugendmuseum Schöneberg (Childhood Museum)
►Children in Berlin

KPM-Welt
►Tiergarten

Labyrinth Kindermuseum
►Children in Berlin

Museum Kindheit und Jugend (Museum of Childhood and Youth)
►Children in Berlin

Museumswohnung WBS 70 (Museum Flat)
►Marzahn

Musikinstrumenten-Museum
►Kulturforum

Puppentheater-Museum
►Children in Berlin

Schwules Museum (Museum of Homosexuality)
Mehringdamm 61 (Kreuzberg)
www.schwulesmuseum.de
U-Bahn: Mehringdamm (U 6, U 7);
bus: 119, 140, 219
Wed – Mon 2pm – 6pm, Sat closes
7pm; admission: €5

Sportmuseum Berlin
Haus des Deutschen Sports
Hanns-Braun-Str. (Charl.)
www.sportmuseum-berlin.de
U-Bahn: Olympia-Stadion (U 2)
Mon – Fri 10am – 2pm
Admission: €1
Special exhibitions only

Shopping

Almost as Good as London

Berlin cannot quite measure up to global shopping capitals like London, Paris and New York, but it is catching up, whether for global brands on the main shopping streets or more individual retail experiences in other locations.

Charlottenburg-Wilmersdorf remains one of the classic places to shop in Berlin: Kurfürstendamm and its side streets such as Savignyplatz, Joachimsthaler Strasse, Kantstrasse and Wilmersdorfer Strasse, Bleibtreustrasse and Mommsenstrasse or Breitscheidplatz and Tauentzienstrasse. The best-known shopping centres in the region are the Europa Center next to the Gedächtniskirche, which has more than 90 shops and is open 24 hours a day. Not to be missed, of course, is **KaDeWe** on Wittenbergplatz, one of Germany's most famous stores, a temple of luxury and indeed excess, particularly with regard to the delicatessen section on the sixth floor (▶Sights from A to Z, KaDeWe). Its counterpart in the east is, meanwhile, **Friedrichstrasse** with shopping arcades at 205 (mainly fashion), 206 (highly exclusive and dear with shows, cosmetics, fashion, accessories and designer goods) and 207, the home of Galeries Lafayette, the first German branch of the famous Parisian store with creations and accessories by famous designers plus leather goods and French delicatessen. Books, music and software are available in KulturKaufhaus Dussmann at Friedrichstr. 90. The arcades at **Potsdamer Platz** have more than 100 shops focussing on fashion and textiles: they are making a great effort to keep up with the major players. Berlin's second-largest shopping mall is Alexa on Alexanderplatz with 180 stores. It should not be forgotten, though, that it is always worth shopping off the beaten track, particularly because it is away from the designer mainstream that really unusual items may be found. Have a look around **Spandauer Vorstadt** – Auguststrasse, Hackesche Höfe, Mulackstrasse, Weinmeisterstrasse (which has become a high-class street of fashion designers) – and check out Simon-Dach-Strasse in Friedrichshain, Kastanienallee in Prenzlauer Berg, Winterfeldtplatz and its environs, Maassenstrasse in Schöneberg and Kreuzberg's Bergmannstrasse.

The **classic souvenir** is the Berlin bear, be it a cuddly toy, cast metal model, or a picture on any other kind of item. Almost as popular are models of the Brandenburg Gate, the Funkturm or the Reichstag.

Shopping streets and centres

Souvenirs

A little bit of Paris on Berlin's retail scene:
Galeries Lafayette

Socialist souvenirs survived the fall of the Wall

There are also souvenirs nowadays related to »**reunification**«, things like the famous East German traffic light figures or »Ampelmännchen«, (real?) pieces of the Berlin Wall, and all kinds of medals and uniform trappings from the East German or Soviet army. Many museums also have copies of their most popular exhibits for sale.

Markets, flea markets

The biggest and best-known flea market in Berlin attracts thousands each weekend to the Strasse des 17. Juni (Sat, Sun 10am–6pm). At Eichenstrasse 4 on the Spree in **Treptow** it's opening time in enormous halls filled with goods ranging from screws to TVs, antique furniture, games, car tyres and even engines. At the **Ostbahnhof** furniture and antiques are bought and sold on Sundays. The flea market in the **Mauerpark** in Bernauer Strasse (Sat, Sun 8am–6pm) is a good place to look for clothes. Books, art and fashion are on offer at weekends on the **Museumsinsel**.

The most interesting food market is the **Turkish market on Maybachufer** in Neukölln (Tue, Fri 12 noon–6.30pm). As well as fruit and vegetables, meat and fish, all kinds of fabrics and haberdashery are on sale here, with African goods a recent addition to the products. sches. The large **food market on Winterfeldtplatz** in Schöneberg (Sat 8am–4pm) draws residents from the surrounding areas. High-quality goods are sold at the organic market on **Kollwitzplatz** in Prenzlauer Berg (Thu 12 noon–7pm). The Saturday market from 8.30am here is the most popular in the eastern part of the city.

Three historic **market halls** are still in operation: the Arminius-Markthalle in Moabit (Arminiusstr. 2), the Eisenbahn-Markthalle in Kreuzberg (Eisenbahnstr. 42 – 43) and the Marheineke-Markthalle, also in Kreuzberg (Marheinekeplatz 15). They were opened in the early 1890s, and are atmospheric surroundings for buying anything from groceries to shoe laces, as well as having food stalls.

Where to shop

COMICS
Grober Unfug
Torstr. 75 (Mitte) and Zossener Str. 32 – 33 (Kreuzberg)
Comics from all over the world, models, DVDs, and exhibitions.

DELICATESSEN
Fassbender & Rausch
Charlottenstr. 60 (Mitte)
www.fassbender-rausch.de
▶MARCO POLO Tip p.211

KaDeWe
Tauentzienstr. 21 – 24, 6th floor (Schöneberg)
www.kadewe.de
A temple to consumption with the biggest delicatessen section in Europe, including 1300 cheeses alone, plus 1200 types of sausage and ham, 2400 wines – and many counters where shoppers can sample the produce

Kadó
Graefestr. 20 (Kreuzberg)
400 kinds of liquorice with unbelievable flavours, sourced from Lapland to Sicily. The house flavour is ginger liquorice.

Königsberger Marzipan
Pestalozzistr. 54a (Charlottenburg)
www.wald-koenigsberger-marzipan.de
Marzipan from Lübeck is famous – but from Königsberg?

HOUSEHOLD AND KITCHEN
DIM
Oranienstr. 26 (Kreuzberg)
www.u-s-e.org

An »Imaginary Manufactory« makes design items in basketry, plus brooms and brushes.

KPM
Wegelystr. 1 (Tiergarten)
www.kpm-berlin.de
In what used to be a production hall of the Königliche Porzellanmanufaktur (Royal Porcelain Factory), fine porcelain and cheaper seconds are on sale.

Küchenladen
Knesebeckstr. 26 (Charlottenburg.)
www.kuechenladen.com
Utensils for people who are serious about cooking

FASHION, SHOES, ACCESSORIES
Claudia Skoda
Alte Schönhauser Str. 35 (Mitte)
www.claudiaskoda.com
Avant-garde knitted fashion, all hand-made from the finest wool

Firma
Mulackstr. 1 (Mitte)
www.firma.net
One of Berlin's most successful labels, originally for men, now for women too

Galeries Lafayette
Friedrichstr. Quartier 207 (Mitte)
Delicatessen with products from all over the world

Ic!Berlin
Oranienburger Str. 32 (Mitte)
www.ic-berlin.de

! *Blackriver* **Insider Tip**

For people who like sports but have no space, the flagship store Blackriver (Boxhagener Str. 14 in Friedrichshain, www.blackriver-ramps.com) is the only shop in Germany selling fingerboards: skatesboards 8cm/3in long for »fingerboarding«, the latest fun sport, for championships are already held.

Internationally successful designers of eye-glasses work and sell in Berlin. Celebrities worldwide go for the spectacle hinge system used here – and the cool sunglasses

Kaviar Gauche
Linienstr 44 (Mitte)
www.kaviargauche.com
A Berlin label that combines luxury with avant-garde fashion

Lala Berlin
Mulackstr. 7 (Mitte)
www.lalaberlin.com
Pullovers, shirts, dresses, silk, Egyptian cotton, mohair by a Berlin label

Luccico
Neue Schönhauser Str. 18 (Mitte)
Classical or bold, this Italian shoemaker guarantees »shoes for a lifetime«

Respectmen
Neue Schönhauser Str. 14 (Mitte)
www.respectmen.de
Designer label that is both chic and suitable for business wear. Other labels are also represented in the shop. Not far away are two other shops called Respectwomen and Respectless.

Sterling Gold
Oranienburgr Str. 32
Heckmannhöfe (Mitte)
www.sterlinggold.de
Vintage evening and cocktail dresses

Trippen
Hackesche Höfe, Hof 4 (Mitte)
www.trippen.com
Hand-made and off-beat

Zeha
Kurfürstendamm 188 –189 (Charlottenburg), Prenzlauer Allee 22 (Prenzlauer Berg), Brunnenstr. 195 (Mitte); www.zeha-berlin.de
Traditional GDR brand, revived by two Berlin designers

MUSIC
KulturKaufhaus Dussmann
Friedrichstr. 90 (Mitte)
www.kulturkaufhaus.de
Wide assortment for all styles of music.

Platten Pedro
Tegeler Weg 102 (Charlottenburg)
www.platten-pedro.de
Berlin's biggest second-hand store with over 110,00 vinyl and several hundred shellack records in all genres.

fSOUVENIRS
Ampelmännchen
Rosenthaler Str. 40, Hackesche Höfe, auch Gendarmenmarkt, Potsdamer Platz und DomAquaree Karl-Liebknecht-Str.
www.ampelmannshop.de

Trippen sell fantastic shoes

The Ampelmännchen is the little green or red man from the GDR traffic lights, now a cult figure that can be bought on a huge range of products.

Bärenstark
S-Bahnbogen 201, under the railway arches at Bahnhof Friedrichstrasse (Mitte)
Berlin's emblem, the bear, in all shapes and sizes.

BerlinStory
Unter den Linden 40 (Mitte)
www.berlinstory.de
Books, kitsch, maps, everything about Berlin and Prussia.

OTHER SHOPS
Erfinderladen

Insider Tip

Lychener Str. 8 (Prenzlauer Berg)
U-Bahn: Eberswalder Str. (U 2)
A shop full of curiosities, from a child's jacket with integrated rucksack to a snacking bag to wear round your neck while driving. The owners' aim is to help inventors to market their products, and customers can test the ideas in this shop.

Ostpaket
Karl-Liebknecht-Str. 13 (Mitte)
www.ostpaket-berlin.de
Food, drinks and household goods from daily life in the GDR, as well as from its old socialist brother countries, on a 300 m² surface.

Fashion Made in Berlin

The website stilinberlin, a blog kept by a fashion hunter since 2006, gets about 70,000 visits per month. It is so successful that it has attracted interest from many companies, and the blogger has hired help.

She goes fashion-stalking through the city, especially around Weinmeisterstrasse, Torstrasse and Mulackstrasse, sometimes hunts her prey in parks, and looks around in cafés to get a picture of what people are wearing in Berlin. The wearers, models for a day, are proud to tell her where they bought their clothes and are pleased to be photographed. They find their discoveries in the shops of local designers and charity depots, wear vintage clothes casually and without inhibitions but not retro, i.e. old items in a new look. They usually wear flat, comfortable soles, as uneven pavements and potholes make high heels an expensive luxury.

Berlin is celebrating its status as a fashion city again, a place where fashion fairs attract leading figures in the business, especially since Bread & Butter, one of the most important fairs, returned to Berlin in 2009 after roaming to Cologne and Barcelona, and now presents all the labels that matter in the field of jeans and streetwear in the halls of the decommissioned Tempelhof Airport.

Premium, a rendezvous for the national and international fashion business, is for trade insiders only. 5 elements.berlin shows underwear and beachwear, and the latest partner of Fashion Week is Thekey.to, environmentally conscious fashion that has long been part of the luxury segment. In nine schools of fashion, each with its own special course of training, the designers of the future learn the trade. There is no lack of famous teachers here. Vivien Westwood, a creator of imaginative and dramatic fashion while remaining uncompromising in craft standards, became world-famous with her punk look and has taught at the Universität der Künste (University of the Arts) since 1993.

Berlin labels

Today there are 3700 fashion companies in Berlin. Some 15,300 work in the business, which has an annual turnover of 1.6 billion euros. Since 1990 the city government has supported 1000 micro-labels and made ateliers available free of charge to the creators of haute couture in Wedding, a district that was once anything but fashion-oriented. Names like Lala Berlin, Kaviar Gauche, Respectman and Sisi Wasabi bring glamour to the fashion world. Some have fought bravely and succeeded in the competitive fashion business, while others burned briefly like comets in the sky and then faded – sometimes because they overestimated themselves, but usually, as their teachers point out, because they regarded activities such as marketing and sales strategies as »uncool«. In the long term the survivors are those who are not above entering into cooperations as a business model. After all, even Karl Lagerfeld has worked for H&M. Many of the well-known designers now work on bags, notebooks and sports products, or advertise for washing powder. In the early years, few can manage without a sponsor. Even though many Berlin labels are sold in Berlin stores, most are not able to run their own boutique.

Looking back

The new fashion boom in Berlin that resulted from German reunification also brought a flood of exclusive stores such as Yves Saint Laurent, Gucci, Prada, Louis Vuitton and Escada, thus taking up a thread from days long gone. In 1927 the trade journal »Der Konfektionär« counted more than 800 companies producing womenswear, concentrated in the area around Hausvogteiplatz, where the Manheimer brothers founded a company in 1837. Others followed their example. Hermannn Gerson, who entered the business in 1836, was running the largest company of this type in Berlin within a few years and became a supplier to the royal court with his luxury range. For this centre of the textile and fur trade and of the tailoring business, it was not long before 100,000 women were working at home in the tenements of north and east Berlin. The First World War brought the most profitable era to an end, but designs from the women's fashion business in Berlin influenced the international scene until the Golden Twenties. Berlin pointed the way in fashion.

Marlene Dietrich had a high opinion of Berlin fashion, and ordered the latest styles from Hausvogteiplatz before she moved to the USA. She arrived in New York with 25 travelling trunks. A few years earlier, in 1912, a whole collection of valuable designs that were intended to promote the Berlin fashion trade in New York went down with the Titanic.

Even before the destruction of Hausvogteiplatz in the Second World War, the racist policy of the Nazis forced many businesses there, most of which were Jewish, to emigrate. The companies were »Aryanized«, then forcibly collectivized after the war. Today only a mirror monument on Hausvogteiplatz serves as a reminder of this golden age.

Fashion week is the climax of the season

Tours and Guides

Explore Berlin

Every day 360,000 visitors wander through Berlin, look at the Reichstag and Kurfürstendamm or stroll around Potsdamer Platz. Many of them like to have a guided tour.

One of the cheapest ways of seeing the city is to catch its major sights by bus on services 100 and 200 run by the local bus authority, the BVG, between Bahnhof Zoo and Alexanderplatz or Prenzlauer Berg – although there is no tour guide of course. One very popular service also provided by the BVG is the Zille Express, an hourly tour bus (German and English) with nine stops, where it is possible to get on and off. The vehicle is a faithful copy of a »Robert-Kaufmann-Wagen« (open-topped double-decker bus), such as plied routes in Berlin from 1916 to 1928. A tour on one of the bright red Top-Tour buses with their open top deck lasts about two and a half hours in all, although you can get on and off at any stop.

Bus tours

MARCO ❂ POLO TIP

A normal bus – with commentary

For a trip on bus route no. 100 you can download an audio-guide at www.culture-to-go.com. It explains what you see by the side of the road.

Insider Tip

The bus companies BBS, Berolina and BVB jointly operate the half-hourly City CircleTour, with 20 stops to hop on or off.

CityCircle-Sightseeing

Boat trips are a relaxing way to see Berlin from a completely different angle. Apart from the usual historic trips, mostly lasting an hour and costing €10 – €11, most operators run night trips or special tours of the bridges, the Landwehrkanal or scenic cruises on the river Havel or Wannsee lake.

Boat trips

Journeys with the normal S-Bahn or U-Bahn trains above ground or on the high-level lines also provide interesting views. For an extremely enjoyable trip, try the U-Bahn-Cabrio: a two-hour tour by night on an open subway train!

Train or underground train

A walking tour with an unusual theme is a way to get to know a completely different side of Berlin. The range of subjects is enormous, and encompasses »In the footsteps of« tours, trips beneath the ground, and much more: special themes are in great demand (▶MARCO POLO Insight p.142).

Unusual tours

Visitors to underground Berlin have to wear a helmet

Themes are in Demand

The classic tour of city highlights still finds plenty of customers, of course – but tours on special themes provide more and more new variations relating to the history and culture of the city.

History, Nature, Underground

The most popular tours include border walks along the course of the now non-existent Berlin Wall (www.stattreisenberlin.de). The guides of the agency Stattverführer visits the sites of German revolutions (www.stattverfuehrer.de), while »Stummfilm Berlin«, one of many themes offered at www.filmstadt-berlin.de, goes to the homes of the stars and directors of the age of the silent movies. By the Spree at the old heart of Berlin, once the site of the Stadtschloss and Palast der Republik, guides go in search of the origins of the city (www.berlin-industriekultur.de).

Bird life in Berlin is the subject of a tour by the Naturschutzbund (League for Nature Conservation) around the Karower Teiche ponds in spring, when migratory birds arrive (http://berlin.nabu.de). A trail to pop music from the early days to the contemporary scene can be followed on foot or by bus (www.musictours-berlin.de), and the secrets of the city's subculture can also ber revealed (www.berlinwasted.de). The »oasis tour« by bike takes in parks, bodies of water, urban wasteland and sites that are not to be found in any history book (www.berlinonbike.de).

Berliner Unterwelten is an association that shows visitors the subterranean sights of Berlin, and Carpe-Berlin caters for the blind and those with limited vision ((http://berliner-unterwelten.de; www.carpediem.com.

Art, Luxury, Speed

A number of agencies, for example Ticket B and Go Art!, take advantage of the know-how of artists and architects to present the buildings and the art of Berlin.

And of course there are more exclusive and expensive ways to explore the city. A limousine picks up guests at the hotel and takes them through Berlin with an experienced chauffeur and a well-informed guide for €275 (www.beringuide.biz). »Berlin-Deluxe« is a culinary tour that starts off with champagne and heads for a Michelin-starred restaurant, or alternatively a fine old apartment with an open fire on a piano nobile, where a harpist gives a musical accompaniment to the meal that a skilful cook prepares on the spot (from 660 € for two persons, www.eat-the-world.com).

Those who are short of time, and nverheless want to see on a single day everything that it takes native Berliners half a lifetime to experience, can join a ten-hour marathon tour that includes a crash course in history as well as curry sausage and local drinks (www.berlinandmore.com)

Sightseeing

BUS TOURS/U-BAHN
Zille-Express
Starts from: Brandenburg Gate
April – Oct Fri, Sat and Sun
10am – 5pm every 75 min., 8 €,
www.bvg.de

TopTour
Departs from: U-Bahnhof Kurfürstendamm / Café Kranzler
Daily from 9.25, every 15 – 20
min., 20 €, www.top-tour-sight-
seeing.de

City Circle Tour
Main departure point: Kurfürstendamm opposite Gedächtniskirche,
Alexanderplatz opposite Park Inn
Hotel
Daily from 10am every 10 – 15
min., 22 €
www.bbsberlin.de, www.berolina-
berlin.com, www.bvb.net

U-Bahn-Cabrio *Insider Tip*
April – Oct every other Fri
Booking tel. 030 25 62 52 56,
u-bahn-cabriotour@bvg.de, 40 €

BOAT TRIPS
Reederei Riedel
Tel. 030 693 46 46
www.reederei-riedel.de

Reederei Bruno Winkler
Mierendorffstr. 16
Tel. 030 3 49 95 95
www.reedereiwinkler.de

Stern- und Kreisschifffahrt
Tel. 030 5 36 36 00
www.sternundkreis.de

THEMED TOURS
Berliner Unterwelten
Brunnenstr. 105, Tel.
030 49 91 05 18
www. berliner-unterwelten.de
Berlin below the ground, e.g. the
flak bunker in Humboldthain, the
cityÄs largest remaining bunker.

CarpeBerlin
www.carpeberlin.com
Free audio-guides to be down-
loaded for the blind and visually
impaired

Go Art! Berlin
Halle am Wasser, Invalidenstr.
50 – 51 (Mitte)
Tel. 030 30 87 36 26, www.goart-
berlin.de
The latest trends in art and fashion, with trips to galleries, fairs
and private collections.

StattReisen Berlin
Malplaquetstr. 5 (Mitte)
Tel. 030 4 55 30 28
www.stattreisen.berlin.de
Broad range of topics including
the Berlin Wall

Ticket B
Tel. 030 4 20 26 96 20
www.ticket-b.de
Architects, all of them members
of the international network
www.guiding-architects.net, organize five classic walking tours or
visits to particular buildings.

TOURS

It is great to explore Berlin from the water: or on one of our routes, for example on the crime trail.

Getting Around in Berlin

By S-Bahn (urban railway), U-Bahn (underground railway) and bus links, it is easy to get to any of the interesting places in the city. It is worth buying a ticket valid for the whole period of your stay for any journey. The only remaining question, then, is what part of town to make your base. Night owls should seek out the city centre, Kreuzberg or Prenzlauer Berg, and either side of Kurfürstendamm there is still plenty on offer, too. After all, who wants to go to bed early in Berlin?

Tour 1 What a History!

Start and finish: Alexanderplatz to the Brandenburg Gate
Duration: 3 hours

This walk through the history of Berlin, following in the footsteps of prince electors, kings, emperors and the rulers of the GDR, is a trip through the history of all of Germany.

View of the city

From the ❶*TV tower, close to the bustling but not particularly attractive Alexanderplatz, at a height of about 200m/650ft, Berlin seems to stretch away endlessly: trees to the west – that is Tiergarten – and high-rise blocks and rail tracks to the east, here and there courtyards on narrow streets, the shining river Spree shines, and church towers visible in-between. There are even some ruins, and the last remaining stretch of the city wall with Zur letzten Instanz, possibly the oldest tavern in Berlin. It is not even 800 years since the city was founded, more or less exactly on the post where the *Nikolaikirche can be made out with its two towers, and it takes some imagination to conceive of the broad crossroads behind as a narrow ford. In the Middle Ages it would have been easy to take in the whole city, which was then no bigger than the old Mitte district.

Where Berlin originated

Passing the ❷*Rotes Rathaus you reach the cradle of the German capital in the ❸*Nikolaiviertel, created in its present form for the 750th anniversary of Berlin in 1987. Almost nothing here is truly old, but narrow streets, signs on the houses and places to eat or drink make for a cosy atmosphere. Here is the Zille-Museum, here you can buy lace from Plauen, and souvenir bears in all sizes. Following a short walk along the Spree and across the Rathausbrücke, an astonishing contrast is presented by a wide open space: ❹*Schlossplatz,

View through the Neptune Fountain to the Rotes Rathaus

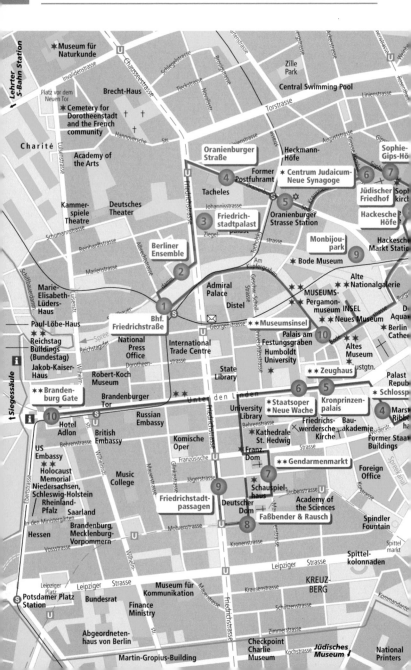

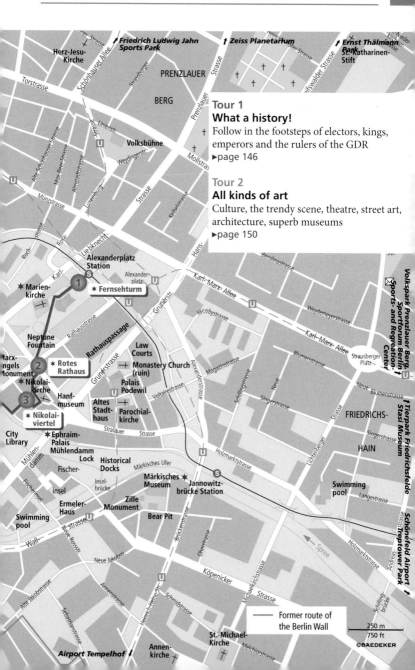

Tour 1
What a history!
Follow in the footsteps of electors, kings, emperors and the rulers of the GDR
▶page 146

Tour 2
All kinds of art
Culture, the trendy scene, theatre, street art, architecture, superb museums
▶page 150

Former route of the Berlin Wall

250 m
750 ft

©BAEDEKER

used as a lawn for sunbathing, also an excavation site. Across the street is the huge cathedral, the Berliner Dom (on the opposite bank of the Spree is the GDR-Museum), and adjacent is the Lustgarten in front of the ***Altes Museum**.

Showcase avenue

Beyond the ****Schlossbrücke**, ****Unter den Linden**, a showcase boulevard, begins on the right with the oldest surviving building on the street at no. 2: the ❺****Zeughaus** (Armoury). No. 1 on the left, the Kommandantur, pretends to be old but is brand new. A historic building, the ❺**Kronprinzenpalais**, comes next, followed by the ❻***Staatsoper** and Schinkel's ❻***Neue Wache** opposite, in front of the glade of chestnut trees. In the middle of the road, Frederick the Great is mounted on his horse: a glance at his followers, their size and their positions reveals a lot about this old king.

Berlin's finest square

Beyond the Humboldt-Universität and Staatsbibliothek turn left into Charlottenstrasse to reach ❼****Gendarmenmarkt**, where the local residents campaigned successfully to keep the spherical trees. This means that you can relax in their shade to enjoy coffee and ice cream, listen to the musicians at Refugium (no. 5) or sit on the steps of the Französischer Dom or Schauspielhaus and note how the surroundings create a festive mood. Chocolate lovers should not fail to look in at ❽**Fassbender & Rausch** (Charlottenstr. 60).

Shopping

The atmosphere in the ❾**Friedrichstadtpassagen** is entirely different. Luxury shops sell fashion, furniture, art, tea and accessories from all over the world. Leave the Passagen via Galeries Lafayette, perhaps after having an exquisite snack in the basement, to return to Unter den Linden. The best place to walk is on the strip in the middle – beneath lime trees, which is what the street name means – to the ❿****Brandenburg Gate**, where there are street performers, horse-drawn coaches and expensive cars in front of the Hotel Adlon; the terrace of Tucher restaurant is a good spot. Again it takes an act of imagination to realize that only 25 years ago, the Berlin Wall and barbed wire blocked the way here.

Tour 2 **All Kinds of Art**

Start and finish: Friedrichstrasse station
Duration: 3 hours, not including museum visits

Theatres, life indoors and outdoors, street art, architecture, traces of Jewish life and the highlights of the Prussian state cultural collections on Museum Island.

Leave **①Friedrichstrasse Station** heading for Schiffbauerdamm on the walkway above the Spree. Here, at least between Easter and October, it seems as if everyone is moving around the city on the water. Countless tourist boats are chugging to and fro. The river bank is a line of restaurant tables as far as the **②Berliner Ensemble** theatre, in front of which its founder, Bertolt Brecht, looks pensive in bronze. Actors cross the courtyard on their way to the canteen, and the curious can follow them to take a snack in unaccustomed company.

On the Spree

Go left down Friedrichstrasse. The **③Friedrichstadtpalast** on the right harks back to the old glory days with its modern shows. At Oranienburger Tor and **④Oranienburger Strasse** you reach a district whose character, users, places to eat and drink and thus atmosphere have changed more quickly than elsewhere, evolving from the stronghold of the alternative scene to a neighbourhood for redevelopment, then to a strip for tourists and drinkers – and is now changing again. The pavements have become cafés, and in winter flaming torches greet the guests. Here the attractive-looking and excellent restaurant Neu in the Heckmannhöfe, behind the sweets factory, is still something of an insiders' tip.

Trendy scene

The **⑤*Neue Synagoge** with its golden domes, the centre of the Jewish community in Berlin, has remained true to itself. Via Krausnickstrasse with its little basement shops you reach the ivy-covered St Hedwig's hospital. Just before Grosse Hamburger Strasse meets Oranienburger Strasse, the **⑥first Jewish cemetery** in Berlin is visible. Turn left, then right straight away into Sophienstrasse, which was prettified in 1987 for the city jubilee with old-fashioned lettering on the shops. No. 21, inconspicuous during the daytime, draws guests in the evenings with colourful lights to the **⑦Sophie-Gips-Höfe**, where Barcomi's café occupies an idyllic spot.

Jewish Berlin

The entrance to the **⑧Hackesche Höfe**, which is closed in the evenings, is also inconspicuous as this is the rear side. Each of the courtyards has an individual design. Here you find a shop selling merchandise with the cult Ampelmann (traffic-light figure), Trippen for extravagant shoes, lots of fashion stores, and finally, when approaching from this side, the most beautiful of the courtyards, with the cinema and Varieté Chamäleon. Pass through Hackescher Markt S-Bahn station and go straight ahead to the bridge – on the right, the weary rest their feet in **⑨Monbijoupark** or Strandbar Mitte a little further up the Spree – where outstanding Russian musicians set the mood for a world heritage site: **⑩**Museum Island**, starting with the **Alte Nationalgalerie**. In front of it is the *Altes Museum**, straight ahead and further on are the **Neues Museum and **Pergamonmuseum**, where two policemen guard the apartment of the

World Heritage

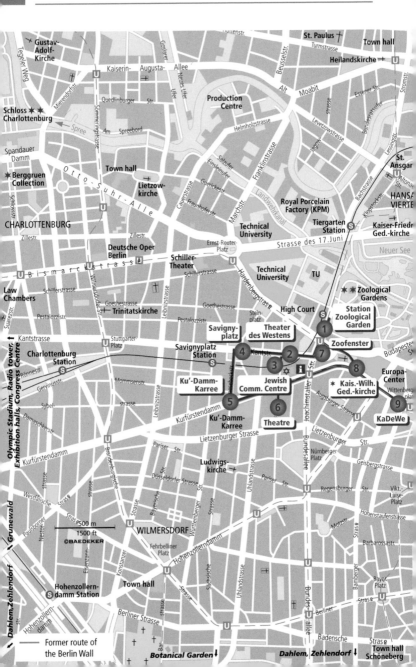

Former route of
the Berlin Wall

Tour 3
The old west
Along Kurfürstendamm and its side streets:
still a cosmopolitan place
▶page 152

Tour 4
A park, art and politics
The heart of German politics, surrounded by
greenery
▶page 153

chancellor of the Federal Republic, and finally the * ***Bodemuseum**. At the next corner you are back on Friedrichstrasse.

Tour 3   **The Old West**

Start and finish: Bahnhof Zoo
Duration: 2–3 hours

Word got around a few years ago: the Kurfürstendamm is making a comeback. This famous street seemed to have gone downhill after German reunification, but that phase is over now, and spectacular architecture is being built here.

Down Kantstrasse

From ❶**Zoologischer Garten** train station go a little way up Joachimstaler Strasse and turn right into Kantstrasse. On the left under the railway bridge take a look at the refurbished Kranzlereck with its shops. On the right the ❷**Theater des Westens** announces that musicals are staged behind its neo-Renaissance façade. Next door, Quasimodo below the Delphi cinema is still a venue where legendary jazz musicians perform. On the left in Fasanenstrasse stands the ❸**Jewish community centre** with the doorway of the old synagogue. Continue along Kantstrasse past the once-legendary Paris-Bar. At Stilwerk across the road you can furnish your home stylishly. Next comes ❹**Savignyplatz**, cut across by Kantstrasse. It is one of the most attractive and spacious squares in the western part of Berlin. Until the fall of the Wall it was a haunt of artists and strollers, then went out of fashion, and is now again a centre of urban life with an outstanding art bookshop beneath the railway arches and well-frequented restaurants. In Zwiebelfisch the nightlife still goes on until the early hours. Along the railway arches a narrow passage lined by small shops leads to Bleibtreustrasse, perhaps the liveliest of the side streets here. Then go under the railway tracks to ❺**Kurfürstendamm**. Zillemarkt, a restaurant on the left, takes its guests back to bygone days.

Along Kurfürstendamm

Between Knesebeckstrasse and Uhlandstrasse the theatres have been moved into the first floor of a new building. In glass showcases on the broad pavements extravagant footwear, elegant hats, elaborate jewellery and fine porcelain point the way to the shops close by. On the right in Fasanenstrasse lie the ❻**Literaturhaus and Wintergarten**, an enchanting coffee garden next to the Käthe-Kollwitz-Museum, with expensive shops opposite. On the left before the junction with Joachimstaler Strasse the red-and-white awnings draw attention to Café Kranzler, which now only occupies one storey – and then the new, so-called ❼**Zoofenster** (Zoo Window) rises to the heavens.

Berliners were outraged – though not for long – when they realized   At the zoo that this new structure would overshadow the ruins of the ❽ **Gedächtniskirche**. The Zoo-Palast, a venue for the film festival in Cold War days, will move into new premises and hopes to revive its days of glamour. Bikini Berlin is the name of the other new building. From its roof terrace there is a view of the camels in the zoo. The Gedächtniskirche (Memorial Church) still stands: the ruins of the old church and the post-war building by Eiermann dating from 1961 with its wonderful windows of blue glass. Around the Weltkugelbrunnen (Globe Fountain, also known as the »Water Dumpling«) gather painters, daydreamers and pickpockets – don't forget that the busy Kudamm is a haunt of thieves! If you still have some energy, take a look around the department store ❾ **KaDeWe**, perhaps on the delicatessen floor. And if you have not yet tried a curry sausage, call in at Fritz & Co on Wittenbergplatz, where the meat is organic and the fries are handcut and seasoned with sea salt.

A Park, Art and Politics

Tour 4

Start and finish: Grosser Stern
Duration: 4–5 hours

This tour leads through and around part of the Tiergarten and then runs past the Kulturforum and Potsdamer Platz to the parliament and government precincts.

Freshly gilded, the figure of Victory shines again on the ❶ *Sie-   Diplomatic gessäule (Victory Column) at the centre of the Grosser Stern. This   quarter walk starts out heading south-west on Fasanerieallee in the park, passing monuments to hunting the European bison, boar and hares, all dating from 1904. At the junction with Grosser Weg turn left, resisting the charms of the pleasant beer garden on the lake straight ahead, and cross busy Klingelhöfer Strasse. Look back at the nearby crossroads to see the green ribbon of the ❷ **Scandinavian embassies** and the party headquarters of the CDU. Walking beneath trees on the park side of Tiergartenstrasse, you pass an architectural gallery of embassies, where the representation of the federal state of Baden-Württemberg has also sneaked in. All the side streets on the right are characterized by tranquillity and the architectural styles of foreign countries.

From Stauffenbergstrasse, with the ❸ **Gedenkstätte Deutscher**   World-class **Widerstand** (Memorial to the German Resistance) on the site of the   culture ministry of defence, follow Sigismundstrasse to the St. Matthäu-

skirche, designed by Stüler. The ❹****Kulturforum**, where the
Gemäldegalerie, ***Kupferstichkabinett, ***Kunstgewerbemuseum**, ***Philharmonie** and ***Musikinstrumentenmuseum** are all
located – the ****Neue Nationalgalerie** is by the road, the Staatsbibliothek opposite – has been awaiting remodelling for some years, and
this oasis of art still has an inhospitable air. For those who prefer not
to visit a museum, ❺****Potsdamer Platz** is a suitable place to take
a break. The first floor of the Potsdamer Platz Arkaden is a destination for everyone with a sweet tooth for one very good reason: Caffè
e Gelato. With luck a table will be free; otherwise get an ice-cream to
take out. In the Kollhoff-Tower with its golden crenellations, the fast-
est lift in Europe takes visitors to the panorama deck in seconds.

**Art in the
Tiergarten**
Then go through the Sony-Center back towards Tiergarten and take
the tunnel into the park heading east. The Tiergarten still seems a bit
wild here. Using five enormous stones from five continents, the
sculptor Wolfgang Kraker von Schwarzenfeld has made his dream of
a Global Stone come true in the face of some derision. From here it
is not far to the ❻****Holocaust Memorial** and the ❼****Brandenburg Gate**.

**Home of
power**
Walk over to the ❽****Reichstag building** to start the last stage of
this tour, which goes on to the ❾***Bundeskanzleramt** (Federal
Chancellery) and the banks of the river Spree. The outdoor tables of
the café of the ❿**Haus der Kulturen der Welt** is a place to take a
break with a view of the ships. Just beyond, a path leads to John-Fos-
ter-Dulles-Allee, with a view of the white ❿***Schloss Bellevue**. Following the Spree or walking parallel through the park, you return to
the Grosser Stern.

Tour 5 Dark Ways

Start and finish: from Moritzplatz U-Bahn station to the Ostbahnhof
Duration: 2 hours

**In 2010 a high-calibre poker game was robbed at Potsdamer
Platz, and jewels disappeared from the KaDeWe department
store. Criminals are at work everywhere. This walk traces
spectacular cases from the past between Kreuzberg and Friedrichshain.**

**Back to the
future**
❶**Moritzplatz** is a strange place: a big, bare circle. Even Berliners are
unsure whether it was in the east or the west. All eight subway exits
led to the west, and the Wall was visible from some of them. Until

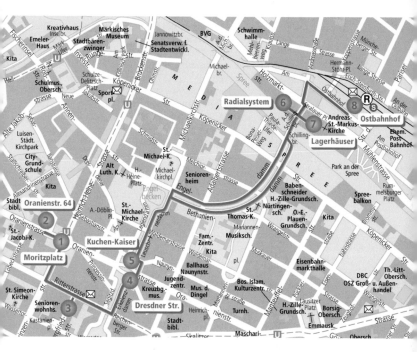

1920 Moritzplatz was the centre of the so-called Luisenstadt. As almost all of its buildings were destroyed in the Second World War, the walk takes different paths to reach the past.

At ❷ **Oranienstr. 64** there was a three-day street battle against the police in July 1863. Some 10,000 local residents took part. The reason was the eviction of the publican Schulze, because he had replaced the tiled stove in his tavern by an iron one. The city court found in favour of the owner of the building, and the outraged publican drew attention to this by putting up posters. His turnover increased along with the solidarity and rage of his guests, who destroyed the owner's apartment. Mounted police intervened. Onlookers arrived on foot and in horse-drawn omnibuses. The destruction and violence did not die down until the police president threatened to use firearms. Of 426 people who were arrested, in the end 109 were sentenced for riot, damage to property and resistance to the police.

Riots

Walk along Prinzenstrasse and Ritterstrasse to reach ❸ **Bergfried-strasse no. 13**, where one of the first contract killings in the Federal Republic of Germany took place in 1988. For 8000 deutschmarks the

Murder

murderer, who had come from the east in 1987 and was heavily in debt, killed the ex-girlfriend and child of the boss of a scaffolding company by stabbing them 42 times. Continue via Ritterstrasse, Segitzstrasse and Erkelenzdamm to Reichenberger Strasse, which leads to Kottbusser Tor. This part of Kreuzberg is firmly in Turkish hands and the number of police patrol cars reveals that they are on the look-out for drug dealers. The ugly ten-storey building called Neues Kreuzberger Zentrum that bridges the road blocks off ❺**Dresdner Strasse**. You have to pass it to the left, then walk past Möbel-Olfe, a trendy bar that used to be a furniture store. The murder that was carried out in 1887 in the house at no. 8 was significant from a legal point of view because it was the first time in Berlin that the perpetrator was condemned entirely on the basis of circumstantial evidence: while leafing through a newspaper the murderer expressed his disappointment, according to the paper vendor, that it contained nothing about the murder – but the body had not yet been discovered at that time.

More Murder   At the end of Oranienplatz, where ❺**Kuchen-Kaiser** is a good place to stop at all times of day, the Luisenstädtischer Kanal between Legienstrasse and Leuschnerdamm has become a park again following the fall of the Wall and extends as far as the Engelbecken basin. Take the Schillingbrücke across the Spree to Friedrichshain. On the left-hand, northern bank there once stood public baths, called the Horst-Wessel-Bad in Nazi days. ❻**Radialsystem** in the old pumphouse is one of the best arts venues in the city today. »Degenerate art« was stored by the Nazis in the ❼**warehouses on the south bank**. In the early 20th century the butcher Carl Friedrich Wilhelm Grossmann disposed of his victims in the river here, professionally dismembered and placed in parcels. He is regarded as a serial killer, accused of killing approximately 100 girls, but he only confessed to three murders when arrested in 1921.

Gangland   In those years Friedrichshain was seen as Berlin's Chicago. In the area around the Schlesischer Bahnhof, the station now called ❽**Ostbahnhof**, robbery and violence on the street were everyday occurrences, and organised gangs gave the police a hard time. But that was a long time ago. Today »Berghain« is a place to go dancing, and the opening of the new main station has given the Ostbahnhof a small-town atmosphere. From platform 10 the S-Bahn trains take you back to the city centre.

Contrasts

Nature and gardens   If the noise of the city gets too much to bear, go out to the suburbs. In the west the place to go is the ***Wannsee**, which can easily be

Highlights in the Outer Boroughs

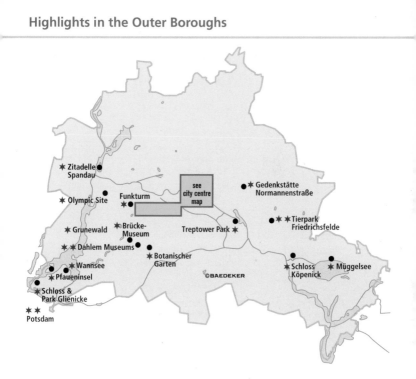

combined with a trip to ***Pfaueninsel (Peacock Island)**. In the east the alternative is a trip through **Köpenick** to the ***Müggelsee**. If gardens are more to your liking, visit the park at ****Schloss Charlottenburg**, the gardens and palaces of **Potsdam** (►from p.344), or the ***Botanical Gardens.**

For a rural idyll, take a trip to the last almost completely intact village within Berlin's boundaries: Lübars (S-Bahn S 1 to Waidmannslust, then bus 222). Its centre is the village green with the thatched Kossätenhaus (Kossäten were farmers from east of the Elbe) and the village tavern, called Alter Dorfkrug. Here or on the family farm in the Fasanerie (Pheasantry) you can get refreshments.

Lübars

BERLIN FROM A TO Z

The Brandenburg Gate is a good starting point for exploring the attractions of Berlin: Unter den Linden, the Tiergarten, the government quarter, Potsdamer Platz... There is a lot to discover.

Alexanderplatz

K 17/18

Location: Mitte
S-Bahn and U-Bahn: Alexanderplatz
(S3, S5, S7, S75, S9, U2, U5, U8)

City centre map:
B 14/15

Alexanderplatz has always struggled to belong to a prestigious capital city. Its characteristic scent is rather that of the simple man, as embodied in literature by Franz Biberkopf in Alfred Döblin's novel Berlin Alexanderplatz.

The home of Franz Biberkopf

The East German government, however, sought to make the square the focal point of East Berlin, rebuilding it according to socialist architectural concepts that transformed the former lively vigour of the old »Alex« into what is now, architecturally speaking, a rather bleak concrete plain. Plans for restructuring the site have been in discussion for years, but they don't really offer much hope of an improvement. Alexanderplatz has existed since the creation of the Georgsspital (St George's Hospital) in front of the Oderberg Gate at the end of the 13th century. In about 1700 a cattle market grew up around the site, which was soon joined by a wool market. After Elector Friedrich III entered Berlin by the gate then called the Georgentor, having declared himself Friedrich I, »King in Prussia«, the gate was renamed the Königstor (King's Gate). As of 1777, at the instigation of Friedrich II, the prestigious Königsbrücke (King's Bridge) stood here. It passed over a channel leading off the Spree that was still visible at the time. A row of colonnades to lead up to the bridge was designed by Karl von Gontard, but they are now situated at the Kleist Park in front of the former headquarters of the Allied Control Council. In 1805 the name of the square was changed from »Ochsenplatz« to its present name in honour of Tsar Alexander I.

A landmark on Alexanderplatz: the global time clock

Among the buildings of the old site – the colossal statue of Berolina, sculpted by Emil Hundrieser in 1895, and the Berlin police headquarters were its greatest landmarks – only the Berolinahaus and the Alexanderhaus to the south remain. Both were erected according to plans drawn up by Peter Behrens between 1928 and 1931. The rest of the area is dominated by modern buildings, the 30-storey Forum Hotel (now Park Inn with the **Base Flyer**, which offers a safe jump of 98m/325ft from the roof) built from 1967 to 1970 and rising to 120m/394ft, the Centrum-Warenhaus building (now Kaufhof), the shallow dome of the Kongresshalle, the 18-storey Haus des Reisens (Travel House) and the red **shopping mall Alexa**. The assault of colour outside gives way to a surprise within: Berlin's second-largest shopping centre with 180 stores is an attractive complex with curved passageways, wood and mosaics. Within this mainstream retail offering the **miniature world of Loxx** appeals to railway fans of all ages: it is one of the world's largest digital model railways, in H 0 gauge, and mainly shows Berlin scenes. The **Brunnen der Völkerfreundschaft** (Fountain of Friendship between Peoples) was created by Walter Womacka in 1969, the same year that the Weltzeituhr (World Time Clock) was built by Erich John.

Miniatur world Loxx: daily 10am–8pm; admission €12.90

Alliierten-Museum
(Allies' Museum)

Location: Clayallee 135, Zehlendorf
U-Bahn: Dahlem-Dorf (U 1), then by X 83 bus
❶ Thu–Tue 10am–6pm

☆ Q 10
www.allierten museum.de
Admission free

The subject of the Allies' Museum in the southwestern suburb of Zehlendorf is the period when West Berlin, at the forefront of the Cold War, was the remotest outpost of western freedom.

The former US Army cinema is used to show the film Outpost about the period between 1945 and 1949 and the museum recalls the period from 1950 to 1994 from the point of view of the western allies, the USA, Britain and France, in the building next door. The US military government and the high command of the Berlin Brigade was based on the other side of Clayallee. The museum covers topics such as the major politics of the age, the Airlift, the Allied Control Council and the war crimes prison in Spandau, as well as the lives of soldiers and West Berliners and the interaction between them. Documents and original artefacts call to mind a time when West Berlin was seen as an island of freedom amid the »Evil Empire«. Exhibits include a British »Hastings« transport plane as used in the Berlin

Airlift, a carriage from a French interzone train, a US jeep, an American spy tunnel and the museum's prized possession, the original guard hut from Checkpoint Charlie (▶p.200).

Alt-Köpenick

✦ **South east N 20**

Location: Köpenick
S-Bahn: Köpenick (S 3), then by tram 60, 62

The suburb of Köpenick, known for the famous story of the Captain of Köpenick (▶Famous People, Wilhelm Voigt), is greener and has more lakes than any other district of Berlin. This is where the Dahme or Wendish Spree flows into the Spree itself and day trippers come to swim in the ▶Müggelsee lake, take a boat trip or ramble in the Müggelberg hills.

The greenest district of Berlin The core of Köpenick, which is an ancient settlement like Cölln and Spandau, was the Koppenik fortress built for the ruler Jaczo de Copnic on what is now called the Schlossinsel (Castle Island). The first recorded mention of the fort is from 1240. In the 19th century the large number of establishments taking in washing led to Köpenick being dubbed »**Berlin's laundry**«. After the empire was established, it attracted factories, elevating Köpenick to one of Berlin's major centres of industry, as witnessed by the industrial sites in Oberschöneweide. The site of the modern Peter Behrens building of the Samsung electronics company was where the National Automobile Company (NAG) manufactured its vehicles until 1933; it then became the AEG-Telefunken factory and during the GDR era it was a factory producing electronics for televisions. Köpenick became a part of Greater Berlin in 1920.

Old quarter The first steps through the old quarter naturally lead to the **Rathaus** or town hall, designed by Hans Schütte and built between 1901 and 1904. On its steps there is a monument to »Köpenick's most famous son«, the Captain of Köpenick, who at the time of his caper in 1906 was a 57-year-old cobbler from Tilsit called Wilhelm Voigt (▶Famous People). Wearing a second-hand captain's uniform he had put together from various sources, he issued orders to twelve grenadiers from the Plötzensee military swimming baths and led them to Köpenick, where they arrested the mayor, confiscated the municipal funds and in the process ex-

> **Insider Tip**
>
> ! *In the Captain's footsteps*
>
> The Berlin Treptow Tourist Association provides tours through the centre of Berlin and out to Köpenick in the footsteps of the famous Captain of Köpenick, tel. 65 48 43 40 to book.

MARCO ⬤ POLO TIP

The magnificent stucco decoration in the Arms Hall at Schloss Köpenick

posed the absurd thrall in which a man in uniform was held in Prussia at that time. A small exhibition in the Rathaus covers details of the heist and the rest of Wilhelm Voigt's life. Alt-Köpenick, the old part of the suburb, mainly spreads out between Kietzer Strasse, Kirchstrasse, Rosenstrasse and Schüsslerplatz. The **Köpenicker Heimat-und Fischereimuseum** (Köpenick Local Museum and Fishing Museum) to the east (Alter Markt 1) covers Köpenick's history.

Exhibition in the Rathaus: to the right on the ground floor, 10am – 6pm daily

Local Museum and Fishing museum: Tue, Wed 10am–4pm, Thu until 6pm, Sat 2–6pm

Something of the idyll of a bygone age is still apparent in the fishing village of Kietz, which was incorporated into Köpenick in 1898. The village had been granted fishing rights as early as 1451. Its prettiest street is Strasse Kietz with its single-storey fishermen's cottages.

Kietz fishing village

In the mid-16th century the elector Joachim II ordered the building of a palatial, Renaissance-style hunting lodge on the site of the Slav's Wasserburg fort on the Schlossinsel. During the Thirty Years' War, Gustav Adolf of Sweden was also quartered there. At the end of the 17th century the Great Elector had the palace remodelled into its current form by Rutger van Langerfeldt. Among the rooms that were

*Schloss Köpenick

built at the time is the magnificent Hall of Heraldry, in which the court martial of Crown Prince Friedrich (later to become Friedrich II) and his friend Lieutenant Hans Hermann von Katte took place from 22 – 28 October 1730 upon the orders of King Friedrich Wilhelm I. Katte had assisted the crown prince in an attempt to flee the country, for which he was condemned to death and executed before Friedrich's very eyes at Küstrin. Since 1963 the palace has housed part of the collection from the **Kunstgewerbemuseum** or Museum of Decorative Arts, which was established in 1867. It is a branch of the museum based at the ▶Kulturforum. Its 29 »epoch chambers« display art from the Renaissance, Baroque and Rococo periods, the highlight being the **Silver Buffet** from the Berlin Stadt-schloss (City Palace). The palace chapel designed by Johann Arnold Nering (1680 – 1690) is also part of the museum.

❶ April–Sep Tue–Sun 10am–6pm, Oct–March Thu–Sun 11am–7pm; admission €6; www.smb.museum

✴ **Berliner Dom**
(Berlin Cathedral)

✦ **K 17**

Location: Lustgarten, Mitte
City centre map: B 13
S-Bahn: Hackescher Markt (S 5, S 7, S 75)
Bus: 100, 200
❶ April –Sept Mon–Sat 9am–8pm, Sun, holidays noon–8pm; Oct–March until 7pm
Admission: €7
www.berliner-dom.de

**Berlin Cathedral, the Berliner Dom, was built on the instruc-
tions of Kaiser Wilhelm II as the foremost Protestant church in
Prussia and to house the graves of the Hohenzollern royal
family.**

It was constructed between 1894 and 1905 according to a design by Julius Carl Raschdorff and replaced a church dating back to the time of Frederick the Great (1747 – 1750, designed by Johann Boumann the Elder). The building with its central ground plan and neo-Baroque style was originally organized in three main sections. In the north was the now demolished memorial church, in the south the nuptial church for christenings and weddings, and in the middle the main parish church, which seats 2000. The building is 116m/381ft high and 114m/125yd long. The dome is covered with mosaics designed by Anton von Werner and its apex is 74.8m/245ft high. The oldest of the cathedral's bells dates from 1532. The building was badly damaged during the war but was renovated between 1974 and

1993. It was reopened with a mass and a dedication ceremony for the massive Sauer's organ (built in 1904, it has 113 stops and 7200 pipes). Its most valuable possessions include a baptismal font by Christian Daniel Rauch and Karl Friedrich Schinkel's wall altar with the 12 apostles, but its prized possessions are the (empty) sarcophagi of the Great Elector and his wife Dorothea (designed by Johann Arnold Nering), Elector Johann Cicero, the magnificent tomb of the first Prussian royal couple Friedrich I and Sophie Charlotte (designed by Andreas Schlüter) and the headstone of Kaiser Friedrich III (by Reinhold Begas). Their actual remains, though, are kept in the **Hohenzollern crypt**, where 94 coffins, dating from the 16th to the 20th centuries, hold the mortal remains of Hohenzollern family members. The crypt is open to the public. **Imperial staircase** The imperial staircase was for the exclusive use of the royal family. It is decorated with bronzed capitals and 13 tempera paintings created by the landscape painter Albert Hertel (1905). The imperial box offers a splendid view of the cathedral interior. Further up the stairs is the Dom-Museum, which catalogues the architectural history of the edifice. **Dome** A maze of stairs and passages leads away from the imperial staircase into the cathedral dome. From the gallery around the dome, 50m/164ft above the ground, it is possible to see the whole of Berlin (MARCO POLO Insight p.192).

Lustgarten

The Lustgarten park, situated between the Dom, Schlossplatz and the Altes Museum (►Museumsinsel) is at the very heart of old Berlin. It was initially created as a kitchen garden in 1573 but was transformed into a decorative garden in 1643. Its design and uses have been altered many times since. Under Friedrich Wilhelm I it became a parade ground, and trees were first planted from 1830 onwards. During the Weimar Republic it was a favoured venue for political gatherings, but under the Nazis it was concreted over and used for marches. The large granite bowl in front of the old museum was polished up between 1827 and 1830 by Christian Gottlieb Cantian using an erratic block that was found in the Brandenburg March. It is 6.9m/23ft in diameter, weighs 75 tons and is nicknamed **»Berlin's biggest soup dish«**.

? *Did you know*

MARCO ⊕ POLO INSIGHT

... that the first potatoes in Prussia were planted in the Lustgarten in 1649?

Dom Aquarée

Dom Aquarée is a new hotel and office development on the other side of the Liebknecht bridge and has three popular attractions: **Sealife** features 30 pools filled with native freshwater and salt-water creatures; **Aquadom** is the world's largest aquarium with a height of 26m/85ft and a diameter of 11.5m/38ft and is remarkable in that it is

The Berliner Dom has a fine reputation for church music

viewed from a lift that runs through its centre; and the **DDR Museum** on the ground floor, which seeks to exhibit »the life and times of the former state in a unique hands-on experience«. The museum includes a complete living room and kitchen from the GDR era, and shows film documentaries which can be enjoyed from an authentic East German cinema seat.

DDR-Museum: daily 10am–8pm, Sat until 10pm; admission €7; www.ddr-museum.de
Sealife: daily 10am–7pm; admission €17.95; www.sealifeeurope.com

** Brandenburg Gate · Pariser Platz
✦ L 15

Location: Pariser Platz, Mitte
S/U-Bahn: Brandenburger Tor (S 1, S 2, S 25, U 55)

Bus: 100, 200
City centre map: B 10

The Brandenburg Gate is Berlin's defining landmark and has come to symbolize the ending of the division in Germany.

Berlin's definitive landmark

It was built on the instructions of King Friedrich Wilhelm II between 1788 and 1791 using a design by **Carl Gotthard Langhans the El-**

der, who took the propylaea of the Acropolis in Athens as his inspiration. It was intended to provide a suitable conclusion to the western end of the Unter den Linden boulevard. Its classical sandstone construction, unique at the time in Berlin, is 26m/85ft high (including the Quadriga statue), 65.5m/215ft wide and 11m/36ft across. On both sides of the gate, front and back, are six Doric columns, between which are five passages for traffic. The central opening is 5.6m/18ft wide and was originally for the exclusive use of the royal family's carriages while the other four side passages (each 3.8m/12.5ft wide) were open to general traffic. The wings built on both sides, with the façades of Doric temples, were given over to the city's toll collectors and guards. On 6 August 1791 the Brandenburg Gate was opened as a public thoroughfare with no great ceremony in the absence of the king. New passages were made between the gate and its side buildings by Johann Heinrich Strack between 1861 and 1868, during which time he also added open galleries of columns to the gatehouses. The gate was very badly damaged during the Second World War and it was not until 1958 that all the damage was repaired. Corrosion and damage caused during the New Year's celebrations of 1989 / 90 resulted in another major renovation. Yet more harm was done when traffic was diverted through the gate after the fall of the Wall. The gate is now only open to pedestrians.

Quadriga

The Brandenburg Gate's sculptural adornment, particularly the Quadriga, the four horse chariot on top of the building, is primarily the work of **Johann Gottfried Schadow**. His plans were carried out by a Potsdam coppersmith by the name of Jury, whose niece Ulrike acted as the model for the statue of the chariot's driver, Irene, goddess of peace, although the statue would later be regarded as representing the goddess of victory, Victoria, after victory laurels were placed in her hands. The Quadriga was lifted onto the top of the gate in 1793, although it was moved to Paris after Napoleon conquered the city in 1806. It was only after the French defeat at the Battle of Leipzig in 1813 that Marshall Blücher was able to arrange for the statue to be returned. It was put back in its rightful place on 14 August 1814. By order of the king, Karl Friedrich Schinkel was commanded to give the goddess of peace a new trophy, a wreath of oak laurels wrapped around the iron cross and crowned with the eagle of Prussia. With this trophy the statue took on a new meaning and was thereby transformed into the goddess Victoria. Along with the laurels there were initially other trophies in the form of a helmet and spear, a breastplate and two shields. The Quadriga was destroyed during the Second World War, leaving nothing but the head of one horse, now on display in the Märkisches Museum (▶Märkisches Ufer). Thanks to plaster casts made in 1942 it was possible for the Noack casting company in Friedenau to fashion a new Quadriga, which was hoisted into place

The goddess of peace became the goddess of victory: Schadow's Quadriga

in September 1958. Shortly afterwards though, the iron cross and the Prussian eagle were removed by order of the East German government.

A witness of German history

Since the entry of the French in 1806 the Brandenburg Gate has witnessed any number of **musters and victory parades**, including the return of the Prussian troops from Denmark in 1864, in 1866 after the campaign against the Austrians, the victors over France in 1871 and the establishment of the German Reich. At the start of the First World War the Berlin garrison marched through it, and Nazi stormtroopers paraded by torchlight to Wilhelmstrasse on 30 January 1933 in celebration of Hitler's takeover.

When the Wall went up on 13 August 1961 the Brandenburg Gate became the symbol of the city's division – the wall ran right next to the western side of it. It was only a few weeks after the opening of the borders on 9 November 1989, though, that the Brandenburg Gate could once again celebrate its official reopening on 22 December.

Under Friedrich Wilhelm I, Pariser Platz was one of three large **Pariser Platz**
squares, the Oktogon (Leipziger Platz), the Rondell (Mehringplatz)
and Quarré, Pariser Platz itself. It gained its present name in 1814. It
was the site of the French and British embassies, and the home of
Max Liebermann and the legendary Hotel Adlon.

The new construction at the site has sought to hark back to this era.
Thus both Haus Liebermann (to the north with J. P. Kleihues as the
architect) and Haus Sommer (Commerzbank) have appeared either
side of the gate. The northern side of the square is now graced by the
Palais am Pariser Platz (Winking/Froh), the Dresdner Bank (Gerkan
& Partner), the French embassy
(Christian de Portzamparc) and finally a new building for the AGB
property company. The US embassy
by More, Rubel, Yudell at the southwest corner opened in 2008 to devas-
tating reviews from the architecture
critics. In contrast next door the
cuboid *DZ Bank has a quiet exteri-
or that belies the fantastic »architectural sculpture« by Frank O. Gehry
(▶ ill. p.42) inside. Next to that, the
glass structure of the Akademie der
Künste (Academy of Arts) (Beh-
nisch/Durth) rather disrupts the historical recreation intended by the
senate, intentions that are fully real-
ized by the new Hotel Adlon. Around the corner from Adlon on Wilhelmstrasse, however, the British embassy by Michael Wilford is a
bolder modern creation.

To the south of the Brandenburg Gate there is now a memorial to the ****Holocaust**
Jews murdered in Europe during the Holocaust. Peter Eisenman's **Memorial**
design features 2711 concrete blocks of varying size to make up a
structure that can be perceived differently from any place within it as
you walk through. According to Eisenman himself, he made this
radical departure from conventional memorial architecture because
»the extent and scale of the Holocaust mean that any attempt to represent it by conventional means is doomed to fail hopelessly. Our
memorial is attempting to create a new concept of reminiscence that
is quite different.« At the southeastern corner of the group of blocks
an **information point** provides information on victims and memorials in Germany and the rest of Europe.

On the other side of the road in the ▶Tiergarten a memorial was **Other**
dedicated to homosexuals who were persecuted in the National So- **memorials**

cialist period; opposite the south façade of the Reichstag is a memorial to Sinti and Roma who were murdered in those years.

❶ Information point: April–Sept Tue–Sun 10am–8pm, Oct–March 10am–7pm; admission free; www.stiftung-denkmal.de

Cemeteries

Many important figures are buried in Berlin's cemeteries. They bear witness to the history of the city itself.

A reflection of the city's history

In the list of dignitaries below the actual locations of the graves are given in brackets wherever possible. Various tour operators (▶Enjoy Berlin, Tours and Guides) offer guided walks through cemeteries.

✳ FRIEDHOF DER DOROTHEENSTÄDTISCHEN UND FRIEDRICHSWERDERSCHEN GEMEINDE

❶ Chausseestr. 126, Mitte (✳ J 16)
U-Bahn: Oranienburger Tor (U 6) Tram: M 1, 12

More than any other cemetery in Berlin, the small and romantic Dorotheenstadt and Friedrichswerder parish cemetery, is well worth visiting. Laid out in 1762 and used for burials from 1770, it is still used for burials of well-known figures from the worlds of art, culture, economics and politics, including the following (directions are given from the main path starting at the entrance):

Johann Gottlieb Fichte († 1814), philosopher (3rd path on the left, right-hand side)

Georg Wilhelm Friedrich Hegel († 1831), philosopher (2nd left, right-hand side)

Christoph Wilhelm Hufeland († 1832), doctor (1st left, left-hand side)

Karl Friedrich Schinkel († 1841), builder (5th left, left-hand side)

Johann Gottfried Schadow († 1850), sculptor (5th left, at the end)

August Borsig († 1854), industrialist (5th left, left-hand side)

Christian Daniel Rauch († 1857),

sculptor (5th left, left-hand side)
Friedrich August Stüler († 1865), architect (5th left, at the end)
Ernst Litfass († 1874), inventor of the advertising pillar (1st left, right-hand side)
Heinrich Mann († 1950), writer (1st left, left-hand side)
Bertolt Brecht († 1956), writer, and his wife Helene Weigel-Brecht († 1971), actress and theatre manager, (1st left, left-hand side)
Johannes R. Becher († 1958), writer, East German culture minister (1st left, left-hand side)
Hanns Eisler († 1962), composer (1st left, right-hand side)
John Heartfield († 1968), graphic designer (3rd left, right-hand side)
Arnold Zweig († 1968), writer (4th left, left-hand side)
Paul Dessau († 1979), composer (1st left, left-hand side)

The double grave for Bertolt Brecht and Helene Weigel in the Dorotheenstädtischer Friedhof

Anna Seghers († 1983), writer (1st left, left-hand side)
Heiner Müller († 1995), dramatist (5th path on the left, right-hand side)
Bernhard Minetti († 1998), actor (5th path on the left, left-hand side)
George Tabori († 2007), theatre director and author (2nd path left, to the back, then right)
Johannes Rau († 2006), state president (last path on the left, left-hand side)
Bärbel Bohley († 2010), painter and civil-rights campaigner (4th path on the left, at the back to the right)
Fritz Teufel († 2010), political activist (1st path on the left, at the back)

FRANZÖSISCHER FRIEDHOF (HUGUENOT CEMETERY)

Right next door (entrance on Liesenstr. or from the Dorotheenstädtischer Friedhof) is the French Cemetery, which was opened in 1780. It includes:
Daniel Chodowiecki († 1801), engraver and illustrator
Madame Dutitre († 1827), a unique character in the city

Friedrich Ancillon († 1837), educator, foreign minister of Prussia in 1832 under Friedrich Wilhelm IV (tomb by Schinkel)
Ludwig Devrient († 1832), actor
Peter Hacks († 2003), dramatist and author
Further north on Wöhlertstrasse (a side street off Chausseestrasse) lies another cemetery for the French community with the grave of Theodor Fontane († 1898) among others.

INVALIDENFRIEDHOF (CEMETERY FOR THE WAR DISABLED)

❶ Scharnhorststr. 33, Mitte (Y 15)
S/U-Bahn: Hauptbahnhof (S 5, S 7, S 75, U 55)

This cemetery beside the Berlin-Spandau ship canal was opened in 1748 to accommodate the deceased from the nearby invalids' home of the Prussian army. It is the final resting place of many officers of the Prussian and German armies. As it lay directly on the border between East and West Berlin, in the 1960s the cemetery was partially levelled to build the Wall and border defences. Since the early 1990s the cemetery has been partially restored, but some of the border installations have been retained. Gerhard Johann David von Scharnhorst († 1813) – with its lion headstone designed by Schinkel and made by Christian Daniel Rauch with reliefs by Friedrich Tieck
General Graf Tauentzien von Wittenberg († 1824)

General Field Marshal Alfred Graf von Schlieffen († 1913)
Manfred von Richthofen († 1918, memorial of 1975) was re-interred in Wiesbaden in 1972 where his sister and his brother are buried.
Colonel-General Hans von Seeckt († 1936)
Colonel-General Werner von Fritsch († 1939)
Berlin's oldest military cemetery, the Alte Garnisonfriedhof, was laid out in 1701 and lies in the Scheunenviertel (▶p.305).

DREIFALTIGKEITSKIRCHHOF (CEMETERY OF THE HOLY TRINITY CHURCH)

❶ Bergmannstr. 39–41, Kreuzberg (O 17)
U-Bahn: Südstern (U 7)

Friedrich Daniel Schleiermacher († 1834), philosopher (B-OA-118)
Georg Andreas Reimer († 1842), book dealer (B-OA-72)
Charlotte von Kalb († 1843), writer and friend of Schiller (B-HA-14)
Ludwig Tieck († 1853), poet (B top 3-3)
Martin Gropius († 1880), architect (C-W.S.-6)
J. G. Halske († 1890), co-founder of Siemens AG (M-HA-1-11)
Theodor Mommsen († 1903), historian (O-UA-36)
Adolph Menzel († 1905), painter (A-W.S.-48)
Georg Wertheim († 1940), store owner (H-HA-31-33)

CHURCH CEMETERIES NEAR HALLESCHES TOR

❶ Between Mehringdamm and Zossener Strasse, Kreuzberg (N 16)
U-Bahn: Mehringdamm (U 6)

From 1735 on, four cemeteries belonging to three different churches were set up near the Hallesches Tor.
Felix Mendelssohn-Bartholdy († 1847), composer (VI-6-7)
Karl-August Varnhagen von Ense († 1858), writer, and his wife Rahel Varnhagen von Ense, writer († 1833; VII-2-38/39)
Heinrich von Stephan († 1897), general post office manager (VII-SA-10)

Dreifaltig-keitskirchhof (Baruther Strasse)

Cemetery I (Blücher-/Zossener Strasse):

Georg Wenzeslaus v. Knobelsdorff († 1753), builder for Friedrich II
Antoine Pesne († 1757), court painter to Friedrich II (1/1 main avenue)

Jerusalems-und Neue Kirchenge-meinde

Cemetery II (Zossener/Baruther Strasse):

August Wilhelm Iffland († 1814), actor (3/1 Erb.)
Henriette Herz († 1847), lady of letters (1/-3-9/10)

Cemetery III (Mehringdamm 21):

E.T.A. Hoffmann († 1822), poet and composer (1/1-32-6)
Adelbert von Chamisso († 1838), poet (3/1-38-1)
Carl Ferdinand Langhans († 1869), builder (2/2-12-16)
Adolf Glassbrenner († 1876), writer (1/2-17-20/21)
Ernst Christian Fr. Schering († 1889), chemicals manufacturer (4/3 Erb.)

ZENTRALFRIEDHOF FRIEDRICHSFELDE

❶ Gudrunstrasse, Lichtenberg (east K 20)
S-Bahn: Lichtenberg (S 5, S 7, S 75, U 5)

This cemetery was laid out by Hermann Mächtig and bequeathed to the state in 1881. It was the preferred resting place of the SED's leading officials and East German painters. Its graves include:

Friedrich Archenhold († 1939), founder of the public observatory in Treptow (urn section at Feuerhalle no. 18)

Käthe Kollwitz († 1945), graphic artist and sculptor (8th urn section, niche 2)

Arnold von Golssenau († 1979), who wrote under the pseudonym »Ludwig Renn« (8th urn section, niche 7)

Socialist Memorial The Socialist Memorial was formerly situated on what is now Row 46. It was created by Mies van der Rohe in 1926 but was destroyed by the Nazis in 1935. In 1951 it was reinstated in an entirely different form near the front of the cemetery close to the administration building. Memorial plaques recall Karl Liebknecht († 1919), Rosa Luxemburg († 1919) and Rudolf Breitscheid († 1944). Among those interred there are Wilhelm Liebknecht († 1900), Franz Mehring († 1919), Wilhelm Pieck († 1960) and Walter Ulbricht († 1973).

The neighbouring graveyard on Pergolenweg has the graves of Adolf Hennecke († 1975), a worker who became famous in East Germany for exceeding production quotas and was hailed as an example to the country, as well as film director Konrad Wolf († 1982).

FRIEDHOF HEERSTRASSE

❶ Trakehner Allee, Charlottenburg (L9 west)
U-Bahn: Olympiastadion (U 2)

The large cemetery on Heerstrasse was opened in 1924 and its grounds are among the loveliest in Berlin. Many artists and actors are buried here :

Paul Cassirer († 1926), art publisher (5C no. 4)

Maximilian Harden († 1927), critic and publicist (8C no. 10)

Arno Holz († 1929), writer (3B nos. 29/30)

Helene Lange († 1930), women's rights campaigner

Joachim Ringelnatz (Hans Bötticher, † 1934), writer (12D no. 21)

Georg Kolbe († 1947), sculptor (2D)

George Grosz († 1959), painter (16B no. 19)

Curt Goetz († 1960), dramatist and actor, with his wife Valerie von Martens († 1986), actress (16G nos. 11/12)

Grete Weiser († 1970), actress (18L nos. 228/229)

Tilla Durieux († 1971), actress (5C no. 4)

Victor de Kowa († 1973), actor (16G Nr. 29)

Hilde Hildebrand († 1976), actress (6F no. 12)

Käthe Haack († 1986), actress (16J no. 27)

Horst Buchholz († 2003), actor (Feld I-Wald-2)

Loriot (Bernhard-Victor Christoph Carl von Bülow, † 2011) humorist, cartoonist, actor and director

ALTER ST. MATTHÄUS-KIRCHHOF (CEMETERY OF THE OLD ST MATTHEW'S CHURCH)

❶ Grossgörschenstr. 12, Schöneberg (N 15)
S-Bahn: Grossgörschen-/ Yorckstrasse (S 1, S 2, S 25)

Jacob and Wilhelm Grimm († 1863 and † 1859; F-s-1/14)
Adolf Diesterweg († 1866), educator (I-s-1)
Wilhelm Loewe († 1886), president of the German national assembly in Frankfurt in 1848 (Erb 270 L-sI)
Ernst Robert Curtius († 1896), historian and philologist (D-17-16)
Rudolf Virchow († 1902), doctor and social scientist (H-s-12)
Max Bruch († 1920), composer (Q-w-85)
There is also a memorial stone to the conspirators of 20 July 1944: Claus Schenk Graf von Stauffenberg, Ludwig Beck, Friedrich Olbricht, Albrecht Mertz von Quirnheim and Werner von Haeften, who were initially buried here but were later exhumed and cremated, their ashes being scattered.

> **MARCO POLO TIP**
> **Insider Tip**
>
> ! *Berlin's only cemetery café*
>
> ... is at the entrance to the Alter Matthäus-Kirchhof: Café finovo, a combination of fin & novo. It serves hot soup and home-made cake, in summer with seating in the pretty garden. Together with the Roter Mohn florist it is a generally happy rendezvous close to walls painted in reminder of the burial vaults and tombs that were demolished to make way for Albert Speer's plans for a new capital city.

WALDFRIEDHOF DAHLEM

❶ Hüttenweg 47, Zehlendorf (Q 9)
U-Bahn: Oskar-Helene-Heim (U 3), then bus no. 111

Erich Mühsam († 1934), writer (2A 144)
Bernd Rosemeyer († 1938), racing driver and his wife Elly Beinhorn († 2007), aviator (11-4a)
Henriette Hebel a.k.a. »La Jana« († 1940), actress (22B 97)
Gottfried Benn († 1956), doctor and lyricist (27W 32)
Karl Schmidt-Rottluff († 1976), painter (10E 11/12)
O. E. Hasse († 1978), actor (23A 7)
Harald Juhnke († 2005), entertainer
Heinz Berggruen († 2007), art collector

WALDFRIEDHOF ZEHLENDORF

❶ Potsdamer Chaussee 75, Zehlendorf (S/ T 7)
S-Bahn: Mexikoplatz (S 1), then bus no. 211

Ernst Reuter († 1953), mayor (VI 18/19)
Willy Brandt († 1992), chancellor (behind Reuter)
Otto Suhr († 1957), mayor (III U 49)
Jakob Kaiser († 1961), federal minister (XIV W 1-5)
Erwin Piscator († 1966), superintendent of the Volksbühne (XX 688-91)
Paul Löbe († 1967), president of the Reichstag (III U 24)
Hans Scharoun († 1972), architect (I U 24)
Helmut Käutner († 1980), actor and director (III U 7)
Hildegard Knef († 2002), actress

Friedhof Nikolassee On the other side of Potsdamer Chaussee east of the Rehwiese stands the protestant church of Nikolassee. The small cemetery opposite the church (Kirchweg 18/420) has the graves of Hermann Muthesius († 1927), architect (family plot 83) Jochen Klepper († 1942), writer who committed suicide with his Jewish wife and daughter (J 1/4), and Axel Springer († 1985), publisher (family plot 98)

SÜDWESTFRIEDHOF

❶ Potsdam, Stahnsdorf (T 6 west)
S-Bahn: Babelsberg (S 7), then by 601, 602 or 603 bus

The Südwestfriedhof belonging to the Berlin synod is near Potsdamer Damm in Stahnsdorf (Rudolf-Breitscheid-Platz), which is part of the Potsdam district. Its graves include:
Werner von Siemens († 1892), industrialist
Gustav Langenscheidt († 1895), publisher
Engelbert Humperdinck († 1921), composer
Lovis Corinth († 1925), painter
Heinrich Zille († 1929), who drew scenes of the Berlin »milieu«
F. W. Murnau († 1931), film director
Erik Jan Hannussen (Hermann Steinschneider, † 1933), famous spiritualist
Rudolf Breitscheid († 1944), SPD Reichstag member

JEWISH CEMETERIES

Note: When visiting Jewish cemeteries it is essential for men to cover their heads (headwear can sometimes be hired on site.

Alter Jüdischer Friedhof Little remains of the oldest Jewish cemetery in Berlin, which was inaugurated in 1672. More than 3000 people were buried there before it closed in 1827. The cemetery was obliterated by the Nazis in 1943. There are now memorial stones commemorating:

Moses Mendelssohn († 1786), philosopher
Veitel Heine Ephraim († 1775), head of the royal mint under Friedrich II
Daniel Itzig († 1799), banker
❶ Grosse Hamburger Str. 26, Mitte a K 17
S-Bahn: Hackescher Markt (S 5, S 7, S 75)

This cemetery was opened in 1827 to replace the cemetery on Grosser Hamburger Strasse, and was used until 1942. The Lapidarium at the entrance, used to exhibit over 60 Jewish gravestones from various cemeteries was built on the remains of the chapel of rest. Burials include:
Giacomo Meyerbeer († 1864), composer
Gerson von Bleichröder († 1893), banker and adviser to Bismarck
Leopold Ullstein († 1899), publisher
Max Liebermann († 1935), painter
❶ Schönhauser Allee 22/23, Prenzlauer Berg, (J 18)
U-Bahn: Senefelderplatz (U 2)

Jüdischer Friedhof Schönhauser Allee

A Jewish cemetery that opened in 1880 and covers an area of some 40ha/100ac. The entrance and mourners hall with its yellow bricks were designed by Hugo Licht. It is the **largest Jewish cemetery in western Europe** and is the last resting place of some 115,000 people. There is a plaque at the gate listing the graves of:
Hermann Tietz († 1907), founder of the Hertie department stores
Rudolf Mosse († 1920), newspaper publisher
Adolf Jandorf († 1931), founder of the »KaDeWe«
Lesser Ury († 1931), Impressionist painter
Samuel S. Fischer († 1934), publisher
Theodor Wolff († 1943), journalist
Stefan Heym († 2001), writer
Urns of 809 concentration camp victims are also kept in the cemetery and there are around 3000 graves of people who committed suicide during the time of Nazi rule. Jewish resistance fighter Herbert Baum († 1943) also has his grave here as well as Alex Tucholsky († 1905), the father of Kurt Tucholsky. His mother died in Theresienstadt. This is a translation of Tucholsky's poem dedicated to the cemetery:

*Jüdischer Friedhof Weissensee

At Weissensee Jewish Cemetery

»*The clock is ticking. Your grave has time, three metres long, three metres wide. You see another three, four cities. You see Grete, naked. Snow twenty or thirty times more – and then: field P – in Weissensee – in Weissensee*«.

⊙ Herbert-Baum- Strasse/Markus-Reich-Platz, Weissensee (H 19)
Tram: M 4 to Anton-Platz

Jüdischer Friedhof Heerstrasse

A small Jewish cemetery was opened in Charlottenburg in 1955 to the west of Scholzplatz, between Heerstrasse and Am Postfenn, and south of the neighbouring British military cemetery. Many headstones from the Spandau citadel are located here, including one from the 14th century. There is also a memorial to Jewish victims of the Nazis. Hans Rosenthal (▶Famous People) is also buried here.

⊙ Charlottenburg / M 9 west
U-Bahn: Theodor-Heuss-Platz (U 2, U 12), then bus no. 149

** Schloss Charlottenburg and Park

✳ **K 10 / 11**

Location: Spandauer Damm 10–24, Charlottenburg
U-Bahn: Richard-Wagner-Platz (U 7)
Bus: M 45, 109, 309
Altes Schloss (Old Palace), tour or audioguide: April–Oct Tue–Sun 10am– 6pm, Nov–March Tue–Sun 10am–5pm; €12
Neuer Flügel (New Wing): April–Oct Wed–Mon 10am–6pm, Nov–March 10am–5pm; €6

Neuer Pavillon: April–Oct Tue–Sun 10am–6pm; Nov–March Tue–Sun noon–5pm; €4
Belvedere: April–Oct Tue–Sun 10am–6pm; €3
Mausoleum of Queen Luise: April–Oct ue–Sun 10am–6pm; €2
Photo permit €3
www.spsg.de

Since the demolition of Berlin's Stadtschloss (▶Schlossplatz), Schloss Charlottenburg has been the finest example of architecture under the kings of Prussia in Berlin and their love of building.

Berlin's most exquisite Baroque palace

In 1695 Brandenburg's royal director of building **Johann Arnold Nering** was commissioned to build a small summer residence for Elector Friedrich III's wife, Sophie Charlotte. Nering died before completion of this »Lietzenburg« palace (named after the district of Lützenburg). Thereafter Martin Grünberg took over supervision of the building work, adding the two side wings to house the palace retinue. Grünberg's successor, **Johann Eosander von Göthe**, a favourite of Sophie

Charlottenburg Castle

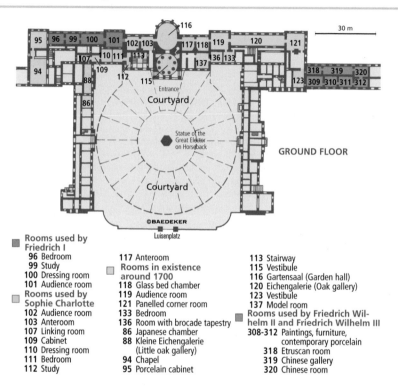

Rooms used by Friedrich I
96 Bedroom
99 Study
100 Dressing room
101 Audience room

Rooms used by Sophie Charlotte
102 Audience room
103 Anteroom
107 Linking room
109 Cabinet
110 Dressing room
111 Bedroom
112 Study

117 Anteroom
Rooms in existence around 1700
118 Glass bed chamber
119 Audience room
121 Panelled corner room
133 Bedroom
136 Room with brocade tapestry
86 Japanese chamber
88 Kleine Eichengalerie (Little oak gallery)
94 Chapel
95 Porcelain cabinet

113 Stairway
115 Vestibule
116 Gartensaal (Garden hall)
120 Eichengalerie (Oak gallery)
123 Vestibule
137 Model room
Rooms used by Friedrich Wilhelm II and Friedrich Wilhelm III
308-312 Paintings, furniture, contemporary porcelain
318 Etruscan room
319 Chinese gallery
320 Chinese room

Charlotte, appended the central projection at the front in order to make space for a domed tower, 48m/157ft in height. After Sophie Charlotte died in 1705, the palace was given its present name in her honour. Between 1709 and 1712 Eosander von Göthe also erected an orangery on the western side. Under Frederick the Great **Georg Wenzeslaus von Knobelsdorff** made plans to supplement an orangery on the eastern side with a new wing (1740 – 46) and in the reign of Friedrich Wilhelm II a small theatre was built in addition to the orangery under the supervision of Carl Gotthard Langhans (1788). This brought the total length of the building to 505m/552yd. Both before and after Sophie Charlotte became the first queen of Prussia, the palace was the scene of many spectacular festivals and balls. In Frederick the Great's time it was used for large family gatherings. During the 19th century it became home to the Countess of Liegnitz, wife of Friedrich Wilhelm

III, and Friedrich Wilhelm IV also lived there for a time. The entire complex suffered serious damage in an air raid on 23 November 1943

* Court of Honour

An entrance flanked with two reproductions of the Borghese gladiator leads to a forecourt with a mounted statue of the Great Elector Friedrich Wilhelm in the centre. The statue is one of the most important equestrian monuments of the Baroque period. The design was commissioned by Friedrich III, son of the Great Elector, from **Andreas Schlüter**. Casting began in October 1700 and the statue was formally unveiled on 12 July 1703, the anniversary of the first Prussian monarch's birth. Friedrich Wilhelm is depicted in a mixture of Roman and contemporary garb featuring a brass breastplate and a flowing wig with his staff of command extended in authoritative fashion. The coat of arms on the marble pedestal has a Latin inscription expressing the gratitude of his son. The figures on chains at each end of the pedestal signify the elector's defeated enemies. The monument was originally situated at the Stadtschloss on the Long Bridge or Elector's Bridge, which is nowadays called the Rathausbrücke. In 1943 it was to be moved to safety by barge but the overloaded vessel sank in Tegel dock. The statue was salvaged in 1949 and erected in its current position three years later.

Altes Schloss (Nering-Eosander Building)

The rooms used by Friedrich I (bedroom, study, the »braided room«, the audience chamber) and his second wife Sophie Charlotte (audience chamber, anteroom, living rooms) are on the western side of the Altes Schloss. The furnishings are mainly painted

View of the Court of Honour at Schloss Charlottenburg

Chinese pieces, or European imitations, or carved and inlaid pieces dating from around 1700. Among the most remarkable of the rooms are the **Porzellankabinett (porcelain cabinet)** with its Far Eastern porcelain of the 17th and 18th centuries, the palace chapel where King Friedrich Wilhelm II entered into a morganatic marriage with Countess Julie von Ingenheim, and the tapestry room (Gobelinraum), which features two hangings from the Grossmogul series made in Jean Barraband II's Berlin studio at the beginning of the 18th century called *Die Teetrinker (The Tea Drinker)* and *Der mongolische Kaiser (The Mongol Emperor)*. The large and fabulously carved and panelled oak gallery in the eastern wing of the palace was constructed in 1713.

In the adjoining »new wing« the ground floor houses the summer residence and the permanent residence of Friedrich Wilhelm III. On the first floor of the same wing are the apartments of Frederick the Great as well as two reception rooms. The walls of the great dining hall (Weisser Saal) are panelled with pink marble stucco and the 42m/46yd-long Golden Gallery leading away to the east, and taking up the entire width of the wing, contains some fabulous gilded stucco decoration. The former **apartments of Frederick the Great** – including the Yellow Atlas Chamber with its Rococo furnishings, specially created by Johann August Nahl in 1744 for the silver dining hall at Schloss Potsdam – include an important collection of paintings from the early 18th century French school, among them Nicolas Lancret's *Magic Lantern Man* and *Shop Sign of the Art Dealer Gersaint*, which is one of the most famous works by Antoine Watteau.

New wing (Knobelsdorff wing)

* CHARLOTTENBURG PARK

The park was laid out as a French-style garden by Siméon Godeau in 1697 and was largely remodelled in English style by Peter Joseph Lenné at the beginning of the 19th century. The »Parterre«, however, has been restored as a Baroque garden.

The Neue Pavillon (Schinkel Pavillon) at the eastern entrance was built in 1824 – 25 to designs drawn up by Karl Friedrich Schinkel and emulates a Neapolitan villa. Friedrich Wilhelm III commissioned the pavilion for himself and his second wife, Princess Liegnitz. It has several paintings on display, including some by C. D. Friedrich.

Neuer Pavillon

The Belvedere at the northern end of the park was built in 1788 by Carl Gotthard Langhans as a tea house. Nowadays it houses the Federal State of Berlin's collection of KPM (Königliche Porzellan Manufaktur or Royal Porcelain Factory) porcelain.

Belvedere

Mausoleum   At the end of an avenue of pines in the west of the park there is a small Doric temple with columns at the front made of erratic granite blocks found in the March of Brandenburg. This is the mausoleum that Friedrich Wilhelm III had built by Heinrich Gentz as the last resting place of Queen Luise (1776 – 1810). It was completed in 1812 and expanded in 1841 and 1889. The sarcophagus and the statue of the queen were created by **Christian Daniel Rauch**. The statue of the queen shows her asleep with her hands folded and dressed in a light dress that falls loosely from her reclining form. Thirty years after its construction her husband was also buried in the mausoleum. His sarcophagus was also designed by Rauch and shows the king in a simple greatcoat. Others were also interred here as time went by, including Prince Albert (1809 – 72), Kaiser Wilhelm I (1797 – 1888) and his wife Augusta (1811 – 90) as well as Princess Liegnitz, second wife of Friedrich Wilhelm III (1800 – 73). The heart of Friedrich Wilhelm IV (1795 – 1861) is kept in a special stone capsule.

Dahlem

✦ P – Q 8 – 10

Borough: Steglitz-Zehlendorf
U-Bahn: Dahlem-Dorf (U 3)

Dahlem, in southwest Berlin, has long been one of the most affluent areas in the city. There is a good reason for this in that Kaiser Wilhelm II was particularly attracted to the area and inspired the institution of an academic quarter.

The results of this are still to be seen in the form of aristocratic villas, the university and some excellent museums accompanied by an almost rural idyll with plenty of green open spaces. The first mention of the locale dates from 1375 where it appears in the Land Book of Karl IV as »Dalm«. It remained as an estate or manor domain until the 19th century when the final owners surrendered it to the district tax authorities. Dahlem has considerable cultural and scientific importance within Berlin nowadays as the home of the Freie Universität (Free University), various institutes belonging to the Technische Universität (Technical University), the Max Planck Society and state museums.

*Botanical   The botanical gardens originated as a kitchen and herb garden for the
gardens   elector's household at the Berlin Stadtschloss in the Lustgarten (►Berliner Dom). The Great Elector decreed in 1679 that a »model garden« be laid out in Schöneberg – in what is now the Kleistpark. This developed into a real botanical garden. At the turn of the twen-

tieth century it was relocated to Dahlem. Botanist Adolf Engler (1844 – 1930; his gravestone is to the left of the main avenue) fashioned this into one of the largest and most important botanical gardens in the world between 1899 and 1910. It covers an area of about 42ha/104ac and features more than 18,000 types of plant. It has a forestry section, a section for cultivated and medicinal plants, 16 greenhouses (the largest hothouse is 60m/66yd long, 30m/33yd wide and 25m/82ft high), a biotope for water and marsh dwelling plants, the Elector's Garden with plants dating from the 17th century as well as a special »touch and smell« garden for the blind and partially sighted.

From 2006 to 2009 the **Grosses Tropenhaus** (Great Tropical House), with a surface area of 1750 sq m/19,000 sq ft and a height of 26.5m/87ft one of the world's largest hothouses without internal supports, was renovated. When it was built between 1905 and 1907 to a design by the royal architect Alfred Koerner the structure, consisting of a roof supported only from the exterior to which glass walls were added, was a sensation. This method of construction allows plant lovers to admire the tropical jungle without supports and pillars to spoil the view. With over 1300 species and over 4000 tropical plants, the Tropenhaus also holds one the world's greatest varieties of plant life and is a veritable Noah's ark for endangered species.

The **Botanisches Museum** (Botanical Museum) next to the entrance from Königin-Luise-Strasse has a herbarium with more than two million plants. The Egyptian section is notable, as is a room that features various types of poisonous and edible mushrooms.

❶ Entrances: Königin-Luise-Str. 6 – 8 (from the Königin-Luise-Platz bus stop) and Unter den Eichen 5 – 10 (approached from the S-Bahn station).

Gardens: Nov–Jan daily 9am–4pm, Feb closes 5pm, Mar and Oct closes 6pm, Sept open till 7pm, April and Aug till 8pm, May, June, July till 9pm; last admission 30 minutes before closing. Hothouses as gardens, at weekends from 10am;

Botanisches Museum: 10am – 6pm daily, admission: €6; www.botanischer-garten-berlin.de

> **?** | **MARCO POLO INSIGHT** | *Did you know …*
>
> … that the tower of St Anne's Church in Dahlem was used as a station on the first optical telegraph route, from Berlin to Koblenz, between 1832 and 1892?

Dahlem-Dorf U-Bahn station

The picturesquely rustic underground railway station, Dahlem-Dorf is a half timbered, thatched building, erected in 1913 at the behest of Kaiser Wilhelm II.

Domäne Dahlem

The Domäne Dahlem opposite the U-Bahn station is still farmed. The harvest is sold in the farm's own health food shop. The open-air museum, »the only farm in Berlin with its own U-Bahn station«, also hosts a varied programme. Historic craft workshops including a blue-printing establishment and bee-keeping with a bee museum can also be viewed, and various other craft skills are regularly demonstrated. The **Gutshaus** or farmhouse is a Baroque building erected in 1680 by Cuno Hans of Willmerstorff and features the Willmerstorff Alliance crest on the gable. As part of the Domäne farm museum it now portrays the agricultural history of Berlin and Brandenburg, with its own nostalgic village shop. The Gothic chapel on the ground floor is also open to the public: its market days and craft festivals seem to attract half of Berlin. Further along Königin-Luise-Strasse is the **St.-Annen-Kirche** (St Anne's Church), built in 1220. Its late Gothic chancel dates from the 15th century while its Baroque pulpit and gallery were added in 1679. In the cemetery **the grave of Rudi Dutschke** can be seen, and the theologian Helmut Gollwitzer (1908 – 93) is also buried here.

Domänenmuseum: 10am – 6pm daily except Tue; the domain itself is freely accessible

✱✱ DAHLEM MUSEUMS

❶ Tue–Fri 10am–5pm; Sat, Sun 11am–6pm
Admission to all museums: €8; www.smb.museum

The main attractions in Dahlem are the Berlin State Museums (run by the Prussian Cultural Heritage Foundation – Stiftung Preussischer Kulturbesitz), which have brought together their ethnographic collections in the village. The split-site locations are at Im Winkel (Museum Europäischer Kulturen – Museum of European Cultures) and the three-storey museum building on Lansstrasse, which was built between 1914 and 1923 by Bruno Paul. It was originally planned to house an Asian museum but has been extended at various times and now houses the Ethnologisches Museum as well as the Museen für Indische und Ostasiatische Kunst (Museums for Indian and Far Eastern Art).

Museum Europäischer Kulturen

The Museum of European Cultures was founded in 1999 to combine the ethnographic collections of the Museum für Volkskunde (Folklore Museum) founded by Rudolf Virchow and the European possessions of the former Völkerkundemuseum. It is divided into two sections, respectively covering the meaning of images in everyday life and the places where those images were perceived.

✱Museum für Asiatische Kunst

The collections from South, Southeast and Central Asia on the ground floor in the left-hand wing include terra-cotta pieces, stone sculptures, bronze work, wood carvings and paintings from India, the countries of the Himalayas and Central and Southeast Asia. The oldest pieces date from the 2nd century BC while the most recent are from the 19th century. Nearly all the major Asian religions including Buddhism,

Hinduism and Jainism are represented. The *Turfan« collection with its murals and sculptures from the 5th to the 12th centuries is the key highlight. They were brought to Berlin from Buddhist temples on the northern part of the Silk Road by four expeditions that took place between 1902 and 1914. The most impressive of the features is the reconstruction of a temple cave in Kizil with an original fresco, The Ring-bearing Doves, painted from 431 to 533. Two computer terminals are provided from which it is possible to learn about the life and works of Buddha. Since 1992 the **Ostasiatische Kunstsammlung** (Collection of Far Eastern Art), founded in 1906, has united in Dahlem the »Far Eastern Collection« established in East Berlin with those pieces that were not transported to the Soviet Union after the war. Most of the collection that once existed nevertheless remains in the Hermitage of St Petersburg in Russia. The current sections – the core of which come from a collection belonging to art dealer Klaus Naumann – cover Chinese archaeology, Far Eastern Buddhist art, Japanese paintings and Chinese, Japanese or Korean arts and crafts including the throne of a Chinese emperor with a screen from one of the emperor's provincial residences, dating from the second half of the 17th century. There is even a complete Japanese tea room.

This is one of the best ethnological museums in the world and is far more extensive than the other two museums in the building. It possesses more than 500,000 exhibits and 60,000 sound recordings from all over the world and presently features ancient American items (ground floor), exhibits from the South Seas (ground floor and upper floor), African items (upper floor) and Far Eastern works (attic). The African exhibition is particularly notable for its terra-cotta sculptures from Ife (western Nigeria, 10th – 13th centuries), **bronze pieces from Benin** (16th century), a royal throne and a collection of masks from the grasslands of Cameroon as well as an initiation mask made by the Chokwe of southwest Congo. The Central and South American section features the »Golden Chamber« with pieces from Columbia, Costa Rica and Peru (including ancient Incan sacrifice dishes). The South Seas section includes an exhibition of boats including an **ocean-going vessel from Luf** as well as original dwellings from New Guinea, the Palau Islands and New Zealand. On the ground floor the exhibition on the North American Indians has impressive items such as artefacts of the Prairie Indians, which include what is probably the oldest leather tepee still in existence (made by the Lakota tribe around 1820/30). Many of the exhibits were collected by Prince Maximilian of Wied, Duke Paul von Württemberg and Balduin of Möllnhausen on their various expeditions. Blind visitors to the museum have a hall of their own where they can touch and examine models of various buildings. The Juniormuseum is aimed at youngsters of eight and under who are interested in ethnology.

**Ethnologisches Museum

✳ Deutsches Technikmuseum
(German Museum of Technology)

✤ **N 15**

Entrance: Trebbiner Str. 9, Kreuzberg
U-Bahn: Gleisdreieck (U 1, U 2, U 12, U 15), Möckernbrücke (U 7)
❶ Tue–Fri 9am–5.30pm; Sat, Sun

10am–6pm
Tours: tel. 030 90 25 41 24
Admission: €6
www.sdtb.de

The German Museum of Technology, originally called the Transport and Technology Museum, cannot match the Deutsches Museum in Munich, but has unique exhibits including aircraft, locomotives and ships, as original items and models, and much more than that.

Old Building

The German Museum of Technology, opened in 1983 as the Museum für Verkehr und Technik (Transport and Technology Museum) on premises used by the city markets and refrigerated storehouses, also includes the site of the Anhalter Bahnhof railway yard and the Anhalter goods yard. The latter will be expanded in the coming years to form a new museum quarter ‚the Technoversum, which will be organized on thematic lines. Six forums will be dedicated to the relationship between humans and technology. The hall built for the horses of the market company in 1908 now accommodates the museum entrance, shop and cafeteria. The first floor is devoted to textile and communications technologies, the second floor to paper and printing, computing and automation. One of the highlights is a replica of the **»Z 1«, the world's first computer**, made by the Berliner Konrad Zuse in 1936.

New building

The themes in the new building, air, space and sea travel, are presented with the latest museum technology. Three whole floors are dedicated to water transport, subdivided into the inland waterways between the rivers Elbe and Oder on the ground floor, where is a 33m/108ft-long barge dating from 1840, and sea shipping on the second floor. Above that the two floors of the air and space department contain a great many original items.

The stand-out exhibits here are **fully restored aircraft** such as a Junkers 52, a Messerschmidt 109 and, on the terrace, one of the famous »raisin bombers« of the Berlin Airlift, as well as a fantastic collection of medals belonging to almost all the ace fighter pilots of the First World War. The evolution of German rocket science is also presented, with attention paid to the appalling conditions of labour of the concentration camp inmates who worked in rocket production.

In the loading sheds of the former freight station an exhibition on cars and other means of road transport has bicycles, motorbikes, coaches and 30 motor cars ranging from the Colani GT (1964) to the Mercedes Nürburg (1930), from a VW Beatle (1951) to a streamlined Saab 92A (1951). There is a special focus on electric vehicles. The two locomotive sheds of 1874 display »33 stages in railway history« including 40 wagons, some going back to 1840, and the Fürstenportal (Princes' Gate) of the Anhalter Bahnhof. A new exhibition examines the role played by the German state railways in the deportation of Jews to the death camps. In the railway offices behind the locomotive sheds departments for photography, films, scientific instruments, production technology and household technology can be seen. This includes the museum's own suitcase manufacture (a popular souvenir) and jewellery workshop. In the park around the museum there are windmills and wind generators, a water wheel and a water tower.

The emblem of the Technikmuseum is a Douglas C-47 Skytrain, one of the aircraft that was used during the Berlin Air Lift

Exhibition Grounds

✦ M 9/10

Location: Hammarskjöldplatz, Charlottenburg
S-Bahn: Messe Süd, Eichkamp (S 5, S 7, S 75),

Messe Nord/ICC (S 41, S 42, S 46)
U-Bahn: Kaiserdamm (U 2)

Major exhibitions and trade fairs such as the International Tourism Exchange and the International Radio Exhibition attract hundreds of thousands of visitors to the exhibition grounds at the base of the Funkturm (radio tower) every year.

The first of the exhibition halls were erected at the beginning of the 1920s. The grounds were expandedin 1936, after 1945 and finally Hin 1999. The oldest parts still standing include the Palais next to the Funkturm, which dates from the 1930s. Between Halls 10 and 12 and along the Messedamm road visitors will find a Japanese garden and the Ursula Sax sculpture Doppel-Looping. Parallel to the Messedamm road is the northern loop of the former **Avus race track**.

*Funkturm The Funkturm or radio tower is another of the city's major landmarks and has been affectionately dubbed »Langer Lulatsch« (beanpole) by Berliners. It was built in 1924 according to plans by Heinrich Straumer and features a steel girder construction mounted on ceramic piers. It first went into service at the third German Radio Exhibition in 1926. In 1930 it broadcast the world's first public television programmes; in 1945 a grenade destroyed one of the main girders but the tower did not collapse. It is 138m/453ft high (150m/492ft including the antennae) and has both a restaurant at 55m/180ft and an observation platform at a height of 121m/397ft, both of which offer fantastic views of the city (▶MARCO POLO Insight p.192).

Viewing platform: Tue–Sun 10am–11pm, Mon until 8pm, admission €5

The **International Congress Centre** (ICC) is linked to the exhibition grounds via a roofed bridge over Messedamm. Before the new development at ▶Potsdamer Platz, it was the largest building project in Berlin built since the war (built 1970 – 79). The overall length of the complex is 320m/350yd, it is 80m/87yd wide and 40m/131ft high. The volume of the building is some 800,000 cu m/1,050,000 cu yd. There are more than 80 rooms and halls for congresses and seminars. The largest hall, Saal 1, accommodates up to 5000 people.

Another legacy of Germany's radio history lies to the north east just outside the exhibition grounds on Masurenallee. The five-storey Haus des Rundfunks (**Broadcasting House**) was built between 1929 and 1931 by Hans Poelzig and features a distinctive entrance hall. A television centre (1965 – 70) is situated to the north of it.

Fernsehturm (Television Tower)

✦ **K 17**

Location: Mitte
S-Bahn and U-Bahn: Alexanderplatz (S 5, S 7, S 75, U 2, U 5, U 8)
City centre map: B 14
Observation platform: March–Oct

daily 9am–midnight, Nov–Feb.
daily 10am–midnight
Admission: €13
www.tv-turm.de

The TV Tower or Fernsehturm has become one of Berlin's most distinctive landmarks.

It came into existence because the East German republic needed a nationwide broadcasting facility, but its size and appearance arose from the GDR leaders' desire for a symbol to represent the socialist part of Germany to the world. It was inspired by Hermann Henselmann, the architect of the Karl-Marx-Allee development

118 m

368 m

203 m   **250 m**

©BAEDEKER

(▶Friedrichshain), who envisioned a »dominating tower of socialism«. Construction began on 4 August 1965 using a design by architects Fritz Dieter and Günter Franke and a team of Swedish engineers. The tower was put into operation as early as 3 October 1969. At 368m/1207ft high (including antenna) it is the tallest building in the city. A viewing platform is placed at a height of 204m/669ft. 4m/13ft below that is the **Telecafé**,

> **MARCO POLO TIP** ⊕
>
> **Insider Tip**
> *A better wurst?*
>
> In the café of the TV tower a socialist alternative to the Western hotdog was invented: the Ketwurst, a name combining the word for »sausage« with »ketchup«. They are no longer sold in the TV tower, but can be enjoyed in the restaurant of the DDR-Museum (▶p.168) and at Friedrichstrasse U-Bahn station.

which makes a complete revolution every half hour. In good weather it is possible to see for 40km/25mi. The Fernsehturm was hailed by the central organ of the ruling party, the SED, as a symbol of »New Germany«, the »Telespargel (TV asparagus)«, but the people themselves gave it several other playfully subversive nicknames including »Imponierkeule« (show-off's club), »Protzstengel« (swank stalk) or »St Walter« (since SED chief and state council leader Walter Ulbricht was said to have chosen the site). The GDR leadership were also mightily displeased the first time the sun shone on the mirrored ball since the reflection took the form of a cross, causing it to be dubbed the »Pope's revenge« on the atheist regime. The phenomenon is apparent every time the sun shines on Berlin (▶MARCO POLO Insight, p.192).

Friedrichshain

✴ K – M 18 – 20

Borough: Friedrichshain-Kreuzberg
S-U-Bahn: S 5, S 7, S 75, S 41, S 42, U 5, U 12

Like ▶Prenzlauer Berg before it, Friedrichshain is undergoing a change from inconspicuous suburb to happening scene.

The traditionally rather dowdy working class district has been discovered by the well-to-do, sporting designer suits; artists, fashion gurus and young academics have also been moving in. The barbers and hairdressers are now hair stylists and busloads of tourists are descending on the fashionable new bars around Boxhagener Platz; Simon-Dach-Strasse, in particular, has become a mecca for pub-lovers and café-goers, and Wühlischstrasse is an address for fashionable boutiques. What was formerly the smallest of Berlin's boroughs also has the former Stalinallee, the epitome of socialist architecture. The park that gives the borough's name is one of the prettiest in the city.

Now a fashionable scene

MARCO ⊕ POLO INSIGHT

Berlin – From Above and Below

When you visit a city for the first time, it's always good to get a bird's-eye view. There are plenty of opportunities to do this in the German capital. And Berlin would not be Berlin if it were not possible to go beneath the ground.

1) Berlin Fernsehturm (TV tower) on Alexanderplatz
Height: 368m/1207ft (Germany's tallest building)
Telecafé 207.5m/681ft , viewing platform (VP) 204m/669ft

2) HiFlyer tethered balloon near Checkpoint Charlie
Flight altitude approx. 150m/492ft

3) Funkturm (radio tower)
at exhibition grounds
Height 147m/482ft, VP 121.5m/399ft

9) Teu
Heigh
above

8) Müggelturm
in Köpenick,
Height 30m/98ft
VP 29m/95ft

10) Gr
Heigh

5) Bell tower in Olympic Park
Height 77m/253ft, VP 77m/253ft

6) Kollhoff-Tower at Potsdamer Platz, **Height 103m/338ft**
VP and café 100m/328ft

4) Park Inn Hotel, Alexanderplatz
Height 132m/433ft,
VP 125m/410ft

7) Gasometer
in Schöneberg
Height 78m/256ft

©BAEDEKER

▶ The lowest-lying districts of Berlin are not below 32m/105ft above sea level.

▶ **How can you go below ground in Berlin?**
Two associations explore and record the world below the city streets, and organize fascinating tours. Our recommendation: book ahead.

Tours with unter-berlin e.V.

• Berlin from above and below
• Archaeology in Berlin
• Line U2 through Berlin's history
• Prenzlauer Berg from below
• Jewish life in Prenzlauer Berg
• Fighting beneath the earth
• Underground GDR

Further information:
www.unter-berlin.de

g im Grunewald
/377ft
el

dturm in Grunewald
84ft, VP 36m/118ft

Bierpinsel in Steglitz
ght 47m/154ft
46m/151ft

**12) Berliner Dom
(cathedral)**
on Museumsinsel
Height 116m/381ft
VP 50m/164ft

17) Grosser Bunkerberg
in Volkspark Friedrichshain
**Height 78m/256ft
above sea level**

16) Französischer Dom
on Gendarmenmarkt
**Height 71m/233ft,
VP 44m/144ft**

14) Zionskirche in Mitte
**Height 67m/220ft,
VP 22m/72ft**

13) Hotel Senator in
Spandau, **Panorama
restaurant 50m/164ft**

15) Siegessäule in Tiergarten
**Height 67m/220ft,
VP 51m/167ft**

Height above sea level: 200m

**18) Reichstag dome
Height 47m/154ft,
VP 40m/131ft**

150 m

19) Schinkel Monument
in Viktoriapark
**Height 66m/217ft
above sea level**

100 m

50 m

The highest ground in the city is the Grosse Müggelberg at 114.7m/376ft above sea level.

Tours with Berliner Unterwelten e.V.

• Dark worlds
• From the flak tower to
  the rubble mountain
• Subway, bunker, Cold War
• Breaches in the Wall
• Tracing U-Bahn line D
• The bunker tour

• »Mother-and-child bunker«
  in Fichtestrasse
• Extreme Humboldthain
• Kindl area in Neukölln
• Operations bunker in Teichstrasse
• Traces of the cemetery railway

Further information:
http://berliner-unterwelten.de

Karl-Marx-Allee

Karl-Marx-Allee, 2.3km/1.5mi long and 90m/100yd wide, was built from 1952 as part of a »National Reconstruction Programme for Berlin«. Initially called **Stalinallee**, it was renamed in 1961; it was built on the site of a high-density rental district that had been utterly destroyed by bombs. The thoroughfare starts from the southeast corner of ►Alexanderplatz in the city centre and runs all the way to Strausberger Platz in Friedrichs-hain. Here begins the section of the development that has gone down in German history: when the site was being built, the resentment of the workers against excessive labour quotas boiled over into rebellion on 17 June 1953. The section between Strausberger Platz, dominated by the two skyscrapers »Haus Berlin« and »Haus des Kindes«, and Frankfurter Tor, with its two tall domes modelled on those on Gendarmenmarkt, is nevertheless that part of the site which most clearly exhibits the ambitions of the East German leadership. It is a »socialist magistral« with cheap but well appointed workers' apartments: giant housing blocks, tiled with Meissner ceramics, in the typical »confectionery style« of the Stalin era that had genuinely remarkable features such as central heating and waste disposal units. Karl-Marx-Allee along with its 200 street lights is now a listed heritage site. New tenants, a young and creative crowd, are starting to revive a street that had been declared dead with their chic offices and galleries. At Café Sibylle at no. 72 an exhibition is devoted to the history of this street. .

Ostbahnhof

The Ostbahnhof to the south of Friedrichshain was called Schlesischer Bahnhof (Silesian station) until 1950 and was at one time the central terminus in Berlin. Until 2006 it was the main inter-city station in the east of Berlin. It was opened in 1842 as the Frankfurter Bahnhof for the line to Frankfurt an der Oder (extended to Breslau/Wroclaw in 1847).

East Side Gallery

A preserved section of the old Berlin Wall, 1.3km/1420yd long, leads away to the southeast of the station along Mühlenstrasse as far as the Oberbaumbrücke. Its design is that of the outer or Vorderland wall, although it was actually situated on the eastern side. It was intended to block off the view from the west, because Mühlenstrasse was on the motorcade route taken by dignitaries visiting the GDR from Schönefeld airport to the centre. After the fall of the Wall, 118 artists painted murals on this section and their works have achieved a kind of fame: the picture of that passionate embrace between Honecker and Brezhnev is known the world over. Thanks to a breach in the

Wall and new jetties for boats opposite the O2-World Arena, the banks of the Spree are to become a park and part of the new Medi-aspree quarter.

At the end of the East Side Gallery, beyond the Oberbaum bridge leading to ▶Kreuzberg, the lights of Warschauer Strasse never went out as this was the site of the Osram factory and of VEB Narva bulbs after the war. The factory was closed in 1992 and Oberbaum City was built on the site as an office and commercial quarter, home to about 70 companies se.

Oberbaum City

The Eierkühlhaus, once a refrigerated store for eggs built in 1928 by Oskar Pusch on the Allee am Spreeufer has also found creative new tenants, the music broadcaster MTV. In the Spree the so-called *Molecule Men* stand for the districts of Kreuzberg, Friedrichshain and Treptow, which meet here (ill. p.50). Beyond them at Eichenstrasse lies the **Badeschiff** (bathing boat) – a barge for inland waterways whose hold has been converted to a swimming pool.

On the Spree

Between Landsberger Allee and Am Friedrichshain in the northern part of the borough is the Volkspark Friedrichshain. In 1840, on the hundredth anniversary of Friedrich II's ascent to the throne, the city magistracy decided to create a park in counterpoint to the ▶Tiergarten. It was laid out during the latter part of the 19th century by Gustav Meyer but its 52ha/128ac had to be redesigned after the Second World War when two hills with views were created from the rubble of two flak bunkers: the 78m/256ft Grosser Bunkerberg and the 30m/100ft Kleiner Bunkerberg. Next to the Königstor at the western entrance is the Märchenbrunnen (fairy tale fountain) built in 1913, featuring figures from the Grimms' fairy tales. In the northern half of the park there is a leisure centre for sports and games and in the east an open-air stage. There are also some political memorials including the Friedhof der Märzgefallenen (Cemetery of the March Revolutionaries) for victims of the fighting on the barricades of the March 1848 revolution. Two exhibitions tell their history and that of the cemetery itself. The west of the park also has a monument to anti-fascist Germans who fell fighting for the International Brigades during the Spanish Civil War.

*Volkspark Friedrichshain

> **? MARCO ⬤ POLO INSIGHT**
>
> *The dictator's fate*
>
> It goes without saying that there was a monument to the eponymous Soviet leader on Stalinallee: on its south side between Andreasstrasse and Koppenstrasse. It was melted down in 1961 and re-cast to make some of the metal animal figures in Friedichsfelde Zoo.

Exhibition in Friedhof der Märzgefallenen: daily 10am–6pm, admission free

✳ Friedrichstrasse

	✦ **K – M 16**
Location: Mitte	**U-Bahn:** U 6 between
S-Bahn: Friedrichstrasse (S 1, S 2,	Hallescher Tor and
S 25, S 5, S 7, S 75)	Oranienburger Tor
City centre map: O – M 10 – 12	

The name still calls to mind the era when it was the centre of Berlin's entertainment district. It is also, however, a name forever associated with the partition of Berlin, since between 1961 and 1989 the street was divided in two by the Wall and the famous Checkpoint Charlie at Zimmerstrasse.

In search of the old glamour
Friedrichstrasse runs for about 3.3km/2mi in a north-south alignment from Oranienburger Tor in the city centre to Mehringplatz by the Hallescher Tor in Kreuzberg. Few traces of the division can be seen nowadays, and the glitter of days past has not yet been recaptured by the somewhat soulless modern buildings on the site.

Fried-richstrasse was constructed under Friedrich Wilhelm I to allow a direct march from the parade grounds on Tempelhofer Feld. Under Wilhelm II too, troops would regularly march along the route to the palace from their manoeuvres. With the founding of the German Empire, or Reich, the boulevard underwent a »colossal boom«, during which the famous Kaisergalerie was built, shortly to be followed by the Friedrichstrassenpassage, which was twice the size. This was the basis from which Friedrichstrasse developed into imperial Germany's foremost shopping street, and even more so to its premier entertainment centre. It had high-class hotels, opera houses, beer halls and revue palaces. Behrenstrasse, the first side street after Unter den Linden, became synonymous with the might of money – the headquarters of the Deutsche Bank and the Berlin branch of the Dresdner Bank both stood there. After the First World War, Friedrichstrasse lost its status as the premier shopping destination to an up-and-coming pretender, Kurfürstendamm, but for those seeking entertainment it still held top slot. A major US air raid on 3 February 1945 destroyed the centre of Berlin including Friedrichstrasse. The partition of Berlin meant the areas either side of the zone borders decayed to frontier wilderness. The East German leadership sought to recapture the flair of a boulevard in a world metropolis by creating such buildings as the Friedrichstadtpalast and the Grand Hotel but their plans were overtaken by events.

Since 1989 the street has seen a positive swarm of investors. Between Friedrichstrasse station in the north and the former Checkpoint Charlie practically every block has been built up with new buildings. Building shells and older buildings dating from the GDR period have mostly been demolished. Architects have had to keep to the historic height limits, but failed to maintain the small-scale character of the old street.

FRIEDRICHSTRASSE NORTH OF UNTER DEN LINDEN

From the crossroads of ▶Unter den Linden and Friedrichstrasse and walking along Friedrichstrasse towards the north, practically the first thing you see is the Dussmann department store on the right. It offers books, videos, CDs and DVDs aplenty, and has its own internet café plus another café with US styling. Not far away, beyond Dorotheenstrasse, the 25-storey Internationale Handelszentrum or International Trade Centre (1978) towers 93m/305ft over the street.

Next is the legendary Friedrichstrasse station, which opened on 1 May 1882 as a suburban station. It quickly became the most important station in the capital of the Reich. Between 1924 and 1926 it was completely refurbished, receiving two parallel train sheds, one for long distance services and the other for S-Bahn trains. After the building of the Wall in 1961 it was the only place in the city where there was a direct connection for inter-city, S-Bahn and U-Bahn services: long-distance travellers from the west and residents of West Berlin using the U 6 underground service, which actually passed under East Berlin, were allowed to take S-Bahn trains to the west, albeit from just two ex-territorial and closely guarded platforms. Those travelling to the east were watched by suspicious East German border guards, in the confined rooms of the so-called »**Tränenpalast**« or Palace of Tears, which has now disappeared behind the dull architecture of the new Spreedreieck (Spree triangle). A newly opened exhibiton recreates this, including narrow passages, a model of the border crossing point and the stories of eye-witnesses.
Tränenpalast: Tue–Fri 9am–7pm, Sat and Sun 10am–6pm; admission free

Bahnhof Friedrichstrasse

> ! **MARCO ⊕ POLO TIP**
>
> *Secret passage* Insider Tip
>
> Beneath the arches of Friedrichstrasse station, on the right-hand side of the road, is a row of antique and junk shops. Go and have a look round – and be amazed at the internal passage that connects all the shops.

Beyond the S-Bahn bridge on the right is the former Haus der Presse (1910) with the cabaret theatre »Die Distel«. In the courtyard at the back stands the **Admiralspalast**, built in 1910 by Heinrich Schweitzer and Alexander Diepenbrock as a swimming baths and skating rink. After 1955 it became home to the Metropol theatre. This is the building in which the forcible merger of the socialist SPD and communist KPD parties of Eastern Germany took place in April

Admiralspalast

The bright lights of the Friedrichstadt-Palast

1946 to create the Socialist Unity Party (SED). The Admiralspalast is now used for readings, music and comedy performances.

Berliner Ensemble — The Weidendammbrücke (1895/96), with Prussian eagles on its wrought iron balustrades, of which Wolf Biermann sang in The Ballad of the Prussian Icarus bridges the Spree. Down on the left is Schiffbauerdamm where the Berliner Ensemble was opened in 1892 under the name »Theater am Schiffbauerdamm«. Among other claims to fame it was the venue for the first performance of the Threepenny Opera. In 1954 Bertolt Brecht and Helene Weigel took it over. She was to remain its manager until 1971. Am Zirkus leads away from Bertolt-Brecht-Platz and provides a reminder of the **Friedrichstadtpalast**, built in 1869 as Berlin's first market hall, which was renamed the »Zirkus« in 1874 and was rebuilt as Germany's largest theatre, the Grosses Schauspielhaus (Great Theatre) in 1919. It had its heyday under Max Reinhardt. The »Palast« was reopened in 1984 on Friedrichstrasse itself opposite the junction with Reinhardtstrasse, where it became the temple of entertainment in East Germany. Even today its revues attract hordes of people. In front of it there is a memorial to Claire Waldoff (▶Famous People).

Go past Reinhardtstrasse, Albrechtstrasse and Schumannstrasse – where Max Reinhardt built the fame of the Deutsches Theater – to reach a site that was established as a plague house by a decree of King Friedrich I on 13 May 1710. This was the original Charité. Since Berlin was fortunate enough to be spared the worst of plague, the site was re-dedicated as a hospital. When the Friedrich Wilhelm University was established in 1810 it was agreed that the manager of the Charité would be declared a professor. The first dean of the hospital was **Christoph Wilhelm Hufeland**, who introduced immunization against smallpox. Others that have succeeded him include **Rudolf Virchow, Robert Koch and Ferdinand Sauerbruch**. Although not for those of a queasy disposition, the Berlin Museum of Medical History, which was co-founded by Rudolf Virchow, invites visitors to view its pathological and anatomical collection. Exhibits include medicinal compounds, surgical instruments and various items that used to be personal possessions of Rudolf Virchow himself.

A short diversion to the Charité

❶ i Tue, Thu, Fri , Sun 10am–5pm, Wed und Sat until 7pm; admission €7; www.bmm.charite.de

FRIEDRICHSTRASSE SOUTH OF UNTER DEN LINDEN

To the south of Unter den Linden is the section of Friedrichstrasse that has seen the majority of the new building work. Right at the crossroads with Unter den Linden is the Lindencorso. This was originally intended as a French cultural centre but now houses a car showroom. Opposite, next to the Grand Hotel, a prestige project for the GDR when it opened in 1987, the main outlet of the legendary Café Kranzler once stood. History was made in the building at Friedrichstrasse 165 (on the corner of Behrenstrasse). This was the »**Haus der Demokratie**« (House of Democracy), where groups such as Neues Forum, who demanded the democratization of East Germany, met. Before that, the SED council leadership for the Mitte district was based here and before the war the building housed a popular cellar pub serving the produce of Munich's Pschorr brewery. Further along the street is the Russisches Haus (Russia House), where the Soviet scientific and culture missions were once located.

The highlight of the new architecture on Friedrichstrasse – in terms of both size and cost – is the completely new Friedrichstadtpassagen, a complex of buildings that cost 1.4 billion deutschmarks. It consists of three blocks connected to each other underground and situated on the left-hand side of Französischerstrasse and Mohrenstrasse. The most northerly of the blocks (architect: Jean Nouvel of Paris), Quartier 207 (as per the old street numbering), rather stands out from the

Friedrich-stadtpassagen

others as the only building made entirely of glass, with its elegantly curved corner. It has been occupied by the Berlin branch of the famous Paris store **Galeries Lafayette**. The spectacular 37m/120ft atrium with its two cones one above the other has often garnered more attention than the shop's own product lines. **Quartier 206** (architects: I. M. Pei, Cobb and Freed, New York) harks back to Art Deco architecture with its expressive façade featuring a myriad strips of lights. The floor of the inner courtyard enchants shoppers with Carrara marble. Beware though, the prices charged by the top-range shops in the building are just as breathtaking. **Quartier 205** (architect: O. M. Ungers, Cologne) is the most muted and formal of the buildings with the square geometry of its stark façade. Its array of stores and fashion boutiques is also on the conservative side.

Deutsches Currywurstmuseum

Who invented Germany's very own fast food, the curry sausage? Which ingredients make the sauce so spicy? Is Berlin's snack-bar culture thriving? To find the answer to these and other questions, visit the Deutsches Currywurstmuseum at Schützenstr. 70

❶ Daily 10am–6pm, admission €11; www.currywurstmuseum.de.

Checkpoint Charlie

The border between the Soviet and the American sectors of post-war Berlin crossed Friedrichstrasse at Zimmerstrasse. The crossing was marked by the famous border post for foreign visitors, Checkpoint Charlie. Nowadays it is hard to believe that the site was once at the very crux of the Cold War. What was at this time a vast empty space has been filled by the American Business Center building. A museum devoted to the Cold War is foreseen for the unoccupied site at the corner of Zimmerstrasse. At the former border crossing, there is just a single sentry tower, where tourists can have their photograph taken with people dressed as border guards, a warning sign, a strip of paving, one outsized picture of a Soviet soldier and a GI plus a copy of the famous guard house. Around Friedrichstrasse, Zimmerstrasse and Schützenstrasse is an exhibition with historic photos of this district. To find out how it once looked and how many desperate attempts were made to cross the border out of East Germany, visit the **Museum at Checkpoint Charlie**. The museum also highlights the human rights movement in the GDR and now possesses many historic artefacts including several whitewashed asphalt fragments, all that remains of the border line between East and West that was once painted across the street at Checkpoint Charlie

❶ Daily 9am–10pm, admission €12.50; www.mauermuseum.de

Berlin's former **newspaper publishing district** around Kochstrasse/ Zimmerstrasse was once home to many large and important newspaper and book publishers. Right at the end of Rudi-Dutschke-Strasse is the **Axel-Springer Tower**, which was quite intentionally built right next to the wall as early as 1966. In front of it stand the sculpture *Balancing Act* by Stephan Balkenhol. In Zimmerstrasse a new publishing and editing centre, the **Mosse-Zentrum** carries on the tradition. Here, as along Kochstrasse and Lindenstrasse, a new art gallery scene is springing up, away from the Spandauer Vorstadt, which is oversaturated with galleries.

Old newspaper distict

** Gedenkstätte Berliner Mauer
(Berlin Wall Memorial)

J 16

Location: Bernauer Strasse Mitte/Wedding	April–OctTue–Sun9am– 7pm, Nov–March
S-Bahn: Nordbahnhof (S 1, S 2, S 25)	Tue–Sun 9am–6pm
U-Bahn: Bernauer Str. (U 8)	**Admission free**
❶ Outdoor site daily 8am – 10pm, documentation and visitor centre	**www.berliner-mauer-gedenkstaette.de**

Nowhere in Berlin is the madness of the Berlin Wall as tangible as in Bernauer Strasse. Those who experienced the Wall themselves will be reminded of it here; those who did not will at least get a feeling for how it was.

The border between the Soviet sector (Mitte) and the French sector (Wedding) ran along Bernauer Strasse. While the buildings on the south side were on the territory of the GDR, the pavement in front of them was part of West Berlin. In the days after the construction of the wall, dramatic scenes occured here when people jumped from windows that had not yet been walled up onto the West Berlin side. In the followng years the GDR perfected the border installation, making them into an insuperable obstacle – which did not prevent a large number of people from trying to escape here.

Bernauer Strasse

Starting at the Nordbahnhof (with an exhibition about Berlin's ghost stations on an S-Bahn and two U-Bahn lines that passed from West

Memorial

The Wall Has Gone!

*But not completely. Many remains of the Wall and other border
installations can still be seen within the city limits. This plan marks
the largest and most interesting of them.*

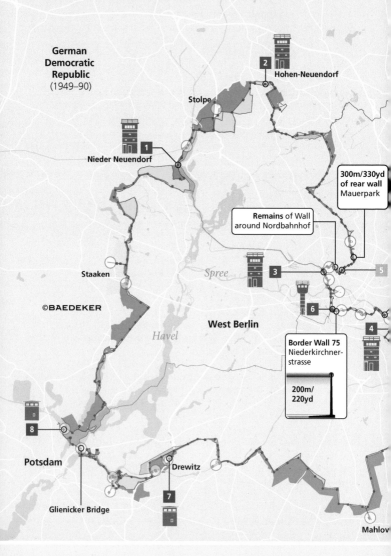

**German
Democratic
Republic**
(1949–90)

Stolpe

2 Hohen-Neuendorf

1 Nieder Neuendorf

**300m/330yd
of rear wall
Mauerpark**

**Remains of Wall
around Nordbahnhof**

3

5

Staaken

©BAEDEKER

Spree

6

West Berlin

Havel

4

Border Wall 75
Niederkirchner-
strasse

**200m/
220yd**

8

Potsdam

Drewitz

7

Glienicker Bridge

Mahlov

Legend Border installations, 1989

- Border and no-go zone
  Authorized persons only
- Border strip/»death zone«
- Walls and fences
- Command posts, watchtowers
- Border crossings for persons, cars, ships and trains

East Berlin
(GDR, 1949–90)

Border Wall 75, East Side Gallery, Mühlenstrasse

1300m/1420yd

450m/492yd of rear Wall
on Rudower Strasse

Schönefeld

5 km

▶ The Border in Numbers

Total length around West Berlin	156km/97mi
Total length of walls	243km/151mi
Total length of fences	191km/119mi
Watchtowers and guard huts	282
Border patrol boats	29
Border soldiers on duty daily	2300 to2500
Dog patrol strips	40.2km/25mi / approx. 425 dogs
Car barriers	88km/55mi

▶ Watchtowers and places of memorial

1 **Nieder Neuendorf command post**
Dorfstrasse, 16761 Hennigsdorf
Visits: 6 April to 3 Oct
Tue–Sun 10am–6pm

2 **Hohen Neuendorf command post**
Naturschutzturm Berliner Nordrand e.V.,
www.naturschutzturm.de

3 **Kieler Eck command post**, »Gedenkstätte Günter
Litfin«, Kieler Strasse 2, 10115 Berlin
March–Oct daily except Fri, noon–5pm

4 **Schlesischer Busch command post**
Puschkinallee/Am Flutgraben 3, 12435 Berlin

5 **Watchtower with border strip**
Gedenkstätte Berliner Mauer, Bernauer Straße
111/119, S-Bahn: Nordbahnhof S1, S2, S25
Exhibition on site all year
Visitor and documentation centre
April–Oct Tue–Sun 9.30am–7pm
Nov–March Tue–Sun 9.30am–6pm

6 **All-round view tower**
Erna-Berger-Str., (near Potsdamer Platz)

7 **Commander's tower at the former Drewitz border
crossing**, »Checkpoint Bravo e.V.«, Erinnerungs-
und Begegnungsstätte Drewitz-Dreilinden,
Albert-Einstein-Ring/Stahnsdorfer Damm,14 May
to 30 Oct, Sun 11am–4pm

8 **Sentry tower** at the former Nedlitz border
crossing (water), Bertinistrasse, 14469 Potsdam

▶ Remains of the Wall online

A website created by Cottbus Technical University
documents the surviving parts of the
border installations.
www.denkmallandschaft-berliner-mauer.de

A Perfidious Construction

It is actually astonishing that there is practically no trace of the former Wall remaining in Berlin. That must surely be a good thing, though. In particular, there is nowhere where the full border facilities have survived. For the Wall was not just one wall; it was a complicated, multitiered installation that was practically impossible to cross. By 1988 the barrier was 155km/96mi long, of which 43.1km/27mi were within the city centre while the rest, 111.9km/69mi followed the border between West Berlin and the neighbouring East German regions..

❶ Outer Wall (Vorderlandmauer)
The wall that faced West Berlin was 106km/66mi long and was made of concrete sheets, 3.6 to 4.1m/12 to 13.5ft high and 16cm/6in thick with a wide concrete tube along the top, which was replaced by metal fencing in places along the rural border.

❷ Vehicle traps
Intended to prevent crossing in vehicles. Total length 90km/56mi.

❸ Sentry strips
Continually raked and kept free of vegetation to make it easier to spot trails. Total length 165km/102.5mi

❹ Access roads
6 to 7m/7 to 8yd-wide two-lane paved roads for vehicles and marching columns. Total length 172km/107m i.

❺ Lights
Rows of lampposts to flood 180km/112mi of the strip in bright light during the night

❻ Watchtowers
190 watchtowers kept watch on the strip and served as control centres. In some sections the watchtowers were accompanied by dog runs.

❼ Tank traps
Chevaux-de-frise (for 1km/0.6mi) or mats of nails (for 20km/12mi) to prevent penetration by vehicles.

❽ Border signalling fence
Set off acoustic and visible alarms when touched. Total length 150km/93mi .

❾ Inner wall (Hinterlandmauer)
Initial barrier on the East German side, frequently only metal fencing. Total length 70km/43.5mi

August 1961: shortly before their windows were walled up, inhabitants of houses on Bernauer Strasse flee across the road to West Berlin. The pavement is already on the western side.

Nine border crossings allowed westerners at least to pass across, although under severe restrictions. Chèckpoint Charlie on Friedrichstrasse was limited to foreigners and diplomats from the West.

The »Vorderlandmauer« ran right behind the Reichstag. Security vessels patrolled the River Spree. A section of the »Hinterlandmauer« can be seen on the bank.

FIN
DU
UR FRANÇAIS

Ende
des französischen
Sektors.

6

8

7

9

The »Vorderlandmauer« did not always follow the border precisely but was occasionally set back a little towards the eastern side, thus some areas that could be accessed by westerners were officially already in East Germany. Two of those places were near the Brandenburg Gate or in Wedding in the French sector, as seen on the right.

©BAEDEKER

Berlin to West Berlin beneath East Berlin), a strip of land extends 1.4km/0.9mi to Schwedter Strasse. It is the only place in Berlin where parts of the Wall have been preserved that show the depth of the installations. Steel rods mark its course; steel rails in the ground show the outlines of demolished houses and the course of tunnels that were dug to escape. Panels with text and sound recordings explain the installations and events. At Ackerstrasse two steel walls enclose a 70m/230ft-long original section of the Wall, which serves as a memorial for the victims and includes the forward wall and the one behind it, the death strip and a watchtower. A little further along, on the site of a church that was blown up in 1985, stands the **Kapelle der Versöhnung** (Chapel of Reconciliation), dedicated in 2000. In the documentation centre opposite the memorial site, visitors can examine films and sound recordings, documents and log books of the GDR border guards, and an exhibition about the construction of the Wall in August 1961; an observation tower gives an overall view of the course of the Wall, showing how it cut through the Sophienfriedhof cemetery. In the visitor centre opposite the Nordbahnhof is a bookshop dedicated to the topic of the Berlin Wall.

Gedenkstätte Deutscher Widerstand

(Memorial to the German Resistance)

✳ M 14

Location: Stauffenbergstr. 13, Tiergarten
Bus: M 29 from U-Bahn Kurfüstendamm (U 1)
City centre plan: C 8
❶ Mon–Wed, Fri 9am–6pm, Thu

until 8pm; Sat, Sun, holidays 9am–6pm
Tours: Sat, Sun 3pm; memorial on application, tel. 030 18 24 22 37
Admission free
www.gdw-berlin.de

The Bendlerblock is now the German defence ministry's Berlin headquarters. Important events in the attempted coup of 20 July 1944 took place here.

The so-called Bendlerblock (named after the road which was then called Bendlerstrasse, but is now Stauffenbergstrasse) was built between 1911 and 1914 at the southern edge of the ▶Tiergarten and housed the Reichsmarineamt (admiralty) until 1918. Afterwards it was the headquarters of the army. It was in the Bendlerblock that Hitler gave his notorious speech to the army leaders laying claim to »living space« in the east on the 3 February 1933. Importantly, though, it was also the scene of events on 20 July 1944: after the unsuccessful assassination attempt on the Führer at his headquarters in eastern Prussia, generals Beck and Olbricht, colonels Graf von Stauffenberg and Mertz von Quirnheim and First Lieutenant von Haeften were shot by firing squad in the courtyard that same night. This event is commemorated by the Gedenkstätte Deutscher Widerstand or Memorial to the German Resistance, created in 1953 by Richard Scheibe. On the second floor a permanent exhibition shows the extent of resistance to National Socialism by communist and Christian groups in Germany. The tragic events of 20 July 1944 form the centre point of the display. At the rear of the site is the Ehrenmal der Bundeswehr, a memorial of the German army.

Claus von Stauffenberg

Gedenkstätte Plötzensee
(Plötzensee Memorial)

✦ L 11

Location: Hüttigpfad, Charlottenburg
U-Bahn: Jakob-Kaiser-Platz (U 7), then by 123 bus
❶ Mon–Wed, Fri 9am–6pm, Thu until 8pm, Sat, Sun, holidays 10am–6pm
Tours: Sun 3pm
Admission free
www.gedenkstaette-ploetzensee.de

Plötzensee too has become a symbol of resistance to the Nazi regime.

Between 1933 and 1945 about 1800 people of various nationalities were executed for political crimes in the former Plötzensee penitentiary. In 1952 the Berlin Senate commissioned a memorial. It includes what was once the execution barracks in which it is still possible to see a ceiling beam with its eight hooks, where victims of Nazi justice were hanged. Subsequent to the attempt to assassinate Adolf

Hitler on 20 July 1944 no fewer than 89 of the conspirators (including Carl Friedrich Goerdeler, and Helmuth James Graf von Moltke) were executed here. In front of the barracks there is a memorial stone and a large stone urn filled with soil from Nazi concentration camps.

Maria Regina Martyrum The unadorned cubic church of Maria Regina Martyrum 3km/2mi to the west is another monument to the victims of the period 1933 to 1945. It was built between 1960 and 1963 according to designs by Würzburg architects Friedrich Ebert and Hans Schädel. The courtyard is lined with bronze sculptures depicting the Stations of the Cross by Otto H. Hajek. The sculpture of Our Lady on the outer wall was made by Fritz Koenig. The remembrance hall is dominated by a large altarpiece by Georg Meistermann, while the crypt-like underground chapel has a pietà by Fritz Koenig. There are sepulchres for Provost Lichtenberg (whose actual grave is in St. Hedwig's Cathedral in the city centre) and Erich Klausener, the leader of Catholic Action, as well as a symbolic grave for all Nazi victims who were denied a burial.

❶ Heckerdamm 230/232
Mar–Oct 9am – 5pm daily, Nov–Feb 9am–4pm daily

✱✱ Gendarmenmarkt

✦ L 16

Location: Mitte
U-Bahn: Französische Strasse (U 6), city centre (U 2, U 6)
City centre map: C 12

Gendarmenmarkt is the finest and most harmonious square in Berlin thanks to three monumental buildings that form a coherent ensemble: the Schauspielhaus (theatre) and the churches known as the Französischer Dom and the Deutscher Dom.

From ►Friedrichstrasse it is just a stone's throw along Taubenstrasse or Jägerstrasse to Gendarmenmarkt, a square that has been in existence since the 17th century, when it was originally called the Esplanade. It then became Lindenmarkt, Mittelstädtischer and Friedrich-städtischer Markt and finally Gendarmenmarkt, because the **guards regiment, »Gens d'armes«** had their guardhouse and stables here between 1736 and 1782. As part of the 250th anniversary celebrations for the Akademie der Wissenschaften (Academy of Science) in 1950 the square, which had suffered serious damage during the Second World War, was briefly renamed »Platz der Akademie«. The square was still un-

der East German control but years of reconstruction work had restored its former appearance, and when the two halves of Berlin were reunited, the square was given back its familiar name. Since then a lively restaurant district has built up around the square, which is fully in keeping with the tenor of the district. It includes the wine lodge **Lutter & Wegner** (Charlottenstr. 56). This is very close to its historic site at the corner of Französische Strasse and Charlottenstrasse, where it stood upon its opening in 1811. E.T.A. Hoffmann, who lived on Gendarmenmarkt itself between 1815 and 1822, and the actor Ludwig Devrient were regulars at the establishment.

At the centre of the square at Gendarmenmarkt stands the Schauspielhaus, one of the finest of Schinkel's buildings. It was built between 1818 and 1821 atop the foundations of the old national theatre that had burned down in 1817. The latter had been constructed in 1802 as a successor to the Französische Komödie building, which was erected by Carl Gotthard Langhans and opened in 1774. The bas-reliefs on the gables and the muses on the roof were mostly made by Schinkel. Christian Daniel Rauch created the gables of the theatre hall itself and the figure of Apollo with a flight of griffins in harness on the top. Christian Friedrich Tieck added the spirits riding panthers and lions either side of the stairway. The opening play in 1821 was Goethe's Iphigenie, and Weber's Freischütz was also premiered here. The Schauspielhaus soon become one of the foremost theatres in Germany. Between 1934 and 1945 its superintendent was Gustaf Gründgens. After the war, though, its tradition as a theatre came to an end. In 1984 a reconstruction with an exterior true to the original was opened on the site under the name Konzerthaus Berlin.

*Schauspielhaus (Konzerthaus Berlin)

It was to be more than 50 years before the Schillerdenkmal (Schiller memorial), which had been erected in front of the Schauspielhaus by Reinhold Begas but removed by the Nazis in 1935, was returned to

Schillerdenkmal

its accustomed place. In 1987, on the 750th anniversary of Berlin itself, the Senate of West Berlin handed the monument over to the East German authorities. The four female figures around the basin of the fountain are personifications of Lyric Poetry (with a harp), Drama (with a dagger), History (with tablets bearing the names of Goethe, Beethoven, Michelangelo and others) and Philosophy (parchment scroll inscribed »Know Yourself«).

*Französi-
scher Dom
The Französischer Dom (French church) on the northern side of the square came into existence between 1701 and 1705 as the parish church for the Friedrichswerder and reformed French parishes and their Huguenots who had come to Berlin in 1685. The architects Louis Cayart and Quesnay took the Huguenot church at Charenton, which had been destroyed in 1688, as their model. The tower is 71m/233ft tall with an allegory of Religion at the top and was constructed by Georg Christian Unger on the basis of plans by Carl Friedrich von Gontard. In its interior is a carillon with 60 bells covering 5 octaves. The balustrade 44m/145ft above the street offers a fine view over Gendarmenmarkt. The Hugenottenmuseum inside the tower relates the history of the Huguenots in France and Berlin-Brandenburg.

❶ Dom: daily 9am–7pm; www.franzoesischer-dom.de
Hugenottenmuseum: Tue–Sat noon–5pm, Sun 11am–5pm; admission €2
Carillon: daily noon, 4pm, 7pm

Illuminations on Gendarmenmarkt

The counterpoint to the French church is the German church, Deutscher Dom. Its builder Martin Grünberg initially created a simple church for the German reformed community during the years 1701 to 1708. The dome is topped with a gilded sculpture 7m/23ft-tall allegory of Virtue. Inside is the grave of Georg Wenzeslaus von Knobelsdorff. The democrats who died on the barricades in 1848, the »Märzgefallenen«, were laid out upon its steps. These events and others make up the theme of an exhibition inside the church called »Wege – Irrwege – Umwege« (ways, lost ways and diversions), which catalogues the development of parliamentary democracy in Germany.

*Deutscher Dom

❶ Exhibition: Tue–Sun 10am–6pm, May–Sept until 7pm; tours every 30 min 11am–5pm; film screenings daily 2pm
www.bundestag.de/
kulturundgeschichte

> **!** MARCO POLO TIP ⊕
>
> Insider Tip
>
> *World of chocolate*
>
> In 1863 Heinrich Fassbender opened a chocolate factory behind Gendarmenmarkt. Today Fassbender & Rausch is Europe`s largest chocolate shop. Their biggest seller is the Diplomat assortment, and as a souvenir the little pieces of Plantagenschokolade (plantation chocolate) are popular (Charlottenstrasse 60, corner of Mohrenstrasse). A competitor has appeared: Ritter Sport has opened a flagship store close by with a chocolate trail, a chocolate workshop and a »Schokolateria« (Französische Strasse 24).

* Schloss Glienicke and Park

⊹ **T 7 west**

Location: Zehlendorf
S-Bahn: Wannsee (S 1, S 7), then by 316 bus

The palace and park of Schloss Glienicke have a wonderful location at the outer southwestern edge of Berlin on the eastern bank of the River Havel where a spit of land divides two lakes, the Jungfernsee and Glienicker See.

A link with nearby Potsdam had already been built at the time of the Humboldts in the form of a bridge, the Glienicker Brücke, famous for its view of the Havel. The present iron bridge over the Havel (Jungfernsee/Tiefer See) was opened in 1907 to succeed a brick construction designed by Karl Friedrich Schinkel. During the GDR period it was renamed »Brücke der Einheit« (Bridge of Unity) and a border post was set up that was the exclusive domain of the allies, East German diplomats, exchanges of secret agents and the transfer of political prisoners. In 1962 American U2 pilot Gary Powers was exchanged here for the Soviet master spy Rudolf Abel. The bridge was the first border crossing to be opened on 12 November 1989.

Glienicker Brücke

The Glienicker Brücke: the icy wind of the Cold War once blew across this bridge

In the first building on the Potsdam side, Villa Schöningen, the Deutsch-Deutsches Museum records the history of the Glienicker Brücke and its role in the years when Germany was divided.
❶ Thu, Fri 11am–6pm; Sat, Sun 10am–6pm; admission €9; www.villa-schoeningen.de

Schloss Glienicke

Schloss Glienicke was expanded into its current form during 1825 and 1826 by Karl Friedrich Schinkel in the late classical style. At that time the building functioned as the summer residence of Carl of Prussia. The main building, the Cavalier wing added in 1832 and the ancillary buildings surround an Italian garden adorned with fountains. The antiquities let into the walls were brought back from his travels by Prince Carl. It is possible to visit the chambers of the prince and his wife as well as see an exhibition about the castles and palaces of Prussia.
❶ Schloss and garden museum: April–Oct Tue–Sun 10am–6pm; Nov–March Sat, Sun, holidays 10am–5pm; admission €5, www.spsg.de

The palace grounds cover 116ha/286ac and are open all year round. **Park Glienicke**
The park passed into possession of the city of Berlin in 1934, since
which time it has officially been called Volkspark Kleinglienicke. It was
laid out in 1814 on the basis of an es-
tate belonging to the Prussian chancellor Fürst Hardenberg. To convert
the cultivated land, Hardenberg commissioned Peter Joseph Lenné in
1816. He was allowed to continue his
work after Prince Carl took possession of the land in 1824. Lenné created a garden landscape around the
Italian styled palace bordered by a so-
called pleasure ground in the west
and an English garden in the north.
This design symbolized the passage
from summery Italy across the Alps
to the fields of northern Europe. The
buildings that were added to the park
on the prince's commission by Schinkel and Ludwig Persius between 1824
and 1840 took up this same theme.
For example Schinkel's hunting lodge
expresses an English styling, while the
Alps are represented by Persius's
Teufelsbrücke bridge. Persius also

> **! MARCO POLO TIP** | *A walk to Nikolskoe* Insider Tip
>
> A pretty route for a ramble:
> through Glienicker Park and
> along the riverside path to the
> Nikolskoe log cabin, which stands
> on a viewing platform created by
> Lenné, high above the Wannsee.
> Friedrich Wilhelm III had the place
> built for his daughter and named
> it after his son-in-law Czar
> Nikolaus. A restaurant and a beer
> garden attract day trippers who
> can also admire the Russian
> Church of St Peter and Paul, built
> by Friedrich August Stüler and Al-
> bert Dietrich Schadow between
> 1834 and 1837. By the way, the
> Pfaueninsel is only a 15-minute
> walk away. A bus can be used for
> the return journey (e.g. line 218
> to Wannsee S-Bahn station).

created the Matrosenhaus, the gardener's lodge and machine shed to
pump water for the park from the Havel, the greenhouse and orange
house plus the Stibadium, a roofed bench built to a Roman pattern,
situated to the south of the palace. Schinkel created the casino, the tea
pavilion and the circular temple he called **»Grosse Neugierde«**
(Great Curiosity) based on the 4th century BC Lysistrata monument
in Athens, as well as the **»Kleine Neugierde«** (Small Curiosity),
which is located in the southwest corner of the park on Königstrasse –
both of which are excellent viewpoints, as their names are intended to
suggest. The lions of the fountain outside the palace take the Villa
Medici as their template. The art of the gardeners and their portraits
are presented in the **Hofgärtnermuseum** (Court Gardening Museum). **Klosterhof** The Klosterhof was built in 1850 by Ferdinand von
Arnim based on Venetian models. What sets it apart are the more than
100 works of Byzantine art, collected by Carl of Prussia.

South of Königstrasse on the northeast bank of the Glienicker Lake **Jagdschloss Glienicke**
stands Jagdschloss Glienicke, a hunting lodge built in 1682/83 for the
Great Elector, remodelled in 1859 and now an international meeting
place for young people.

✳ **Grunewald**

✦ O – Q 7 – 9

Location: Wilmersdorf/Zehlendorf
S-Bahn: Grunewald (S 7)

»Grunewald« means more to Berliners than just the name of one of their most popular local leisure spaces, it is also one of the plushest places to live in the city. The best proof of this is the collection of villas clustered around Grunewald S-Bahn station.

The forest covers 32 sq km/8000ac stretching from the east bank of the Havel between Heerstrasse and ▶Wannsee. The name dates back to 1542 when the elector Joachim II had a hunting lodge built here, which he called »Zum grünen Wald« (in the green wood). This appellation for the woodland was only officially adopted at the end of the 19th century, when it became a leisure destination; it had previously been known as the Spandau Forest. In the fierce winters that followed the end of the Second World War and during the blockade of Berlin, 70% of the trees were felled for heating fuel. Nowadays the wood has been fully replanted and is home to game such as fallow deer and roe deer, wild boar (in the Saubucht) and European mouflon. A watercourse formed by the melting of ice-age glaciers runs through a landscape of moor and fen. In the east are innumerable lakes (Hundekehlesee, Grunewaldsee and Schlachtensee, Krumme Lanke) and 9km/5.5mi of river bank along the Havel in the west provides plenty of opportunity for bathing in both large and small havens, although Teufelsberg, Grunewaldturm, Schildhorn and Jagdschloss Grunewald are the places that attract most visitors. What was originally Germany's first race track, the Avus built in 1921, also runs between Nikolassee and Grunewald.

Grunewald station
✦ N / O 9

The S-Bahn station at Grunewald is among those places in Berlin that are tainted by an association with the Nazi terror. It was from here and the neighbouring Grunewald goods yard that tens of thousands of Berlin Jews were transported to death camps between 1941 and 1945. A memorial erected in front of the station in 1991 and one unveiled on platform 17 in 1998 testify to these terrible events. From the S-Bahn station pass under the Avus and turn left to reach the **Waldmuseum** (forest museum) of the Waldschule Grunewald, which is devoted to forests as a habitant and to their plants and animals.

❶ Königsweg 4, Tue–Fri 10am–3pm, Sun 1pm–4pm, admission €1.50; www.waldmuseum-waldschule.de

*Jagdschloss Grunewald
✦ P 9

From the bus stop it is only a twenty-minute walk through the Grunewald to reach the hunting lodge on the lake known as Grunewaldsee. It was commissioned by Joachim II, elector of

Brandenburg, and built by Caspar Theyss in 1542. Originally a simple Renaissance building, it has seen many alterations. The gazebo was added to the rear façade in 1593 under Elector Johann Georg. Under King Friedrich I of Prussia (1657 – 1713), the palace was completely refurbished and altered before final modifications were made under Frederick the Great (1712 – 1786), when the service yard and barns for hunting gear were built. The Great Hall with its painted wooden ceiling remained in its Renaissance condition. The palace endured many troubled days: in 1814 the boxed components of the quadriga from the Brandenburg Gate were brought here when they were returned to Berlin, having been appropriated by Napoleon Bonaparte. They were kept here till they could be reassembled on top of the ▶Brandenburg Gate. The attractions of the palace include not only the Great Hall but the collection of German and Dutch portraits from the 15th to the 19th centuries, including works by Barthel Bruyn, Lucas Cranach the Elder, van Haarlem, Anton Graff, Jacob Jordaens, Franz Krüger and Antoine Pesne. In the **Jagdzeugmaga-zin** (hunting stockroom) there is a collection of hunting weapons and trophies.

> **! No trespassing ...** Insider Tip
>
> MARCO ⬥ POLO TIP
>
> ... is the usual rule for what used to be a military site on the Teufelsberg. But on a guided tour it is possible to explore the old, slowly decaying listening post. See www.berlinsightout.de

❶ U-Bahn Dahlem-Dorf (U 3), then bus X 83, 183 to Königin-Luise-Str., then on foot
April–Oct Tue–Sun 10am–6pm, Nov, Dec and March only Sat, Sun until 4pm and on holidays only as part of a tour at 11am, 1pm, 3pm; admission €6,; www.spsg.de

From the bus stop at Königin-Luise-Str./Clayallee it is not far north-ward along Clayallee to the Bussardsteig, where a bungalow built in a style reminiscent of the Bauhaus movement (no. 9, built 1967) houses the Werner Düttmann archive and an exhibition featuring the expressionist artists' collective »Die Brücke«, founded in Dresden in 1905. The museum was inspired by Berlin artist and former exponent of the Brücke group, Karl Schmidt-Rottluff, who donated most of the works. Among the Brücke artists represented are Erich Heckel, Ernst Ludwig Kirchner, Otto Mueller and Max Pechstein. The pieces are presented in changing exhibitions.

*Brücke Museum ✛ P 10

❶ daily except Tue 11am–5pm; admission €5; www.bruecke-museum.de

It is about a half hour's walk from either of the S-Bahn stations at Grunewald or Heerstrasse to the leisure park around Teufelsberg at the northern edge of the Grunewald forest. The Teufelsberg is a mound 115m/377ft in height that consists of 25 million cu m/33 mil-

Teufelsberg

The Grunewaldturm stands at the exact mid-point between Berlin and Potsdam

lion cu yd of rubble, heaped between 1950 and 1972 from the ruins of a former defence faculty. By the mid-1960s a ski-lift and two ski-jumps had already been installed, but the fun didn't last long, as the Americans set up a listening post on top of the mound with five listening domes that could spy on telephone and radio communications deep inside the Soviet Union. The mound was fenced off for military use but, even so, a world cup slalom event was still held here in 1986. With the ending of the Cold War the Americans abandoned the station and the Teufelsberg has reverted to leisure use, becoming a popular destination in both winter and summer.

Grunewald-turm The Grunewaldturm is a tower built on Havelchaussee and was formerly known as the »Kaiser Wilhelm Tower« as it was erected in honour of the Prussian king (later emperor) Wilhelm I. It is 56m/184ft tall and towers 104m/340ft above the Havel. 205 steps lead up to the top. It was built from red bricks in 1897 and 1898 by Franz Schwechten at the exact mid-point between Berlin and Potsdam. Following lengthy restoration, the observation deck at a height of 36m/117ft is now open again. Boats on the Havel also dock at the jetty underneath the tower.

❶ i Bus 218 from U-Bahn Theodor-Heuss-Platz (U 2)
Daily 10am–10pm; admission €1

✳ Hamburger Bahnhof · Museum für Gegenwart

(Contemporary Art)

✦ J 13

Location: Invalidenstr. 50–51,
Tiergarten
S-Bahn: Hauptbahnhof (S 5, S 7, S 75)
❶ Tue–Fri 10am–6pm

(Thu until 8pm),
Sat and Sun 11am–6pm
Admission: €14
www.smb.museum

The Hamburger Bahnhof, the oldest surviving passenger railway station in Berlin, is a branch of the Neue Nationalgalerie (New National Gallery; ▶Kulturforum) and one of Europe's leading museums of modern art.

North of the Spreebogen precinct on Invalidenstrasse the Neoclassical Hamburger Bahnhof was built between 1845 and 1847 according to plans by Friedrich Neuhaus and Ferdinand Wilhelm Holz. The concourse by Borsig was of purely iron construction and became a template for stations all over Germany. It has been many years, though, since trains passed through the station. After the new Lehrter Bahnhof opened right next door in 1879, Hamburger Bahnhof was closed to traffic by as soon as 1884. In 1906 Prussian minister of state Budde gave the site over to a building and transport museum. Its exhibits remained there after 1945 but under the control of the Reichs-bahn and the GDR they remained inaccessible until 1984. Some of these items are now displayed at the ▶ Deutsches Technikmuseum.

Collections

Since rebuilding by Josef Paul Kleihues, the museum, called the Museum für Gegenwart (Museum of the Present Day), has highlighted contemporary art from the years since 1960, including works from the collections of Erich Marx, Egidio Marzona and Friedrich-Christian Flick, supplemented by pieces from the New National Gallery itself. The rearrangement in 2009 gave a fine setting for works by artists such as Anselm Kiefer, Richard Serra the Junge Wilde in the main hall, Joseph Beuys in the west wing, as well as Andy Warhol, Cy Twombly and Robert Rauschenberg.

Flick Collection

The Friedrich Christian Flick Collection opened in the Rieck-Hallen at Hamburger Bahnhof in September 2004. The collection includes 150 works of late 20th-century art, especially exhibits from the Documenta shows, including installations by Pipilotti Rist, Wolfgang Tilman's military series and Nam June Paik's Fluxus objects.

✳ Jüdisches Museum
(Jewish Museum)

✦ **M 17**

Location: Lindenstr. 9 – 14, Kreuzberg
U-Bahn: Hallesches Tor (U 1, U 15, U 6)
Bus: M 29, M 41, 248
❶ Daily 10am–8pm, Mon until 10pm, closed on Rosh Hashana and Yom Kippur (in Sept / Oct) and Christmas Eve
Admission: €8
www.jmberlin.de

Few of Berlin's new buildings have caused as much furore as Daniel Libeskind's Jewish Museum – it had hundreds of thousands of visitors after completion in 1999 even before the actual museum opened in 2001.

Radical architecture

This expressive building, built to a floor plan that zigzags like a lightning bolt, radically differs from the mainstream of modern architecture. Thanks to its zinc façade with irregular, strip-like windows cut into it, the building has a highly abstract and objective character. The rooms inside are mostly accessed by ramps that guide visitors through the strikingly irregular ground plans and acute angles of the various halls. In some rooms it is only possible to see through narrow slits into nothingness (»voids«), which seek to symbolize the absence of victims of the Holocaust, thus making them even more strongly present. When it opened in September 2001 the exhibition gave Berlin its first Jewish museum for more than 60 years: an earlier museum opened in January 1933 on Oranienburger Strasse but was closed down by the Gestapo in 1938.

An underground passage from the entrance in the Baroque Kollegienhaus leads to the cellar of Libeskind's building. Three corridor axes lined with showcases cross here: the »Axis of Exile« leads out into the E.T.A. Hoffmann Garden, the »Axis of the Holocaust« leads to a steel door in front of the dark and empty Holocaust Tower. The »Axis of Historical Continuity« then leads to the actual exhibition, which is divided into 13 so-called epochal images depicting two thousand years of German-Jewish history. This journey through the museum begins on the second floor with a copy of the first documentary mention of Jews in Germany in a decree made by the Roman Emperor Constantine in AD 321. It introduces important Jewish figures such as Moses Mendelssohn and Emil Rathenau and ends with developments subsequent to the Second World War. Altogether some 4000 items are exhibited, often with multimedia background presentations – although, in conjunction with the asymmetric architecture, this makes it difficult to follow the thread of the museum's content.

The angular architecture of the Jewish Museum

The entrance and service area incorporated into the Jewish Museum is composed of the former superior Court of Justice building, the »Kollegienhaus« built by Philipp Gerlach in 1734/35, which has the Prussian coat of arms on its gables with the goddesses Justicia and Veritas (Justice and Truth) above them. Since 2007 a glass roof borne by four free-standing steel supports has covered the 670 sq m/7200 sq ft, U-shaped inner courtyard. The support construction takes its inspiration from the form of a tree, which continues as a network of lines in the roof. With this design Daniel Libeskind makes reference to the Jewish Sukkot festival, or Feast of the Tabernacles, for which a hut is clothed in foliage.

Kollegien-haus

The new Berlinische Galerie, the state of Berlin's museum of modern art, photography and architecture, is about ten minutes' walk from the Jüdisches Museum. It stages changing exhibitions.

Berlinische Galerie

❶ Alte Jakobstrasse 124–128; Wed–Mon 10am–6pm; admission €8, www.berlinischegalerie.de

KaDeWe (Kaufhaus des Westens)

✦ **L 14**

Location: Wittenbergplatz, Schöneberg
U-Bahn: Wittenbergplatz (U 1, U 2)
City centre map: D 6

Berlin's equivalent to London's Harrods is KaDeWe – the city's foremost consumer palace.

Berlin's most famous department store is the largest of its kind on the European continent. Adolf Jandorf founded the shop in 1907. 20 years later it passed into the hands of »department store king« Hermann Tietz. It has 60,000 sq m/15 acres of shop floor on eight storeys and provides practically anything the heart could possibly desire. The food department on the sixth floor remains a top attraction with its inconceivable range of produce, which can be sampled in-store at any of the counters or in the restaurant beneath the glass dome.

Kreuzberg

✦ **N – M 15 – 20**

Borough: Friedrichshain-Kreuzberg
U-Bahn: U 1, U 6, U 7, U 8

For many years Kreuzberg was synonymous in Berlin with an alternative lifestyle, for an outstanding pub scene, where the nights never seem to end, and for its continuing experiment in multi-cultural urban living (▶MARCO POLO Insight p.222).

Kreuzberg was also notorious for speculation in housing, squats and riots, which commonly took place on 1 May. Little of this holds true today, for Kreuzberg itself has changed dramatically. With the fall of the Berlin Wall it is no longer frontier territory where many an alternative bloom could grow, sometimes supported by senate money. Now located right in the centre of the big city, Kreuzberg has been rediscovered, this time by higher earning individuals who have almost turned the old suburb into a chic city centre address that still has the great pubs and bars. A new clientele now comes on cheap flights from all over Europe to go partying here – sometimes on the street and not always to the delight of residents. The alternative and radical types have relocated to other districts, leaving behind the large Turkish population, which represents the largest Turkish community in Germany and the largest ethnic group in Kreuzberg. The district thus offers plenty to do in the evenings, e.g. on Oranienstrasse between Oranienplatz and Heinrichplatz, along Adalbertstrasse and around the Schlesisches Tor U-Bahn station. Top-quality chefs have opened restaurants on Paul-Lincke-Ufer, Fichtestrasse and round the Südstern. There is also a good deal to see in addition to the main sights: the ▶Deutsches Technikmuseum, ▶Topographie des Terrors, the ▶Jüdisches Museum and several ▶cemeteries.

Kreuzberg came into being as a borough in 1920 in a merger of Friedrichstadt to the south, Luisenstadt and the suburb of Tempelhof. Its characteristic features are the U-Bahn, not underground here but running on elevated pillars above the streets, as well as the Landwehr canal, which bisects the district on a line from east to west.

Kreuzberg's elevated railway and canal

Rote Harfe, a pub in the Kreuzberg scene with a tradition of protest

Multicultural Berlin

Berlin is an international melting-pot. Almost all the peoples of the earth are represented in the German capital. Its economy would grind to a halt without them. But how are they spread around the city, and where are their centres? Who really lives in Berlin?

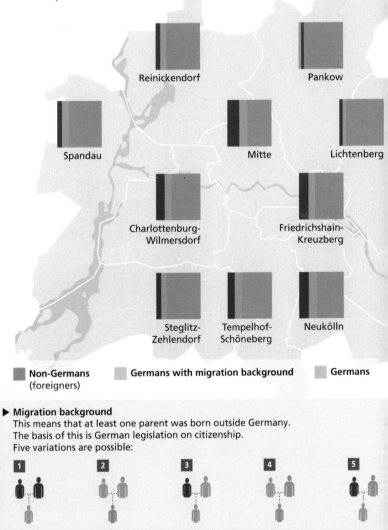

Reinickendorf

Pankow

Spandau

Mitte

Lichtenberg

Charlottenburg-Wilmersdorf

Friedrichshain-Kreuzberg

Steglitz-Zehlendorf

Tempelhof-Schöneberg

Neukölln

Non-Germans (foreigners)   **Germans with migration background**   **Germans**

▶ **Migration background**
This means that at least one parent was born outside Germany.
The basis of this is German legislation on citizenship.
Five variations are possible:

1   **2**   **3**   **4**   **5**

Berlin

466,000
foreigners
(14 %)

422,000
migration
background
(12 %)

2.5 Mio.
Germans
(74 %)

Marzahn-
Hellersdorf

©BAEDEKER

Treptow-
Köpenick

How many nationalities live in Berlin?
190 of the 194 nations recognized by the
United Nations are represented in Berlin.

■ Nationalities represented in Berlin
■ Nationalities not represented in Berlin

▶ **Vitality of the economy**
Without foreigners, Berlin's economy would not
work. A much higher proportion of foreigners
are self-employed than Germans and thus make
an enormous contribution to the wealth of the
whole of Germany. (Figures date from 2010)

32,373 32,373 foreign entrepreneurs
in Berlin

12.4 % 12.4% of Berlin companies
are run by foreigners

▶ **Which continents are most represented in Berlin?**

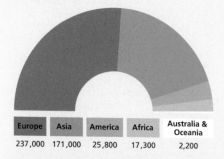

Europe	Asia	America	Africa	Australia & Oceania
237,000	171,000	25,800	17,300	2,200

▶ **Which countries are most represented in Berlin?**
The breathtaking number of different nationalities
in Berlin means that it is impossible to list them all
in a small space. We have therefore limited
ourselves to the top ten, which account for over
55% of the foreigners in Berlin.

✝ approx. 1000 people

Turkey
✝✝✝✝✝✝✝✝✝✝✝✝✝✝✝✝✝✝✝✝
✝✝✝✝✝✝✝✝✝✝✝✝✝✝✝✝✝✝✝✝
✝✝✝✝✝✝✝✝✝✝✝✝✝✝✝✝✝✝✝✝
✝✝✝✝✝✝✝✝✝✝✝✝✝✝✝✝✝✝✝✝
✝✝✝✝✝✝✝✝✝✝✝✝✝✝✝✝✝✝✝✝
✝✝✝

Poland
✝✝✝✝✝✝✝✝✝✝✝✝✝✝✝✝✝✝✝✝
✝✝✝✝✝✝✝✝✝✝✝✝✝✝✝✝✝✝✝✝
✝✝

Serbia
✝✝✝✝✝✝✝✝✝✝✝
✝✝✝✝✝✝✝✝✝✝

Italy
✝✝✝✝✝✝✝✝✝✝
✝✝✝✝✝✝✝

Russia
✝✝✝✝✝✝✝✝✝✝
✝✝✝✝✝✝

France
✝✝✝✝✝✝✝✝✝✝✝
✝✝✝✝

Vietnam
✝✝✝✝✝✝✝✝✝✝
✝✝✝

USA
✝✝✝✝✝✝✝✝✝✝
✝✝✝

Bulgaria
✝✝✝✝✝✝✝✝✝✝

United Kingdom
✝✝✝✝✝✝✝✝✝✝

Kreuzberg (Viktoriapark)
✦ O 15 / 16

The name of the borough comes from the eponymous 66m/217ft hill, located towards the south near Berlin's Tempelhof airport (▶Tempelhof). It was given to the Franciscans around 1300, when the hill was still known as Tempelhofer Berg. It was dubbed the »Runde« or »Götzesche Weinberg« due to the vineyards that existed on its slopes until 1740. Those slopes are now decked by the Viktoriapark laid out from 1888 to 1894 by director of gardens Hermann Mächtig and extended in 1913/14. It features the »wolf gorge« (Wolfsschlucht), a toboggan course and an artificial waterfall modelled on the Zackelfall in the Riesengebirge mountains. The vineyard tradition has also been reanimated in the park, although its white wines are only given to official guests of the senate.

The summit of the Kreuzberg hill is topped with a 20m/66ft memorial to the wars of liberation from 1813 – 15, which was erected to a Schinkel design between 1818 and 1821. Twelve statues symbolize the major victories and carry a procession of the outstanding figures of the struggle.

New high-class housing

At the southern foot of the hill is the castle-like Schultheiss brewery, built in 1862 and now refurbished as luxury flats. These and the expensively refurbished flats in the late 19th-century buildings next to Riehmers Hofgarten, as well as similar homes on Chamissoplatz and new buildings next to the Viktoriapark, are among the most sought-after and exclusive on the Berlin property market.

*Riehmers Hofgarten

It is possible to experience a small chapter in the history of Berlin's domestic housing a little to the north of the Viktoriapark between Hagelberger, Grossbeerenstrasse and Yorckstrasse, where the atmosphere of old Kreuzberg can still be savoured beneath the gas lamps. Master bricklayer Riehmer had a three-winged housing estate built here between 1891 and 1899 that made a pleasant change from the barrack-like tenements of the time. The houses are grouped around a cobbled, tree-planted inner courtyard.

Bergmannstrasse
✦ O 16

South of Gneisenaustrasse U-Bahn station (U 7) lies Bergmannstrasse. Once an authentic slice of Kreuzberg, a mix of young, multicultural, alternative and everyday, this has now become an upmarket strip. The best parts are Chamissoplatz, a little further south, and Marheinekeplatz with one of the four remaining market halls of the 14 that once existed in Berlin.

The Oberbaumbrücke links Kreuzberg and Friedrichshain

The 10.3km/6.5mi of the Landwehrkanal bisect Kreuzberg from east to west and connect the Upper Spree (at Schlesisches Tor) with the Lower Spree (at Charlottenburg). The canal was built between 1845 and 1850 according to plans by Peter Joseph Lenné in place of the existing Flossgraben and Schafgraben channels and was expanded from 1883 to 1889. The channels were originally border ditches and were mentioned as early as 1450. The canal has made a major contribution to Kreuzberg in the past but nowadays it is little used, at least in economic terms. It nevertheless remains an important leisure feature and the best walks along its banks and tow paths are on Fraenkelufer, which passes the buildings put up for the IBA event in 1987 and Paul-Lincke-Ufer, where there are several nice bars and cafés. Maybachufer across the canal hosts the famous »Türkenmarkt« on

Landwehr-
kanal
✦ N 16 – 19

Tuesdays and Fridays. Next to the Turkish market, Neukölln with a few pubs and fashion boutiques is on the up and increasingly finding favour under the name **»Kreuzkölln«**.

Mehringplatz
✦ **N 16**

▶Friedrichstrasse comes to an end in Kreuzberg at Mehringplatz, which was formerly called Rondell, then Belle-Alliance-Platz. It was designed by Hans Scharoun as a ring-shaped housing estate although the results were not particularly inviting. The Friedenssäule or peace column in the middle is a memorial to the wars of liberation.At the corner to the west of Mehringplatz where Wilhelmstrasse and Stresemannstrasse form a sharp angle, Germany's social democratic political party, the SPD, commissioned architect Helge Bofinger to design them a spacious headquarters, the **Willy-Brandt-Haus**. Its atrium is dominated by a large sculpture of Willy Brandt himself, created by Rainer Fetting (▶ill. p.57).

*Oberbaum-
brücke
✦ **M 20**

A little to the north of where the Landwehrkanal flows into the Spree stands the Oberbaumbrücke, a bridge that links Kreuzberg with Friedrichshain. The bridge is 30m/100ft wide with two massive towers designed in Gothic style using bricks from the March and erected in 1896. The name of the bridge dates from the days when an »Oberbaum«, a wooden barrier suspended under the bridge, was laid across the channel to prevent passage. When the Wall was erected, only pensioners in possession of appropriate passes were allowed to use the bridge. On 9 November 1989, shortly after the announcement that the border was to be opened, tens of thousands of East Berliners stormed the bridge. Five years later it was renovated and opened for traffic, including the reinstated underground railway line U 1. Today it is in the hands of the Easyjet party crowd.

> **? MARCO ⊕ POLO INSIGHT**
>
> *Georg-von-Rauch-Haus*
>
> The building at Mariannenplatz 1A is a monument to Berlin's history of protest. Once a nurses' home called Bethanien, on 8 December 1971 it was the first house in Berlin to be occupied by squatters, and was named after Georg von Rauch, who was shot during a hunt for the RAF terrorist group. Today it is still an autonomous youth and arts centre.

Mariannen-
platz
✦ **M 18**

Mariannenplatz was designed in 1853 by Peter Joseph Lenné and is situated in the northern part of Kreuzberg between Adalbertstrasse and Waldemarstrasse (U-Bahn: Görlitzer Bahnhof; U 1). The former Bethanien hospital is situated on the western side of the square. Built between 1845 and 1847, it was the first large building in this area. From 1848 to 1849 Theodor Fontane worked there as an apothecary. The northern side of the square is occupied by the neo-Romanesque Thomas-Kirche (Church of St Thomas).

Fontane-Apotheke: Tue 2–5pm

✶✶ Kulturforum

⬥ **M 15**

Location: Tiergarten
S- and U-Bahn: Potsdamer Platz
(S 1, S 2, S 25, U 2)
Bus: M 29, M 41, M 48, 200

City centre map:
N 8 / 9
www.smb.museum

The Kulturforum is the site for exhibiting the European art in the collection of the Staatliche Museen Preussischer Kulturbesitz (State Museums for Prussian Cultural Legacy), its second site after ▶Museum Island. The idea of building a new cultural focus in the western part of the city is attributed to Hans Scharoun (1893 – 1972).

In the area between the southern edge of the ▶Tiergarten, the Landwehrkanal and ▶Potsdamer Platz, which was completely flattened during the Second World War, first to make way for the new

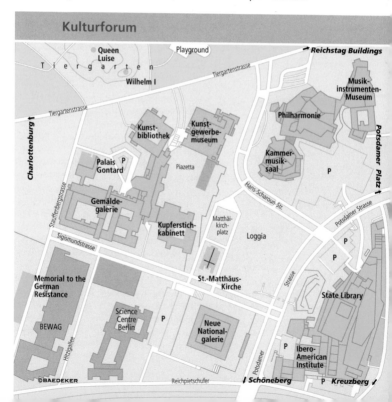

Kulturforum

capital that Hitler was planning for the Third Reich, then by allied bombs, first of all the Philharmonie (1960 – 63) was erected as the eastern cornerstone of the site, then the Staatsbibliothek (1966 – 78), the Neue Nationalgalerie (1965 – 68) appearing at the southern edge. The Staatliches Institut für Musikforschung (State Institute for Research into Music) with its museum of musical instruments then sprung up to the northeast of the Philharmonie between 1979 and 1984, to be joined by the Kunstgewerbemuseum (Museum of Decorative Arts) west of the Philharmonie and between 1984 and 1987 by the Kammermusiksaal (Hall for Chamber Music), adjoining to the south. On Matthäikirchplatz by 1994 the Kupferstichkabinett (Prints Collection) and the Kunstbibliothek (Arts Library) had been constructed. The western side of the square has been completed by the buildings of the Gemäldegalerie (Galleries of Painting) since 1998. The forum in the midst of all these buildings was designed by the Austrian Hans Hollein. The Romanesque **St.-Matthäus-Kirche** (St Matthew's Church) by August Stüler (1846) is the only remaining historic building here.

** GEMÄLDEGALERIE (PICTURE GALLERY)

❶ Tue–Fri 10am–6pm, Thu until 10pm, Sat and Sun 11am–6pm; admission €10

The Gemäldegalerie (Picture Gallery) opened in the Altes Museum on the ▶Museumsinsel in 1830. It emerged from the collections of the Great Elector and of Frederick the Great. Wilhelm von Bode, its director between 1890 and 1929, expanded it into a museum of international renown and its exhibits were displayed from 1904 onwards in what is now the Bodemuseum (then Kaiser-Friedrich Museum). In spite of serious losses incurred during the Second World War, the gallery still counts as one of the finest collections of European art from the years up till the end of the 18th century. The works had been distributed after the war among the museums in Dahlem and on the Museumsinsel but have now been reunited at the Kulturforum. The latest plans foresee transferring the Old Masters to the Bode-Muse um on Museum Island and installing a collection of

Don't miss

- Albrecht Dürer: *Madonna with a Siskin*
- Lucas Cranach the Elder: *The Fountain of Youth*
- Hans Holbein the Younger: *Portrait of the Merchant Georg Gisze*
- Pieter Brueghel the Elder: *Dutch Proverbs*
- Rembrandt: *Portrait of Hendrickje Stoffels, Samson and Deiliah*
- Rembrandt's studio: *The Man with the Golden Helmet*

Gemäldegalerie

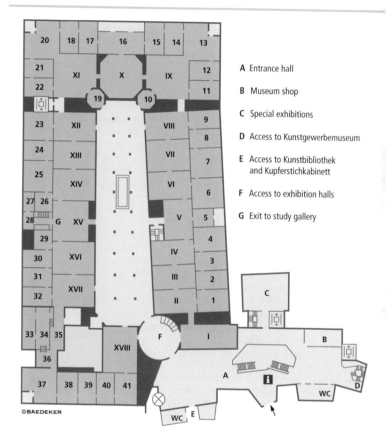

A Entrance hall

B Museum shop

C Special exhibitions

D Access to Kunstgewerbemuseum

E Access to Kunstbibliothek
and Kupferstichkabinett

F Access to exhibition halls

G Exit to study gallery

©BAEDEKER

I-III / 1-4
German painters
(Dürer, Cranach)

V-VI / 5-7
Dutch painters
(Van Eyck, Bruegel)

VII-XI / 8-19
Flemish and Dutch
painters (Rubens,
Rembrandt)

20-22
English, French and
German Painters
of the 18th century

XII-XIV / 23-26, 28
Italian, French and
Spanish painters

XV-XVII / 29-32
Italian painters
(Raphael, Titian)
34
Miniatures

XVII / 35-41
Italian painters
(Giotto, Botticelli)

27, 33, 42 (study gallery)
Digital gallery

Surrealist art at the Kulturforum. Art from the 19th century can be seen in the Alte Nationalgalerie on the ▶Museumsinsel.

The new gallery building, opened in 1998, is from a design by Rolf Gutbrod that proved highly controversial, so that the interior has been reconfigured by Munich architects Hilmer and Sattler. Its core is the three-winged lobby, which is completely empty apart from one installation by Walter de Maria but leads into the other halls in which approximately 1000 works are displayed. Another 400 paintings are on show in the Studiengalerie in the basement.

German paintings

The highlight of the collection of old German masters are the **eight works by Albrecht Dürer**, including *Madonna with a Siskin*, the *Young Venetian Girl* as well as the famous portraits of Hieronymus Holzschuher and Jacob Muffel. Martin Schongauer's *Birth of Christ* is one of his few altar pieces. Among the works of Lucas Cranach the Elder, *The Fountain of Youth* is clearly the outstanding piece. Almost as famous is Hans Holbein the Younger's *Portrait of the Merchant Georg Gisze*. German paintings of the 18th century, including those of Johann Heinrich Tischbein, can be seen later on in rooms 20, 21 and 22.

Dutch and Flemish painters

Paintings from Spain's Dutch territories as well as independent Holland form a core aspect of the collection. Madonna in the Church is one of the early oil paintings by Jan van Eyck. Other representatives of Dutch and Flemish painters from the 15th and 16th centuries include Hugo van der Goes, Hans Memling (*Mary with Child*), Gerard David, Rogier van der Weyden (*Woman with Wimple*), Hieronymus Bosch of course, and **Pieter Bruegel the Elder** with his wonderful depiction of *Dutch Proverbs*.

The high-point of the entire collection is formed by the Dutch and Flemish masters of the 17th century, in particular the **✴✴ works of Rembrandt and his studio** in room 10, including *Samson and Delilah*, *The Mennonite Preacher Anslo and his Wife*, *Susanna and the Elders*, *Portrait of Hendrickje Stoffel* and *The Man with the Golden Helmet*, even though it has now been proven that the latter was not painted by the master himself but was »only« a product of his studio. In addition there are portraits, genre paintings and landscapes Frans Hals (*Malle Babbe*), Thomas de Kayser, Jakob van Ruisdael, Salomon van Ruisdael (*Landscape with Thieves*), Jan Vermeer van Delft (*The Wine Glass*), Jan Steen and naturally Peter Paul Rubens.

Italian paintings

All the most renowned names in Italian painting are represented, starting with religious scenes from the 13th century and taking in Botticelli's *Madonna with Child and Chorus of Angels*, Raphael's *Madonna Colonna*, Titian's *Venus and Organist* and Caravaggio's outstanding *Amor as Victor*, and extending into the 18th century with works by Tiepolo and Canaletto.

French painting is much less well represented but there are still high-quality works including three paintings by Nicolas Poussin, a landscape by Claude Lorrain, works by Georges de La Tour, the Le Nain brothers and 18th-century artists such as Antoine Pesne, Jean Restout and Antoine Watteau (*The French Comedy*).

French paintings

Among the works of Spanish painters are Mater Dolorosa by El Greco, Velázquez's *Portrait of a Woman*, Murillo's *Baptism of Christ* and Zurbarán's *Portrait of Alonso Verdugo*. English artists are represented by fine portraiture such as Thomas Gainsborough's *Portrait of an Old Woman* and Joshua Reynolds' *George Clive and Family*.

Spanish and English paintings

✳ KUPFERSTICHKABINETT AND KUNSTBIBLIOTHEK (COPPER ENGRAVING MUSEUM AND ART LIBRARY)

❶ Tue–Fri 10am–6pm, Sat and Sun 11am–6pm; admission €10

The story of the Kupferstichkabinett or Copper Engraving Museum began in 1652, when the Great Elector obtained some 2500 drawings and watercolours for the court library at the Berlin Stadtschloss. In 1831 the Prussian Kupferstichkabinett opened as part of the Altes Museum. The archives presently hold more than 110,000 drawings, some 550,000 printed sheets, printers' plates and illustrated books from the 14th to the 21st centuries, plus several hundred incunables. This makes the Kupferstichkabinett one of the world's four largest collections of prints. The pride of the collection is the early Italian, Old German and Dutch graphic work and drawings (including works by Botticelli, Dürer, Brueghel and Rembrandt) along with pieces by Schinkel and Menzel. The **Kunstbibliothek** or Art Library was founded in 1867 from the guild museum of the Berlin craftsmen's guild, the Berliner Handwerkerverein. It currently possesses around 350,000 books and graphic works covering the history of art and culture of Europe.

✳✳ KUNSTGEWERBEMUSEUM (MUSEUM OF DECORATIVE ARTS)

❶ Tue–Fri 10am–6pm, Sat and Sun 11am–6pm; admission €10

The Kunstgewerbemuseum (Museum of Decorative Arts) opened in 1867 and was the first of its kind in Germany. Until 1921 it was incorporated into the Martin-Gropius-Bau (►p.326) and later moved to the Berlin Stadtschloss, where it remained until 1939. Part of the collection was reassembled after the war in Schloss Köpenick (►Alt-Köpenick), where 29 rooms are arranged by era, while the rest was housed in the palace of Schloss Charlottenburg until 1984 but moved to a new building at the Kulturforum designed by **Rolf Gutbrod** in

1985 . Schloss Köpenick and its 29 »epoch rooms« are still considered part of the museum. The building at the Kulturforum has four storeys displaying important examples of European decorative applied art from the early Middle Ages to the present day. Exhibits that should not be missed include the **»Welfenschatz«** (44 relics, monstrances and crucifixes from the 11th to the 15th centuries, formerly treasures of the St. Blasius Cathedral in Brunswick) and the treasure trove of the former Dionysius trust of Enger/Herford (including the so-called purse relic, probably a baptismal gift from Charlemagne to the Saxon earl Widukind at the end of the 8th century). Further highlights are the collection of Spanish and Italian maiolica ceramics (16th century), the silver of the Lüneburg council (15th/16th century), the emperor's trophy by Wenzel Jamnitzer (1564), the celestial bowl of Jonas Silber (1589) and a dressing table by Abraham Roentgen (18th century). After renovation which was finished in late 2014 there is a new department showing classical design and a large fashion gallery with costumes and accessories from 18th to 20th centuries.

✱ PHILHARMONIE

❶ Tue 1pm lunch-time concerts of chamber music, admission free;
www.berliner-philharmoniker.de

The Berlin Philharmonie is known not only to aficionados of classical music: the name also resonates in the world of architecture. The building was considered revolutionary when it was built between 1960 and 1963 (▶ill. p.48). **Hans Scharoun** designed the asymmetrically shaped building covered by a tent-like concrete roof. The concert hall has a stage ringed by groups of seats that rise up in the nature of an amphitheatre and seat some 2200 people. At the time this was a new idea, although it has come to be accepted, not least because of its outstanding acoustics. Because of this unusual shape and the name of the chief conductor of the Philharmonic orchestra in those days, the hall was dubbed »Karajan's circus«. Adjoining it to the south is the Kammermusiksaal for (1984 – 87), which has come to be known as the »Little Philharmonie« and seats 1000 people.

> **!**   *Midday music*   Insider Tip
>
> **MARCO ⊕ POLO TIP**
>
> Tuesday is the day for lunch-time concerts at the Philharmonie, free of charge in the foyer. The performers are members of the Berlin Philharmonic Orchestra, the Deutsches Symphonie-Orchester and the Staatskapelle Berlin, or holders of scholarships at the orchestra academy.
> Payment has only to be made for the lunch that follows, but the prices are reasonable (Tue 1pm; there is a summer break).

St.-Matthäus-Kirche and Neue Nationalgalerie

* MUSIKINSTRUMENTEN MUSEUM (MUSEUM OF MUSICAL INSTRUMENTS)

❶ Tue, Wed, Fri 9am–5pm; Thu until 10pm; Sat, Sun 10am–5pm; tours: Thu 6pm, Sat 11am; admission €6; www.sim.spk-berlin.de

The Museum of Musical Instruments was founded in 1888 and its building adjoins the Philharmonie. Most of its 800 or so exhibits from total holdings of 3200 items are exquisitely made European instruments from a period covering the 16th century into the 20th, including some unique pieces from the Renaissance and Baroque eras. The instruments are not solely for viewing, but can also be heard on the accompanying audio-guides. The main attraction is **the largest cinema or theatre organ in Europe, »The Mighty Wurlitzer«**, ordered from Siemens in 1929 by cinema organist Werner Ferdinand for his own private use. It is played every Saturday at noon.

** NEUE NATIONALGALERIE (NEW NATIONAL GALLERY)

❶ Closed for renovation

The New National Gallery was erected between 1965 and 1968 according to a design by **Ludwig Mies van der Rohe**. The steel and glass building is a hall constructed on a pedestal. Adjoining it to the west is a courtyard for sculptures featuring pieces by Alexander Calder, Henry Moore, Joannis Avramidis and George Rickey. From 2015 on the building is undergoing renovation and is expected to be **closed for several years**.

The collection unites works of art from genres including Expressionism, Cubism, Bauhaus, Surrealism, Verismus and New Objectivity, plus a very fine collection of US paintings from the 1960s and 70s. Among the most important of the artists represented are Edvard Munch (*The Frieze of Life, Portrait of Graf Kessler*), Ernst Ludwig Kirchner (*Potsdamer Platz*), George Grosz (*Pillars of Society*), Max Beckmann (eleven works by him alone including Portrait of the George Family), Paul Klee, Max Ernst (*Capricorne*), Dalí, Miró, Penck and Baselitz. Cutting edge contemporary art is on display at the ▶Hamburger Bahnhof.

STAATSBIBLIOTHEK ZU BERLIN (BERLIN STATE LIBRARY)

❶ Mon–Fri 9am–9pm, Sat 9am–7pm; www.staatsbibliothek-berlin.de

The Berlin State Library was constructed between 1967 and 1978 according to a design by Hans Scharoun. Originally the library was based on that part of the inventory of the Prussian state library that was stored in western Germany. The rest remained in East Berlin at the Deutsche Staatsbibliothek. Today both sections have been reassembled as possessions of the »Staatsbibliothek zu Berlin – Preussischer Kulturbesitz«, although the two venues now have differing objectives. The library at the Kulturforum is a reference and lending library for literature published since 1956, while the former East German site on ▶Unter den Linden is now a research library for literature produced up until 1955.

* # Kurfürstendamm

✳ **M/N 10/12**

Location and course: In Charlottenburg and Wilmersdorf between Rathenauplatz and Breitscheidplatz
S-Bahn: Zoologischer Garten (S 5, S 7, S 75)

City centre map: C 1 – 5
U-Bahn: Kurfürstendamm (U 9, U 15), Uhlandstrasse, Adenauerplatz (U 7), Zoologischer Garten (U 2, U 9)
www.kudamm2011.de

When West Berlin was an island of capitalism in the midst of the communist empire, Kurfürstendamm became the place to promenade and shop. It was, in a very real sense, the »shop window of the free world«.

Elegant stores and boutiques, hotels, restaurants, bars and cafés with outdoor seating, cinemas and theatres, and a bustling lifestyle that lasted well beyond midnight brought a taste of the big wide world to the Cold War front. After German reunification the gloss of »Ku'damm« slightly faded, as Friedrichstrasse, Unter den Linden and Potsdamer Platz became competitors once again. Nevertheless the street is still able to persuade you to part with large amounts of your money and there are plenty of shops where the prices can make anyone earning an average wage dizzy just to look at them. Nevertheless, amid the Gucci and Versace, there are increasing numbers of discount stores creeping in and the closure of traditional establishments such as Café Möhring

? **MARCO POLO INSIGHT**

Arithmetic of house numbers

Kurfürstendamm begins opposite the Kaiser-Wilhelm-Gedächtniskirche with number 11. Numbers 1 to 9 were lost in 1925 when this section was renamed Budapester Strasse, and number 10 was lost to the enlargement of Breitscheidplatz after the Second World War. Numbers 77 to 89 never existed, so number 90 at Lehniner Platz comes straight after number 76. The house with the highest number on Kurfürstendamm is number 237 at the corner of Rankestrasse.

An emblem of Berlin and a memorial against war: the Kaiser-Wilhelm-Gedächtniskirche

and some of the cinemas as well as the relegation of Café Kranzler to a rooftop restaurant above a fashion store is all indicative that the real world is putting its stamp on Kurfürstendamm. In spite of that, the Ku'damm is among the world's leading shopping destinations. In 2011 the street celebrated its 125th anniversary with real conviction, as its retailers were more satisfied with the previous years than might have been supposed. The number of luxury shops has increased again. With new buildings such as the Zoofenster and Bikini Berlin, and other exclusive developments, the old centre of the West plans to regain its commercial supremacy. The Ku'damm is 3.5km/2mi long and over 53m/58yd wide. It was laid out in 1542 to allow Elector Joachim II to ride to his hunting lodge in ▶Grunewald, but only after 1875 was it transformed into a prestigious boulevard on the orders of Bismarck. Almost half the buildings on the street had been utterly destroyed by the end of the Second World War and the rest were all damaged to a greater or lesser degree. The only survivors of the street as it once was are the **Iduna-Haus** (nos. 59/69, dating from 1905) and nos. 201, 213 to 216 and 218, the latter built in 1896.

Memorial plaques

Various plaques are affixed to some of the buildings in memory of former inhabitants, including writers Max Hermann-Neisse (no. 215), Robert Musil (no. 217) and composer and cabaret performer Rudolf Nelson (no. 186). No. 68 was the site of the former Alhambra Lichtspiel cinema and a plaque records that this was where the world's first movie with sound was premiered in 1922.

Sculpture boulevard

In conjunction with Berlin's jubilee celebrations in 1987 a line of modern sculptures was erected as the »sculpture boulevard of Kurfürstendamm and Tauentzien Strasse«: **Tauentzien/ Breitscheidstr.** on the central reservation of Tauentzien between Marburger and Nürnberger Strasse is the work Berlin by Brigitte and Martin

Matschinsky-Denninghoff; at Breitscheidplatz stands Two Lines Eccentric Joined With Six Angles by George Rickey; **Kurfürstendamm** on Joachimstaler Strasse is the 13. 4. 1981 installation by Olaf Metzel, a composition of outsized police barriers. Josef Erben's Pyramide adorns Bleibtreustrasse and the corner of Schlüterstrasse/Wielandstrasse boasts Large Shadow on a Pedestal by Frank Dornseif. Albrecht-Achilles-Strasse has Large Figure of a Woman, Berlin by Rolf Szymanski and Concrete Cadillac by Wolf Vostell is at Rathenauplatz.

ACROSS KURFÜRSTENDAMM TO KANTSTRASSE

The best place to start a stroll down Kurfürstendamm is from Breitscheidplatz, where Kurfürstendamm meets Budapester Strasse, Kantstrasse and Tauentzienstrasse. Towering 63m/207ft over the square is the ruined tower of the neo-Romanesque Kaiser-Wilhelm Memorial Church, built from 1891 to 1895 in memory of Kaiser Wilhelm I using a design by Franz Schwechten. The church was hit in a bombing raid on 23 November 1943 and for years after the war it was scheduled for demolition. In the intervening period, however, it developed into a West Berlin landmark and a war memorial. For this reason, architect **Egon Eiermann** designed a new church building consisting of a blue-glazed octagon with a flat roof and a hexagonal tower (built from 1959 to 1961) alongside the ruin. This has remained as a monument opposing war and destruction and now houses mosaics, architectural fragments and photographs of the old church. The centrepiece of this collection is a statue of Christ from the old church alongside a crucifix from Coventry Cathedral, which was obliterated by German bombers during the war. Directly adjacent to the Gedächtniskirche is the Zoofenster, at 118m/390ft the tallest building in the western part of the city. Offices from the 16th floor upwards have a fine panoramic view, and the building, completed in 2012, is also home to a luxury hotel, The Waldorf Astoria.

*Kaiser-
Wilhelm-
Gedächtnis-
kirche

Breitscheidplatz also has the Europa-Center, built from 1963 to 1965 on the site of a former Romanesque café to a design by K. H. Pepper and rising to 86m/280ft in height (103m/338ft with the Mercedes star on top). The Europa-Center remains a popular meeting place – not least thanks to its landmark fountain featuring a globe, popularly known as the »Wasserklops«.

Europa-
Center

The »Bahnhof Zoo« railway station at Hardenbergerplatz was the city's premier inter-city station until 2006 It gained a sorry fame in the 1980s with the release of the autobiographical *Wir Kinder vom Bahnhof Zoo*, in which the 14-year-old Christiane F (the English version is simply known under her shortened name) revealed her expe-

Zoologischer
Garten
station

riences as a child in the Berlin drug scene. Jebensstr. 2, behind Bahnhof Zoo, houses the **Museum of Photography**. The building was once a club for army officers. The museum takes particular pride in a collection of more than 1000 pieces on permanent loan from the **Helmut Newton Foundation**. Newton was a native of Berlin.

❶ i Tue–Fri 10am–6pm, Thu until 10pm, Sund and Sat 11am–6pm; admission €10; www.smb.museum

Bikini Berlin

Between Bahnhof Zoo and Elefantentor, around the former Bikinihaus (so-called as its second floor was open), an ambitious new architectural landscape called Bikini Berlin has been built. It includes a hotel, shops and places of entertainment.

Neues Kranzler Eck

From Breitscheidplatz head westward along the Ku'damm. On the right-hand side of the road, a glass building called the Neues Kranzler Eck by Helmut Jahn rises some 50m/164ft above the crossroads with Joachimstaler Strasse. It completely dwarfs the once legendary Café Kranzler building, which now houses two fashion boutiques. The original café was on Unter den Linden but this subsidiary outlet gained special fame. It still clings on in the round red and white building from the 1950s but only as a restaurant on the roof.

Fasanenstrasse

The next street to cross the Ku'damm is Fasanenstrasse. Fasanenstrasse 23, to the south of Kurfürstendamm, is an apartment building from 1873 that has been home since 1986 to the **Literaturhaus Berlin**, which sponsors various exhibitions and readings; it includes the Wintergarten restaurant and a café in its splendid front garden. No. 24, the oldest dwelling on Fasanenstrasse, now houses the **Käthe-Kollwitz Museum**, which possesses some 200 works by the artist, most of them from the collection of painter and art dealer Hans Pels-Leusden. Finally, no. 25 was built in 1891/92 as **Villa Grisebach**, and was once the abode of architect Hans Grisebach. It is now home to the Kunstgalerie Pels-Leusden. To the north of Ku'damm it is worth going as far as the **Jüdisches Gemeindehaus** (no. 79/80), a meeting hall for the Jewish community that was built in 1959 on the site of the 1912-built synagogue, which was burned down by Nazis on the »Kristallnacht« of 9/10 November 1938. The façade incorporates surviving parts of the original building. The space in front of the site features a sculpture of a broken roll from the Torah and the pillared hall includes names of people incarcerated in concentration camps and Jewish ghettos.

Käthe-Kollwitz-Museum: daily 11am–6pm

The area between Kurfürstendamm and Uhlandstrasse, as far as Lietzenburger Strasse to the south, is due to be redeveloped by 2015 to plans by the English architect David Chipperfield. and Knesebeckstrasse, the southern side of the road was until 2006 occupied as far as Lietzenburger Strasse by the Kurfürstendamm-Karree. The Theater am Kurfürstendamm will remain, and the multimedia show The Story of Berlin will be accommodated in the new building.

New Kurfürsten-damm-Karree

❶ Story of Berlin: daily 10am– 8pm, admission until 6pm), €10; www. story-of-berlin.de

If the mood takes you, carry on as far as Knesebeckstrasse (or Bleibtreustrasse with the Schrill department store) and go beneath the S-Bahn arches straight to the square. Though it is situated so close to busy Ku'damm and the heavy traffic on Kantstrasse, the spot still has the air of the old urbane Berlin as it once was, particularly at the time around 1968. It was and is still the heart of the Charlottenburg scene that is so popular with students. It is surrounded by bars, including some smart new ones but including many traditional, almost legendary places such as Zwiebelfisch, Dicke Wirtin, Terzo Mondo, run by a pub landlord in a well-known TV soap opera, and Diener, where painter George Grosz, a proponent of New Objectivity, drank himself to death.

Savignyplatz

> **!** MARCO ☉ POLO TIP
>
> *Open secret*   Insider Tip
>
> This is no secret bar known only to insiders. On the contrary, it is known far and wide, yet anyone seeking an untrammelled pub, a glass of pils or a coffee at a price that is pretty reasonable by Charlottenburg standards need only try out *Zwiebelfisch* on the corner of Savignyplatz and Grolmanstrasse.

Next, go back to Breitscheidplatz along Kantstrasse, which a large number of Chinese restaurants, shops and snack-bars have turned into »Peking-Allee« – the first Chinese restaurant in Germany opened here in 1923. At Fasanenstrasse the road passes the **Theater des Westens**, now a theatre for musicals, though when it was built in 1895/96 it was designed to house classical operetta and is reminiscent of some confectionery palace from a fairy-tale such as Cinderella. Next to the theatre stands another Berlin institution, the **Quasimodo** jazz bar. The **Kantdreieck** office block on the corner of Fasanenstrasse is most conspicuous for its giant silver weather vane, designed by architect J. P. Kleihues apparently in homage to Josephine Baker, who appeared at the Theater des Westens across the way in 1926. Along Fasanenstrasse in the direction of Hardenbergstrasse is the **Ludwig-Erhard-Haus** (headquarters of the Berlin chamber of commerce and the Berlin stock exchange, the Börse), one of the fascinating new building projects to have been undertaken in the west part of the city centre. The steel ribs of the building arch across the heavens like the scales of a giant armadillo, giving it a highly expressive, organic look.

Kantstrasse

Leipziger Strasse

✦ M – L 15 – 17

Location: Mitte, between
Spittelmarkt and Leipziger Platz
U-Bahn: Stadtmitte (U 2, U 6)

Spittelmarkt (U 2)
City plan: C 10 – 13

Leipziger Strasse, which runs east from Leipziger Platz to Spittelmarkt, was a lively shopping street with department stores and fashion shops before the Second World War.

From Leipziger Platz to Wilhelmstrasse

Today, with residential blocks built in the 1970s, it presents a completely different appearance, especially because it has become the main route between the east and west of the city since the fall of the Wall. It starts at the octagonal Leipziger Platz, which was once surrounded by large town houses and together with ▶Potsdamer Platz was Berlin's principal hub of road traffic. At no. 7 an exhibition entitled »**Dalí** – Die Ausstellung am Potsdamer Platz« displays 400 works by the Spanish Surrealist, including drawings, graphic work, sculptures and book illustrations An old guard tower from the Wall stands at Erna-Berger-Strasse, south of Leipziger Platz. On Leipziger Strasse on the right is the so-called Preussisches Herrenhaus, which was completed in 1904 and is now home to the **Bundesrat**, the house of representatives of the Bundesländer (federal states) and second chamber of the German parliament. Practically the whole length of the street opposite the building was formerly occupied by Kaufhaus Wertheim, in its day the largest department store in Europe.

Dalí-Ausstellung: Mon–Sat noon–8pm, Sun from 10am; admission €11; www.daliberlin.de

Bundesfinanzministerium

Also on the right, the huge building that stretches around the corner along Wilhelmstrasse (▶MARCO POLO Insight p.322) built from 1934 to 1936 as Goering's Reichsluftfahrtministerium or Ministry of Aviation. It was later used by the East German government as their »Haus der Ministerien«, when several ministries were housed there. It is now the headquarters of the Bundesministerium für Finanzen, the German Finance Ministry. A glass-covered memorial recessed into the ground in front of the building recalls the revolt of 17 June 1953.

*Museum für Kommunikation Berlin

Shortly afterwards, beyond Wilhelmstrasse, at the corner of Mauerstrasse stands the former ministry for post and telecommunications, which is topped by a group of giant statues flanked by allegorical pieces representing science (left) and transport (right). It is now home to the Berlin Museum of Communication. This is the new name of the former Reichspostmuseum established in 1875 at the instigation of postmaster general Heinrich von Stephan (1831–1897). The museum began modestly but in 1898 moved to Leipziger Strasse with a grand opening. It is **the oldest postal museum in the world**. The exhibition includes a range of exhibits from quaintly nostalgic items right through to the latest telecommunications technology. Much of the exhibition is interactive. Underneath the foyer is a treasure trove featuring the most valuable items, including the legendary **red and blue Mauritius** penny stamps.

❶ Tue 9am–8pm, Wed–Fri 9am–5pm, Sat and Sun 10am–6pm; admission €4; www.mfk-berlin.de

As it approaches Spittelmarkt, Leipziger Strasse crosses Friedrichstrasse and Jerusalemer Strasse. This junction was once the site of the famous Hermann Tietz department store. Just before reaching Spittelmarkt, which gets its name from a hospital (Spital der hl. Gertrude) that originally stood here, note part of the **Spittelkolonnaden** built by von Gontard in 1776, which have been reconstructed using parts of the original colonnades. From Spittelmarkt the old **Gertraudenbrücke** – on the left below the road bridge – leads across to the Fischerinsel, one of the sites where Berlin first grew (▶p.247).

Spittelmarkt

Lichtenberg

✴ **L 20 east**

Borough: Lichtenberg
U-Bahn: U 5

Lichtenberg, a district dominated by industry since the early 20th century, has relatively little to attract visitors – except for those with an interest in history.

What was once the borough of Lichtenberg extends on both sides of Frankfurter Allee, which used to be the main road to Frankfurt (Oder) and leads eastwards away from the city. It has now been merged with the district of Hohenschönhausen, its neighbour to the north, to form a new borough. Since the beginning of the 20th century, the area has largely been industrial in character and therefore has relatively little to offer tourists, unless, that is, they take a special interest in history.

Normannenstrasse was once synonomous with the Ministerium für Staatssicherheit (MfS), the notorious and ubiquitous East German »Stasi«. This was the site of the **Stasi headquarters.** On 15 January 1990 an angry mob of citizens stormed the complex. Only a week

*Forschungs- und Gedenkstätte Normannenstrasse

later, the so-called central round table decided to re-establish the building as the Normannenstrasse Research Centre and Memorial, investigating human rights breaches during the GDR era. Part of the building is now home to the »Bundesbeauftragter für die Unterlagen des Staatssicherheitsdienstes« (Federal Office for the Documentation of the State Security Service). Haus 1, where Erich Mielke was the last minister to preside, accommodates the research centre and place of memorial that is better known as the Stasi Museum. Visitors can inspect the former offices of Stasi chief Erich Mielke as well as conference rooms and secretariat offices. Exhibits reflect such aspects as bugging technology and include flags, medals, busts, a van for the transport of prisoners and various documents

● U-Bahn: U 5 to Magdalenenstrasse, entrance from station exit to Ruschestrasse; Mon–Fri 10am–6pm, Sat and Sun noon–6pm; admission €5; www.stasimuseum.de

*Museum Berlin-Karlshorst

In the former officers' club of the Wehrmacht's Pionierschule 1 a page of world history was written: on the night of 8 and 9 May 1945 army chief Keitel, General von Friedeburg and Colonel General Stumpff signed the unconditional surrender of German forces in the presence of the Soviet Marshall Zhukov, British Air Marshal Tedder, US General Spaatz and French General de Lattre de Tassigny. For a period thereafter, the head of the Soviet military administration in Germany had his offices here and it was here that the Soviets granted powers to the East German administration in 1949. During the GDR era, the building was made into a museum, literally entitled the »Museum of the Capitulation of Fascist Germany in the Great War of the Fatherland 1941 – 1945«. After the end of the East German regime, a German-Russian commission of experts devised a new concept. The museum now features 16 rooms primarily covering Germany's campaign against the Soviet Union featuring countless documents, original items and films. The room where the surrender took place and Zhukov's study are also open to visitors.

● Zwieseler Str. 4; S 3 to Karlshorst or U 5 to Tierpark, then bus 296; Tue– Sun 10am–6pm; admission free, Sun 3pm free guided tour; www. museum-karlshorst.de

---

MARCO ⊕ POLO TIP

Insider Tip

Little Vietnam – on a large scale

The language spoken in the Dong Xuan Center (Herzbergstr. 128 – 129) is Vietnamese. 200 traders in eight halls sell an overwhelming variety of jewellery, bling and artificial flowers, trousers with a traditional cut and other clothing, mountains of mangoes, bitter cucumbers, ladies' fingers, giant sacks of aromatic rice and spices. The locals meet in the food stores, and have their own restaurants and hairdressers, driving schools and lawyers (tram M 8, Wed–Mon 11am–8pm).

Marienkirche
(Church of St Mary)

K 17 · B 14

Location: Karl-Liebknecht-Str. 8, city centre

S-Bahn and U-Bahn:
Alexanderplatz (S 3, S 5, S 7, S 75, U 2, U 5, U 8)
❶ Oct–March daily 10am–6pm,
April–Sept until 9pm

Organ concerts:
Thu and Fri 1.30 pm
(admission free)
www.marienkirche-berlin.de

The Marienkirche or church of St Mary, seat of the bishops of the Lutheran diocese of Berlin-Brandenburg, is the second-oldest parish church in Berlin after the Nikolaikirche (▶Nikolaiviertel).

The earliest written evidence of the church dates from 1294. By 1340 it had been expanded into a Gothic hall church with a five-sided choir to the east. This church burned down in 1380 but reconstruction was completed only a few years later. The pyramid tower that was added between 1790 and 1792 by Carl Gotthard Langhans is in a mixture of Gothic and classical styles. In front of the entrance there is a stone penitence cross erected in 1726 to recall the murder of church provost Nikolaus von Bernau in 1325. Inside, the first feature that demands attention is a 2m/6.5ft-tall and 22.60m/24yd 2ft-long fresco, the **»Totentanz«** or »Dance of Death« in the hall at the base of the tower. This was probably inspired by an outbreak of the plague that took place in 1484. There are fourteen groups depicted and vers-

Marienkirche

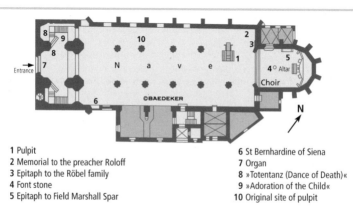

1 Pulpit
2 Memorial to the preacher Roloff
3 Epitaph to the Röbel family
4 Font stone
5 Epitaph to Field Marshall Spar

6 St Bernhardine of Siena
7 Organ
8 »Totentanz (Dance of Death)«
9 »Adoration of the Child«
10 Original site of pulpit

es in Middle Low German relate how death plucks all classes of society into his domain. The fresco was plastered over in 1730 but was rediscovered in 1860 by August Stüler. The bronze baptismal font of the Marienkirche dates from 1437 and has an inscription in Low German. The pulpit in the main aisle is a Baroque piece made in 1703 by Andreas Schlüter, while the organ front was added in 1722. Apart from the Protestant tombs, the carved image of St Bernhardino of Siena (15th century) and the bas-relief of the Holy Family attributed to Lucas Cranach the Elder are all worthy of attention, too.

● Oct – March daily 10am – 6pm, April – Sep daily 10am – 9pm

Luther statue Until 1975 a statue of Martin Luther stood next to the church, the remains of a large monument to the reformation, erected in 1895 and initially situated at Neuer Markt, although it was damaged during the Second World War. The original featured not only Luther but Johannes Reuchlin, Philipp Melanchthon and Ulrich von Hutten. The statue can now be seen at the Dorotheenstadt cemetery (▶p.172).

✳ **Märkisches Ufer · Märkisches Museum**

✦ L 17/18

Location: Mitte, southern bank of the Spree between the Inselbrücke and Jannowitzbrücke
S-Bahn: Jannowitzbrücke (S 5, S 7, S 75)

U-Bahn:
Jannowitzbrücke (U 8),
Märkisches Museum (U 2)
City centre plan: C 14/15

The south bank of the Spree, now known as Märkisches Ufer, is one of the original settlements that gave birth to Berlin. It was first dubbed »Neu-Cölln on the water«, since it was actually part of Cölln, the oldest residential district of which was on the Fischerinsel island on the opposite shore.

An original Eight beautifully restored houses from the 18th century between two
nucleus of bridges, the Inselbrücke and Rossstrassenbrücke, hint at the atmos-
Berlin phere of old Berlin. The best view is from the opposite bank on the Fischerinsel. The prettiest of them is number 11, a copy of the upper-class residence named **Ermelerhaus** that was demolished in 1966 at Breite Strasse 11 on the Fischerinsel. It originated at the end of the 17th century and underwent restoration in 1724 before being rebuilt in Rococo style with a fine classical façade between 1760 and 1762. From 1824 to 1918 it was owned by the family of tobacco dealer Wilhelm Ferdinand Ermeler, who had it furnished most artistically;

some of the furnishings can be admired in the café and the restaurant. Also on the Fischerinsel, at Friedrichsgracht 15, was the original of house no. 12. The photographic archive of the Berlin State Museum is housed in the neo-Baroque houses at nos. 16 and 18. Two other buildings on Märkisches Ufer are also of historical interest: no. 48 near the Jannowitzbrücke is where the staff of the revolutionary peoples' navy had its headquarters during the revolution of 1918/19; the German trades union congress, the Allgemeine Deutsche Gewerkschaftsbund, built its headquarters in 1922/23 on the corner of Wallstrasse and Inselstrasse.

> **MARCO ⊕ POLO TIP**
>
> **! *History from the water*** Insider Tip
>
> From May to September a boat on river Spree and Landwehrkanal starting from Historischer Hafen and lasting approx. three hours illuminates many aspects of the history of Berlin. Information: www.berliner-geschichts-werkstatt.de

Near the Inselbrücke and on the shores of the Fischerinsel, 28 old inland shipping vessels are moored, including the steam tug (and flagship) »Andreas«, launched in 1950, the buoy tender »Phoenix«, built in 1910, the motor tug »Gesa »from 1905, and the »Renate-Angelika«, a barge from 1910 which features an exhibition covering 250 years of river shipping on the Spree and the Havel.

*Historischer Hafen Berlin

❶ Summer: Sat and Sun 1pm–6pm; admission €2; www.historischer-hafen-berlin.de

Wallstrasse leads to the Märkisches Museum is the main site for the Berlin City Museums Trust and covers the history of the city from its founding to the present day. The Märkisches Provinzialmuseum, the forerunner of the present Märkisches Museum, was founded in 1874. It moved into its distinctive building in Köllnischer Park in 1908. Architect Ludwig Hoffmann evoked the brick architecture of the March: the tower is based on Ratzeburg Cathedral; the southern gable with its fan tracery is reminiscent of St Katharine's in Brandenburg; the Roland statue in front of Wallstrasse is a copy of one created in 1474 for the Neustadt Rathaus in Brandenburg. The architectural quotes continue inside with a Gothic chapel, great hall and arms room. Outstanding exhibits include a reconstruction of a hunter's cottage from the 6th and 7th centuries BC, a model of Berlin as it was in 1750 that covers an area of 15 sq m/160 sq ft (the same hall also has two giant paintings by Anton von Werner and Ferdinand Keller), the **original head of one of the horses – the last remaining original piece – in Gottfried Schadow's quadriga** on the ▶Brandenburg Gate, remains of the Berlin Stadtschloss after its demolition by explosives, a fabulously furnished parlour and a self-portrait by Lovis Corinth and a portrait of murder victim Walter Rathenau, also by Corinth. There are also numerous examples of Berlin arts and crafts

*Märkisches Museum

and a unique collection of mechanical music devices (called automatophones), which are demonstrated every Sunday at 3pm. A new exhibition is devoted to the theme of childhood and youth.

❶ Am Köllnischen Park 5; Tue–Sun 10am–6pm, admission €5 (free admission on the 1st Wed in the month); www.stadtmuseum.de

Köllnischer Park and bear compound
The little Köllnischer Park behind the Märkisches Museum includes a lapidarium belonging to the museum and a bronze memorial to Heinrich Zille (▶Famous People) by H. Drake (1965). One curiosity is the bear compound dating from 1939, which is still home to the two Berlin city bears, Schnute and her daughter Maxi.

Fischerinsel
A walk along Fischerinsel-Ufer on the Spree Canal leads to Schlossplatz, passing the Jungfernbrücke, Berlin's last drawbridge. On the right here, although today only residential blocks up to 21 storeys high can be seen, was one of the sites where Berlin's history began. On the southern tip of an island in the Spree, the Fischerinsel, fisherfolk and Spree boatmen lived in the days when Berlin-Cölln was founded. The nine lanes of the district known as Fischerkiez were destroyed in the Second World War.

The Ermeler-Haus (left) and the house at Friedrichsgracht no. 15 (right) were moved from the Fischerinsel to Märkisches Ufer

Marzahn

✴ **F 20 east**

Borough: Marzahn-Hellersdorf
S-Bahn: Marzahn (S 7)
Tram: several stops on line M 6

What was to become the 19th Berlin borough was raised on the sandy soil of Brandenburg from 1977. Marzahn was a prestige project for East Germany, intended to realize an ideal of »socialist living conditions«.

Since then the hamlet of Alt-Marzahn has been encircled by eleven-storey towers with a total of 57,000 apartments – the largest prefabricated housing estate in Europe. After German reunification Marzahn got a reputation as a place of unemployment and crime. If this was ever true, it is no longer the case today. Many of the prefabricated blocks have been renovated or reduced to three- to six-storey buildings where »completely normal« people live. To find out what life was like in one of the GDR residential blocks, visit Hellersdorfer Str. 179, which was built in 1986 and now contains the Museumswohnung, an apartment furnished in the style of those years.
Museumswohnung WBS 70: Sun 2–4pm; admission free; www.stadt undland.de/33_Museumswohnung.htm

New estate with a historic centre

> **!** *Don't be surprised ...*   *Insider Tip*
>
> **MARCO⊕POLO TIP**
>
> ... if you come across a Frank-Zappa-Strasse in Marzahn – there is even more, and you can hear it: no. 19–20 is »Berlin's noisiest concrete block«. Here, in the former Orwo factory, are the rehearsal rooms for about 700 Berlin musicians. Every year in early July, the ORWOhaus Festival shows whether they have practised enough (www.orwohaus.de).

The suburb's main landmark is the windmill built in 1719 at the corner of Landsberger Allee and Allee der Kosmonauten. Pretty Alt-Marzahn, with its brick church, village tavern and a school building from 1911 all clustered around a village green, seems a tad forlorn. Nevertheless, in addition to the local **museum for Marzahn-Hellersdorf** in the old school, it does have a historic farmyard ensemble with rare domestic animals, paddocks for horses and donkeys, goats, turkeys, geese and sheep, a yard with small animals and poultry, an educational cereal garden and old rustic equipment at the foot of the hill on which the mill stands.
Local museum: Mon–Fri 10am–5pm, Sun 11am–5pm, admission free; www.museum-marzahn-hellersdorf.de

Alt-Marzahn

Gärten der Welt (Gardens of the World) started out as a garden show in the Wuhle valley around the Kienberg hill that was laid out in 1987

Gärten der Welt

The largest Chinese garden outside China: the Garden of the Regained Moon in Marzahn

for Berlin's 750th anniversary celebrations. Among its attractions is a fairy-tale garden for children. One authentic highlight is the Garten des wiedergewonnenen Mondes (Garden of the Regained Moon), the largest Chinese garden outside China. It was created by experts from the Beijing Institute for classical garden architecture in a northern Chinese style. The garden has since been supplemented by a Japanese Garden of Confluent Waters, a Balinese Garden of the Three Harmonies, an oriental Garden of Four Rivers and the Korean Seoul Garden. In 2007 a maze was added, based on that at Hampton Court in London. Since 2008 an Italian Renaissance garden has demonstrated European garden styles form the 14th to the 16th century, and the remodelled Karl-Foerster-Garten presents contemporary horticulture. There are also a Christian European garden, an Italian garden and a secret garden.

❶ Main entrance: Eisenacher Strasse, bus 195 from S-Bahn Marzahn; daily from 9am; admission: €4; www.gruen-berlin.de

In Hellersdorf, neighbouring Marzahn to the east, from 1960 Charlotte von Mahlsdorf a.k.a. Lothar Berfelde collected furniture and household goods of the Gründerzeit, the period from 1870, in the manor house Gutshaus Mahlsdorf. Charlotte (1928 – 2002) was awarded the Federal Republic of Germany's major honour, the Bundesverdienstkreuz, and revealed to have been a Stasi informer shortly before her death. She left behind nine fully furnished rooms in Mahlsdorf, the most impressive of which is the »**Mulackritze**« room from 1890, taken from the last of Berlin's taverns from the milieu of Heinrich Zille

Gründerzeit-museum Mahlsdorf

❶ Hultschiner Damm 333; Wed, Sun 10am – 6pm;admission €4.50; www.museumsportal-berlin.de

＊ Müggelsee

—————————————————— ✳ O 20 southeast

Location: Köpenick
S-Bahn: Friedrichshagen (S 3), then tram 60 to Müggelseedamm

Where West Berlin had the Wannsee, the East Berliners were well served by the Müggelsee. It is not only a place for swimming, since about 160km/100mi of paths range through its woods.

Covering an area 7.5 sq km/1850ac and reaching a depth of some 8m/26ft, the lake east of ▶Alt-Köpenick is the largest in the metropolitan district. Its woods were among the most best-stocked hunting grounds between the Elbe and the Oder until well into the 18th century. It goes without saying that boat trips round the lake are on offer.

Berlin's biggest lake

From the S-Bahn take the tram or a walk through the suburb of **Friedrichshagen** on Bölschestrasse to the lake. Friedrich II had 1200 mulberry trees planted here in a gap in the forest in the year 1753 and built workers' dwellings for employees of his planned silk spinning factory, which did not actually get off the ground. What remains is the broad Bölschestrasse avenue, flanked with limes. It is a lovely place for a walk because the route has plenty of nice shops, bars and restau-

> **!** *A boat trip with sunshine* Insider Tip
>
> MARCO ⊕ POLO TIP
>
> Glide across Müggelsee without noise, emissions or a skipper's licence. The starting point is Köpenick via Müggelspree, and the electric boats are driven by solar power. Rent one from the Solarbootpavillon Köpenick, Müggelheimer Strasse 1d; Mon–Fri noon–7pm; Sat, Sun from 10am; tel. 303 94 11 38; www.solarwaterworld.de; 1 hour from €10

Did you know?

Long before the Fernsehturm was erected at Alexanderplatz there was a plan to build a tower on the Müggelberge hills. It was to be 130m/430ft high. Construction work began in May 1954, but was called off in November 1956 – the planners had overlooked the fact that it would have stood right in the approach path for Schönefeld Airport. The stump of the tower, today a directional radio station, is visible a few hundred metres from the Müggelturm.

rants, many in attractive single storey cottages. The avenue ends at the Köpenicker Bürgerbräu building, from where a left turn followed by another quick right leads to the approach road for the 120m/130yd-long **Spree tunnel**, which dips underneath the Müggelspree river spur to come out on the eastern shore of the Müggelsee lake. Friedrichshagen also has its own museum: it is situated a little out of town towards the east (Müggelseedamm 307). Its exhibition, in an old watermill at the **Friedrichshagen waterworks**, tells the story of supplying water to Berlin from the Middle Ages to the present day. The museum is particularly proud of its machine hall from 1893.

❶ Apr–Oct Fri and Sat 10am–6pm, Sun until 4pm; Nov–March Fri–Sun 11am–4pm, admission €2.50; www.museum-im-wasserwerk.de

*Neu-Venedig
Further along, the Müggelseedamm leads past the Müggelsee beach, Strandbad Müggelsee, to Rahnsdorf, part of which is called Neu-Venedig or New Venice. This is an allotment site, criss-crossed by drainage channels where many a Berliner has bought an idyllic weekend home. The highly picturesque spot came into existence in the 1920s during the building of a ship canal.

*Müggel-berge
There are many ways of getting to the southern shore of the lake: on foot from Friedrichshagen, by bus X69 from Köpenick S-Bahn station, by car via Müggelheimer Damm or by steamship right across the lake to the »Rübezahl« jetties or Hotel Müggelsee. From there, various paths lead up to the Müggelberg hills, which reach a height of 115m/377ft. Routes lead over the moors around the Teufelssee and come to an end at the **Müggelturm**, an old tower that is a popular destination for Berliners taking a day trip, although it is now somewhat in need of repair. Originally there was a wooden tower at the site, built in 1899, but when it burned down in 1958 it was replaced by a modern building. Between 1928 and 1933 there was a tented camp for workers not far away from the Müggelseeperle bus stop, which gained fame with the release of the eponymous film *Kuhle Wampe*, with a screenplay written by Bertolt Brecht.

✳ Museum Berggruen

✳ **K 11**

Location: Schlossstr. 1,
Charlottenburg
S-Bahn: Westend (S 41, S 42, S 46)
U-Bahn: Richard-Wagner-Platz (U 7)
Bus: M 45, 109, 309

🕐 Tue–Fri 10am–6pm,
Sat and Sun
11am–6pm
Admission: €8
www.smb.museum

**With the help of government funds, what began as a loan
from an émigré to the city of his birth has become a major institution: one of the most important private collections of
modern art. Two further attractive art museums are close by.**

The collection was assembled by **Heinz Berggruen**, who was compelled to emigrate to the USA in 1936, remaining there until 1996.
Under the theme **»Picasso and his times«** it exhibits over 100 paintings by Pablo Picasso, a personal friend of Berggruen. They include
Seated Harlequin from 1905, The Painter and His Model and The
Yellow Pullover, 1939. In addition, there are 60 pieces by **Paul Klee**
alongside works by Henri Matisse, Giacometti and African sculpture.
The collection is exhibited in the west wing of Friedrich August Stüler's »cavalier building« opposite ►Schloss Charlottenburg, which
features a wonderfully light stairway designed by Stüler. There are

**Almost modern art in its own right: the stairway in the Museum
Berggruen**

plans to build an extension. Heinz Berggruen himself occupied an apartment on the top floor until his death in 2007. His grave is in teh Waldfriedhof in Dahlem (►p.177).

Scharf/ Gerstenberg collection

The Sammlung Scharf/Gerstenberg in the eastern part of Stüler's building is a major collection of modern painting and includes more than 200 works by the Surrealists and their predecessors - for example by Goya as well as Paul Klee and Max Ernst In the Sahuré Room, which remains from the Egyptian Museum that occupied the building before German reunification, Surrealist films are screened.

❶ as Museum Berggruen

Bröhan Museum

The Bröhan Museum (Regional Museum for Art Nouveau, Art Deco and Functionalism) opened in a former infantry barracks next to the ► Museum Berggruen near Schloss ►Charlottenburg in 1983. It contains the private collection that Karl H. Bröhan bequeathed to the city of Berlin in 1982, and exhibits paintings, graphic and sculptural items, furniture, porcelain, ceramic, glass, tin and silver works of art from the period 1889 to 1939. The ground floor features a sequence of rooms dedicated to specific artists and cataloguing their styles that illustrate the diversity of furniture, art and crafts from Art Nouveau to Art Deco. On the first floor there are paintings, silverwork and French Art Deco, including paintings by Walter Leistikow, Hans Baluschek and Karl Hagemeister. The third floor includes two cabinets dedicated to Henry van de Velde and one of the founders of the Vienna studios, Josef Hoffmann.

❶ Tue–Sun 10am–6pm; admission €8; www.broehan-museum.de

✴ Museum für Naturkunde
(Natural History Museum)

✳ H 15/16

Location: Invalidenstr. 43, Mitte
U-Bahn: Naturkundemuseum (U 6)
Tram: M 6, M 8, 12
❶ Tue–Fri 9.30am–6pm, Sat and Sun

10am–6pm
Admission: €6
www.naturkunde museum-berlin.de

The director of the British Museum in London praised the Museum für Naturkunde in 1893, as »a remarkable illustration of the absolute revolution in ideas for the design of museums«.

The collection of the Museum für Naturkunde, the Natural History Museum of Humboldt University, possesses more than 25 million items, based initially on a teaching collection started by the Berliner Bergakademie (mountaineering school) in the 18th century. As of

The pride of the Museum für Naturkunde are its dinosaur skeletons

1810 the museum was located in the university on Unter den Linden. Expedition finds and donations by Alexander von Humboldt and Adelbert von Chamisso, among others, caused the collection to expand immensely, so that a new building was conceived in 1875 and opened on Invalidenstrasse in 1889. Much of it was damaged by air raids during the Second World War and many truly valuable pieces were destroyed, including the Hall of Anatomy with all its skeletons and the Whale Hall, containing skeletons of great whales and other marine mammals. Today it is once again among the world's premier natural history museums. Its newly designed sections provide a tour through the history of nature on earth. The main attraction is the Dinosaur Hall with original fossil skeletons from Upper Jurassic strata in Tanzania (c150 million years old), including the **largest mounted authentic dinosaur skeleton on the globe, a brachiosaurus brancai** 23m/75ft long and 13.27m/41ft high. So-called »Jurascopes« bring the world of the dinosaurs to life. Another highlight is the original fossil of the ancient bird-like dinosaur **archaeopteryx** from the Solnhofen slates, the best example of the twelve fossils of the species found to date. The zoological collections use dioramas and taxidermy to provide an insight into the animal world. One particularly interesting diorama – one of the first in the world – concerns the »Bavarian Alps«. Another fascinating exhibit is the stuffed model of the gorilla »Bobby«, who was a popular inhabitant of Berlin's ▶Zoologischer Garten between 1928 and 1935. The Hall of Minerals exhibits the third largest collection of meteorites in Germany. It has largely been maintained in its 19th-century state and includes pieces collected by people such as Alexander von Humboldt himself. A new and slightly grisly section is the »wet collection« in the reconstructed east wing: 12.6km/8mi of shelves hold 276,000 glass vesels with specimens preserved in alcohol – fish and spiders, crabs, worms and reptiles, some of them over 200 years old.

** Museumsinsel
(Museum Island)

✳ K 16/17

Location: Am Kupfergraben, Mitte
S-Bahn: Friedrichstrasse (S 1, S 2, S 25, S 26, S 5, S 7, S 75), Hackescher Markt (S 5, S 7, S 75)
City centre plan: B 12/13

U-Bahn:
Friedrichstrasse (U 6)
Tram: M 1, M 12
Bus: 100, 200
www.smb.museum
(including ticket orders)

The world-famous Museumsinsel or Museum Island, situated between Kupfergraben and the Spree, was declared a World Cultural Heritage Site by UNESCO in 2000. It is among the world's leading centres of art.

Designation as World Heritage by UNESCO was justified partly on the grounds of the uniqueness of this »ensemble of museum buildings that illustates the development of modern museum design over more than a century«. Museum Island originated in 1830 with the opening of the Altes Museum (Old Museum), endowed by King Friedrich Wilhelm III in order to give the public at large access to the art treasures of the royal palaces. Friedrich Wilhelm IV declared in 1841 that the whole of the site beyond the museum would be given over to forming a **»district dedicated to the study of art and the science of antiquity«**. Between 1843 and 1855 the Neues Museum (New Museum) was erected on the other side of Bodestrasse. The Nationalgalerie or National Gallery, slightly set back on the right, was opened in 1876 and in 1904 the Kaiser-Friedrich Museum, now the Bodemuseum, opened on the other side of the railway line. In 1909 work started on construction of the Pergamonmuseum, although it was not opened until 1930. Under the aegis of **Wilhelm von Bode** (1845 – 1929), who managed the museums between 1872 and 1920 and was named as General Director of Museums in 1905, the collections were to become world class, comparable with those of the Louvre in Paris, the Hermitage of St. Petersburg or London's British Museum and Victoria and Albert Museum. During the Second World War, though, the buildings on the Museum Island were 70% destroyed. The art treasures had earlier been shipped to safety and largely survived the war, but they were distributed throughout various parts of the now divided Berlin. Far-reaching architectural changes are taking place on Museum Island. A **master plan passed in 1999** (see 3D model on the lower floor of the foyer of the Pergamon Museum) foresees a new main entrance building between the Neues Museum and Kupfergraben (James-Simon-Galerie) and a fourth wing for the Pergamon Museum designed by O.M. Ungers. A good deal of water will flow down the Spree by the time of the intended completion of these projects in 2025.

✳ ALTES MUSEUM (OLD MUSEUM)

❶ Entrance: Lustgarten; Tue–Sun 10am–6pm, Thu until 8pm; admission €10

The Altes Museum or Old Museum was designed by **Karl Friedrich Schinkel** and opened in 1830. Alongside the Fridericianum in Kassel (1779) and Klenzes Glyptothek in Munich (1816 – 30), it is among

Albert Wolff's »Boy Riding« in front of the Altes Museum

A Home for Art and Antiquities

This unique and fabulous cultural landscape has been declared a UNESCO World Heritage site. The Museumsinsel or Museum Island, one of the largest museum complexes in the world, is wholly dedicated to art and archaeology. One day is not enough to take it all in, but the Pergamon altar, the bust of Nefertiti and the Alte Nationalgalerie (Old National Gallery) are not to be missed. An entrance ticket is valid for all the museums. One curious thing is that railway trains and S-Bahn units constantly rattle through the middle of the island.

❶ Bode-Museum

The Bode-Museum opened as the Kaiser-Fried-rich-Museum in 1904 but was renamed after its founder, Wilhelm von Bode, when it reopened in 1956. It includes the coin collection in the Münzkabinett as well as ancient and Byzantine artefacts in the Museum für Spätantike und Byzantinische Kunst.

❷ Pergamonmuseum

The Pergamonmuseum was completed in 1930 and actually comprises three museums: the Antikensammlung (Collection of Antiquities), Vorderasiatisches Museum (Near East Museum) and the Museum für Islamische Kunst (Museum of Islamic Art). A new fourth wing facing Kupferstrasse by O.M. Ungers is planned.

❸ Alte Nationalgalerie

The Old National Gallery (built from 1866 to 1876 according to plans by Friedrich August Stüler and Johann Heinrich Strack) was originally intended as a teaching and entertainment venue for German art. It is designed in the form of a Corinthian temple on a high base. After a long rebuilding period, the gallery now displays brilliant paintings and sculpture from the 19th century.

❹ Neues Museum

Friedrich August Stüler built the »new« museum from 1843 to 1847. It has now been fully restored and presents the collections of the Egyptian Museum and the Museum for Pre-History and Early History, including Heinrich Schliemann's collection of Trojan antiquities.

❺ Altes Museum

The Altes Museum came into existence on the northern edge of the Lustgarten between 1824 and 1830 under the aegis of Karl Friedrich Schinkel and takes the form of a Greek temple with the Royal Museum. It is considered Schinkel's finest work.

❻ New Main Entrance

Designed by David Chipperfield

❼ Archäologische Promenade

The »Archaeological Promenade« is to link the Bode-Museum and Pergamonmuseum with the Altes and Neues Museums via underground passages to allow rapid transit between the key exhibits of all four.

In 2013 Museum Island had 2.75 million visitors, of whom 1.4 million went to the Pergamonmuseum. Which is nowhere near enough to make it one of the world's five most visited museums:
- Louvre, Paris: 9.3 million
- British Museum, London: 6.7 million
- Metropolitan Museum, New York: 6.2 million
- National Gallery, London: 6.0 million
- Vatican Museums, Rome: 5.9 million

©BAEDEKER

Local trains pass across the island. Passengers can even look into the windows of the museum.

Nefertiti has a view from the northern dome room through the Hall of the Niobids, the Bacchus Room and the Roman Room to the southern dome of the restored Neues Museum.

The heart of the Pergamonmuseum is the Altar of Zeus from Pergamon

the oldest museum buildings in Germany and is certainly **the oldest museum in Berlin**. Two sculptures flank the stairs to the foyer – Albert Wolff's Youth on Horseback on the left, and Mounted Amazons by August Kiss. The foyer itself is supported by 18 Ionic columns. A Latin inscription at the entrance dedicates the building to »the study of antiquity and fine arts«. At the museum's heart is the fabulous 23m/75ft rotunda, modelled on the Pantheon in Rome. The gallery that runs around it is supported by 20 Corinthian columns.

*Antiken-sammlung

The **Collection of Antiquities** largely goes back to the Antiquarium founded in 1830 and has been divided between the Pergamonmuseum and the Altes Museum, where art and sculpture of the Greeks and Romans is displayed, with a new thematic arrangement since 2011. The theme of the upper floor is the most influential pre-Roman civilization in Italy, that of the Etruscans. The south-east room presents the rise of this culture with the biconic urn and warrior grave of Tarquinia (8th century BC), grave goods, fragments of textiles and stone tomb guardians. In the eastern gallery, colourful roof terracottas, drinking vessels, mirrors, ear-rings and candelabras are on display. Life-sized statues of seated mothers with swaddled babies come from the sanctuary of Fondo Patturelli near Curti/Capua. Family tombs and sarcophaguses lead to theme of »Life and Death in Rome«: statues of Apollo, Dionysos and Antinoos are on show. The subject of luxury is presented with the Hildesheim silver hoard arranged as a buffet. A sensual garden with erotic depictions is followed by the faces of empire in the shape of portraits of Caesar and Cleopatra.

The main floor presents art from the Greek world, beginning with the Heroic Age (9th–7th century BC). Sacred sites are represented with an arrangement of archaic statues from Samos, Miletos etc. The coloured Berlin Goddess, a kore, has a counterpart in the Naxos Kouros. In a separate room, ancient coins and arts and crafts illustrate trade in the Mediterranean world. Classical sculpture, around the Praying Boy from Rhodes (4th century BC), is a further spatial and thematic focus. This is followed by daily life and the cult of death in classical Athens, and by theatre sculpture from Greece and southern Italy, including the Enthroned Goddess of Tarento. The circuit is completed with a show entitled »350 Years of the Collection of Antiquities«.

NEUES MUSEUM (NEW MUSEUM)

❶ Entrance: Bodestr.; daily 10am–6pm, Thu until 8pm; admission €12, timed ticket recommended as few are available on the day at the ticket desk!

The Neues Museum or New Museum was erected between 1843 and 1847 according to designs by **Friedrich August Stüler**. Its interior, including a towering and grandiose staircase, was not completed until 1855, however. The building was badly hit during the Second World War, and attempts at repairing the damage did not begin until 1986. When it was first opened, the Neues Museum was regarded as a universal museum, a composition of architecture, interior decoration and exhibits, the most modern museum of the day.

Today, after a long process of restoration, it is at one and the same time **a historical gem and a modern museum space**. Restored colourful frescoes from the original decoration can be seen alongside coolly monumental exhibition halls of freestone. The reopening of the museum in 2009 was preceded by years of debate, and David Chipperfield's concept of archaeological restoration, which did not exclude new designs, as in the case of the famous stair hall, has not met with unanimous approval.

The re-opening brought the Egyptian Museum back to its original location. The limestone bust of Queen **Nefertiti** (from around 1350 BC), wife of the pharaoh Akhnaton. The bust was discovered in 1912 and its presence here has led to Nefertiti herself being described as Berlin's most famous daughter. She is now on display in the perfectly lit north domed room, looking towards monumental statues of the late Roman imperial period from Alexandria under the south dome. Other outstanding pieces are the so-called family stele, depicting Nefertiti and Akhnaton with three of their six daughters, as well as »A Walk in the Garden« (a painted relief showing the royal couple in their youth), portrait masks from the sculptors' workshops of Thutmos in Amarna, a small ebony head of Queen Tiy, mother of Akhnaton (from around 1370 BC), an almost perfectly preserved but incomplete statue of Pharaoh Akhnaton plus the »Green Head of Berlin« (c500 BC).

∗∗
Ägyptisches Museum and Papyrus Collection

The Museum for Pre-History and Early History surveys the **civilizations of the ancient world** from the Stone Age until the Middle Ages. The exhibits range from hand-axes to the famous **Berlin Golden Hat**, and from the beginnings of human settlement in Europe through Roman time to the Middle Ages. Silver vessels, weapons, ceramic figures and skeletons are arranged in a chronological circuit; the highlights apart from the golden hat include the Le Moustier Neanderthal and above all **Heinrich Schliemann's renowned collection of Trojan antiquities.**.

∗Museum für Vor- und Früh- geschichte

In the Greek Court of the Neues Museum (beneath the Schievelbein Frieze with its depiction of the destruction of Pompeii), 20th-century sculptures found in 2010 near the Rotes Rathaus during excavations for construction of a subway line are on display. They have been identi-

Griechischer Hof

fied as works confiscated in 1937 from various German museums, having been classified by the National Socialists as »Degenerate Art« .

** ALTE NATIONALGALERIE (OLD NATIONAL GALLERY)

❶ Entrance: Bodestr.; Tue–Sun 10am–6pm, Thu until 8pm; admission €8

The Old National Gallery building was designed by Friedrich August Stüler und Johann Heinrich Strack and built during the period 1866 to 1876. Above the entrance is an equestrian statue of King Friedrich Wilhelm IV fashioned from bronze in 1886 by Alexander Calandrelli. The Nationalgalerie suffered during the war, but also under the Nazi regime itself. A large part of its collection of German Expressionists was shipped to Munich to be shown at a notorious exhibition entitled »Entartete Kunst«, or »Degenerate Art«. Afterwards the pieces were sold at give-away prices. Another part of the collection was burnt while in storage at a bunker in Friedrichshain.

Museum tour A tour begins in the Sculpture Hall, in the middle of which is Schadow's famous statue of the two princesses, Crown Princess Luise and Princess Friederike (▶ill. p.46). To the left, the museum takes up the topic of realism and the highlights of this section are works by Adolph Menzel, starting with his Flute Concert in Sanssouci (▶ill. p.367) and including The Balcony Room, then finally Iron Mill from 1875. Next come paintings from the 19th-century period under the rule of Wilhelm II, where the outstanding pieces are those of Max Klinger. The two rooms after that are concerned with the Secession group and the turn of the 20th century and include Franz von Stuck's The Sin and Tilla Durieux as Circe as well as Max Beckmann's Death Bed. Around the staircase leading to the first floor there is a frieze featuring figures from German history, art and science. This floor starts with the so-called Germano-Romans Arnold Böcklin (Island of Death), Anselm Feuerbach, Hans von Marées and Adolph von Hildebrand, leading on to a room of French impressionists that includes masterpieces such as Manet's Winter Garden or Cézanne's Mill on the Couleuve near Pontoise, which was the first of his works ever to hang in a museum. Other rooms cover Wilhelm Leibl, realism in Germany and Austria (Hans Thoma, Spitzweg), Max Liebermann, the Munich school, historic paintings and salon idealism. The second floor takes the visitor through the times of Goethe, Romanticism and Biedermeier. Most of these rooms include some of Schinkel's fine landscape paintings or works by Caspar David Friedrich (among them Abbey in the Oak Wood). Three rooms feature views of Berlin by such figures as Eduard Gaertner and J. E. Hummel. Finally come the boards for the frescoes in the Göttessaal at the Munich Glyptothek by Peter Cornelius.

** PERGAMONMUSEUM

❶ Entrance: Kupfergraben; daily 10am–6pm, Thu until 9pm, admission €12

Alfred Messel and Ludwig Hoffmann's Pergamonmuseum took shape between 1909 and 1930. It too is one of the oldest museums of its kind in the world. It combines the Antikensammlung (Collection of Antiquities) with the Vorderasiatisches Museum (Museum of the Near East) and Museum für Islamische Kunst (Museum of Islamic Art).

The **Collection of Antiquities** covers most of the Pergamonmuseum's main floor. According to the masterplan of 1999 the hall containing the Pergamon Altar as well as the north wing and the gallery of Hellenistic art will be closed for renovation until 2019.

**Antiken-sammlung

The centrepiece will still be the reconstruction of the altar to Zeus from Pergamon in Asia Minor (now Bergama in Turkey). 35m/115ft wide and 33m/110ft deep, it was probably a votive offering to Zeus and Pergamon's patron god Athena by King Eumenes. Made during a period from 180 to 160 BC, the altar was brought to Berlin by Carl Humann in 1902. The artistry of its Greek masons is most apparent in the frieze showing the battle between gods and titans that once ran around the whole altar. Other important exhibits include valuable examples of early Hellenic architecture from Priene, Magnesia and Miletos as well as sculptures from Milet, Samos, Naxos and Attica.

Closure of the Pergamon Hall and the gallery of Hellenistic art until 2019

The Pergamon Altar cannot be visited until 2019

Pergamonmuseum

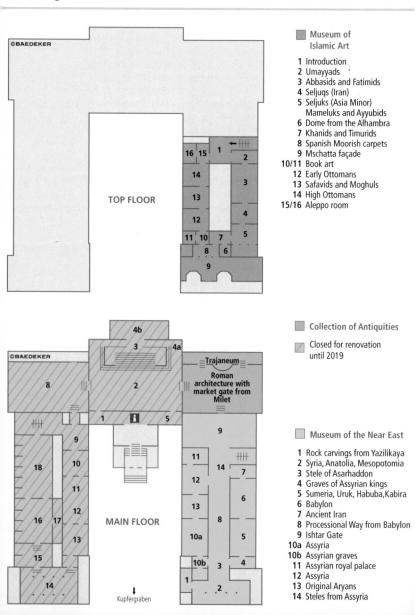

©BAEDEKER

TOP FLOOR

16 15 1
14
13
12
11 10 7
8
6
9
2
3
4
5

Museum of Islamic Art

1 Introduction
2 Umayyads
3 Abbasids and Fatimids
4 Seljuqs (Iran)
5 Seljuks (Asia Minor) Mameluks and Ayyubids
6 Dome from the Alhambra
7 Khanids and Timurids
8 Spanish Moorish carpets
9 Mschatta façade
10/11 Book art
12 Early Ottomans
13 Safavids and Moghuls
14 High Ottomans
15/16 Aleppo room

©BAEDEKER

MAIN FLOOR

8
1
9
18
10
11
16 17 12
13
15
14

4b
3
2
4a

Trajaneum
Roman architecture with market gate from Milet

5
9
11
12
13
10a
10b
1
2
14
7
6
8
5
3
4

↓ Kupfergraben

Collection of Antiquities

Closed for renovation until 2019

Museum of the Near East

1 Rock carvings from Yazilikaya
2 Syria, Anatolia, Mesopotomia
3 Stele of Asarhaddon
4 Graves of Assyrian kings
5 Sumeria, Uruk, Habuba, Kabira
6 Babylon
7 Ancient Iran
8 Processional Way from Babylon
9 Ishtar Gate
10a Assyria
10b Assyrian graves
11 Assyrian royal palace
12 Assyria
13 Original Aryans
14 Steles from Assyria

The magnificent **market gate of Miletus is not affected by the closure.** It dates from Roman times (165 BC) but clearly displays Hellenic influences. Another wonderful item is the 3rd-century BC Roman floor mosaic from Gerasa (Jerash in modern-day Jordan).

MARCO POLO TIP

Don't miss   Insider Tip

- Pergamon Altar: the battle of the gods and giants **(closed)**
- Market gate of Miletus
- Ishtar Gate and processional way from Babylon
- Giant bird statue from Tell Halaf
- Desert castle from Mshatta
- Aleppo Room

The Pergamon's Vorderasiatisches Museum (**Museum of the Near East**), located in the right-hand wing on the main floor, provides a comprehensive insight into 4000 years of history, art and culture in the Near East. Its items are mainly archaeological finds from digs undertaken by the German Oriental Society (Deutsche Orientgesellschaft) from 1898 to 1917. Its most fabulous and monumental pieces are the Ishtar Gate (▶ill. p. 272) and Processional Way as well as parts of the royal palace façade from Babylon at the time of Nebuchadnezzar II (603 – 562 BC). Other examples of ancient monumental architecture from the Near East include a mosaic wall (from c3000 BC) and a brick façade (c1415 BC) from the Inanna shrine in Uruk. Another unique item is the giant bird statue from Tell Halaf (c900 BC): Also featured are the victory stele of Assyria's King Asarhaddon (680 – 669 BC) and the great Lion Gate from the fortress at Zincirli.

The **Museum of Islamic Art** on the top floor was founded by Wilhelm von Bode in 1904. The occasion was after the donation of what is still its finest treasure, the façade of the desert castle of Mshatta in Jordan (8th century), to Emperor Wilhelm II by the Sultan of Turkey. It also features the Aleppo room from the early 17th century, a prayer niche from the Maidan mosque in Kashan (13th century), a decorated Qur'an and prayer niche of the Safavid dynasty (16th century), Iranian stone stair pillars from the 14th century, Persian and Indian miniatures, plus carpets and carvings.

*Museum für Islamische Kunst

✳ BODE-MUSEUM

❶ Entrance: Kupfergraben / Monbijoubrücke; Tue–Sun 10am–6pm, Thu until 8pm; admission €10

The domed Bode-Museum, designed by Ernst von Ihne, projects into the Spree at the north end of Museum Island. It reopened in 2006 after renovation. Now daylight shines again onto the equestrian statue of the Great Elector in the great hall beneath the dome and onto the five medallions depicting Prussian monarchs who sponsored the arts. The marble inlays in the floor of the basilica-shaped building have been reconstructed, as has the Tiepolo cabinet, around which is a collection of **some 1700 sculptures** belonging to the Skulpturensammlung (Sculpture Collection), the Museum für Byzantinische Kunst (Museum of Byzantine Art) and the Gemäldegalerie (Picture Gallery). The sculptures date from late antiquity right up to the end of the 18th century, and include superb works by Riemenschneider. There are also about **150 paintings**, as well as the **Münzkabinett** (Coin Cabinet). It is planned that the Gemäldegalerie will move from the ▶Kulturforum to Museum Island.

Neukölln

 ✦ T – V 17 – 20

Borough: Neukölln
U-Bahn: U 7, U 8

The Neukölln borough in the south of Berlin was called Rixdorf until 1912. It comprises the areas of Neukölln itself in the north plus Buckow, Britz und Rudow in the south. Its rustic, almost village character makes it attractive for trippers.

Hasenheide
Volkspark
(O 18/17)

The park on Columbiadamm (U 7, U 8 to Hermannplatz) covers some 56ha/140ac. It was an enclosure for breeding hares at the time of the electors but in 1838 Peter Joseph Lenné laid the area out as a park. As of 1878, though, its function changed again and it became a

Idyll in Neukölln on the Böhmischer Gottesacker

garrison shooting range until it was converted back into a park between 1936 and 1939, and today has many animal enclosures to delight Berlin's children. The Hasenheide park is associated with the »father of gymnastics«, Friedrich Ludwig Jahn, who founded **Germany's first open-air gymnastic arena** here in 1810. A memorial erected at the northern edge of the park by Erdmann Encke in 1872 recalls the fact. There are

MARCO POLO TIP

Knight of the Black Pudding Insider Tip

Marcus Benser was awarded this title by the French fraternity Confrérie des Chevaliers du Goûte Boudin. This means good business for his Berlin black pudding factory, including orders from top chefs (Blutwurstmanufaktur, Karl-Marx-Platz 9–11, www.blutwurstmanufaktur.de).

plans to construct a Buddhist temple opposite. The papal nunciature lies on the eastern margin of the park, just inside Kreuzberg.

The Bohemian village (Böhmisches Dorf) around Richardplatz (U 7 to Karl-Marx-Strasse) is an unexpected oasis of seclusion in the midst of Berlin. The village still has its 18th century smithy, the oldest in Berlin, and it is possible to rent horse-drawn carriages for a nostalgic ride. King Friedrich Wilhelm I allowed the village to be built in 1737 for the settlement of Bohemian religious refugees. »Bohemian Rixdorf« remained independent until 1873. Nowadays its community still carries on customs such as the Easter walk to the Bohemian cemetery. The most idyllic spot in this idyll is the **Comenius Garden**, which recalls the teachings of the Bohemian brotherhood's last bishop, Johann Amos Comenius (1592 – 1670).

*Böhmisches Dorf (P 20)

Britz is bounded to the north by the Teltowkanal (U 7 to Parchimer Allee). This is where Bruno Taut and Martin Wagner built their **Hufeisensiedlung** (horseshoe estate), one of the most famous major housing projects from the time of the Weimar Republic, and a World Heritage site since 2008. The nucleus of the 1024 dwellings on the estate is formed by the buildings on Louise-Reuter-Ring, built between 1924 and 1927. The centre of the old village between Britzer Damm and the street called Alt-Britz is dominated by the **Britzer Dorfkirche** or village church, which picturesquely overlooks the scene from a hill that rises away from the village pond. The stone building dates from the 13th century, though a crypt (now the sacristy) was added in 1766. Among the church's possessions is an altar donated in 1720 and a late medieval font made from Nuremberg brass. Schloss Britz and park To the west of the village centre on Fulhamer Allee is ***Schloss Britz**. It dates from 1547 and gained its present appearance in 1706 at the instigation of the lord of the manor, Field Marshall von Erlach. The stables have been converted to accommodate the Museum Neukölln, a music school and an open-air stage. Teams of young trainees run the hotel and restaurant. To the

Britz (Q 20)

> ! *Neuköllner Opera* Insider Tip
>
> Real opera aficionados go to the Staatsoper Unter den Linden as well, but the name »Neuköllner Oper« makes their eyes sparkle. The stage at Karl-Marx-Straße 131-133 is among the most experimental of the German opera scene – to be experienced every year at the Neuköllner opera competition, among other occasions (U 7 to Karl-Marx-Straße; tel. 030 68 89 07-0, www.neukoellneroper.de).

south of Britz, the broad parkland of the **Britzer Garten** extends between Buckower Damm and Mohriner Allee (U 7 to Britz-Süd, then by 144 bus). It is a popular leisure destination and has some unique features, such as the »Katastrophenbrunnen« (Catastrophe Fountain) or the »Rhizomatischen Brücke« (Rhizome Bridge). On Buckower Damm at the eastern edge of the park stands the Britzer Mühle, a Dutch windmill dating from 1865.

Museum Neukölln: Tue–Sun 11am–6pm; www.museum-neukoelln.de; www.schloss-britz.de

Britzer Garten: U 7 to Britz-Süd, then bus 181 to the entrance on Mohriner Allee; daily from 9am; admission €3 ; www.gruen-berlin.de

Buckower Dorfkirche

The **parish church of Buckow village** (U 7 to Johannisthaler Chaussee, then by X 11, 172 or 736 bus) was built between 1220 and 1250. The early Gothic stone blocks of the present gabled building date to the 19th-century period of Wilhelm II, although the late Gothic cross vault is 15th century. The west tower is the only one in Berlin which has remained unaltered since the 13th century. It also has a bell dating from the time it was built. A second bell has been dated to 1322. An impressive epitaph to Johann von Hohenlohe, who was killed in the battle of Kremmener Damm in 1412, is considered the **oldest panel painting in Berlin**.

✷ Nikolaiviertel

✦ **L 17**

Location: Mitte
S-Bahn and U-Bahn: Alexanderplatz (S 3, S 5, S 7, S 75, S 9, U 8)

City centre plan: C 13/14

The Nikolai Quarter, which now exudes the atmosphere of old Berlin, with all kinds of shops and taverns to attract tourists, is indeed a historic nucleus of the city.

Distilled idyll

In the area around where the Nikolaikirche later came into existence, the eastern part of the twin settlement of Cölln-Berlin grew up alongside a ford on the Spree. In 1981 the site southwest of the Rotes Rathaus (▶Rathaus Buildings), bounded by Spandauer Strasse, Molkenmarkt, Mühlendamm, Rathausstrasse and the Spree, was selected by the East German government for the building of an »Island of Old Berliner Milieu« that was to be completed in time for Berlin's 750th anniversary celebrations in 1987. The project was to assemble various historic features, some of which had originally been situated at other sites in the city. Where no suitable original was available, a modern equivalent was to be built to emulate its historic predecessor.

A mixture of nostalgia and genuine history in the Nikolaiviertel

The Nikolaikirche or Church of St Nicholas, **the oldest ecclesiastical building in Berlin**, is aligned in an east-west direction at an angle to the street grid of the original settlement. The original church was a Romanesque stone basilica dedicated in 1230 to St Nicholas, patron saint of mariners and merchants. The western part of this building remains in existence. A new building was begun in 1380 and completed in 1470. It comprised a late-Gothic brick hall with an overarching gabled roof and twin towers standing in close proximity to one another. The interior was rebuilt in 1817 by F. W. Langhans and the building was renovated again from 1876 to 1878, at which time the towers took on their present form. The Lady Chapel with a stepped gable roof abutting the front of the towers on the right-hand side dates from 1452. In 1809 Berlin's first elected city council was sworn in in the Nikolaikirche, and in 1991 the first freely elected chamber of deputies for the whole of Berlin assembled here for its constitutive meeting. In the Second World War air raids destroyed much of the interior. Some remnants of late medieval murals have been exposed in the choir. The Kötteritz Chapel, a masterpiece of the late Renaissance, and the Krautsch tomb, one of Berlin's finest 18th-century funeral monuments, are reconstructions. Other interesting features include the grave of Daniel Männlich by Andreas Schlüter and the Renaissance epitaphs for Paul Schultheiss and Johann Zeideler. Several other notables are buried here including the teacher of natural law Samuel Pufendorf (1632 to 1694; his grave is on the outside of the choir) and the pietist Philipp Jakob Spener (1635 – 1705). Paul Gerhardt (1607 – 76), composer of several Lutheran hymns, was vicar of the Nikolaikirche from 1657 to 1666. There is an exhibition by the Stadtmuseum Berlin up in the gallery that features him and various other personalities that have been associated with the church.

*Nikolaikirche

❶ Daily 10am–6pm; admission €5 ; www.stadtmuseum.de

Lessinghaus   Nikolaikirchplatz no. 10 was the home of German author Gotthold
Ephraim Lessing from 1752 to 1755. It has been reconstructed and is
now no. 7.

»Zum   Hearty Berlin specialities, such as Eisbein (knuckle of pork), sauer-
Nussbaum«   kraut and mashed potatoes are all available in the »Zum Nussbaum«
restaurant, situated in a gabled house at the corner of Nikolaikirchplatz and Propststrasse. One of the tavern's appreciative guests in
former times was Heinrich Zille, although in those days the building
was located on the Fischerinsel, where it is known to have stood since
about 1570.

Propststrasse   The life and works of Heinrich Zille are illustrated in the **Heinrich-
Zille Museum** at Propststr. 11 At the end of Propststrasse stands the
bronze **Drachentöter** statue of St George killing the dragon, created
by August Kiss in 1856. As of 1865 the statue stood in the first courtyard of the Berlin Stadtschloss. It was moved to the Volkspark in
Friedrichshain after the Second World War.

❶ Zille-Museum: Mon–Sat 11am– 6pm, Sun 1pm–6pm; admission €6; www.
zillemuesum-berlin.de

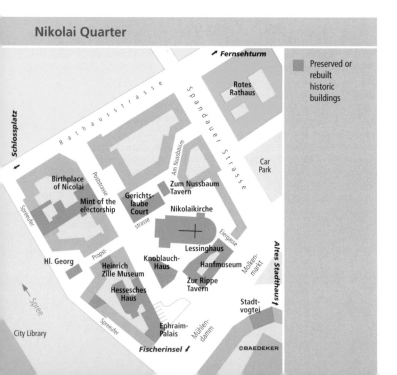

Nikolai Quarter

Preserved or rebuilt historic buildings

Fernsehturm

Schlossplatz

Rathausstrasse

Spandauer Strasse

Rotes Rathaus

Car Park

Birthplace of Nicolai

Poststrasse

Am Nussbaum

Spreeufer

Mint of the electorship

Gerichts-laube Court

Zum Nussbaum Tavern

strasse

Nikolaikirche

Eiergasse

Lessinghaus

Altes Stadthaus

Hl. Georg

Propst-

Knoblauch-Haus

Hanfmuseum

Molken-markt

Spree

Heinrich Zille Museum

Zur Rippe Tavern

Hessesches Haus

Stadt-vogtei

Spreeufer

Ephraim-Palais

Mühlen-damm

City Library

Fischerinsel

©BAEDEKER

Some of the buildings on Poststrasse have been at their current loca- **Poststrasse**
tions throughout their history. No. 4 was the birthplace of the book-
seller and publisher Friedrich Nicolai (1733 – 1811), no. 5 was the
city's mint at the time of the electors and no. 12 is an original too,
going by the name of the Hessesche Haus. Diagonally across from the
entrance to the church is the **Gerichtslaube**, the old town hall or
Rathaus in the Middle Ages (now a restaurant). Its original location
was 200m/220yd further to the north but the building was demolished in 1870. Afterwards a reconstruction was built in the park at
Schloss Babelsberg (▶p.366). As such the Gerichtslaube building in
the Nikolaiviertel is actually a copy of a copy. The *Knoblauchhaus**
at the corner of Nikolaikirchplatz and Poststrasse was reconstructed
in 1989 on its original site. The building was initially commissioned
by pin-maker Johann Christian Knoblauch and was built between
1754 and 1760. The well-to-do family – Eduard Knoblauch, architect
of the new synagogue on Oranienburger Strasse (▶p.303) is a more
recent descendant – received many prominent visitors in the house,
including Lessing, Mendelssohn, Wilhelm von Humboldt, Scharnhorst and Baron vom Stein. An exhibition focuses on the history of
the family during the 19th century and is located in rooms furnished
in the original style of the times.

Knoblauchhaus: Tue, Thu–Sun 10am–6pm, admission free; www.
stadtmuseum.de

At the corner of Poststrasse and Mühlendammbrücke the Ephraim ***Ephraim**
Palais, which was demolished in 1935, has been reconstructed some **Palais**
16m/50ft from its original location. Originally known as the »Ton-
nenbindersche Haus«, it was modified and expanded in 1763/64 for
Nathan Veitel Heine Ephraim (1703 – 75), master of the mint in the
time of Friedrich the Great. The result was a four-storey city mansion
in fine Rococo style with a façade that was rounded at the corners, as
well as some magnificent balconies. It was dubbed **»the prettiest
corner in Berlin«**. The interior is no less beautiful, particularly the
stairway and a copy of Schlüter's ceiling from the Wartenberg Palais.
Here the Stadtmuseum Berlin puts on changing exhibitions and displays part of its prints collection.

❶ Tue, Thu–Sun 10am–6pm, Wed noon–8pm); admission €5;
www.stadtmuseum.de

Mühlendamm leads along the front of the Ephraim Palais past a recon- **Hanfmuseum**
struction of the »Zur Rippe« tavern, originally established in 1665, to
another reconstructed town house (no. 5). This contains Germany's
only Hanfmuseum or **Museum of Hemp**, which tells visitors all there
is to know about this inestimably useful yet oft ignored plant.

❶ Tue–Fri 10am–8pm, Sat and Sun noon–8pm ; admission €4.50,
www.hanfmuseum.de

MOLKENMARKT

Molkenmarkt

Molkenmarkt, which once bore the name Alter Markt, was perhaps the original core of Berlin. The name comes from the Low German word »Mollen«, referring to the mills (German: Mühlen) of Mühlendamm. This was where Berlin's earliest settlement was situated, along with its first town hall or Rathaus. From here the original river crossing, Mühlendamm itself, linked the two settlements Berlin and Cölln on either side of the Spree. There is nothing of this to be seen nowadays. Berlin's earliest core is submerged beneath the massive interchange between Mühlendamm and Spandauer Strasse. Rising 80m/260ft above the drone of traffic is the tower of the **Altes Stadthaus**. The administrative building was built between 1902 and 1911 according to a design by Ludwig Hoffmann for the city's local services. It later became the base for the East German Council of Ministers and is now the headquarters of the internal senate. Molkenmarkt was previously the site of a building known as Alter Krögel and the city bailiwick, but they were demolished in 1935 to make way for the **Reichsmünze** (National Mint). This later became the headquarters of the East German culture ministry. It has now become a cool locations, especially during fashion fairs. The front of the building has a copy of a frieze Gottfried von Schadow made from sketches by Friedrich Gilly and modelled on murals that were made for the earliest mint building on Werderscher Markt. The original is now situated in Charlottenburg on the building at Spandauer Damm 42 – 44. The mint building also incorporates Palais Schwerin, designed by de Bodt in 1704.

> **!** *Not guilty...* Insider Tip
>
> MARCO ⊕ POLO TIP
>
> You don't have to be the accused to take a look at the wonderful Art Nouveau stairway in the law courts in Littenstrasse.

Parochial-kirche

Parochialstrasse leads through the gap between the Altes Stadthaus and the Neues Stadthaus down towards the Parochialkirche (parish church). This was begun by court builder Grünberg in 1695 using plans by Johann Arnold Nering and was completed by Philipp Gerlach in 1714. It was **Berlin's first Baroque church**. It suffered serious damage during the Second World War but the tower was preserved. The tower once contained a Dutch glockenspiel with 37 bells, installed there for Friedrich Wilhelm I. It played for the first time in 1715 but since 1944 it has not been heard again. The church cemetery contains the grave of Kaspar Wegely († 1764), founder of the Königliche Porzellan-Manufaktur (Royal Porcelain Factory).

Remnants of city wall, »Zur letzten Instanz«

Behind the church on Waisenstrasse there are some remnants of Berlin's medieval city walls from the 13th/14th century. Waisenstr no. 16 is allegedly the **oldest tavern in Berlin**. Its name, »Zur letzten Instanz«, a reference to the court of ultimate resort, is explained by the tavern's proximity to Berlin's municipal court. Now, as then, hearty Berlin specialities are on the menu.

The 13th-century church on Klosterstrasse was part of the Franciscan monastery founded in 1254, which stood on land belonging to a neighbouring park. In 1574 it became a school called the »Gymnasium im Grauen Kloster«. Its alumni included Gottfried Schadow, Friedrich Schleiermacher, Karl Friedrich Schinkel and Otto von Bismarck. Friedrich Ludwig Jahn was not only a pupil but became a teacher as well. Its ruins are now a memorial repudiating war; there is an exhibition of sculptures here by Berlin artists.

Franziskaner-klosterkirche

✳ Olympic Site

✳ **M 9 west**

Location: Olympischer Platz, Charlottenburg
S-Bahn and U-Bahn: Olympiastadion (S 5, S 75, U 2)

The XIth Olympic Games took place in Berlin in 1936. For the ruling Nazis it was a welcome opportunity to portray the Third Reich as a peaceful and tolerant nation.

Wherever would you find a blue tartan track? In Berlin's Olympic Stadium, where else?

Most of the events were held at the so-called Reichssportfeld in the western part of Charlottenburg. It comprised the Harbig Sporthalle, the Sportforum built between 1926 and 1928 and the Haus des Deutschen Sports (House of German Sport) from 1932. The swimming stadium was situated to the north of the site with the hockey stadium and the equestrian arena to the south. The site as a whole still exudes the monumental character implicit in the art and architecture of the Third Reich, from its sculptures fashioned by prominent Nazi artists to the massive Olympic arena beyond the Olympic Gate. The centrepiece of the site is the Olympic stadium itself, built between 1934 and 1936 according to plans by Werner March, although Hitler himself and his favourite architect, Albert Speer, both had considerable input. It was built as a replacement for the Deutsches Stadion, which had been built in 1913 by Werner March's father Otto on the same site. The new stadium was designed to accommodate 100,000 spectators (it seats 76,000 today). The stadium oval rises to only 16.5m/52.5ft as seen from the outside, as the actual playing fields were sunk by some 12m/39ft. The Marathontor, the gate at the west of the site, bears the names of all the Olympic champions from 1936. After the Second World War the Sportforum was used as a headquarters by the British and the Maifeld playing fields were given over to polo and cricket. Nowadays the stadium has been newly renovated, roofed and equipped with a blue tartan track. It hosts both athletics events and concerts and is the home ground of Hertha BSC Berlin football club. Each May it also serves as the venue for Germany's football cup final.

❶ Daily 9am – 7pm; June – mid-Sep until 8pm; Nov – mid-March until 4pm. Tours €7; www.olympiastadion-berlin.de

Maifeld   The Maifeld playing fields were used for equestrian dressage and polo matches, though it was later employed as a parade ground. To the west of the fields stands a bell tower some 77m/253ft high that was originally called the »Führerturm«. It was destroyed during the war but was rebuilt in 1962. The old bell is now situated in front of the southern entrance to the stadium. Its observation platform provides a fabulous view that stretches as far as Potsdam and the Müggelberge hills. The Langemarckhalle under the stands was intended as a tribute to the dead at the battle of Langemarck (1914), primarily school scholars and students who had joined volunteer regiments. Nazi propaganda heralded the battle as an »example of selfless courage and sacrifice«. Nowadays an exhibition recounts the history of the stadium and screens a film about the development of the Olympic Games.

Bell tower: April–Oct daily 10am–6pm; admission €4; www.glockenturm.de

Waldbühne   To the north of the Maifeld in the Murellenberge hills, Werner March built the Waldbühne, an open-air theatre in the form of an amphitheatre seating 20,000 people. It was completed in 1936 and used by the Nazis for their so-called »Thing plays«. Nowadays it is a popular venue for. Bob Dylan and the Rolling Stones are among those who have played there and contributed to the fact that the site is no longer associated with the evil sentiments of its builders.

** Parliament and Government Precinct

✳ **J/K 15**

Location: Tiergarten, Mitte
Bus: 85, 100
S-Bahn: Unter den Linden

(S 1, S 2, S 25, S 26)
City centre plan:
A/B 9/10

Germany's parliament, its ministries and offices are scattered across the city centre, mainly in the districts Tiergarten and Mitte, and are accommodated in various buildings, old and new.

The government quarter extends from the Bundesinnenministerium (interior ministry) at the Moabiter Spreebogen Center in the west as

The Bundestag, the German parliament, meets in the Reichstag building

DEM DEUTSCHEN VOLKE

far as the Auswärtiges Amt (foreign office) on Werderscher Markt in the east, and from the Bundesfinanzministerium (finance ministry/treasury) in the south at Leipziger Strasse to the Bundeswirtschaftsministerium (economics ministry) on Invalidenstrasse in the north. The place where power in the land is really concentrated is on the site between the Reichstag building and the Spree, known as the **Spreebogen**. Until the Second World War this was a middle class housing district called the Alsenviertel. However, during the Nazi dictatorship, Hitler's architect Albert Speer devised plans to build his Grosse Volkshalle here, a gigantic domed building 290m/950ft in height. By 1942, before Berlin had suffered from its really major air raids, most of the area had already been demolished. The only building that has survived from that time is the Swiss embassy. The land remained desolate after the war until a general plan for the site by architects Axel Schultes and Charlotte Frank – incorporating the so-called **»Band des Bundes«**, a strip of land running from east to west across the Spreebogen site – conceived the new chancellery (Bundeskanzleramt) and offices for members of parliament.

** REICHSTAG BUILDING · BUNDESTAG

History of the Reichstag When the establishment of the German Empire or »Reich« was proclaimed on 18 January 1871, Prussian capital Berlin was declared capital of the new German state. Its new parliamentary body, the Reichstag, needed a prestigious building to replace its temporary home at Leipziger Strasse 74 in the Royal Porcelain Factory. **Paul Wallot** was commissioned to realize the new building, which he built between 1884 and 1894 in the style of a squat neo-Renaissance palace. The Kaiser himself laid the foundation stone. 30 million Reichsmarks were diverted from the war reparations paid by France in 1871. It was not until 1916, though, that the famous inscription was added to the gable: »Dem Deutschen Volke«, »For the German People«. On 9 November 1918, power really did accede in a sense to the German people when, from the Reichstag building itself, Philipp Scheidemann declared Germany a republic. **Reichstag fire** On the evening of 27 February 1933 the Reichstag caught fire. The »Reichstag fire« entered the pages of history but the cause of the fire has never been indisputably established. The Nazis suggested that the blaze was the result of a plot by the German communist party, the KPD. However, this was called into question when two of the suspects, **Georgij Dimitroff and Ernst Torgler**, were cleared of arson by a Leipzig court in December 1933, even though one other suspect, **Marinus van der Lubbe** was convicted and sentenced to death by the same court. The alternative theory, championed most loudly by the KPD, was that the Nazis started the fire themselves in order to use it against their political opponents, though this too has never been proven. Nevertheless, the political consequences of the Reichstag fire were drastic. The crime was used as an excuse to declare the **»emergency law to protect the people and state«** on 28 February 1933, which suspended German citizens' basic rights and gave the National Socialists the opportunity to persecute and eliminate their opponents shortly before the Reichstag elections took place on 5 March 1933. Subsequent to the fire, the building fell into disuse and was not renovated. The Reichstag's elected officials moved into the **Krolloper** building in the Tiergarten (where the Kongresshalle now stands, ▶p.315) – although under the Nazis parliament lost all semblance of importance anyway. On 30 April 1945 two soldiers of the Soviet Red Army hoisted the Soviet flag over the ruins of the Reichstag building. That same day, Hitler committed suicide in his »Führerbunker« just a few hundred metres away (information board on Vossstrasse).

Reconstruction of the building was not finished until 1970. Even then it was decided not to rebuild the dome blown up by a demolition team in 1957. For symbolic reasons the West German parliament, the Bundestag, held regular sittings in the Reichstag, evoking equally regular protests from the Soviet Union and the East Germans. On 4 October 1990, a body comprising members of both the Bundestag and East Germany's Volkskammer held its very first sitting in the plenary hall and 17 January 1991 saw the first constitutional meeting of a pan-German parliament voted for by the reunited German people in the election held on 2 December 1990. The Bundestag held its first sitting in the newly reconstructed Reichstag building, an inaugural ceremony for the new edifice, on 19 April 1999.

Reconstruction

> **MARCO ⊕ POLO TIP**
>
> **!** *Art for architecture* **Insider Tip**
>
> 111 artists have worked on the parliament buildings, and their work can be viewed on free tours. Make a booking at: besucherdienst@bundestag.de; dates:
> Reichstag building: Sat, Sun, holidays 11.30am
> Jakob-Kaiser-Haus: Sat, Sun, holidays 2pm and 4pm
> Marie-Elisabeth-Lüders-Haus: Sat, Sun, holidays noon and 2pm

During the latest rebuilding, an event took place that would draw the eyes of the entire international art world to Berlin. In June and July 1995 the whole building disappeared for two weeks under 100,000 sq m/25ac of glittering silvery fabric. The American-Bulgarian artist Christo and his wife Jeanne-Claude had doggedly pursued their **»Wrapped Reichstag«** idea since 1971, and on 20 June 1994 the Bundestag finally voted that it could take place. The outstanding success of the project was a thorough vindication of the artists' vision.

More Deputies = More Democracy?

In relation to the population of the country, the Bundestag is one of the world's biggest parliaments. This is especially clear from the comparison of how many people are represented by one member of parliament. Is this more democracy? It certainly means more bureaucracy.

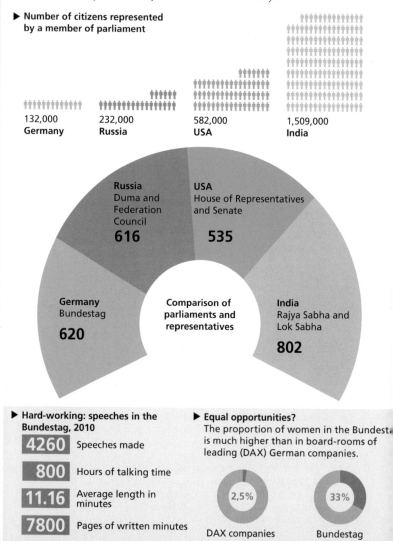

▶ **Number of citizens represented by a member of parliament**

132,000	232,000	582,000	1,509,000
Germany	**Russia**	**USA**	**India**

Russia
Duma and Federation Council
616

USA
House of Representatives and Senate
535

Germany
Bundestag
620

Comparison of parliaments and representatives

India
Rajya Sabha and Lok Sabha
802

▶ **Hard-working: speeches in the Bundestag, 2010**

4260	Speeches made
800	Hours of talking time
11.16	Average length in minutes
7800	Pages of written minutes

▶ **Equal opportunities?**
The proportion of women in the Bundesta is much higher than in board-rooms of leading (DAX) German companies.

2,5% — DAX companies

33% — Bundestag

Employees of the Bundestag, federal ministries and Bundesrat (upper house)
Directly employed by the Bundestag: 28,430, Bundestag budget 682 million €

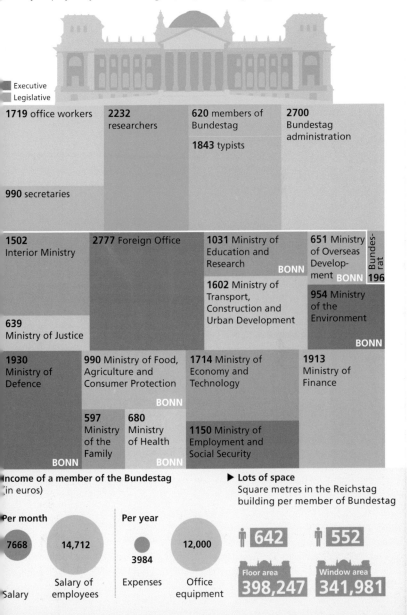

Executive
Legislative

1719 office workers

2232 researchers

620 members of Bundestag

1843 typists

2700 Bundestag administration

990 secretaries

1502 Interior Ministry

2777 Foreign Office

1031 Ministry of Education and Research BONN

651 Ministry of Overseas Development BONN

Bundesrat **196**

1602 Ministry of Transport, Construction and Urban Development

954 Ministry of the Environment BONN

639 Ministry of Justice

1930 Ministry of Defence BONN

990 Ministry of Food, Agriculture and Consumer Protection BONN

597 Ministry of the Family BONN

680 Ministry of Health BONN

1714 Ministry of Economy and Technology

1150 Ministry of Employment and Social Security

1913 Ministry of Finance

Income of a member of the Bundestag (in euros)

Per month
7668 — Salary
14,712 — Salary of employees

Per year
3984 — Expenses
12,000 — Office equipment

▶ **Lots of space**
Square metres in the Reichstag building per member of Bundestag

642   552

Floor area **398,247**   Window area **341,981**

Seat of German Parliaments

Inaugurated in 1894 and burned down in 1933. Bombarded in 1945 but since 1990 the seat of parliament for all of Germany. The history of the Reichstag building has been rich and varied. Its new dome has become a Berlin landmark.

❶ Dome

The glass dome is 23.5m/77ft high and its base has a diameter of some 40m/131ft. Two ramps wind up the inside in different directions as far as an observation platform (and back down again). The objective of the dome is to allow entry of air into the building and its mirrored design directs light into the plenary hall.

❷ Roof terrace

In the roof garden restaurant you can take a break (reservation recommended, tel. 22629933)

❸ Plenary hall

The plenary hall houses parliamentary sessions. Seen from where the members sit, the seats occupied by the government are on the left of the lectern and the parliament's president, while officials of the Bundesrat (house of the Bundesländer) sit on the right.

❹ Party meeting rooms

The north and the south wing contain rooms for party meetings; the office of the parliament's president is in the south wing.

❺ Modern Art

Contemporary artists have donated works of art to the Reichstag, including the colours of the German flag in the entrance hall in a work by Gerhard Richter as well as a floor relief by Ulrich Rückriem in the atrium.

❻ Graffitti

Some inscriptions carved into the newly conquered walls by Soviet troops have been preserved.

❼ Security gates

Everyone has to pass through a security gate before going up to the dome in glass lifts.

The Reichstag in 1930 with the original dome by Paul Wallot

an eagle (nicknamed the
«   » or »Fat Hen«) is made
        ing 2.5 tons. It was
    e 1950s by Ludwig Gies.
    version was made by the
    amp metals and machine
    tory in the Münsterland.

2

3

4

5

7

At the base of the dome there is an exhibition on the history of the Reichstag.

The Ge[...]
»Fette Her[...]
of aluminiu[...]
designed in [...]
The curren[...]
Trende[...]
f[...]

©BAEDEKER

1

4

5 **6**

Press photographers have an excellent view of all that goes on.

The new design | The latest version of the Reichstag building was designed by the British architect **Norman Foster**. Keeping only the exterior walls, the resulting edifice is now a highly functional, modern parliament building, and there are few places where the original fabric peeks through. The finest architectural feature is undoubtedly the glass ****Dome** dome. Illuminated at night, it has become a landmark, a symbol of the new Berlin and one of its biggest tourist attractions: a spiral ramp leads up the inside of the structure to an observation platform with excellent views of the city. To visit the dome, register at least two days in advance, giving your name and date of birth.

❶ Dome reservations: www.bundestag.de/besuche or Deutscher Bundestag, Besucherdienst, Platz der Republik 1, 11011 Berlin

OTHER BUILDINGS IN AND AROUND THE SPREEBOGEN

*Bundeskanzleramt | The Bundeskanzleramt, the new chancellery opposite the Reichstag building, forms an intriguing architectural counterpoint. Axel Schultes and Charlotte Frank designed a structure with two long rows of offices, some 18m/60ft high and 335m/366yd long in the case of the southern wing, linked by a nine-storey cube rising to 36m/120ft. This is where the power behind the German government is really concentrated. On the sixth floor is the cabinet room with the office of the chancellor above it. To the east there is a courtyard adorned with Eduardo Chilida's »Berlin« sculpture. Towards the west the office wings reach all the way to the Spree, although a bridge then leads across the river to the Kanzlergarten or Chancellor's Gardens on the opposite bank. The monumental character of the building has come in for some rough criticism. The populace themselves, though, have treated it with rather more humour, dubbing the chancellery with nicknames such as the »Bundeswaschmaschine«, (federal washing machine) due to the circular windows in the central cube, or the »Kohlosseum«, a reference to former chancellor Helmut Kohl, who was the building's prime champion.

?

The phantom of the Bundestag

The delicate-looking link between the Marie-Elisabeth-Lüders-Haus and Paul-Löbe-Haus across the Spree is unofficially called Jakob-Mierscheid-Steg. Who was Jakob Mierscheid? A worthy parliamentarian? Seemingly not – he is a phantom, invented by his real-life colleagues. Nevertheless, he has managed to get an entry in the Bundestag handbook (www.bundestag.de).

Swiss embassy | The most exclusive address for any diplomat, at least in terms of proximity to the seat of power in Germany, can be claimed by the Swiss. Their building was the only one to survive the destruction during the war and is now the immediate neighbour of the Bundes-kanzleramt, although the great slab-like presence of the new building hardly sets off the neighbouring palais from 1870 to best effect.

Across the Spree rises the Hauptbahnhof, a huge glass train station that was opened in 2006. On the site of a modest earlier station, the Lehrter Stadtbahnhof, the architect Meinhard v. Gerkan built what is Germany's fourth-busiest passenger station, arranging the tracks on different levels in a cross shape: the upper station shed for urban and long-distance trains with six platforms, 15m/50ft above street level, stretches 321m/350yd from east to west; the north-south hall lies 15m/50ft below street level and has eight long-distance and two subway platforms (▶p.171). In-between are three storeys with shops, gastronomy and service; above the upper train level are two 46m/150ft office towers.

Hauptbahn-hof

North of the Reichstag building stands the massive but seemingly transparent Paul-Löbe building, designed by Stephan Braunfels and named after formed social democratic president of the pre-war Reichstag Paul Löbe (1875 – 1967). The eight-storey building with its high, turned up canopy accommodates nearly 1000 offices, meeting rooms and the Bundestag's visitor services.

Paul-Löbe-Haus

A catwalk leads from the Paul-Löbe-Haus across the Spree to the Marie-Elisabeth-Lüders-Haus. This is another Braunfels-designed building that houses the Bundestag's library and its research services. The name of the building recalls the liberal politician Marie Elisabeth Lüders (1878 – 1966).

Marie-Elisa-beth-Lüders-Haus

The largest of the new buildings on the Bundestag site, at least in terms of area covered, is named after a co-founder of Germany's conservative CDU party, Jakob Kaiser (1888 – 1961). The building was conceived by a group of architects' bureaux and stretches beyond the Reichstag down both sides of Dorotheenstrasse, providing direct access to Pariser Platz alongside the ▶Brandenburg Gate. Among the offices in the building is that of the Bundestag president.

Jakob-Kaiser-Haus

Wherever power is assembled, the media is never far away. Germany's national broadcaster **ARD** has its main studio beyond Wilhelmstrasse, directly adjoining the Jakob-Kaiser-Haus on the river bank next to the Reichstag. Further east, directly below Friedrichstrasse station, is the Bundespresseamt or national press office, while Germany's second public TV channel **ZDF** is based at Unter den Linden 36 – 38. The **Bundespressekonferenz**, an association of journalists, has its headquarters to the north of the Lüders building on Schiffbauerdamm.

Bundes-presseamt

ARD-Hauptstadtstudio: for tours register at www.ard-infocenter.de or tel. 030 22 88 11 10

* Pfaueninsel

✳ T 8 southwest

Location: Zehlendorf
S-Bahn: Wannsee (S 1, S 7), then by 218 bus and ferry

The »pearl of the Havel lakes is one of the Berliners' favourite destinations for a day trip and a World Heritage site. Here King Friedrich Wilhelm II created his own personal Arcadia.

The Pfaueninsel is an island some 1.5km/1mi in length and 500m/550yd wide, situated midstream in the river Havel at the southwestern tip of Berlin. It is now a protected nature reserve with centuries-old trees and rich bird-life. The 98ha/242-acre islet was dubbed Pfaueninsel in the 17th century, but unexpectedly the name does not derive from the modern German word for a peacock, »Pfau«, but from the Middle Low German word »page« meaning »horse«. Before being so named, the island was used by the Great Elector for breeding rabbits, at which time it was known as the Kaninchenwerder or »rabbit eyot«. Also under the Great Elector, a spot on the eastern side of the island was used by alchemist **Johann Kunckel von Löwenstern**, who produced his highly coveted ruby water here in 1685. Remains of his laboratory were discovered in 1972.

Palace In 1793 Prussia's King Friedrich Wilhelm II rediscovered the island and commissioned master carpenter Alfred Brendel to fashion a love nest for himself and his mistress Wilhelmine Encke, later to be known as the Countess Lichtenau. The small wooden **palace** with painted imitation of masonry, which can still be seen today, was built during the period 1794 to 1797 and was allegedly based on a sketch by the countess herself. As the king wanted to enjoy a rustic idyll with cows and farm hands, Brendel built a dairy in 1795, in the same romantic ruined look as the little palace. Friedrich Wilhelm III and his wife Queen Luise were also fond of the island. It was during their time that the island actually was populated with peacocks, and the descendants of these birds inhabit the eyot today. The little pleasure palace is constructed in the style of a romantic ruin. Its two towers are connected by a bridge that was originally made of wood, but was replaced with an iron structure in 1807: the ironwork is an early example of the skill

! **Audio guide** *Insider Tip*

MARCO ⊕ POLO TIP

At five significant spots on the island, visitors can get to know aspects of the history of the Pfaueninsel, downloading onto their mobile phones sound collages on topics such as »Games and Festivities«, »Queen Luise and the War« or »The Royal Menagerie«. The files are available free of charge at www.luise.tomis.mobi.

Pfaueninsel

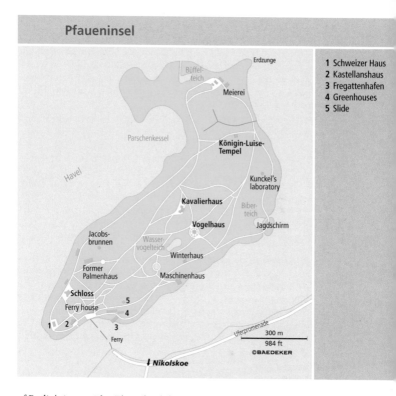

1 Schweizer Haus
2 Kastellanshaus
3 Fregattenhafen
4 Greenhouses
5 Slide

of Berlin's ironsmiths. The splendid interior of the palace shows exquisite taste and testifies to the craftsmanship that was a hallmark of Berlin and Potsdam in the late 18th century and early 19th centuries. The most beautiful examples are the classical Great Hall on the upper floor and the iron spiral staircase.

❶ April–Oct Tue–Sun 10am–5pm; (only with a tour); admission €3; www.spsg.de

Park

Peter Joseph Lenné designed the park between 1821 and 1834. A menagerie that was set up by Friedrich Wilhelm III but abandoned in 1842 was to form the basis for the collection at the ▶Zoologischer Garten. Schinkel's Palmenhaus burned down at the end of the 19th century and a rose garden was moved from here to the park at Sanssouci. What did remain were such unusual trees as Weymouth and Swiss pines, giant sequoia, ginkgos and cedars as well as native plants. There are other buildings as well as the little palace. The southern part of the island has Schinkel's Schweizerhaus (1830), the Russian slide and the Fregattenhafen while another Schinkel building, the Kavaliershaus, graces the centre of the island. The latter was rebuilt between 1824 and 1826 with the façade of a Gothic town house, the Patrizierhaus from Danzig (Gdansk). A memorial temple for Queen Luise in the northern part of the island has the original sandstone portico from the mausoleum in the park around Schloss ▶Charlottenburg (1829).

❶ Nov–Feb 10am–4pm daily, March, April, Sep and Oct 9am–8pm, May–Aug 9am–8pm

✳✳ Potsdamer Platz

✦ **M 15**

Location: Tiergarten
S-Bahn and U-Bahn: Potsdamer Platz (S 1, S 2, S 25, U 2)
City centre plan: C 9 / 10

None of the building work undertaken in the »new Berlin« has caused as much interest as the reconstruction of Potsdamer Platz, at least in terms of the extent of the project. The plan was to redesign from scratch a prime slice of inner city that had lain desolate for decades between the Berlin Wall and the »death strip« parallel to the Wall, and to restore it to its former status as the vibrant heart of one of the world's great cities.

Centre of the new Berlin

Potsdamer Platz was laid out in the 18th century under the name »Platz vor dem Potsdamer Thor« (Thor = gate), receiving its current shortened name in July 1831. Before the Second World War it was the **busiest square in Europe** and, along with neighbouring Leipziger Platz (▶Leipziger Strasse), it formed a hinge between the eastern and western parts of Berlin. Its most memorable landmark was its Verkehrsturm or traffic watchtower, from which a policeman would supervise the vehicles being controlled by the traffic lights that had been installed in 1924, the first such installation in Germany. All around the square there were popular hotels and restaurants such as the **Haus Vaterland**, which was the biggest restaurant in Europe, seating 2000 people, or Hotel Esplanade, where Greta Garbo and Charlie Chaplin would stay and where Wilhelm II hosted men-only sessions in the Kaisersaal. During the Nazi era the notorious Volksgerichtshof or people's court was based next to the hotel. Second World War bombs entirely obliterated the whole square. Practically nothing remained of the earlier buildings, including the Potsdamer Bahnhof station that had been built in 1872 but had to be ripped down after the war. Only **Weinhaus Huth** on the old Potsdamer

Strasse and the **Kaisersaal** of the Esplanade hotel testified to the Berlin that had been there before. Some of the square was honeycombed with underground rooms and passages. This subterranean labyrinth was the reason that the East German government drew the double lines of its Wall so far apart at this point, when they were erecting it in August 1961, so that no one could use the tunnels to escape to the west. The same thinking was behind the decision to withdraw train services to Potsdamer Platz S-Bahn station overnight and wall up its entrances. The Wall had made the square a **no-man's-land** between the twin lines of wall leading south to the Brandenburg Gate. Tank traps, barbed wire, watchtowers and death zones were the features that dominated this desolate space.

After the fall of the Wall, the Berlin senate sought investors and insti- **New life**
gated an architectural contest. The competition was won by Munich architects Hilmer and Sattler, who presented a design based on Berlin's previous street grid. On the basis of this plan, the main investors – Daimler, Sony, Hertie, ABB and Haus Vaterland AG – commissioned internationally renowned architects to create their new buildings on the site. Daimler chose Renzo Piano, Richard Rogers, Arata Isozaki and Hans Kollhoff; Sony went for Helmut Jahn, and ABB for Giorgio Grassi. For years the area was dubbed **Europe's biggest building site** and became a top attraction for the public. The construction work required some major actions, such as the temporary diversion of the Spree. The site became into a completely new district where, amongst primarily commercial buildings, 20% of the new structures are given over to housing, albeit of the most luxuri-

Potsdamer Platz as it was in 1933 with its traffic lights in the centre

ous sort. The main axis of the development is the Neue Potsdamer Strasse, which divides Daimler City from the Sony Center and finishes at Potsdamer Platz itself. Here the roofs of the U-Bahn and S-Bahn stations rise up and there is even a replica of the old traffic light installation. The **Park Kolonnaden** arcades by Giorgio Grass stretch away to the south although, to an extent, they are overshadowed by the Daimler and Sony buildings. At the northern end the decidedly bulky **Beisheim Center** with the Ritz Carlton luxury hotel dominates the scene.

QUARTIER POTSDAMER PLATZ

The first of the major developments to be opened, then called Quartier Daimler Chrysler, was unveiled in 1998. Its focus is Marlene-Dietrich-Platz at the end of Alte Potsdamer Strasse. Various public buildings are concentrated in this area, such as the Grand Hyatt hotel (architect: Rafael Moneo), the Spielbank Berlin casino, the Stage Theater am Potsdamer Platz (Bluemax Theater, Musical Theater and the cinema used for the Berlinale film festival) with its 35m/115ft-high glass foyer (architect: Renzo Piano), its kinked structure abutting against the back of the Staatsbibliothek library by Hans Scharoun at the ▶Kulturforum. Towards the river bank, the Reichpietschufer, is Piano's debis building, a tower rising to some 83m/272ft, panelled in ochre terra-cotta and topped by the green logo of Daimler's now-defunct subsidiary debis.

Marlene-Dietrich-Platz

The Potsdamer Platz Arkaden building, a three-storey shopping mall, largely featuring rather expensive shops, runs from Eichhornstrasse behind the Bluemax Theatre to Haus Huth. In its middle level there are two models that show the plans of the area from 1993 and the results of the development from 1999.

Potsdamer Platz Arkaden

Looking a little forlorn opposite the north entrance to the Arkaden, but still here in its traditional location, is Haus (formerly Weinhaus) Huth. Nowadays it contains the offices of Daimler with art in the Galerie **Daimler Contemporary**, Diekmanns restaurant and a wine dealer, as before.

Haus Huth

❶ Daily 11am–6pm; admission free; www.sammlung.daimler.com

Hans Kollhoff designed the building that stretches from here to Neue Potsdamer Strasse and includes the Cinemaxx cinema (with its 19 screens) and the Kollhof Tower, in which there is a **panorama platform on the 24th and 25th floors**, to which an original piece of the Berlin Wall was taken by helicopter in 2010 to form part of an open-air exhibition about the history of the site. There is also a café.

Kollhoff Tower

Panoramapunkt: daily 10am–8pm; admission €6.50; www.panoramapunkt.de

Various sculptures and installations from the Daimler corporate art collection are spread all over the site: Riding Bikes by Robert Rauschenberg, Méta-Maxi by Jean Tinguely, Galileo by Marc di Suevo, Light Blue by François Morellets, Nam Sat by Nam June Paik, Boxer by Keith Haring and Balloon Flower by Robert Rauschenberg.

Sculptures

Here is also a touch of Hollywood in Berlin: on the strip in the middle of Neue Potsdamer Strasse is a red (asphalt) carpet on which

Boulevard der Stars

The roof of the Sony Center changes colours at night

goldene stars celebrate the big names of the German film and TV business. A trick camera projects the stars like holograms so that fans can have a picture taken with their hero.

SONY CENTER

Forum

In contrast to the Daimler site's conscious reference to traditional urban forms, the buildings in Sony's plan, completed in 2000, can evoke awe in a way that Daimler City's polished dullness does not really achieve. The landmark building here is a 103m/338ft-high glass tower which is now occupied by Deutsche Bahn AG. The Sony Center's seven buildings, as devised by Jahn, cluster around an oval plaza covering 4000 sq m/43,000 sq ft and covered by a light, tent-like sail suspended at a height of 40m/130ft. The roof is particularly impressive under its nightly illumination. Underneath there are cafés, restaurants, Sony's own store, the Cinemaxx multiplex and much more.

Kaisersaal

Part of the Esplanade Hotel with its famous Kaisersaal meeting room was spared destruction from the bombs of the Second World War and this too is now part of the Sony development. It was floated in its entirety on an air bag foundation and moved some 75m/82yd from its previous location to its new site in March 1996. Enclosed in steel and glass and completed by the addition of rebuilt breakfast and silver dining rooms, it now forms part of a new hotel, the Esplanade Residenz.

*Filmmuse-um Berlin

In the direction of the new Potsdamer Strasse are the Filmhaus Berlin with its Mediathek, the German Film and Television Academy and the Arsenal cinema for independent art films. The highlight here, however, is the film and TV museum (Deutsche Kinemathek-Museum für Film und Fernsehen). Anybody taking an interest in film will find this outstandingly designed museum unmissable. It utilizes clever computer and video technology, more than 200 film clips are shown on 84 monitors, and the history of German film is illustrated in a building whose architecture is as fascinating as its contents. Yet even the technology takes second place to the exhibits from the life of Marlene Dietrich: film costumes, her feather boa, a cigarette holder, her own make-up case, even love letters from Jean Gabin, Erich Maria Remarque and Ernest Hemingway. It is almost enough to make you forget that the museum also features other original items, such as the set designs for the first and famous expressionistic film *The Cabinet of Dr. Caligari* and a costume worn by Romy Schneider for her famous role of Empress »Sissi« of Austria.

❶ Tue–Sun 10am–6pm, Thu until 8pm; admission €6; www.deutsche-kinemathek.de

Prenzlauer Berg

✦ H – J 17 – 20

Borough: Pankow
U-Bahn: Senefelderplatz, Eberswalder Strasse, Schönhauser
Allee (U 2)

»Prenzl. Berg« has been transformed; first of all from a work-ing-class quarter to a centre of alternative sub-culture, is now on the way to becoming an upmarket residential area. Some 80 per cent of its residents have moved in recently.

Prenzlauer Berg is one of the most densely populated areas of Berlin. Its five-storey rented apartment buildings are characteristic of what was once a typical working class suburb. It came into existence at the start of the 19th century and was incorporated into Berlin in 1920. During the Second World War the borough suffered little from the bombing apart from at its eastern side, but what the bombs and gre-nades failed to achieve was soon accomplished by the »Magistrat« of East Berlin. Other than a few carefully maintained prestige buildings such as those on Husemannstrasse, little was spent on the upkeep of the buildings. On the other hand, in the dying days of East Germany and certainly in the years since reunification, many of the flats were occupied by young people. In the era of the East German regime of Erich Honecker, any kind of alternative culture was strictly pro-scribed and suppressed, particularly the nascent scene in Prenzlauer Berg, which became a centre of opposition to the GDR government. Nevertheless the autonomously alternative era of »Prenzl. Berg« is almost at an end. The chic ambience of newly renovated housing is attracting prosperous young people from the west, driving the truly alternative out to ▶Friedrichshain.

From workers' suburb to in-quarter

The elevated railway rattling across its steel arches dominates the main thoroughfare of Prenzlauer Berg, Schönhauser Allee. It starts at Senefelderplatz, where there is a monument to **Alois Senefelder** (1771 – 1834), inventor of lithography. The new **Kulturzentrum Pfe-fferberg** is located here in a former brewery, the beer garden of which is listed for protection. A little further to the north there is a Jewish cemetery on the right (▶Cemeteries), which was laid waste by the national socialists in 1943. Opposite the right turn down Wörther Strasse is the Segenskirche (Church of Blessings, 1905/1906), which is fully incorporated into the terraced front of the street. Next comes Sredzkistrasse, with the entrance to *KulturBrauerei the Kultur-Brauerei. This was built by Franz Schwechten for the Schultheiss beer brewers in 1892, at which time it was the biggest lager brewery in the world. The architect was the same man who had designed and built

Schönhauser Allee

Karaoke in the Mauerpark, every Sunday

the Kaiser-Wilhelm-Gedächtniskirche (▶p.237). The KulturBrauerei is now one of Berlin's best venues and includes stages, restaurants and a multiplex cinema as well as being a fine testament to the industrial architecture of the period of Wilhelm II's reign. Under the elevated railway at the intersection of Schönhauser Allee, Danziger Strasse and Kastanienallee it is possible to get a bite to eat at **Konnopke**, a snack bar which is a veritable Berlin institution. It has been owned by the same family since 1930 and its »Currywurst« (▶MARCO POLO Insight p.96) is really well worth trying, although there are plenty more dishes on offer.

Kastanien-allee
Kastanienallee with its eccentric shops and cafés that serve a full breakfast even in the afternoon is changing. The residents are trying to resist upgrading to luxury accommodation, but there are good reasons why the street now has the nickname »Castingallee«. There is still a lovely beer garden, the oldest in Berlin: Prater, opened in 1837. Kastanienallee ends at Zionskirchplatz. In the cellar of the church. consecrated in 1873, an environmental library was founded in 1986 die Umweltbibliothek and became a cell of early protests against the ruling SED party. The library closed in 1998.

Mauerpark
A little further to the west along Eberswalder Strasse is theMauerpark, formerly occupied by a section of the Berlin Wall between Prenzlauer Berg and Wedding. The park is in a shabby condition, but

a flea market is held here at weekends from 7am with karaoke on Sundays, and a few remnants of the Wall remain.

The Gethsemane-Kirche (Gethsemane Church) was opened on Stargarder Strasse near the S-Bahn/U-Bahn station at Schönhauser Allee in 1893. In the final years of the GDR, opponents of the government representing all political viewpoints would meet there.

Gethsemane-Kirche

Wörther Strasse leads from Schönhauser Allee to Kollwitzplatz. A monument erected there by Gustav Seitz in 1959 is in memory of Käthe Kollwitz. She lived in what was then Weissenburger Strasse 25 (now Kollwitzstrasse) from 1891 till the destruction of her house in 1943. On the other side there is a copy of her statue The Mother. Kollwitzplatz is now the centre of Prenzlauer's more up-market scene and is appropriately ringed by bars and cafés, of which Restauration 1900 and Trattoria Lappreggi are among the very best, and Pasternak among the most unusual.

Kollwitzplatz

Husemannstrasse leads from Kollwitzplatz. During the GDR period, the street was expensively renovated for Berlin's 750th anniversary celebrations, but now the ravages of time are beginning to make their presence felt once more. **Dunckerstrasse** is a continuation of Husemannstrasse. At no. 77 an exhibition about life in Prenzlauer Berg around 1900 shows the house that the joiner Brunzel built and furnished in 1895.

Dunckerstrasse: Mon–Sat 11am–4.30pm; admission €2; www.ausstellung-dunckerstrasse.de

Rykestrasse runs parallel to Husemannstrasse. No. 53 contains the only **synagogue** in all of Germany that was not destroyed by the Nazis on »Kristallnacht« or Pogrom Night in 1938. Nevertheless it was later misused as a camp by the Wehrmacht. Its exterior was reconstructed between 1976 and 1978. After expensive restoration it reopened in 2007 and accommodates 1200 worshippers, which makes it the largest German synagogue to have survived the Nazi atrocities. Rykestrasse leads southwards to the premier landmark of Prenzlauer Berg, the tower of the water works built in 1856. The thick round tower itself was added to the plant in 1873. Nazi stormtroopers converted the machine house into a torture chamber in 1933. The hill, a popular meeting place in the summer months, was planted with vines in 2005.

Rykestrasse

Synagogue: Thu 2–6pm (tours 2pm/4pm), Sun 1–5pm (tours 1pm/3pm); admission €3/5

To the east, beyond the heart of the Prenzlauer Berg scene, the former site of a city gas works that closed in 1981 stretches between Danziger Strasse and Greifswalder Strasse. The area has now been made into

Zeiss-Grossplanetarium

the **Ernst-Thälmann-Park**, named after the leader of the communist party who was born in 1886 and murdered at Buchenwald concentration camp in 1944. A bronze memorial to him, created by Soviet sculptor Lew Kerbel and verging on the monumental, has managed to survive reunification. At the northern edge of the park is the spherical dome of the Zeiss-Grossplanetarium, opened in 1987. With the help of a planet projector built by the company Carl Zeiss Jena the explains the workings of the universe.

❶ Prenzlauer Allee 80, Wed–Fri 9am–noon and 1–5pm, Fri also 6–9.30pm, Sat 2.30–9pm, Sun 1.30–5pm; admission €5; information and booking, tel. 42 18 45 0; www.sdtb.de

Rathaus Buildings

As the city has grown from many smaller settlements, Berlin has many town halls. Each district is governed from its own town hall (»Rathaus« in German).

One city, many town halls

The oldest Rathaus for the government of Berlin is said to have been situated at the location of the present-day Rotes Rathaus back in the 13th century. The building was rebuilt several times after fires in 1380, 1448 and 1581. The square in front of its court building, the Gerichtslaube, which was demolished in 1868, was used for executions until 1694. Between 1307 and 1442, when the administrations of Cölln and Berlin were combined, both towns were ruled from a Rathaus next to the bridge, the Lange Brücke (now called the Rathausbrücke). The building was knocked down in 1514. Cölln Rathaus was located on Breite Strasse and was chosen as the seat of a common administration in 1709 when Berlin, Kölln, Friedrichswerder, Friedrichstadt and Dorotheenstadt were combined. Berlin's Rathaus became the base for the city administration. The Rotes Rathaus was used as the seat of the Magistrat and the mayor of Greater Berlin until the end of the Second World War. When the city was divided, East Berlin laid claim to the use of these historical appellations. On 1 October 1991 the administration of the reunited Berlin – the senate – moved back to the Rotes Rathaus, which has been considered the official city hall of Berlin ever since. When the city was booming between 1885 and the start of the First World War, many of the boroughs erected their own prestigious Rat-haus buildings, like the Art Nouveau structure at Charlottenburg, which has the highest Rathaus tower in Berlin (88m/289ft), or those in Köpenick (►Alt-Köpenick) and Steglitz, both fine examples of the neo-Gothic style.

The Rotes Rathaus was built between 1861 and 1869 to a neo-Renaissance design by Hermann Friedrich Waesemann that featured a tower rising up to 74m/243ft. King Wilhelm I took part in the laying of the foundation stone on 11 June 1861. The first sitting of the Magistrat was held at the end of 1865. The name of the Rotes Rathaus literally means »Red City Hall«, the name not being bestowed on the basis of any particular democratic ideal, but simply because of the red colour of its brick façade. The so-called **Steinerne Chronik** runs around the building at about first floor height. This is a frieze of 36 terra-cotta reliefs with scenes from the history of Berlin. In front of the Rotes Rathaus as far as the ▶Fernsehturm and the ▶Marienkirche there is a park that features two sculptures by Fritz Cremer – Trümmerfrau and Aufbauhelfer (Woman Searching in the Rubble and Reconstruction Helper). Furthermore there is a major landmark in Reinhold Begas's **Neptunbrunnen** or Neptune fountain from 1891, which originally stood between the Stadtschloss and the Marstall or royal stud. Its statues represent the sea god Neptune and his court, including four female figures representing the rivers Elbe, Oder, Rhine and Vistula.

*Rotes Rathaus
✢ L 17 • B 14

On the other side of Spandauer Strasse by what was the rear wall of the Palast der Republik (▶Schlossplatz) stands the **Marx-Engels-Forum**, which opened in 1986 and features a statue with Karl Marx (seated) and Friedrich Engels (standing) cast in bronze as well as various metal pillars with etched photographs depicting the »History of Class War«. Shortly after the fall of the Wall one wit added a slogan to the base, declaring »Wir sind unschuldig« – »it's not our fault.« Also known as Sacco and Vanzetti, the two of them have been temporarily moved while the new U-Bahn line 5 is being constructed.

Marx-Engels-Forum

❶ S-Bahn, U-Bahn: Alexanderplatz (S 5, S 7, S 75, U 2, U 5, U 8)

The tower of the Rotes Rathaus stands proudly even in the shadow of the Fernsehturm

Rathaus
Schöneberg
(O 13)

The Rathaus for the borough of Schöneberg was built between 1911 and 1914 and served between 1949 and 1990 as the headquarters for West Berlin's mayor and the seat of its council meetings. It thus has great symbolic importance in terms of the history of West Berlin.To the left of the main entrance there is a **plaque recalling the visit of US President John F. Kennedy**, who in 1963 delivered his famous speech from these steps, in which he declared he too could proudly utter the words, »**Ich bin ein Berliner**« (▶ ill. p.38). The 70m/230ft tower of the Rathaus contains a »freedom bell« paid for by the USA and modelled on the Liberty Bell in Philadelphia. It was handed over on United Nations Day (24 October 1950) by General Lucius D. Clay. It is inscribed with the words »Möge diese Welt mit Gottes Hilfe die Wiedergeburt der Freiheit erleben« – a variation on Abraham Lincoln's theme in his Gettysburg Address: »… this nation, under God, shall have a new birth of freedom«.

❶ U-Bahn: Rathaus Schöneberg (U 4)

✳ Schlossplatz · Werderscher Markt
✦ L 18

Location: Mitte
S-Bahn: Hackescher Markt (S 5, S 7, S 75)
City centre plan: B/C 12/13
Bus: 100, 200

The site occupied until 1950 by the Berliner Stadtschloss, the City Palace, and then until 2009 by the Palast der Republik , is now an empty space where only the Humboldt-Box stands. This state of affairs will remain until the Stadtschloss has been reconstructed.

The Stadtschloss originated under Elector Friedrich II as a castle, built between 1443 and 1451. The massive building was 200m/220yd in length and 120m/130yd wide; it also had a dome 70m/230ft high. The Baroque design of the palace was widely praised and its magnificent interior was the result of a refurbishment conducted in around 1700 under Andreas Schlüter. After 1945 all that was left of the palace was a burnt-out ruin, although there were plenty of good reasons for it to be rebuilt. However, the East German government viewed the building as a symbol of a »feudalistic and imperialist« past and ordered that the remains be blown up. That order was carried out in 1950. There remained a broad, empty space used for parades and demonstrations. It was appropriately called Marx-Engels-Platz.
The **Palast der Republik** (Palace of the Republic) was erected from 1973 to 1976 according to a design by Heinz Graffunder. It was a

prestige building for the GDR and, perhaps for that very reason the public response was not as fulsome, evoking nicknames such as »Palazzo Prozzo« or »Erichs Lampenladen« (Erich Honecker's lamp shop). The building measured 180 x 85m (200 x 93yd) and was the seat of East Germany's parliament (Volkskammer) as well as being a popular venue for events. After the fall of the Wall it was intended that the palace be used as a cultural centre, but in 1990 it became necessary to close the building due to the asbestos used in its construction. After the asbestos was removed various artists' groups were able to use the building before it was finally demolished in 2009.

Schlossplatz in around 1905. In the bottom left-hand corner the »Octagon Café«, a famous Berlin urinal.

The debate about what should be built in place of the Palast der Republik, and in particular whether the Stadtschloss should be recreated, raged for years. A commission of experts recommended the reconstruction in a report at the beginning of 2002. They suggested calling the building the **Humboldt Forum**, a new structure behind a façade recreating the appearance of the Stadtschloss to accommodate the non-European parts of the collections now held by the city's museums in ▶Dahlem. The Italian architect Franco Stella won the competition to built the new Stadtschloss, which is scheduled for completion in 2013 – at least according to the optimists.

Reconstruction of the Stadtschloss

The Humboldt-Box informs visitors about the appearance of the Humboldt-Forum and what will be displayed there. The foundation and friends' association of the Berliner Schloss – Humboldtforum and its future users, the Staatliche Museen, Berliner Landesbibliothek and Humboldt-Universität, put on changing exhibitions. From the viewing platform on the roof there is a view of the excavated foundations of the Stadtschlosses. The Humboldt-Box will be demolished in 2019.

❶ Daily 10am–6pm, Thu until 10pm; admission €4; www.humboldt-box.com

In front of the reconstructed palace, facing Schinkelplatz (▶p.334), a new monument to freedom and unity, the Freiheits- und Einheits-denkmal, will be erected. The design was not produced by artists or architects but by a communication and event agency in cooperation with the choreographer Sasha Waltz. The corresponding result is a huge see-saw onto which people can walk. Depending on the number of visitors and their movement it will rise or fall. The monument is

Einheits-denkmal

intended to symbolize »citizens in movement« and to demonstrate how people can bring about changes together.

Former Staatsrat building

The southern side of the square is occupied by the building of the East German Staatsrat (Council of State). Its façade includes the only surviving piece of the Stadtschloss (»Portal IV«), from which Karl Liebknecht declared Germany a socialist republic in 1918.

Marstall

On Breite Strasse, which runs past the left of the former Staatsrat building, there is a building called the Neue Marstall (1896 – 1901), both wings of which incorporate sections of an older Marstall building from 1670. Marstall refers to the royal stud or court stables and the building is the only remaining example of the early Baroque period in Berlin.

*Ribbeckhaus

Further along is a four-gabled building called the Ribbeckhaus, which was built in 1624 for the aristocratic Brandenburg family of von Ribbeck, immortalized in the literature of Theodor Fontane. This is the only remaining Renaissance dwelling in Berlin and now hosts the **Zentrum für Berlin-Studien**, a centre for the study of Berlin and the first port of call for anyone interested in all aspects of the city. Rubbing shoulders with the Ribbeckhaus is the **Stadtbibliothek** (City Library). Its door is decorated with 117 different versions of the letter A, a design by Fritz Kühn.

Brüderstrasse

Neumannsgasse leads from Breite Strasse toBrüderstrasse, where Andreas Schlüter once lived at no. 33. No. 10 is the so-called **Galgenhaus**, built in 1688 for von Happe, a councillor of the Board of Domains. It is one of the few buildings in Berlin itself that still has a Baroque town house at its core. There is a story that one of the councillor's maids was hanged outside the building for the alleged theft of a silver spoon, which she had not taken (thus the name Galgenhaus, meaning gallows house). No. 13 was built in 1709 but modified in 1787 by Carl Friedrich Zelter for writer, critic and publisher **Christoph Friedrich Nicolai** (1733 – 1811), who also had a bookshop in the building. This was also the meeting point for the intellectual elite of the time and a centre of the Enlightenment. It attracted such figures as the aforementioned master builder, musician and intimate of Goethe, Zelter, as well as Moses Mendelssohn, Gottfried Schadow and Daniel Chodowiecki. In 1892 the bookshop was relocated to Dorotheenstrasse.

Auswärtiges Amt

From Brüderstrasse, take Sperlingsgasse to the Jungfernbrücke, **Berlin's last remaining lifting bridge**, which was built in 1798, cross the Spree Canal and then go right and upwards past the Aussenministerium (Foreign Ministry) to Schinkelplatz (►p.334). Further ahead on Brüderstrasse beyond Gertraudenstrasse are the Fischerinsel (►p.247) and opposite it the ►Märkische Ufer.

Schloss Schönhausen

$\bigstar$ E 18

Location: Tschaikowskistr. 1,
Pankow
S-Bahn, U-Bahn: Pankow
(S 4, S 8, U 2), then tram M1
❶ Tours April–Sept Tue–Sun

10am–6pm,
Oct–March only Sat,
Sun 10am–5pm
Admission: €6
ww.spsg.de

Schloss Schönhausen was built in 1664 as a manor for the Countess
von Dohna. Johann Arnold Nering (as of 1691) and Eosander von
Göthe (as of 1704) modified the building on behalf of Elector Friedrich III. From 1740 to 1797 Elisabeth Christine, wife of King Fried-rich
II, lived in the palace at the behest of her royal spouse, although the
building was ravaged by Russian troops in 1760 and had to be rebuilt
by Johann Boumann the Elder. After the death of Friedrich Wilhelm
III, Countess Liegnitz moved into the palace. When the new East German state was established in 1949, the palace served as the residence of
the nation's first president, Wilhelm Pieck, until 1960 when it was used
to accommodate guests of the government. In the dying days of the
GDR, the state and its people met at a round table discussion in the
building and it was also here that the decisive **»Two plus Four« talks**
took place. It was reopened for visitors in 2009. Some of the apartments
of Queen Elisabeth Christine on the ground floor have been furnished
in authentic period style. On the upper floor Wilhelm Pieck's study,
which has been preserved fully intact, and a guest apartment occupied
by Fidel Castro and Indira Gandhi among others, can also be viewed.
❶ Opening hours:Tue – Sun 10am – 5pm

Spandau

$\bigstar$ U 7 west

Borough: Spandau
U-Bahn: Altstadt Spandau, Rathaus Spandau, Zitadelle (U 7)

**Spandau developed thanks to its position in the Middle Ages
on the eastern border of the German Reich. The citadel is
therefore the most interesting sight here.**

The old fortress town of Spandau, which was independent of Berlin
until 1920, is situated at the confluence of the Spree and Havel rivers.
Between 1160 and about 1200, the Havel formed the border of the
German Holy Empire. As the border was moved eastward, the town
of Spandau, which receives its first known mention in 1197, became
a rearward base and was granted a town charter in 1232. The town

Former
border post

arose on the island where the present Altstadt or old town is located. The fortress was on the island where the citadel stands. The rise of Berlin rather passed Spandau by, and by the end of the 19th century it was still only a middle-sized town. Spandau had a certain notoriety on account of its prison, which was located in the Altstadt until the end of the 19th century. The jail for war criminals some way outside the town, where the four powers oversaw the imprisonment of the one remaining inmate, **Rudolf Hess**, until he committed suicide in 1987, was torn down and replaced by a shopping centre.

Old town Spandau's old town is located on the western bank of the Havel river. Air raids and the construction of an underground railway have left little trace of its earlier buildings, but around Reformationsplatz, in particular, the small scale has at least been retained. Reformationsplatz in the centre is the site of the **St. Nikolai** St. Nikolai church, a brick hall church dating from the first half of the 15th century that was built over an earlier 13th-century building. The hall is most conspicuous for its altar, which is 8m/26ft high and made of limestone and stucco with rich decoration in the form of paintings and sculptures. This **masterpiece of the late Renaissance** was financed in 1582 by the master builder of the town's fortifications, Rochus Graf zu Lynar, who is buried beneath the altar. Other noteworthy features include the baptismal font from 1398 and the Baroque pulpit, originally fashioned for the chapel of the Potsdam City Palace, the Stadtschloss, in around 1700. The house opposite the church is occupied by the **Museum Spandovia Sacra**, which has an exhibition on the history of the church community and the town. The **Gotisches Haus** (Gothic House) at Breite Str. 32 is considered to be the oldest non-ecclesiastical building in the Berlin region. Remains of Gothic brickwork suggest that it may have been constructed in the 15th century; a room on the upper floor holds an exhibition on the history of Spandau. The so-called **Wendenschloss** (Jüdenstr. 35), an elaborate house for a city-dwelling farmer, was built in around 1700. It was broken up in 1966 and replaced, but the façade of the new building was designed to match that of its historical predecessor. The river embankment at Viktoria-Ufer still has a 116m/127yd remnant of the 14th-century **town walls**.

Spandovia Sacra: Wed, Fri–Sun 3pm–6pm; admission free; www. nikolai-spandau.de

Gotisches Haus: Mon–Sat 10am–6pm, admission free; www.museumsportal-berlin.de

MARCO ◉ POLO TIP

**! ** *Florida, nice and cold*   Insider Tip

When they hear the word »Florida«, Berliners think of ice cream and come from all quarters of the city to Klosterstrasse in Spandau for a scoop or two. Ice-cream maker Olaf Höhn has a second ice-cream parlour in Ellipse at the Rathaus Spandau U-Bahn station.

In the village of Gatow lying to the south of the Altstadt on the western bank of the Havel a military airfield, Militärflugplatz Gatow, came into existence in 1935. After the war it was taken over by the British. It is now the site for the German forces' **Luftwaffenmuseum** (German Air Force Museum) and includes 100 military aircraft dating from the First World War until the present day. Among them are many that formerly belonged to East Germany's military forces, the Nationale Volksarmee.

Luftwaffen-museum

❶ Bus 135 from Rathaus Spandau towards Alt-Kladow until Seekorso/ Kurpromenade, then approx. 700m/800yd walk; Tue–Sun 10am–6pm, Nov–March 9am–4pm; admission free; www.luftwaffenmuseum.de

ZITADELLE SPANDAU

❶ Daily 10am–5pm, admission €4.50; tours March–Oct Sat, Sun, holidays 11am, 1pm, 3pm; www.zitadelle-spandau.de

The Spandau Citadel is the **only remaining Renaissance fort in Germany** and testifies to early Italian fortress building skills. The Italians were the first to design their forts as sharply angled bastions rather than in the rounded bastion style that had been common until then. The earliest building on the site was an island fortress built by the Ascanians (12th century). Elector Joachim II had the Spandau Citadel erected as of 1560 for the defence of Berlin. Christoph Römer and the Venetian Chiaramella di Gandino were in charge of the building, while Rochus Graf zu Lynar took over in 1584 and completed construction in 1594. The basic form has remained unchanged since then. It is a square protected by moats on every side, each side being approximately 200m/220yd long with bastions at each corner that bear the names King, Prince, Crown Prince and Brandenburg. The citadel was considered impregnable. During the Thirty Years' War it was occupied without a fight by Swedish-troops after negotiations between King Gustavus Adolfus of Sweden and Brandenburg's minister Adam Graf Schwarzenberg. When the Aus-

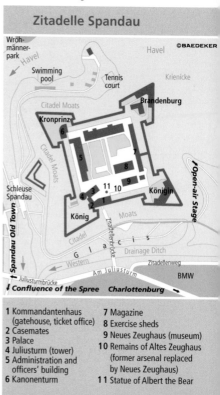

Zitadelle Spandau

©BAEDEKER

1 Kommandantenhaus (gatehouse, ticket office)
2 Casemates
3 Palace
4 Juliusturm (tower)
5 Administration and officers' building
6 Kanonenturm
7 Magazine
8 Exercise sheds
9 Neues Zeughaus (museum)
10 Remains of Altes Zeughaus (former arsenal replaced by Neues Zeughaus)
11 Statue of Albert the Bear

The Kommodantenhaus and the Juliusturm of the Spandau Citadel

trians invaded Brandenburg in 1757, the king and his court sought refuge here. In 1806 the fortress was surrendered without bloodshed to Napoleon's French forces. It continued to be used for military purposes until 1945.

The citadel bridge leads to the so-called **Kommandantenhaus** (the 16th-century gatehouse). It was furnished with a new façade in 1839. Its pediment features a coat of arms depicted in relief with symbols of all the constituent parts of Prussia at the beginning of the 18th century, encircled by the British Order of the Garter. The castle commandant lived on the upper floor, where nowadays an exhibition describes the history of the citadel.

Zitadellenhof Straight ahead of the entrance is the Zitadellenhof, where the army's »Heeresgasversuchsanstalt« (gas experimentation station) has left an unpleasant legacy. At the end of the war remains of its weaponry were thrown into the wells. To the right there is a monument to Margrave Albrecht the Bear. The courtyard is used for open-air concerts and other events; medieval-style meals are served in the Zitadellen-Schänke in the vaults of the Kommandantenhaus.

Palas Diagonally opposite the Kommandantenhaus is the Palas, the living quarters of the fortress, built in around 1350 but remodelled at the beginning of the 16th century as well as in 1821, then altered into an officers' casino in 1936. The newly renovated Gothic hall is used as a venue for a variety of events. At the base of the building on the southern side it is possible to see gravestones (13th/14th century) with inscriptions in Hebrew. They date from Spandau's Jewish cemetery that was ravaged around 1510 and its stones used, as here, for building materials. In the west curtain wall behind the Palas, the excavated remains of a late Slavic fortification can be seen.

The tower known as the **Juliusturm** is the oldest part of the citadel. It was built as early as the beginning of the 14th century as a watchtower and refuge. Its name is probably a corruption of »Judenturm« or »Jewish Tower«. This goes back to 1356 when Margrave Ludwig gave the lucrative job of running the tower to his servant »Frizen the Jew«. The tower was the **repository of the German Reich's war treasury**. In 1874 Chancellor Otto von Bismarck deposited gold to the value of 120 million marks here, money that had been received as war reparations from the French after their defeat in the Franco-German war of 1870/71.

MARCO ⊕ POLO TIP

! *Nocturnal flyers*   Insider Tip

Spandau Citadel is one of the largest hibernation sites in Germany for bats. Tours to the bats are held all year round (dates and bookings: tel. 030 36 75 00 61 or www.bat-ev.de). Every day from noon until 5pm the cellar in which exotic species of bats live is open.

Other buildings

The Neues Zeughaus (1856 – 1858) contains the **Stadtgeschichtliche Museum Spandau** (Museum of the History of Spandau), displaying various historic finds from Spandau. The casemates in the King bastion are open to visitors. The north western boundary of the citadel is formed by the Crown Prince bastion with its »Kavalier« defence, a massive semi-circle intended for defence against heavy artillery bombardment. To the north is the Brandenburg bastion. The ruins of the **Heeresgasversuchsanstalt** from 1940 can still be seen here.

It is possible to walk along the moat around the citadel, offering excellent views of the Havel. Such a walk passes the **Schleuse Spandau** (Spandau lock), which was opened for traffic in 1910. An original lock had already been built here as early as 1723.

Fort Hahneberg

It is less well known that the Spandau district also has a second fortress. Fort Hahneberg was constructed between 1882 and 1888 and was the **last German artillery fort**. After the division of Germany, it spent more than 40 years in a kind of Sleeping Beauty slumber, because it was directly on the border strip between the villages of Staaken-West (East Germany) and Staaken-Ost (West Berlin). Nowadays it is rather overgrown and derelict, and rather spooky.

❶ Approach via Heerstrasse/B 5 and Reimerweg/Weinmeisterhornweg; tours: April–Oct Sat, Sun, holidays 2pm und 4pm, admission €4; www.forthahneberg.de

✳ Spandauer Vorstadt · Scheunenviertel

✦ K 15 – 17

Location: Mitte
U-Bahn: Oranienburger Tor (U 6), Weinmeisterstrasse, Rosenthaler Platz (U 8), Rosa-Luxemburg-Platz (U 2)

S-Bahn: Oranienburger Str. (S 1, S 2), Hackescher Markt (S 5, S 7, S 75)
City centre plan: A 9 – 15

Now an attractive district with the highest concentration of bars in Berlin, the Scheunenviertel was once a ghetto of poverty and criminality: the area was home to low-skilled workers, the proletariat, Jewish refugees from the East, prostitutes and pimps, petty criminals and grafters. Alfred Döblin's novel *Berlin Alexanderplatz* **describes it all.**

The home of Franz Biberkopf   The region to the northwest of modern-day Alexanderplatz and north of the River Spree was called Spandauer Vorstadt when it was first settled around 1700. As early as 1672 a fire prevention decree by the Great Elector had already stipulated the building of 27 barns for the storage of flammable materials: the name »Scheunenviertel« comes from the German word for a barn. With the coming of indus-

A fixture of the Spandauer Vorstadt scene, the Hackesche Höfe

trialization, the area was given over to low-rent, barrack-like dwellings, squalid housing with entire families in a single room and a shared privy for each floor. To this »**backyard of Berlin**« came floods of eastern European Jews taking flight from the pogroms of the 19th century. A uniquely fascinating mixture of eastern Jewish culture, proletarian poverty and big-city crime was the result. Around the main thoroughfares of Dragonerstrasse (now Max-Beer Strasse) and Grenadier-

MARCO❂POLO TIP

Beth-Café   *Insider Tip*

Not a place to go in the evening (it closes at 8pm), but well known for its authentic kosher dishes: the orthodox Adass Jisroel community's Beth-Café at Tucholskystrasse 40 (closed Fri and Sat).

strasse (now Almstadtstrasse), Yiddish was spoken as often as German, matzo bread and rissoles were on sale and the beer flowed in bars like the well-known Mulackritze. The Nazis brought an end to all this with their destruction of the Jewish culture, which simultaneously meant lumping the whole area up to the edge of the Spandauer Vorstadt district around Oranienburger Strasse with the notorious Scheunenviertel, in order to bring discredit on the Jews living there. Finally the Jews were transported and taken to death camps from an assembly point on Grosse Hamburger Strasse. Anything that still remained at the end of the Nazi era disappeared during the GDR epoch. After reunification, the area did experience a brief alternative spring until it was refurbished with costlier flats and became a haven for celebrities, the nouveau riche and tourists spoilt for choice by the plethora of bars.

A WALK THROUGH SPANDAUER VORSTADT

Jewish culture has indeed made a return, and a walk through the district should not miss the memorial sites or the reawakened Jewishness of Berlin. A good place to start is the junction of Friedrichstrasse and Oranienburger Strasse, full to bursting with restaurants and bars.

Oranienburger Strasse

Almost immediately on the right comes the ruin that houses the art centre called Tacheles. The building was constructed from 1907 to 1909, when it was a large shopping arcade. Its ruins were occupied as of 1990 by artists and denizens of the alternative society. New owners took over for a symbolic rent of €1 per year, but the contract expired in 2008. The future of the site is still uncertain. The café and courtyard were bought from the previous operators for one million euros and separated from the rest of the ruin by a wall.

Tacheles

A little further on is the junction with Tucholskystrasse (formerly Artilleriestrasse). On the corner stands the former **Postfuhramt**,

Tucholskystrasse

built by Carl Schwatlo as a central post office and parcel delivery centre between 1875 and 1881. The magnificent brick edifice, now converted to a hotel, is decorated with terra-cotta. Two other buildings on Tucholskystrasse are of interest: two cornucopiae and the head of the Lion of Judah mark the fact that no. 9 once housed the College for the Study of Judaism, where lessons were still being given by the last of its teachers, **Leo Baeck**, until 1942. No. 40 is the community centre for the Israeli synagogue community, **Adass Jisroel**. A few steps away on Oranienburger Strasse is the entrance to the **Heckmann-Höfe**, a beautifully renovated shopping parade that goes as far as Sophienstrasse. There are some interesting and unusual shops and a **sweet factory** .

*Neue Synagoge

The magnificent gold dome of the New Synagogue glitters some 50m/164ft above the street and is visible from quite a distance away. The building was designed in a Moorish/Byzantine style by Eduard Knobloch between 1857 and 1859 and completed in 1866 by Friedrich August Stüler. It was the place of worship for what was at that time Germany's largest Jewish community. When it was inaugurated on 5 September 1866, even the Prussian king numbered among the 3000 people gathered in its main prayer hall. The synagogue was plundered and desecrated during the pogrom of 9 November 1938 but a courageous intervention by **Wilhelm Krützfeld** , head of the Hackescher Markt police precinct, prevented the Nazi stormtroopers from setting the building ablaze. It did burn, though, five years later, but this time on account of an allied bomb. In 1958 the prayer room had to be detonated due to the threat of collapse. Rebuilding efforts began in 1988 with the foyer, the male vestibule, the main stairway, room of representation and the upper ladies' gallery. The main prayer room was however not reconstructed. Its former location is now marked by white gravel paving in the present-day courtyard. The synagogue is now known as the **Centrum Judaicum** and functions not only as a place of prayer but also as a memorial, museum, community hall, library and archive for the Jewish community. An exhibition entitled »Tuet auf die Pforte« relates the history of the New Synagogue and Berlin's Jewish community as a whole.

● April–Sept Sun–Mon 10am–8pm, Tue–Thu until 6pm, Fri until 5pm or 2pm in March and. Oct; Nov–Feb. Sun–Thu 10am–6pm, Fri until 2pm; admission €3.50, www.cjudaicum.de

Grosse Hamburger Strasse

Beyond the former General Archive of German Jews (no. 28) and the Kunsthof art establishment (no. 27) lies Grosse Hamburger Strasse. On the right is a fenced piece of land dotted with trees. This is all that remains of the first Jewish cemetery that was ravaged by the Nazis. **Moses Mendelssohn** is one of the figures who was buried here. A new gravestone was dedicated to him, and other grave slabs are next to the wall. A memorial plaque and a bronze sculpture at the front of the site are in memory of the persecution and murder of Jews. This was previously the location of the Jewish Old Folks Home, which became an **internment camp for Berlin's Jewish population** as of 1941. It was from here that people were transported to the death camps. No. 27 was once the site of the Jewish boys' school, of which Moses Mendelssohn was among the founders. On the other side of the road an installation by Christian Boltanski entitled The Missing House evokes the Jewish inhabitants of a house that no longer exists. At the end of the road is St Hedwig's hospital, which became Berlin's first Catholic hospital when it opened in 1844.

Shortly before there, a drive leads off to the right up to the Sophien-kirche, a church that was endowed by Queen Sophie in 1712. Its Baroque tower, finished in 1734, is probably one of the finest in Berlin. The cemetery has the graves of builder and composer Carl Friedrich Zelter († 1832; on the left-hand side of the church) and historian Leopold von Ranke († 1886; gravestone in the wall on the right) among others.

*Sophien-kirche

Sophienstrasse is a turning off Grosse Hamburger Strasse. The **Sophie-Gips-Höfe** at no. 21 is the name of an art centre illuminated at night in bright, fluorescent colours that leads through to Gipsstrasse. Here, visitors can peruse the private **Sammlung Hoffmann** (Hoffmann collection) of contemporary art. Between 1864 and 1905 the house at Sophienstrasse no. 15 was the meeting hall of the craftsmen's union that was founded in 1844. When the union had to leave to make way for the new Wertheim store in 1905, it purchased nos. 17/18. It was in the meeting rooms of this building, known as the Sophiensäle, that the communist movement made its mark in history with Karl Liebknecht's declaration of a **proletarian revolution** in October 1918. In November 1918 the Spartacus league was constituted here and in 1920 the KPD and USPD parties were merged. The building is now used as a theatre.

Sophien-strasse

Sammlung Hoffmann: tours Sat 11am–4pm, booking required: tel. 030 28 49 91 20; admission €8.

Sophienstrasse opens into Rosenthaler Strasse. At the end by nos. 40/41 turn right into the Hackesche Höfe, once the largest combined work and housing complex in Europe. The development was completed in 1908 (decoration by August Endell) and consists of eight courtyards (Höfe), of which the first (actually the last when entering from Rosenthaler Strasse), still retaining its Art Nouveau design, has now become one of the most happening places on the Berlin scene. The other courtyards extend as far as Sophienstrasse and contain many shops (bookshops, jewellers, various fashion labels and such

*Hackesche Höfe

amusing establishments as a shop devoted to the »Ampelmän-nchen«, the hat-wearing figure of a walking man that lit up on pe-destrian crossings in East Germany), as well as workshops. From courtyard no. 1 exit to lively Hackescher Markt, where cafés and restaurants have started up in front of the old train station dating from 1882.

Otto Weidt's blind workshop
Go left up Rosenthaler Strasse. In the courtyard of no. 39 – the only unrestored court, and it is planned to leave it that way – there was once a small brush factory (Blindenwerkstatt Otto Weidt) that Otto Weidt founded in the early 1940s. He employed deaf and blind people, Jews and non-Jews, and, since the business was recognized as »vital to the war effort«, it was often a last place of refuge for persecuted indi-viduals and their dependents. Fur-ther up Rosenthaler Strasse, pass Gormannstrasse, which is crossed by Mulackstrasse. Now occupied by elegant shops for well-off customers, it was once the heart of the Scheunenviertel. Turn left into Mu-lackstrasse, then right into Kleine Rosenthaler Strasse to reach Berlin's oldest military cemetery, laid out be-tween 1701 and 1705, the Alter Garnisonfriedhof. It is the final resting place of Adolph von Lützow († 1834, plot I), leader of Lützow's Frei-korps, and the poet and army officer Friedrich de la Motte-Fouqué.

> **MARCO ◉ POLO TIP**
>
> **! Tea to go** *Insider Tip*
>
> Chaja is Berlin's first tea-to-go shop. Water at temperatures of 70°C/160°F and 95°C/200°F in green to golden-brown boilers is poured over black tea, green tea, herb teas and fruit teas, and even lovers of oolong, matcha and white tea will find what they are looking for (Chaja, 1st Tea to go, Oranienburger Str. 27).

❶ Blindenwerkstatt Otto Weidt: daily 10am–8pm, tours Sun 3pm; admission free; www.museum-blindenwerkstatt.de

August-strasse
The last of the trendy streets, Auguststrasse, runs from Kleine Rosen-thaler Strasse back to Oranienburger Strasse. It too features plenty in the way of art, shopping and bars. The primary art venue goes by the name of **Kunst-Werke Berlin** (no. 69). Another place that has be-come popular, not with the older generation but with modern young-sters, is the old ballroom of **Clärchens Ballhaus**. No. 11– 13 was a Jewish girls' school.

Rosa-Luxem-burg-Platz
Turn right off Rosenthaler Strasse to reach Neue and Alte Schön-hauser Strasse. Passing lots of restaurants and pubs you reach Rosa-Luxemburg-Platz. Here in the Volksbühne theatre, opened in 1914, director Erwin Piscator once made a furore (Frank Castorf does the same), and this is the site of the Karl-Liebknecht-Haus, formerly the headquarters of the Communist Party, today of Die Linke (Left Par-ty). Beyond Torstrasse lies ▶Prenzlauer Berg.

Tegel

✦ F – G 9 – 12

Borough: Reinickendorf
U-Bahn: Alt-Tegel (U 6)

Two names are associated with Tegel, those of Humboldt and Borsig. The Humboldt brothers grew up here and August Borsig laid the foundations of an engineering empire, to which the Borsigturm, the double tower of his factory gates from 1898, bears witness.

North of the Tegeler Hafen docks on Adelheid-Allee stands Schloss Tegel. In 1550 this was a manor in the possession of Elector Joachim II. Later it became a hunting lodge for the Great Elector and since 1765 it has been owned by the Humboldt family. Wilhelm von Humboldt had it rebuilt in Classical style by **Karl Friedrich Schinkel** between 1822 and 1824. The latter is also responsible for the painting in the vestibule, the blue salon and the library. The four towers at the corners were designed by **Christian Daniel Rauch**. They feature bas-reliefs of the eight wind gods of antiquity. The collection of originals and casts of ancient sculptures was gathered by Wilhelm von Humboldt during his time as ambassador in Rome.

Schloss Tegel (Humboldtschlösschen)

> **MARCO ⊕ POLO TIP**
>
> ❗ *Fat Marie*   Insider Tip
>
> Berlin's largest tree can be seen by wandering northward along the riverbank from the Tegel docks. In a bay called Grosse Malche grows a 900-year-old oak, now 26m/85ft tall and popularly known as »Dicke Marie«.

The park was laid out as a Baroque garden in 1792 and modified by Schinkel 32 years later. An avenue of lime trees leads past a pond called the Humboldtteich to a *mausoleum that Wilhelm von Humboldt had built for his family by Schinkel after the death of his wife Caroline († 1829). In the middle there is a granite Ionic column with a copy of Hope by the Danish sculptor Bertel Thorvaldsen.

❶ i Tours of the house: May–Sept Mon 10am, 11am, 3pm und 4pm; park Mon 10am–6pm

The site of the present-day airport had once been used as a shooting range for the fusiliers in around 1870. In 1909 Graf Zeppelin landed here with his Z 3 airship. It then became an exercise ground for the Berlin airship battalion. In 1931 it was used for the first rocket test experiments of **Hermann Oberth and Wernher von Braun**. The area was first used as an airfield during the blockade of Berlin and the Berlin Airlift of 1948/49. It involved building a runway and apron 2400m/2625yd long, the longest in Europe at the time. The site was then used by the French as a military airfield, but opened for passen-

Berlin Tegel Airport (Flughafen Otto Lilienthal)

ger services in 1960. The present airport took shape in 1969 using designs by architects von Gerkan, Marg and Nickels. It was officialy opened on 1 September 1975. When the new airport in Schönefeld is complete, Tegel Airport will close down and the site will be used as a research and industrial park for future technology.

Tempelhof

⊹ O – Q 16 – 18

Borough: Tempelhof-Schöneberg
U-Bahn: U 6

Tours: Mon–Thu 4pm,
Fri 1pm, 4pm; Sat,
Sun, 11am, 2pm; €12

Tempelhof gets its name from the Knights Templar, who founded the settlement in 1247. The borough stretches a considerable distance towards the south and its buildings, ranging from airport to farmhouse, run the full gamut of architectural forms, for both commerce and transport.

Ullsteinhaus

One of its landmarks is the **Ullsteinhaus** on the other side of the Teltow Canal. Built in 1927 and measuring 76m/250ft in height, it was the first steel-reinforced concrete skyscraper in Berlin, clad in red brick. Culture is represented by the **ufa-Fabrik** events venue at the end of Tempelhofer Damm.

Berlin Tempelhof Airport

Tempelhofer Feld was another former exercise ground for troops that attracted pioneers of aviation: in 1883 the painter **Arnold Böcklin** sought to get airborne with two unpowered biplane-type structures that he had built himself, but gusting winds put paid to the attempt. In 1908 the Wright brothers themselves managed a 19-minute powered flight from the field. By 1923, the site was in business as a commercial airport and during 1936 to 1939 **one of the largest linked buildings on the planet** was constructed in the typical monumental style of the Third Reich, using designs by Ernst Sagebiel: the building shaped in the form of a 90° circle arc measures as much as 1.2km/1300yd and the terminal itself is 400m/450yd long. After the Second World War, the Americans took over the airport. Civil flights were not reinstated until 1950 with Tempelhof's central air-

? *Did you know*

During the eleven-month blockade, 250,000 flights delivered 2,324,257 tons of goods to West Berliners. 222 American, 110 British and 48 other aircraft were used in the airlift, and 41 Britons, 31 Americans and five Germans died while taking part. Freight planes landed not only in Tempelhof but also in Tegel and Gatow, while flying boats even made use of the Wannsee.

The days of Tempelhof Airport are numbered, but its monumental architecture will remain

port service opening for business again a year later. However, after 1975, commercial flights were redirected to Tegel airport. Tempelhof remained a military airfield until the fall of the Berlin Wall. After that it was a regional airport until the extensions to Schönefeld were completed. The last plane took off here on 30 September 2008. Since then Berliners have taken over the 355ha/850-acre site and are quarrelling with urban planners who want to create a Tempelhofer Park, starting with an international garden exhibition in 2017.

Since 1951 a monument has recalled the blockade of 1948/49 and its consequences. Between June 1948 and May 1949 US generals Clay and Wedemeyer organized an air lift of supplies to provide the citizens of West Berlin with the essential food and goods they needed and thus managed to defeat the Soviet blockade. Eduard Ludwig's 20m/66ft sculpture called **Hungerkralle** (Claws of Hunger), erected in front of the main airport entrance, symbolizes the three air corridors that linked Berlin with the West Germany. Identical monuments stand at Frankfurt airport and the military air base at Celle.

Tempelhof's monument to the Berlin Airlift

Three pretty churches attest to the origins of Tempelhof as a village. The **Tempelhof village church** on Reinhardtplatz (U-Bahn: Alt-Tempelhof) with its early Gothic apse dates from 1250. Its altar (1596) is copy of Lucas Cranach the Elder's St Catherine's Altar from Torgau of 1506.

Churches

The **Mariendorfer Kirche** (U-Bahn: Alt-Mariendorf) was built in the early 13th century. In its Baroque west tower, crowned by a curved copper onion dome, a bell dating from 1480 still tolls. The **Marienfelder Dorfkirche** (S-Bahn: Buckower Chaussee, S 2) is one of the oldest in the March of Mark Brandenburg and Berlin. Around 1220 Templars built it from stones found on the fields. In 1318 the Order of St John took it over, and in 1435 it was handed to the municipality of Berlin and Cölln.

∗ Tiergarten

✷ L/M 13 – 15

Location: Both sides of Strasse des 17. Juni
S-Bahn: Tiergarten, Bellevue (S 5, S 7, S 75)

City centre plan: A – C 5 – 10
U-Bahn: Hansaplatz (U 9)
Bus: 100, 106

The Tiergarten is to Berlin what Hyde Park and Regent's Park are to London's: a green oasis at the heart of the city.

In about 1700 Elector Friedrich III transformed a hunting enclosure outside the city gates into a park and had the avenue of Unter den Linden extended through the park towards Charlottenburg along what is now Strasse des 17. Juni. Friedrich the Great commissioned the park to be laid out along French lines but his successor Friedrich Wilhelm II had it altered to an English pattern. It was between 1833 and 1838 that the famous landscape designer **Peter Joseph Lenné** remodelled the public park in its present form. Although it was badly hit during the Second World War, and then felled bare by Berliners seeking firewood to keep warm in the winters that followed, the park was reconstituted from 1949, many of its new trees being donated by towns elsewhere in Germany, as commemorated by a memorial stone on Grosser Weg. It now has 25km/16mi of rambling paths and offers boat rides on the Neue See plus one of the biggest beer gardens in the city alongside the lake, both of which are major attractions that regularly tempt Berliners out of their homes on summer weekends.

MONUMENTS AND MEMORIALS

Siegesallee

The Tiergarten has a great many memorials. The trend began in 1901 when Kaiser Wilhelm II presented the Siegesallee to his capital. It features 32 emotionally depicted groups of figures with crowned heads and was intended to demonstrate the magnificence of the

Prussian empire along a route from Königsplatz (Platz der Republik) to what is now Kemperplatz. The marble parade – dubbed by one contemporary a »snow-white open-air panopticon« – was mocked and scorned abroad, and even the Berliners themselves made jokes about it. »Going down to the dollies« became their way of describing a saunter along the avenue. After the war, the statues, even the undamaged remnants, were taken away. Some fine sculptures remain in the Tiergarten, though, among them the **Goethe Monument** by Fritz Schaper (1880), which stands at the east end of the park, its base depicting allegorical figures of Lyric Poetry (and Amor), Drama (spirit with a symbol of death) and Science. Then there is the **Monument to Queen Luise** by Erdmann Encke (1880). The relief on its base shows scenes from the life of a soldier and women tending to the wounded, representing Queen Luise's own deeds during the war of 1806/07. The **Monument to Friedrich Wilhelm III**, created by Friedrich Drake, was unveiled on 3 August 1849, making it one of the oldest statues in the Tiergarten.

> **MARCO POLO TIP**
>
> **! Insider Tip**
> *In the open air and free!*
>
> A museum open all year round and 24 hours a day, and admission is free? Where on earth could you find such a thing? In Berlin of course – or to be more precise, in the Tiergarten. Along the route through the park from the Berlin Pavillon to the Schleusenbrücke, as well as on Joseph-Haydn-Weg, a hundred gas lamps from the whole of Europe – dating from 1826 to the 1950s – can be examined in the Gaslaternen-Freilichtmuseum (Gas Lamp Museum).

Two other monuments refer to an entirely different time of history. Right under the Lichtensteinbrücke bridge on the right-hand bank of the Landwehrkanal stands a sculpture dedicated to Rosa Luxemburg who, together with Karl Liebknecht, founded Germany's communist party KPD. After the failure of the Spartacus uprising of 15 January 1919, she was murdered by soldiers of the Freikorps and her body was thrown into the canal from the bridge. Karl Liebknecht was also shot on the same day by the Neue See, and his memorial, the counterpart to Rosa Luxemburg's, is located at the lake.

Monuments to Karl Liebknecht and Rosa Luxemburg

GROSSER STERN AND SIEGESSÄULE

Grosser Stern is not precisely in the middle of the Tiergarten, but it is the focus of all the routes through the park. In its midst, surrounded by the roar of traffic, stands the Siegessäule or Victory Column. It is some 69m/226ft tall and was erected in memory of the three victorious campaigns against Denmark in 1864, Austria in 1866 and France in 1870/71. Its unveiling was on the 3rd anniversary of the battle of Sedan, on 2 September 1873, accompanied by a military parade in the pres-

*Siegessäule

Green Berlin

Although Berlin does not look as good as some other European capital cities in terms of its area of green space, it can point to other successes – the number of shops selling organic and fair-trade products is growing, and there is even a wind generator, admittedly a controversial one.

▶ **Second to last**
Green space in Berlin in comparison
to other European capitals

total area   green space

Rome 11,1 %

Paris 0,8 %

Moscow 16,8 %

Berlin 6,2 %

London 13,9 %

▶ **Street trees in Berlin**

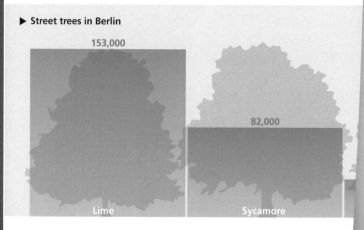

153,000

82,000

Lime   Sycamore

Berlin's first wind generator
- Location: Pankow district
- Official inauguration: June 2011
- Total height: approx. 180m/590ft
- Rotor diameter: 82m/270ft
- Power: 2000 kW
- Annual production:
  4000-45,000 MW hours
- Provides energy for more than
  1000 4-person households

▶ **Organic Berlin**
Read about organic food in
Berlin on this blog:
bioberlin.wordpress.com

Berlin green zone
The border of the
green zone is the inner
circle of rail tracks
(»the big dog's head«).
Only vehicles with the
green sticker (4) may
enter this area.

Gesundbrunnen

Ostkreuz

Westkreuz

Südkreuz

Inner circle of rail tracks

Cycling in Berlin
No European city of comparable size has so
much bicycle traffic.

▶ **Bike hire in Berlin:**
www.callabike-interaktiv.de
www.fahrradstation.com

13 % Berlin   2 % London   57 % Amsterdam   2 % Paris
(centre)

Proportion of cycling in total
traffic volume per city

©BAEDEKER

5,000   25,000   21,000
Oak   Plane   Chestnut

ence of Kaiser Wilhelm I. At that time it was located on Königsplatz, where it remained until 1938, when it was moved to make way for Speer's designs for »Germania«, his planned capital of the Third Reich. The shaft of the Siegessäule incorporates rifles that were seized as spoils of war and stands on a tall granite base with bronze bas-reliefs showing scenes from the three wars. The lower part includes a mosaic designed by Anton von Werner that symbolizes the unification of the various parts of the German Empire or »Reich« in 1870/71. At the top, the statue known as **»Goldelse«** surveys Berlin. The 8m/26ft figure of Victoria, goddess of victory, was fashioned by Friedrich Drake. The Siegessäule can be climbed: a staircase of 285 steps leads to an **observation platform at 51m/166ft** (MARCO POLO Insight, p.192).

❶ i April–Oct Mon–Fri 9.30am–6.30pm, Sat and Sun until 7pm; Nov–March until 5pm or 5.30pm); admission €2.50

Monuments on the roundabout The roundabout at Grosser Stern also features the national monument to Bismarck, created in 1901 by Reinhold Begas. Alongside him are General Field Marshall Moltke (by Joseph Uphues, 1905) and war minister von Roon (by Harro Magnussen, 1904). These three statues were also originally located in front of the Reichstag.

SCHLOSS BELLEVUE

Schloss Bellevue, north-east of the Grosser Stern, has been the main seat of the president of the Federal Republic since 1994. The summer palace of Prince August Ferdinand, the youngest brother of Frederick the Great, was built in 1785 and destroyed in the Second World War. During reconstruction the oval banqueting hall, designed in 1791 by Carl Gotthard Langhans, was restored true to the original. The western part of the palace park (20ha/48 acres) in the style of an English landscape garden is open to the public. Exhibitions and concerts are held in the thatched park house. In the part and immediately south-west of the palace is the Federal President's Office, an elliptical structure clad in black granite, the work of the Frankfurt architects Martin Gruber and Helmut Kleine-Kraneburg

The official seat of the president of the Federal Republic

THE NORTHERN PART OF THE TIERGARTEN

The Königliche Porzellan-Manufaktur or Royal Porcelain Factory of Berlin has been situated at Wegelystr. 1 since 1868. Its origins go back to 1751 when WilhelmKaspar Wegely founded Berlin's first porcelain factory, which was taken over by Frederick the Great himself in 1763. It was the great king who introduced the still-extant trademark showing the blue sceptre of the Brandenburg electorship. Among the older buildings, some turning and forming mills, dating from 1871, have survived alongside the Spree. The factory is still producing high-quality porcelain for domestic use or for decoration. The full range of pro-ducts and the history of the factory are celebrated in an exhibition at Wegelystrasse no. 1; there are salesrooms at Wegelystrasse, Kurfürstendamm 27 and Friedrichstr. 158.

Königliche Porzellan-Manufaktur (KPM)

❶ Mon–Sat 10am–6pm, admission €10; www.kpm.de

Haus der Kulturen der Welt literally means »house of the world's cultures«. The building in the northeast corner of the Tiergarten is seen as a forum for the countries of the Third World and promotes regular exhibitions and concerts. The perfect backdrop is provided by the former Kongresshalle, a milestone in modern architecture. It was designed by Hugh A. Stubbins with the assistance of Werner Düttmann and Franz Mocken he being the US contribution to the International Building Exhibition of 1957, and built on the site of the former Kroll opera house, where the German parliament sat after the burning of the Reichstag building in 1933. The startling curved roof of the building has led to the Kongress-halle being nicknamed the »**Schwangere Auster**« or »Pregnant Oyster«. A sculpture entitled Two Forms that stands in the pool in front of the hall stems unmistakably from Henry Moore. In the summer of 1980, the Kongresshalle's roof collapsed. It was rebuilt and reopened in time for the city's jubilee celebrations in 1987. The Haus der Kulturen der Welt Museum moved in to the building in 1989 (programme of events at www.hkw.de). Next to the Kongress-halle stands a bell tower 42m/138ft high, which contains the fourth biggest **carillon** in the world (the biggest in Europe). The carillon chimes every day at noon and 6pm.

Haus der Kulturen der Welt (Kongress-halle)

The Soviet memorial on the northern side of Strasse des 17. Juni, not far from the ▶Brandenburg Gate, was built in 1945/46. It has a bronze casting of a Red Army soldier in full combat dress, by Lev Kerbel. Two Soviet tanks that took part in the conquest of Berlin in 1945 flank the monument, in which 2500 Soviet soldiers who died in the battle for Berlin are buried. There is much larger Soviet monument in ▶Treptower Park, and one more on the Schönholzer Heide in Pankow.

Soviet memorial

| »Der Rufer« | On the central reservation of Strasse des 17. Juni, in between the Brandenburg Gate and the Soviet monument, there is a 3m/10ft-high bronze sculpture by Gerhard Marcks by the name of Der Rufer, meaning the Caller. Its granite base has an inscription quoting the Italian poet Petrarch (1304 – 74): »I walk through the world and call: ›Peace, peace, peace.‹« |

| Memorial to Sinti and Roma | When in front of the Brandenburg Gate, walk left to reach the Reichstag (▶p.274). Opposite it to the south, on Scheidemannstrasse, is a memorial designed by Dani Karavan dedicated to the Sinti and Roma who were murdered in the Nazi period. |

| Memorial to persecuted homosexuals | Walking to the right when in front of the Brandenburg Gate, on the left you see the Holocaust Memorial (▶p.171). Opposite it a memorial to the homosexuals who were persecuted by tha Nazis was unveiled in May2008. The Danish and Norwegian artists Elmgreen and Dragset created a concrete cube with windows through which a film of two men kissing is visible. |

THE SOUTH OF THE TIERGARTEN

| Diplomats' quarter ▶MARCO POLO Insight p. 317 | To the south of Tiergartenstrasse between Stauffenbergstrasse and Klingelhöferstrasse is an area that was called the **Diplomatenviertel** or diplomats' quarter at the time of the Third Reich. After the war, which only the Italian and Japanese embassies survived, the latter severely damaged, the site was a wasteland, and now further embassy buildings (Austria, India) and the representation of the federal state of Baden-Württemberg, which is anything but modest, have been built there. The so-called Tiergarten Triangle between Stülerstrasse, Klingelhöferstrasse and the Landwehrkanal has also gained new embassies (Scandinavia, Mexico). Here the federal headquarters of the Christian Democratic Union political party sails into the intersection like a glass ship's bows. |

✳ Tierpark Friedrichsfelde

✦ **L 20 east**

Location: Lichtenberg
U-Bahn: Tierpark (U 5)
❶ April–mid-Sept daily 9am– 7pm, Nov–mid-March until 5pm; first half of March, second half of September and Oct until 6pm
Admission: €12
www.zoo-berlin.de/tierpark

The Friedrichsfelde zoo was opened in the grounds around Schloss Friedrichsfelde on 2 July 1955 as East Berlin's much larger answer to

More Bold than Diplomatic?

While the construction of the government quarter, Potsdamer Platz, the Jewish Museum and new buildings on Pariser Platz was transforming Berlin into a prestigious capital city, it also gained, unnoticed by some, a world-class architectural exhibition.

120 countries and the 16 states of the Federal Republic of Germany have built their embassies and representative offices, and in doing so have set their stamp on Berlin. These buildings can be interpreted as an expression of the true or desired importance of the state concerned. They are proclamations of wealth or modesty, even of architectural boldness, and in some cases seem more avant-garde than diplomatic.

Striking and New

The **British Embassy** (architect: Michael Wilford & Partners) wittily gets around the demands of Berlin's urban planners in respect of height and the use of stone: everything is as desired, with a sandstone façade and sloping roof, and above the plain entrance there is a hole through which pale blue and violet architectural elements thrust into the street façade. An English oak grows in the paved courtyard, steps lead to the second courtyard and the viewer sees the historic entrance of the old embassy, which stood on this site and was destroyed in the war. Many embassies hide their greatest charms behind inhospitable walls: the **French Embassy** (by Christian de Portzamparc and Steffen Lehmann), for example, gives its occupants a view of the Brandenburg Gate from every office through windows that look like arrow-slits. Those who enter it from Wilhelmstrasse pass sequestered courtyards with beautiful sculptures on the lawns. To see the diplomatic quarter, take a walk in the southern part of Tiergarten, which had this role before the Sec-

A break with convention: the British Embassy

BRITISH EMBASSY

ond World War. The marks of war have been obliterated almost every-where, except where they have been integrated into the new buildings as stone witnesses to history. The **Nordic Embassies** (Berger and Parrkinen), which share a complex of buildings behind the blades of a band of green copper, amount to a little diplomatic village. In this way Denmark, Norway, Finland, Iceland and Sweden aim to express their geographical, historical and political connections in the so-called Felleshus, which catches the eye on busy Klingelhöferstrasse at the corner of Rauchstrasse. However, the **Mexican Embassy** (González de Leon) steals the show, especially at night, when the illuminated concrete strips of the façade tilt mysteriously in varying directions according to the angle of view. Curious passers-by can look inside through the glass wall behind the concrete supports, and the cylindrical atrium with a roof entirely of glass allows a view out from some 400 bull's-eye windows.

Return to Tradition

The old diplomatic quarter also extends along Tiergartenstrasse. Lovely, shady paths have been laid, but the built-up side of the street opposite, which rose out of more or less romantic ruins after the fall of the Wall, is more interesting. The **pink palace of the Italian Embassy** in the monumental style characteristic of its period (1939–41) has a ground floor clad in travertine stone from Rome; the **Indian Embassy** displays glowing red sandstone from Rajasthan,

which has been cast into the slabs of the façade in rough, broken chunks; the **Austrian Embassy** by Hans Hollein on the corner of Stauffenbergstrasse looks like an architectural exclamation mark behind its skin of green copper, as its colourful red volume rises two storeys with large windows facing the Tiergarten next to austere cubes. The **base of the Japanese diplomats** in Hiroshimastrasse, by contrast, rebuilt in the 1980s, resembles a fortress: the main entrance, with traditional Japanese design features, gilded grilles with Buddhist motifs and stone vases, presents the imperial seal in the form of a stylized chrysanthemum, but the garden in the courtyard, one of the most beautiful Japanese gardens in Berlin, remains invisible, as visitors are not welcome.

Fairy-tale Realm by the Tiergarten

Take just a few steps, as far as Hiroshimastrasse no. 18–20, and you are in a different world. With its conspicuous corner and central blocks, the **Embassy of the United Arab Emirates** (Krause Bohne) is a palace from 1001 Arabian Nights between the delegations of the federal states of North Rhine-Westphalia and Bremen. Columns with gilded capitals bear halls that are adorned with palm trees. Guests in the banqueting hall on the garden side, which is surrounded by galleries and has a glazed garden front, tread an enormous, colourful carpet as if walking on velvet.

The Mexican Embassy has opted for lighting effects

Southern Refinement

For a truly enjoyable trip around the world, don't miss the refinement of southern lands. At Auguste-Viktoria-Strasse 74–76, at the border of Schmargendorf and Grunewald, the copper roof of the **Israeli Embassy** (Samuel Willenberg) glows from afar through the trees above an exterior of shell limestone. This monumental structure is divided inside by an ochre-coloured wall of so-called Jerusalem stone. Six cubic elements in the façade are a reminder of the six million Jews who died in the Holocaust. **Thailand**, by contrast, has given itself an urban look in Lepsiusstrasse in Steglitz, though with a Buddhist shrine in the front garden, while **Ethiopia** has opted for a site on the other side of the Teltow Canal in Lichtenberg. **Macedonia** has settled in without much ado between Königsallee and Hubertusstrasse, and the **Embassy of the Polish Republic** hunkers down in a forbidding castle-like structure in Furtwänglerstrasse. At Hagenstrasse 56, on the corner of Teplitzer Strasse, this architectural walk has returned to the orient: the magnificent and theatrical **palace of the Emirate of Qatar** (John S. Bonnington) hides behind high smooth walls with arched openings and white crenellations. The complex is built of concrete and steel but imitates marble thanks to the use of polished white granite from Spain. In Dahlem, at Clayallee 82, the **Embassy of the Sultanate of Oman** (Hierholzer) lies behind a European façade of dark brick, but opens a dialogue of the cultures by means of traditional elements taken from Arab architec-ture: a classic three-part front and the arrangement of the rooms around an atrium as in an Omani dwelling. The **Embassy of the Islamic Republic of Iran** (Diba and Sfavardi) at Podbiel-skiallee 65–67 also builds bridges between cultures and nations, employing such characteristics of Iranian architecture as geometry, transparency and simplicity. Built like its neighbour of light-coloured limestone, this elongated structure fits into the surroundings in terms of its height and volume. A concave concrete wall emphasizes the entrance and is intended to convey hospitality, but the barriers in front of it have not yet been removed.

Tierpark Friedrichsfelde

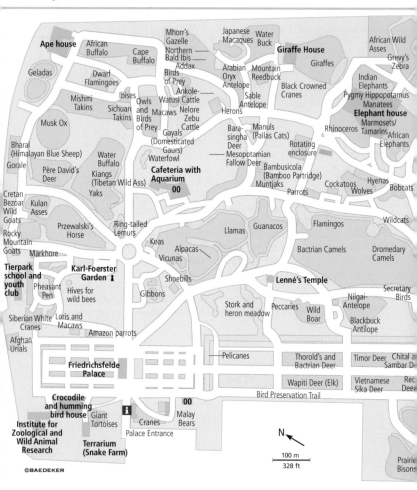

Ape house
African Buffalo
Cape Buffalo
Mhorr's Gazelle
Japanese Macaques
Water Buck
Giraffe House
African Wild Asses
Grevy's Zebra
Geladas
Dwarf Flamingoes
Northern Bald Ibis
Addax
Birds of Prey
Arabian Oryx
Mountain Reedbuck
Giraffes
Indian Elephants
Mishmi Takins
Ibises
Owls and Birds of Prey
Watusi Cattle
Ankole-Nelore Cattle
Antelope
Sable Antelope
Black Crowned Cranes
Pygmy Hippopotamus
Manatees
Sichuan Takins
Macaws
Herons
Elephant house
Marmosets/Tamarins
Musk Ox
Gayals (Domesticated Gaurs)
Bara-singha Deer
Manuls (Pallas Cats)
Rhinoceros
African Elephants
Bharal (Himalayan Blue Sheep)
Water Buffalo
Waterfowl
Mesopotamian Fallow Deer
Rotating enclosure
Gorale
Père David's Deer
Kiangs (Tibetan Wild Ass)
Cafeteria with Aquarium 00
Bambusicola (Bamboo Partridge)
Muntjaks
Cockatoos
Hyenas
Cretan Bezoar Wild Goats
Kulan Asses
Yaks
Parrots
Wolves
Bobcats
Rocky Mountain Goats
Przewalski's Horse
Ring-tailed Lemurs
Llamas
Guanacos
Flamingos
Wildcats
Markhore
Keas
Alpacas
Vicunas
Bactrian Camels
Dromedary Camels
Tierpark school and youth club
Karl-Foerster Garden
Shoebills
Lenné's Temple
Pheasant Pen
Hives for wild bees
Gibbons
Stork and heron meadow
Peccaries
Wild Boar
Nilgai-Antelope
Secretary Birds
Siberian White Cranes
Loris and Macaws
Amazon parrots
Blackbuck Antelope
Afghan Urials
Pelicans
Thorold's and Bactrian Deer
Timor Deer
Chital
Friedrichsfelde Palace
Wapiti Deer (Elk)
Vietnamese Sika Deer
Sambar Deer
Red Deer
Bird Preservation Trail
Crocodile and humming bird house
Giant Tortoises
Cranes
Malay Bears
Institute for Zoological and Wild Animal Research
Palace Entrance
Terrarium (Snake Farm)

N

100 m
328 ft

Prairie Bisons

©BAEDEKER

the ►Zoologischer Garten in the west. The buildings and enclosures were designed by the man who was director of the park for many years, Heinrich Dathe. Compared to the western zoo, the Tierpark grounds are much more expansive and much less cramped in terms of both the outdoor enclosures and the animals' stables and hutches. The Alfred-Brehm-Haus tropical house, for example, has a huge hall

»The New Africanum«

Hartmann's Zebra
Chapman's Zebra
Aviary for birds of prey
Humboldt and Jackass Penguins
Lions
Prairie dog hill
Goliath Herons
Tigers
Reindeer
Storks
Maned Wolves
Alfred-Brehm-Haus (tropical house)
Big cats' outdoor enclosure
Poitou Donkey
Donkeys
Ponies
Snack bar
Shetland Cattle
Open-Air Stage
Gulls' flight dome
Pets' Corner
Ducks
Pig-tailed Macaques
Turkoman
Eagle Owls
Geladas
Barbary Apes
00
Pandas
Dovecote
Playground
Pot-Bellied Pigs
Monument for Wuhlheide Concentration Camp
Children's Animal Park
Rodents
Tierpark sponsors
Budgerigars
American Bison
Goats
Terrace Café
Polar Bears
00
Family mausoleum of the Treskow family and others
Spectacled Bears
American Black Bears
ment (opean Bison)
Directorate
00
Golden Eagle
Siberian Brown Bear
Bear Window Entrance

where almost 100 species of birds can fly, alongside an extraordinarily large house for large feline predators with extensive enclosures inside the hall where the animals can wander freely. The pride of the collection of big cats is its breeding programme for **Indian lions and Siberian tigers**. Its elephant house contains not only pachyderms but also rhinoceroses and hippopotamuses. It also contains a large viewing pool with rare West Indian **manatees** (sea cows) from the Caribbean. The Tierpark has been particularly successful with breeding programmes for rare hoofed animals, such as the Takin from Burma, sometimes called the beestung moose. The snake farm boasts the largest selection of poisonous snakes in Europe.

The park around Schloss Friedrichsfelde was laid out by Benjamin Raulé at the end of the 17th century. He had been in charge of the navy under the Great Elector. The palace itself was built in around 1695 according to plans by Johann Arnold Nering and extended in 1719. In its present form it is an early Neoclassical gem, as designed from 1800 for Duchess Catharina von Holstein-Beck. Its most prominent guest was King Friedrich August I of Saxony in 1814, who had been taken prisoner in the Battle of the Nations at Leipzig in 1813. Some of the finest rooms are open to visitors.

Schloss Friedrichsfelde

❶ Tue, Thu, Sat, Sun and holidays 11am–5pm; included in admission to the Tierpark

✳ Topography of Terror

✦ **M 16**

Location: Niederkirchnerstr. 8, Mitte
S-Bahn and U-Bahn: Potsdamer
Platz (S 1, S 2, S 25, S 26, U 2)
City centre plan: D 10

❶ Daily 10am–8pm;
admission free
www.topographie.de

The heart of the SS state was a city block at the south end of Wilhelmstrasse. An exhibition entitled Topographie des Terrors preserves the memory of the place from which Nazi crimes were directed.

Exhibition centre

On the so-called Prinz-Albrecht-Gelände, the site bounded by Niederkirchnerstrasse (formerly Prinz-Albrecht-Strasse), the part of Wilhelmstrasse (▶MARCO POLO Insight p.323) that runs south of it, Anhalter Strasse and Stresemannstrasse (formerly Saarlandstrasse), stood the headquarters of the SS, Gestapo and Main Reich Security Office. The main addresses on this site included: Prinz-Albrecht-Straße no. 8, formerly a school of arts and crafts (1901–05) and from 1934 the Gestapo headquarters; Prinz-Albrecht-Straße no. 9, built in 1887–88 as Hotel Prinz Albrecht and then named SS-Haus, seat of the SS leadership; Wilhelmstrasse no. 102, the Prinz-Albrecht-Palais, constructed in 1737 as the town house of Baron Vernezobre and acquired in 1830 by Prinz Albrecht of Prussia, son of King Friedrich Wilhelm III, which was first of all the headquarters of the Sicherheitsdienst (SD; Security Service) of the SS and from 1939 seat of the Reichssicherheitshauptamt (Main Reich Security Office). Excavations begun by a citizens' initiative found cellar walls along Niederkirchnerstrasse in 1986 and revealed the cell floors of the Gestapo's in-house prison. This gave rise to a provisional exhibition about the crimes committed on the site. Only after embarrassingly lengthy disputes was a new building opened in May 2010. Its displays shed light on the history of the site and the functions of the Nazi offices that worked here. Panels on the site provide information about the locations of the principal buildings and the open-air exhibition »Berlin 1933–1945« outlines the story of Nazi rule in the city.

THE SURROUNDING AREA

Prinz Albrecht area

The Martin-Gropius-Bau at Niederkirchnerstrasse 7 a huge brick building, is a pillar of Berlin's cultural life, as it is regularly the venue for exhibitions of the highest calibre. Built in Hellenic Renaissance style from 1877 to 1881 by Martin Gropius – great uncle of Walter Gropius, one of the founders of the Bauhaus movement – along with

A Stage for German History

From the foundation of the Empire, the German Reich, in 1871 until the end of Nazi rule in 1945, Berlin was the capital city. The most important ministries, chancelleries and embassies were concentrated on and around Wilhelmstrasse, which runs south from Pariser Platz.

This district, called Friedrichstadt, developed from 1688 as an independent place south of Berlin and Cölln, and was incorporated into the capital of Prussia in 1710. In the reign of Friedrich Wilhelm I, in the first half of the 18th century, several aristocratic mansions were built here, and were converted to government buildings after the foundation of the Reich in 1871. In the second third of the 19th century, the further growth of Berlin as capital of the kingdom of Prussia led to much construction work in the Friedrichstadt, which thus became the government quarter and the »highest-class residential district«, as the Baedeker guide to Berlin of 1878 noted. In the Weimar Republic the government buildings were used unchanged, but the National Socialists trans-formed the appearance of the area with gigantic new structures: the Neue Reichskanzlei (New Reich Chancellery) on Vossstrasse and the Reichsluftfahrtministerium (Reich Air Ministry). In order to erase these memories, after the Second World War, the leadership of the GDR built residential blocks along the whole west side of the street between Pariser Platz and Vossstrasse, in a line 20m/22yd further back from the old, now ruined façades, and named the street after Prime Minister Otto Grotewohl. Directly behind this was the border, with multiple security installations, facing Potsdamer Platz.

Close to the old no. 77, today the corner with An der Kolonnade, a memorial unveiled in 2011 honours Georg Elser, who tried to assassinate Hitler.

An SS detachment in Wilhelmstrasse in the funeral procession for President Paul von Hindenburg in 1934.

Looking Back

Apart from the former Reich Air Ministry, nothing remains of the pre-war buildings on this section of Wilhelmstrasse. The plan and the street numbers below reproduce the situation in 1939.

The right-hand side of Wilhelmstrasse (the »Reich side«):

No. 70: from 1884 the British embassy, formerly the residence of Dr Strousberg; now the newly built British embassy.

No. 72: residence of Prince August Wilhelm of Prussia (1735), Ministry of Agriculture and Food in the Third Reich.

No. 73: built in 1734–37 for Count Schwerin, from 1872 Ministry of the Royal House, from 1919 seat of presidents Friedrich Ebert and Paul von Hindenburg. After the death of Hindenburg in 1934 it was unused until 1939, when it became the official home of the foreign minister.

No. 74: built in 1731 for Privy Councillor v. Kellner, in 1848 Prussian Ministry of State, then Reich Chancellery, until 1919 Reich Interior Ministry, then headquarters of the Foreign Office along with no. 75 (formerly the court printing works Decker, used from 1882 by the Foreign Office) and no. 76 (Foreign Office from 1870).

No. 76: built in 1735 for Colonel v. Pannwitz, Bismarck's official residence until 1877.

No. 77: built in 1736–39 for General v. d. Schulenburg, from 1795 residence of Prince Radziwill, rebuilt 1875–76, then Reich chancellor's residence, until 1890 also Bismarck's private apartment. In 1878

the Congress of Berlin was held here.

No. 78: Neues Palais of Prince von Pless, first used as part of the Reich Chancellery, demolished in 1927 and rebuilt in 1931, then integrated into the New Reich Chancellery.

No. 79: first Ministry of Trade, later headquarters of the Reichsbahn (railways).

No. 80: Reich Ministry of Transport.

No. 82–97: Reich Air Ministry, built in 1935–36 on the site of the Prussian Ministry of War; the only remaining building from the old government quarter south of Unter den Linden. In the GDR years it was the House of Ministries, then seat of the Treuhandanstalt, which privatized the East German economy after reunification (called Detlev-Rohwedder-Haus after the head of the Treuhandanstalt who was murdered by terrorists), and is now the Federal Finance Ministry.

Prinz-Albrecht-Strasse no. 5 on the left round the corner was the Prussian Chamber of Deputies. In 1934–35 it temporarily housed the Volksgerichtshof, an infamous Nazi law court, before Göring made it the »Airmen's House«. Today it is the seat of the Berliner Abgeordnetenhaus, the parliament of the federal state of Berlin. The building on Leipziger Strasse next to the Finance Ministry, once the Herrenhaus (upper chamber) of the Prussian parliament, is now occupied by the Bundesrat, the parliamentary upper chamber of the Federal Republic of Germany.

No. 102: Prinz-Albrecht-Palais, built in 1737 for Baron Vernezobre and bought in 1830 by Prince Albrecht of Prussia, son of King Friedrich Wilhelm III. From 1939 it housed the Main Reich Security Office of the SS. Many other buildings on this section of Wilhelmstrasse and Prinz-Albrecht-Strasse also accommodated departments of the SS and Gestapo and were the centre of the »SS State«.

The left-hand side of Wilhelmstrasse (the »Prussian side«):

No. 65: the Ministry of Justice, first of Prussia, then of the Reich.

No. 64 and 63: Prussian Ministry of State and »liaison staff of the Führer's deputy«, Rudolf Hess.

No. 62: former seat of the Colonial Ministry, during the Weimar Republic the Ministry for Reconstruction.

No. 61a and Wilhelmplatz 8–9: Wilhelmplatz 8–9 was built in 1737 for the grand master of the Knights of St John and remodelled by Schinkel in 1827–28, then enlarged in 1937–39. Along with Wilhelmstrasse 61a seat of Goebbels' ministry for »People's Education and Propaganda« and of the Reich Chamber of Culture.

No. 60 and 61: originally Wilhelmplatz 1, planned as the Foreign Office, then Reich Treasury, finally Reich Finance Ministry.

No. 55: Hitler's private chancellery.

Vossstrasse

Several government departments were once based here, for example at no. 1 (Borsigsches Palais) the Preussische Pfandbriefbank, in nos. 4 and 5 the Reich Justice Office and the office of the Berlin Gauleiter of the Nazi Party (no. 11).

Buildings in existence before 1933
Buildings erected by National Socialists
—— Route of the Berlin Wall before demolition

Niederkirchnerstrasse is the former name of Prinz-Albrecht-Strasse (pre 1945). The numbers are the house numbers of the various buildings.

Hitler commissioned his favourite architect, Albert Speer, to build the New Reich Chancellery (completed in 1939) along the whole north side of Vossstrasse (nos. 1–19). This 430m/475yd-long structure was an architectural manifestation of the megalomania of the National Socialists. After the end of the war, the building, although only moderately damaged, was blown up. During the construction work for Potsdamer Platz several SS guardrooms of the Reich Chancellery came to light and were sealed up again.

Heino Schmieden, it was home to the Prussian Museum of Decorative Arts until 1921. It was badly damaged in the Second World War and restoration only began in 1979, faithfully recreating the rich decoration on the west, east and south façades. The northern side facing Niederkirchnerstrasse, right next to the course of the Berlin Wall, was only restored after reunification, though the soot-blackened and damaged figures around the portal were retained as a war memorial. The interior is impressive with its encircling gallery and imposing proportions.

❶ Wed–Mon 10am–7pm; www.museumsportal-berlin.de

Berliner Abgeordneten- haus

Opposite the Martin-Gropius-Bau. practically back to back with the former seat of Prussian government and the current Bundesrat (▶Leipziger Strasse), stands the Prussian Landtag building, built from 1892 to 1897. It is now the headquarters of the current Berlin state council and is now called the Berliner Abgeordnetenhaus (Berlin House of Representatives). Here is also the **memorial to the Baron Karl vom und zum Stein** by Hermann Schievelbein. It was unveiled in 1870 a little further east along Leipziger Strasse in front of what was then the Prussian Abgeordnetenhaus. The memorial was badly damaged during the Second World War, but was erected once again in 1981 by East German authorities at the top of Unter den Linden. It has now been returned to somewhere at least close to its original site.

Anhalter Bahnhof

The Anhalter Bahnhof was once a magnificent railway station, Berlin's gateway to the south. Nowadays only a section of the façade and

The site of Gestapo terror is now devoted to education and information about Nazi crimes

the portico on Askanischer Platz testify to its former glory. The first station to be called Anhalter Bahnhof was opened in 1839 and in 1841 **August Borsig's first locomotive** steamed out of the station, pulling a train to Jüterbog. The commission for the building of a much larger station was given to architect Franz Schwechten, who had designed buildings including the Kaiser-Wilhelm-Gedächtniskirche and the AEG factory, along with engineer Heinrich Seidel, who had also made a name for himself in the world of literature with his autobiographical novel Leberecht Hühnchen. The train shed was 170m/186yd long and 60m/66yd wide, its iron roof covering an area of some 10,200 sq m/2.5ac. Along with the brick, terra-cotta and dressed stone adorned entrance hall, it was considered to be the exemplary railway station. The first train left for Lichterfelde on 15 June 1880. The golden age of the station was after 1900, with 58 trains running in and out every day, and 40,000 people embarking and disembarking. The station was so badly hit by an air raid on 23 November 1943 that all long-distance traffic had to be abandoned. The building fell into decay after the war and it was demolished in 1961. After reunification, the long neglected site was redefined as a sports facility. **Tempodrom** Since December 2001 life has returned to the location with the legendary Tempodrom finding a new home here in its tent-like new building. This is a venue for concerts, circus performances, theatre and musicals. On the station site facing Schöneberger Strasse, an air-raid bunker remains in existence. Its history and various items that have been found there are exhibited in its basement. On the floors above, **the Berliner Gruselkabinett** or Cabinet of Horrors contains a full complement of mannequins, skeletons and artificial blood to strike terror into the heart of even the bravest visitor (opening hours: 10am – 7pm every day except Wed, Fri closes 8pm, Sat opens noon).

❶ Berliner Gruselkabinett: closed Wed; admission €9.50; www.gruselkabinett-berlin.de

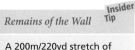

> **!** *Remains of the Wall* **Insider Tip**
>
> MARCO⊕POLO TIP
>
> A 200m/220yd stretch of the Berlin Wall runs along Niederkirchnerstrasse. The street is named after a Communist resistance fighter, Käthe Niederkirchner, who was murdered in 1944 in Ravensbrück concentration camp.

✳ Treptower Park

✦ N 20

Location: Puschkinallee, Treptow
S-Bahn: Treptower Park (S 8, S 9, S 41, S 42)

The Treptower Park is a long stretch of open woodland with a rose garden and extensive lawns by the river Spree.

The Treptower Park and the Plänterwald forest that neighbours it to the east were created by Berlin's municipal director of gardens, Gustav Meyer, a pupil of Peter Joseph Lenné. Meyer created the park between 1876 and 1882 and in 1896 the »Great Berlin Exhibition of Commerce« was held at the site. Towards the end of the rule of the Kaisers and during the period of the Weimar Republic, Treptower Park often hosted large workers' rallies. Treptower Park itself is a long, slightly wooded green space alongside the Spree, with rose gardens and broad lawns.

On the banks of the Spree   Close to the S-Bahn station there is a dock for the Spree steamboats. Behind the station rises the 125m/419ft-high Allianz Treptower. Walk along the banks of the Spree to the **Zenner** tavern, which is popular with day trippers. The tavern took the place of the »Neues Gasthaus an der Spree« built here in 1821/22 by Carl Ferdinand Langhans. On the opposite bank is the Abteiinsel, an island that belonged to the local abbey but which is now termed the Insel der Jugend or Island of Youth. Close to Zenner is the entrance to the natural woodland called Plänterwald.

*Soviet monument   The main attraction in Treptower Park is its huge Soviet monument, built between 1947 and 1949 according to a design by Yevgeny V. Vuchetich and Yakov B. Belopolsky to provide a central monument for the Soviet soldiers killed in the struggle for Berlin in 1945. The main part of the installation is made from Swedish granite that had been stored by the Nazis, in order for it to be used to construct a triumphal arch in Moscow. The figure of a woman on the access avenue is known as Mother Homeland and is sculpted from a single 50-ton granite block. A wide promenade planted with weeping birches leads to the Ehrenhain (honour grove), where two red granite walls symbolize flags lowered in mourning. The main section of the grove, which is the last resting place of 7000 Soviet soldiers, is made up of five lawns bounded by cast laurel wreaths. On both sides of the grove stand eight walls featuring bas-reliefs. The central feature of the monument is a hill of honour with a cylindrical mausoleum that emulates the ancient warrior tombs of the Don plains and includes the main monument to the Soviet soldiers. A figure of a soldier 11.6m/38ft

The Soviet memorial to its heroes in Treptower Park

high carries a child in its left arm and stands on a shattered swastika. The domed hall under the 70-ton monument is decorated with mosaic pictures by the painter Gorpenko on the theme »the representatives of all the republics of the union remember their dead«. The roof also bears the emblem of the Soviet Union's Order of Victory. There are other Soviet memorials in the ▶Tiergarten and on the Schönholzer Heide in Pankow.

Behind the monument lies the Archenhold Observatory. It was built in 1896 and named after its founder, astronomer Friedrich Simon Archenhold. Its main attraction is the **largest refracting telescope in the world**, 21m/69ft long and weighing 130 tons, with a lens 68cm/27in in diameter. The accompanying Himmelskundliche Museum relates the history of the observatory as well as covering other astronomical themes.Next to the observatory is a spot called the **Hain der Kosmonauten** or »Cosmonauts' Copse« that recalls the Soviet space missions. It includes busts of Yuri Gagarin, the first man in space, and East German cosmonaut Sigmund Jähn, the first German in space.

Archenhold Observatory

❶ Wed–Sun 2–4.30pm; tours: Thu 8pm, Sat and Sun 3pm; admission €2.50; information tel. 536 06 37 19; www.astw.de

✶✶ **Unter den Linden**

✦ **L 16/17**

Location: Mitte, between Schlossbrücke and Pariser Platz
S-Bahn: Western end: Brandenburger Tor (S 1, S 2, S 25, U 55);
eastern end: Hackescher Markt (S 5, S 7, S 75)
City centre plan: B 11 – 13
Bus: 100, 147, 200

1400m/1550yd long and 60m/65yd wide, the most famous street in Berlin, if not in all Germany, runs between the Schlossbrücke bridge and Pariser Platz. A place for both Berliners and tourists to promenade, it is the prestigious avenue of the high and mighty: Unter den Linden.

It succeeds an equestrian thoroughfare established during the era of the electors in 1573, which led through the sand of the March to the hunting grounds beyond the city gates. It was the Great Elector who instructed his court gardener Hanff and architects Dressler and Grünberg to plant the stretch leading from the castle to the Tiergarten with six rows of walnut trees and limes in 1647. The walnuts later disappeared but the limes remain. The first buildings along the road were domiciles, commercial buildings and state offices alongside a

Berlin's most famous thoroughfare

couple of palatial mansions, but the Zeughaus or arsenal that was built under Friedrich I was to hint of greater magnificence to follow. Until 1734 the road only went as far as what is now Schadowstrasse, but was extended to Pariser Platz in that year. Friedrich II finally commissioned **Georg Wenzeslaus von Knobelsdorff** to create a prestigious forum, the Forum Fridericianum. However, the architect was soon to lose favour with the king and was only able to complete the opera house, now the Staatsoper on Unter den Linden. Others, though, continued the work he had begun. St Hedwig's Cathedral was built between 1747 and 1773 and the library that came to be known as the Alte Bibliothek was built by Georg Christian Unger. Between 1789 and 1791, Langhans gave Unter den Linden the prime architectural feature that provides a fitting culmination to the road, the ▶Brandenburg Gate. Karl Friedrich Schinkel's Neue Wache was to follow between 1816 and 1818. In the 1920s Unter den Linden and Friedrichstrasse made up the key arteries of republican Berlin. The Second World War ruined Unter den Linden. However, new trees were replanted as early as 1946. In 1958 reconstruction work began on the Forum Fridericianum and many new buildings were erected, particularly to the west of Charlottenstrasse. The object was to make Unter den Linden the prestigious boulevard of the GDR, an evocation of history featuring embassies and ministries. After reunification, the cranes and diggers were back again, building new banks, parliamentary offices, embassies, hotels, company headquarters and, not least, plenty of quality restaurants.

FROM SCHLOSSBRÜCKE TO BEBELPLATZ

*Schloss-
brücke

Starting from ▶Schlossplatz, first the Kupfergraben is bridged by **Karl Friedrich Schinkel's** Schlossbrücke, planned in 1819 and built between 1822 and 1824. It was preceded by a wooden bridge, known to have existed in the 16th century, by the name of the Hundebrücke, so-named because hunters would gather there with their hounds before riding into the game reserves around the city. ****Statues on the bridge** The eight sculptural groups that look down from their white Carrara marble plinths were created between 1845 and 1857 by eight different sculptors using designs by Schinkel himself. Facing towards Unter den Linden they are as follows: **Right-hand side**: Iris, bearing the fallen hero to Olympus (August Wredow, 1841 – 57); thronging youths under the guardianship of Athena (Gustav Bläser, 1854); Minerva accompanies a soldier off to war (Albert Wolff, 1853); Nike, supporting a wounded warrior (Ludwig Wichmann, before 1857). **Left-hand side**: Nike crowns the victor (Friedrich Drake, 1857); Athena arms a warrior for his first battle (Heinrich Möller, 1846 – 50); Pallas Athena teaches a boy to throw the javelin (Hermann Schievelbein,

View from the Schlossbrücke to the Zeughaus

1853); Nike teaches the history of heroism (Emil Wolff, 1847). The sculptures were all taken down during the Second World War and were only returned to the East Berlin senate from West Berlin in 1981.

On the right hand side straight after the bridge stands the former Zeughaus or arsenal, **the largest and most impressive Baroque building in Berlin**. Building began in 1695 using designs by Johann Arnold Nering but it was only completed by Martin Grünberg, Andreas Schlüter and Jean de Bodt. The building was temporarily authorized for use as early as 1706 although it was not completely finished until 1730. From then until 1877 the ground floor was used as an arsenal for heavy artillery, while the top floor stored infantry weapons and trophies of war. For this reason, the Berlin revolutionaries elected to attack the building on 14 June 1848. After the new »Reich« was established in 1870, Kaiser Wilhelm I had the building made into a war and armaments museum for the Brandenburg-Prussian army. The building was badly damaged in the Second World War and rebuilding was not completed until 1965. The façade is 90m/100yd long with a clearly delineated structure; projections and recesses break the uniformity. Its designer was de Bodt. The outstandingly sculpted decoration was mainly provided by Andreas Schlüter, as were the ancient helmets on the cap stones over the windows outside. The allegorical figures on the plinths that project from

the front entrance are by Guillaume Hulot and represent the art of making fireworks along with arithmetic, geometry and mechanics. Hulot also made the trophy sculptures on the roof and the group featuring Mars to designs by Jean de Bodt. Nevertheless, it is the heads of the **22 dying warriors** in the courtyard, the so-called Schlüterhof, which are considered the outstanding example of Baroque architectural sculpture in Germany. ***Deutsches Historisches Museum** Until September 1990 the Zeughaus was home to the German History Museum, the Museum für Deutsche Geschichte, which had been the leading historical museum in East Germany since being established in 1952. This has now been included in the Deutsches Historisches Museum. Its chronology begins in the west wing of the upper floors with the early ages of antiquity up until about 1500. The tour then passes through a second set of selections leading up to 1918/19 in the south wing of the upper floor. It continues in the east wing on the ground floor with the period from the Weimar Republic until the Second World War, then covers the post-war period up until reunification and the withdrawal of the allies in 1994 in the west wing. The annex, designed by I. M. Pei with a spectacular spiral glass stairway outside it, is intended to accommodate rotating exhibitions.

❶ **Deutsches Historisches Museum:** 10am – 6pm daily; admission €6; www.dhm.de

Beyond the Zeughaus stands the Neue Wache or new guardhouse.   *Neue Wache
This was created between 1816 and 1818, with **Karl Friedrich Schinkel** once more the designer. It replaced the earlier Königswache. In front of the castle-like brick building, Schinkel designed a portico of Doric columns, reminiscent of a Greek temple; the bas-relief on the gable is by August Kiss. The German president Paul von Hindenburg declared that the Neue Wache was to be used as a war memorial for the fallen of the First World War, and the redesign that this entailed was completed in 1931 according to plans fashioned by Heinrich Tessenow: the walls of the halls were lined with limestone panels around a tall black granite block under a skylight. On the block there was a silver and gold wreath in the shape of oak-leaf laurels. The East German leadership had the building remodelled again, this time as a memorial to the victims of fascism and militarism. It included an eternal flame over the urns of an unknown concentration camp victim and an unknown soldier. At the end of 1993, it was inaugurated as the central memorial for the whole of the German Federal Republic and it now contains a more than life-sized bronze pietà by Käthe Kollwitz to recall the victims of war and totalitarianism. The original smaller figure by Hermann Haacke was recreated in four times its original size.

❶ daily 10am – 6pm

Magnificent adornment of the Zeughaus entrance

Kastanien-
wäldchen

Behind the Neue Wache there is a wood of chestnut trees, the »Kastanienwäldchen«. The Palais am Festungsgraben (palace by the moat), built in 1753 and redesigned in 1860, is situated amid the trees. Until 1945 it was the residence of the Prussian finance ministers. It now houses the Museum des Heimatvereins Berlin-Mitte, the local museum for the centre of Berlin. The neighbouring Maxim-Gorki Theater was designed in Neoclassical style by Schinkel's pupil Ottmer and built in 1827 as the vocal academy of Carl Friedrich Zelter. Its concert hall was famed for its acoustics at the time and it was used in 1829 for the performance by Felix Mendelssohn-Bartholdy of the St Matthew Passion that had been thought lost after the death of Johann Sebastian Bach (1750), but which had been rediscovered by Zelter.

Schinkelplatz

Opposite the Zeughaus a tower block that housed the East German foreign ministry. stood from 1967 to 1995 on the site of the **Kommandantenhaus,** the house of Berlin's city commandant from 1653, which had been badly damaged during the war. Its external design is now reflected in the new Bertelsmann-Stiftung building that replaced the skyscraper after its demolition in 1995. Beyond it, stretching as far as Werderscher Markt (►Schlossplatz), is Schinkelplatz, now restored to its former layout and adorned once again with its old familiar monuments, including one to Karl Friedrich Schinkel himself and one for agricultural reformer Albrecht Thaer (1752–1828) and one for industrialist Christian Wilhelm Beuth (1781 – 1853). At its southern end some masonry and a printed textile sheet simulate Schinkel's **Bauakademie** (Academy of Architecture), which a sponsor is planning to rebuild.

At the south end of the square on the right stands the Gothic Revival **Friedrichswerdersche Kirche,** built with its two towers from 1824 to 1830 and designed by Karl Friedrich Schinkel. Inside, beneath the starry vault of the hall church, the **Schinkelmuseum** presents a selection of Neoclassical sculptures to illuminate the work of Karl Friedrich Schinkel in Berlin. New Year plaques cast in iron by the Berliner Eisengiesserei are also on show.

The new building opposite the Akademie is the lobby of the **Foreign Ministry**. It conceals the Reichsbank, building, constructed from 1934 to 1938 and used from 1958 by the Central Committee of the ruling SED party. It is now the seat of the Foreign Ministry.

Schinkelmuseum: Tue–Sun 10am–6pm; admission free; www.smb.museum

Kronprinzen-
palais

Beyond the Kommandantenhaus is the palace of the crown price, the Kronprinzenpalais, built by Johann Arnold Nering (1663/64). It passed into the possession of Friedrich Wilhelm I in 1732 and he had it rebuilt by Philipp Gerlach. It was the home of Prince August Wilhelm, brother of Frederick the Great, who became Crown Prince Friedrich Wilhelm after 1793. He lived here with his wife Luise. In

1856 the man who was to become Kaiser Friedrich III moved in with his wife Viktoria. Wilhelm II, the last of the German »Kaisers«, was born here on 27 January 1859. During the Second World War, the building was badly damaged and nowadays there are no longer any copies of the original plans in existence. Thus Richard Paulick's reconstruction of 1968/69 was forced to use only old engravings as its source. The result was a cultural centre and a guesthouse for dignitaries visiting East Germany that was renamed »Palais Unter den Linden«. It was here that the reunification treaty between East and West Germany was signed on 31 August 1990.

The neighbouring Prinzessinnenpalais, another faithful reconstruction by Paulick, was originally built between 1733 and 1737 according to plans by Friedrich Wilhelm Dietrich and was linked to the crown prince's palace by Heinrich Gentz's gatehouse in 1811. It was the home of Friedrich Wilhelm III's three daughters until they were all married and this is where it gets its name. In the **Prinzessinnengarten** are statues of Generals Blücher, Gneisenau, Scharnhorst and Yorck by Christian Daniel Rauch.

Prinzessin-
nenpalais

FORUM FRIDERICIANUM

The Forum Fridericianum begins with the Staatsoper Unter den Linden. It was initially planned that the area around what is now Bebelplatz (formerly Opernplatz) was to be laid out according to Frederick the Great's concept of a cultural focal point for the Prussian capital.

In building the opera house or Staatsoper between 1741 and 1743, Georg Wenzeslaus von Knobelsdorff opened up the way for classicism in Germany. It was **the first theatre in Germany outside a palace of the nobility** and was also the largest theatre in Europe at the time, although all of its 2000 seats were reserved for invited guests only. An inscription on the gable portico leaves no doubt as to the ambitions of the commissioning monarch: FRIDERICUS REX APOLLINI ET MUSIS (Friedrich, king over Apollo and the muses). In 1789 the opera house was opened to the general public but on the night of 18–19 August 1843 the building burned down, only to be resurrected just a year later by Carl Ferdinand Langhans. Meyerbeer, Lortzing and Richard Strauss all had major successes here. During the Second World War an incendiary device reduced the building to a shell and, although it was quickly restored, it was finally obliterated in February 1945. Another reconstruction was started in 1951 under the aegis of Richard Paulick and Kurt Hemmerling, and on 4 September 1955 the building was officially reopened with a performance of Richard Wagner's Meistersinger.

*Deutsche
Staatsoper
Unter den
Linden

*Sankt-Hedwigs-Kathedrale

The Baroque Cathedral of St Hedwig at the southeast corner of Bebelplatz is modelled on the Pantheon in Rome and is the seat of the Catholic bishop of Berlin. Building started in 1747 using designs by Georg Wenzeslaus von Knobelsdorff. The necessary money for the project was collected by the Carmelite monk Mecenati from predominantly Catholic countries and the land was donated by Frede-rick the Great. St. Hedwig's is the only one of Berlin's churches that was built during his reign. After the Seven Years' War, building continued under Johann Boumann the Elder from 1772 onwards, and the church was inaugurated on 1 November 1773. It was named after Hedwig (1174 – 1243), wife of Duke Heinrich of Silesia, who was well revered in that region. When Silesia was conquered by Frederick, it was the first area with a consolidated Catholic population to fall into Prussian hands. St Hedwig's Cathedral burned to a shell during 1943 and its reconstruction lasted from 1952 to 1963. The newly designed interior may seem a little naked but the historical reconstruction of the dome is faithful.

> **MARCO POLO TIP**
>
> **!** *View* *Insider Tip*
>
> From the roof terrace of the Hotel de Rome (formerly Dresdner Bank) next to St Hedwig's there is a good view of the cathedral, Humboldt University, Zeughaus and TV tower (▶photo p.66). In good weather the terrace is open to all from noon until 10pm for coffee or a drink.

Alte Bibliothek

The western side of the square is occupied by the Alte Bibliothek or Old Library, built between 1775 and 1780 as a royal library using a design Fischer von Erlach had originally intended for the Michaelertrakt wing of Vienna's Hofburg palace. Its effectively curvaceous Baroque façade led to it being dubbed the »Kommode«. By 1914 it had served its purpose as a library and was being used as a university. It burned down in 1945 and restoration was not begun until 1967, being completed only in 1969. It is now occupied by the law faculty of Humboldt University.

Altes Palais

Adjoining the Alte Bibliothek is another reconstructed building in the form of the Altes Palais, which is nowadays also part of Humboldt University. It was formerly the home of Wilhelm I, who lived here for 50 years – throughout his time as crown prince, king of Prussia, and emperor of Germany – till his death in 1888. The last window on the left-hand side of the ground floor is the so-called »historic window« from which Wilhelm I is said to have observed the changing of the guard every day at noon. He himself gave the following reason for sticking to this routine: »The people await my greeting – it says so in Baedeker.«

Memorial to the burning of books

A monument by artist Micha Ullmann was unveiled in the centre of Bebelplatz during 1995 to recall the burning of books that was perpetrated here by the Nazis on 10 May 1933. It portrays the vacuum left by the exodus of artists who were dubbed »degenerate« in the form of an underground library with empty shelves. The room can be seen through a glass pane in the ground.

A huge mounted statue of Frederick the Great, which including its pedestal towers rises 13.5m/44ft above the central reservation of Unter den Linden, was designed by **Christian Daniel Rauch** and dates from 1851. In 1950 it was taken to the park at Sanssouci and it was only restored to something like its original location in 1980. Rauch's masterpiece shows the king of Prussia in his coronation vestments and jackboots, carrying a trident and cane, while mounted upon his favourite horse, »Condé«. Four panels on the plinth beneath bear the names of 60 leading contemporaries of the king. The central section shows Prussia's generals, the western end under the horse's tail covers men of politics, art and science, while the corners feature other mounted figures including Prince Heinrich of Prussia, Duke Ferdinand of Brunswick and Generals Friedrich Wilhelm von Seydlitz and Hans Joachim von Ziethen. The upper section is decorated with bas-reliefs depicting scenes from Friedrich's life.

*Equestrian statue of Frederick the Great

Humboldt University is marked by the rare ginkgo trees in its front garden and the marble statues of the brothers Alexander und Wilhelm von Humboldt in front of the entrance. The university dates from an endowment of King Friedrich Wilhelm III that enabled Wilhelm von Humboldt to establish it as an educational institution. The building was originally intended to be a palace for Prince Heinrich, the brother of Frederick the Great, and had been built between 1748 and 1766 by Johann Boumann using plans by von Knobelsdorff. In 2006 a monument to Max Planck by Bernd Heiliger was placed in the courtyard.

Humboldt University

FROM BEBELPLATZ TO PARISER PLATZ

Beyond Humboldt University the avenue passes the Staatsbibliothek or State Library. The original »Churfürstliche Bibliothek zu Cölln an der Spree« dates back to the electorship days of 1661 when the library was housed in the Apotheken wing of the Berliner Stadtschloss. It was renamed the Royal Library in 1701. In 1780 the library of that name relocated to the Alte Bibliothek building (see above). Until 1902 the present Platz der Bibliothek was occupied by the Marstall or royal stud, built between 1687 and 1700 by Johann Arnold Nering und Martin Grünberg. This later housed the Akademie der Wissenschaften (Academy of the Sciences) and Akademie der Künste (Academy of the Arts). The Rotes Saal or Red Hall is known as the venue

Staatsbibliothek zu Berlin

MARCO ☉ POLO TIP

! *Berlin Story* Insider Tip

This may look like an enormous souvenir shop, but those who take a closer look will discover a rich source of Berlin literature, city maps, illustrated books, CDs etc – and plenty of souvenirs and kitsch, too (Unter den Linden 40, daily 10am–7pm).

of **Johann Gottlieb Fichte's** Lectures to the German nation in 1807 and 1808. The present building was built between 1903 and 1914 by Ernst von Ihne in neo-Baroque style and gained the name »Preussische Staatsbibliothek« or Prussian State Library after the First World War. Subsequent to the Second World War, Berlin was divided and its library collections along with it. The building on Unter den Linden was now given over to East Berlin's »Deutsche Staatsbibliothek«, while in West Berlin the »Staatsbibliothek Preussischer Kulturbesitz« was established (▶Kulturforum). The two libraries were merged after reunification to form the »Staatsbibliothek zu Berlin – Preussischer Kulturbesitz« (Berlin State Libraries – Prussian Cultural Heritage). The building on Unter den Linden is now used as a research library for pre-1955 literature.

Neues Gouverneurs-haus
Opposite the library and next to the Alte Palais there is a plot that was formerly occupied by the Niederländische Palais or Dutch Palace, which was completely destroyed in the Second World War. The Neue Gouverneurshaus or New Governor's House that replaced it features decoration on its façade originating from the old Kommandantenhaus, which once stood on the corner of Rathausstrasse and Jüdenstrasse.

Crossroads with Friedrichst-rasse
The crossroads between Unter den Linden and Friedrichstrasse was one of the liveliest places in Berlin before the Second World War. The southeast corner was occupied by the famous and traditional Café Bauer, which was supplanted by the Lindencorso during the GDR era. Since reunification, a new Lindencorso building has been erected. The northeast corner was once the site of the Hotel Victoria and its café; later on Café König stood here. The **Haus der Schweiz** (1936) is one of the few buildings in this area that survived the war almost intact. At the southwest corner of the crossroads, urbanites used to flock to the world famous **Café Kranzler**. This too was destroyed in the war and has been replaced by a new building.

Towards Pariser Platz
The crossroads with Friedrichstrasse also marks the end of the regal section of Unter den Linden. During the 19th century the stretch between Friedrichstrasse and Pariser Platz developed into a boulevard flanked by shops, cafés, restaurants and hotels, and the pedestrian path along the central reservation really did pass under an avenue of linden (lime) trees. Nothing remains from this period of history. On

the northern side of the road, there has been a huge amount of building work in recent years, with new offices including German broadcaster ZDF's headquarters in the capital (nos. 36 – 38) and the long façade of the Bundestag offices. At the corner of Schadowstrasse the **Willy Brandt Foundation** has moved from the Schöneberger Rathaus into considerably more spacious premises. An exhibition there outlines the political career of Brandt, who was ruling mayor of Berlin for many years, and later federal chancellor and chairman of the Social Democratic Party. Among the items on display are the official document of his Nobel Peace Prize and the watch of party founder August Bebel, which Brandt possessed. Next door, in what was the Polish embassy, the German branch of **Madame Tussaud's** waxworks has opened up. One building that harks back to a historic forerunner is the **Russian embassy** (no. 65 on the south side). Its site was previously occupied by the palace of Princess Amalie, Frederick the Great's sister. In 1832 the Russian ambassador moved into the palace and after the October revolution the Soviet ambassador took his place until 1941. The building was bombed into oblivion during the Second World War. In the post-war years it was the first building to be restored on Unter den Linden (1950–53) and it then continued in its role as the Soviet embassy to East Germany. It is still used as an embassy by the present-day Russian Federation. From here it is only a stone's throw across Wilhelmstrasse and past **Hotel Adlon** to Pariser Platz and the ▶Brandenburg Gate.

Willy Brandt Foundation: Tue–Sun 9am–6pm, admission free
Madame Tussaud's: daily 10am–7pm, admission €19.90; www.madametussauds.com/berlin

* # Wannsee

🔆 **T 7 southwest**

Location: Zehlendorf
S-Bahn: Wannsee (S 1, S 7)

With its magnificent detached houses set in large, well-tended gardens, Wannsee is one of the best residential districts in Berlin. But Wannsee, which refers to both the lake and the district, means more than that: it is the most popular recreational area in the west of Berlin.

The area has many attractions: the beach, Strandbad Wannsee, opened in 1907 and extended in 1930 to make it the largest open-air bathing facility in Berlin; other beaches featuring sailing, rowing and other water sports clubs; and the Wannseeterrassen and many other similar taverns on the banks of the lake or nearby. There are plenty of

The greatest crime in human history was prepared here

walks too. The Wannsee area, a relic of the ice age, covers 260ha/640ac where the Havel forms a broad bay. Around the main Wannsee lake, the Grosser Wannsee, there are a number of smaller linked watercourses: Kleiner Wannsee, Pohlesee, Stölpchensee (with beach), the Prinz-Friedrich-Leopold-Kanal and Griebnitzsee, where the Teltowkanal begins.

Wannsee village

The village of Wannsee is one of the longest settled areas in Berlin and was formed in 1899 from the amalgamation of three other villages: Stolpe on Lake Stölpchensee, which is first documented in 1299, the colony around the railway station and the Alsen colony of villas established on the west bank in 1863 by a member of the Chamber of Commerce, a certain Herr Conrad.

The road Am Grossen Wannsee runs along the west bank of the lake. The house on the corner of Colomierstr. (no. 3, **Liebermann Villa**) was the summer home of Max Liebermann for 25 years starting in 1910. 400 of his paintings and drawings were produced there. It is now a museum with the artist's studio and a lovely garden. The large villa at nos. 56–58 dating from 1914/15 was the scene of a notorious event on 20 January 1942. It hosted a conference for which the theme was »The Final Solution to the Jewish Question«. Under the chairmanship of Reinhard Heydrich, leading Nazis gave official sanction to the extermination of Europe's Jews that had already been under way since mid-1941. The meeting and its consequences are documented in an exhibition in the *Haus der Wannsee Konferenz** entitled The Wannsee Conference and the Genocide of the European Jews. In the accompanying Mediathek facility, it is possible to view reports including videos of survivors relating their experiences

❶ Liebermann-Villa: bus 114 from S-Bahn Wannsee, April–Oct Wed–Mon 10am–6pm, Thu until 8pm; Nov–March Wed–Mon 11am–5pm; admission: €6; www.liebermann-villa.de
Haus der Wannseekonferenz: bus 114, daily 10am–6pm, admission free; www.ghwk.de/

On the eastern shore of Kleiner Wannsee, on Bismarckstrasse between two boathouses not far from the S-Bahn station, is the **grave of Heinrich von Kleist**, who committed suicide here on 21 November 1811 along with Henriette Vogel. It was remodelled in 2011 to commemorate the bicentenary of Kleist's death.   **Kleist's grave**

★★ Zoologischer Garten
(Zoological gardens)

⊹ M / L 13

Location: Tiergarten
S-Bahn and U-Bahn: Zoologischer Garten (S 5, S 7, S 75; U 2, U 9)
City centre plan: B/C 5/6
Entrances: Hardenbergplatz 8 (Löwentor), Budapester Str. 34 (Elefantentor)

❶ April–Sept daily 9am–7pm, Oct–March until 5pm; aquarium all year daily 9am–6pm
Admission: zoo and aquarium €20, separate tickets €13 each
www.zoo-berlin.de

The famous zoological gardens lie in the western part of the inner city, right next to Bahnhof Zoo and bounded by the railway, by Budapester Strasse and the Landwehrkanal.

Building of the zoo began in 1841 when King Friedrich Wilhelm IV donated to the city all of the animals from his pheasant pens in the Tiergarten as well as all the animals that had been housed on the

Zoological Garden

Berlin Technical University

Lower lock

Flamingos

Sea Birds

Cassowaries

Nursery

Pheasant pen

Children's Zoo

Emus

Commercial enclosure

Birds' House

Herons

Station Car Park (Berliner Verkehrsgesellschaft)

Domestic Animals

Polar Bears

Hertzallee

Eurasian spoonbill

Maned Wolves

Wolves

African Wild Dogs

Camels

Tropical Bears

Brown Bears

Wald-schänke

Wading Bird Panorama

Llamas

Hippopotami

Children's Playground

00

Cranes

Beavers

Gnus

Rhinoceroses

Antelopes

African Buffalo

Hippo house

Penguins

Tapirs

Birds of Prey

Pigs

Bantengs

Water Buffalo

Wild Asses Zebras

Zoo-logischer

Lion Gate Entrance

Anoas

Cattle

Seals

Antelope

Garten

Tahrs

Owls

Wisents

Bisons

Deer

Wading

Zebras

Station

Barbary Sheep

Alpacas

Ibex

Deer

Bird Meadow

00

Elephant house

Florentin Pigeons

Antelopes

Deer

BUS

Giraffes

Antelope house

Deer

Zoo administration

Flamingos

Flamingos

Vierwald-stätter See

Antelope

Cormorants

Tigers

Lemurs

Monkeys

Sea Lion Pond

Panda Predator house

Restaurant

Zoo-Palast Cinema Centre

Apes

Japanese Macaques

Nocturnal Animal House

Ducks

Rodents

Ape house

Lions

Geese

Gibbons

Stork aviary

Ducks

Ducks

Monkeys

Bobby the Gorilla (statue)

Gibbons

Iguanodon (statue)

Red Pandas

Zoo school

Asian enclosure

00

Aquarium

Budapester Strasse

Elephant Gate

Elephant Gate entrance

Ernst-Reuter-Platz

Zoofenster

100 m

©BAEDEKER

Kantstrasse

Kurfürstendamm

▶Pfaueninsel. The gardens opened on 1 August 1844 and were **the first zoological gardens in Germany**. However, it was not until 1 October 1869 that Heinrich Bodinus was appointed to be the zoo's first proper scientific director. The job was taken on by Ludwig Heck from 1888 and he considerably increased the variety of animals,

Neuer
See

Grosser Weg

Fountain

Café am
Neuen See

Lichtensteinallee

Thomas-Dehler-Str.

African
Animals

Przewalski's
Horse

Lichten-
stein-
brücke

South American
Animals

Antelope

Kangaroos

Drakestrasse

Eastern Grey
Kangaroos

**Pumping
house**

Serows

Wading Birds

Lützowufer

Eastern Grey
Kangaroos

Rauchstrasse

Okapi

-Bongos

P

Rhinoceroses

Landwehr-

Hotel
Inter-
Continental
Berlin

Antelope

Cornelliustr.

Kulturforum ↑

00

Geese

Neptun-
teich

Cornelius- Stülerstrasse
brücke

Swans

Budapester Strasse

Hotel
Schweizerhof

Kanal

Lützowufer

making Berlin Zoo one of the most varied zoos in the world. Under his son and successor Lutz Heck, the first large enclosures with no bars or fences between animals and visitors were established. By 1939 the zoo owned more than 4000 mammals and birds with a total of over 1400 species. Fighting during the Second World War destroyed much of the zoo and killed many animals, and rebuilding work was not begun until long after the end of the conflict. Even the Elefantentor, the elephant-shaped gatehouse from 1899 that had been destroyed in the war, was reconstructed. A counterpart to this zoo, ▶Tierpark Friedrichsfelde, was also opened in 1955 in East Berlin's Lichtenberg district during the division of the city.

The zoo currently has some 13,700 animals of about 1390 species. The main attractions are the apes, the lion enclosure, the elephant herd, the hippo house and, of course, the very rare **giant panda**, now the only panda in any German zoo since the death of his female companion. The **aquarium** (with its crocodile hall and insectarium) boasts about 500 species.

POTSDAM
FROM A TO Z

Just half an hour's S-Bahn ride away from the centre of Berlin,
visitors to Potsdam enter a world of Prussian glory.

POTSDAM

S-Bahn: Potsdam Hbf. (S 7)	Potsdam Hbf., Charlottenhof or
Regional train: RE 1 to	Park Sanssouci

Nowadays 155,000 people live in Potsdam home, a town on the Havel river at the point where it broadens into various lakes and canals. The Prussian kings established a summer residence here, a tradition that was continued by the German emperors, and the king most associated with Potsdam is Frederick the Great. The name Potsdam still conveys undertones of »old Prussia«, although today it is the capital of the federal state of Brandenburg.

Potsdam's array of palaces and gardens is what led it to be adopted onto UNESCO's list of World Heritage Sites in 1990. The bombardment of April 1945 did do serious damage to the historic town centre and East Germany's town planners chose to tear down many of the ruins rather than restore them, but there are still many charming corners. However, it is Potsdam's **unique collection of great parks and palaces** created by the finest landscape gardeners, architects, painters and sculptors of their day that make the town special.

History   Potsdam was first documented in 993, when it was called Poztupimi. It is described as a town from 1317 onwards. The small country town only really expanded, though, when Elector Friedrich Wilhelm selected it as the site of a second residence after his palace in Berlin. The Stadtschloss (Potsdam City Palace) was built to his commission between 1664 and 1670. Under the strict regime of Friedrich Wilhelm I, the »Soldier King«, Potsdam began a transformation that was to make it an administrative centre and garrison town. Friedrich II continued the building work. The Stadtschloss was expanded, and work began on the palace of Schloss Sanssouci and the Neue Palais (New Palace). Whole suburbs were demolished and reconstructed. During Friedrich's reign, Potsdam attracted many writers, musicians and philosophers, in particular Voltaire. In 1838 Prussia's first railway line opened between Berlin and Potsdam. 21 March 1933

!

MARCO◉POLO TIP

Potsdam Programme   Insider Tip

The town centre and Schloss Sanssouci should definitely be on the itinerary: both are easily reached on foot. Those wishing to walk across the entire park to the Neue Palais will need to be a bit fitter – or jump on the bus. The same applies to the Neue Garten and Schloss Cecilienhof. The coordinates given in the following section refer to the map of Potsdam's town centre printed on the back of the enclosed Berlin city map.

Potsdam has a lot to offer – not only palaces and gardens.

became known as »Tag von Potsdam« or **»The Day of Potsdam«**, when Hindenburg and Hitler signified a symbolic bond between the German nation and the National Socialist party at the garrison church, an event seen by many as the beginning of the Third Reich. But Potsdam is also closely associated with its ending: in August 1945 allied leaders Truman, Churchill (and later Attlee after his election in Britain) and Stalin met at Schloss Cecilienhof to sign the **Potsdam Agreement**, which sealed the fate of Germany. Since reunification, Potsdam has been the capital of the federal state of Brandenburg and has experienced a cultural, political and economic boom period, helped not least by its proximity to the national capital.

✴✴ City Centre

✦ C/D 3/4

The following description is a walking tour around Potsdam's city centre. From the main station Potsdam Hauptbahnhof, which has now been incorporated into the gigantic Potsdam Center, cross the Lange Brücke (Long Bridge) to Alter Markt (Old Marketplace).

Alter Markt was the centre of Potsdam. This is where the Great Elector had the Stadtschloss built between 1664 and 1670. An air raid on 14 April 1945 hit the Stadt-schloss and it was gutted by fire. The ruins

*Alter Markt

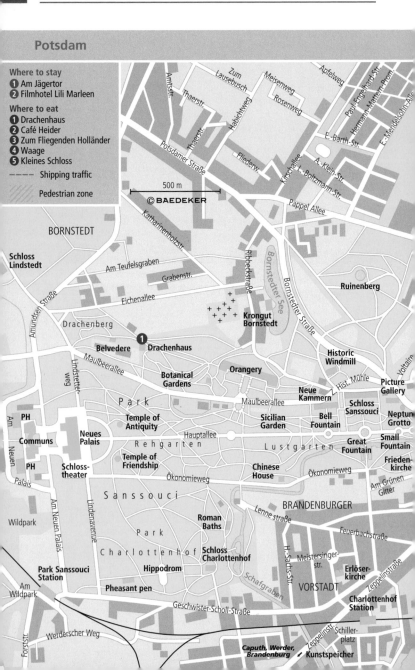

Potsdam

Where to stay
1. Am Jägertor
2. Filmhotel Lili Marleen

Where to eat
1. Drachenhaus
2. Café Heider
3. Zum Fliegenden Holländer
4. Waage
5. Kleines Schloss

----- Shipping traffic

///// Pedestrian zone

500 m

© BAEDEKER

Amtstr.

Zum Lausebusch

Meisenweg

Apfelweg

Thaerstr.

Rosenweg

Paul-Engelhard-Str.

Hermann-Maetern-Prom.

Habichtweg

E.-Barth-Str.

E.-Mendelsohn-Allee

Thaerstr.

Friedenw.

A.-Klein-Str.

Potsdamer Straße

Kirchallee

L.-Boltzmann-Str.

Pappel Allee

Katharinenholzstr.

BORNSTEDT

Schloss Lindstedt

Am Teufelsgraben

Grabenstr.

Ribbeckstraße

Bornstedter See

Bornstedter Straße

Ruinenberg

Amundsen Straße

Eichenallee

+ +
+ + +
+ + +

Krongut Bornstedt

Drachenberg

1 **Drachenhaus**

Belvedere

Maulbeerallee

Botanical Gardens

Historic Windmill

Lindstetter weg

Orangery

Z. Hist. Mühle

Voltaire

Picture Gallery

Neue Kammern

Schloss Sanssouci

Neptun Grotto

Am Neuen Palais

PH

Temple of Antiquity

Sicilian Garden

Bell Fountain

Small Fountain

Communs

Neues Palais

Hauptallee

R e h g a r t e n

L u s t g a r t e n

Great Fountain

PH

Temple of Friendship

Chinese House

Ökonomieweg

Frieden-kirche

Schloss-theater

Ökonomieweg

Am Grünen Gitter

S a n s s o u c i

Lindenavenue

Roman Baths

Lenne straße

BRANDENBURGER

P a r k

Feuerbachstraße

Wildpark

C h a r l o t t e n h o f

Schloss Charlottenhof

H.-Sachs-Str.

Meistersinger-str.

Park Sanssouci Station

Hippodrom

Schafgraben

VORSTADT

Erlöser-kirche

Zeppelinstraße

Am Wildpark

Pheasant pen

Geschwister-Scholl-Straße

Charlottenhof Station

Forststr.

Werderscher Weg

Zeppelinstr.

Schiller-platz

Caputh, Werder, Brandenburg

Kunstspeicher

were demolished in 1959–60. Rows of poplars now mark where the walls once stood. In 2002 the Fortuna-Tor, a gate designed by Jean de Bodt in 1701 when Prussia was first made a kingdom, was rebuilt. Reconstruction of the palace to make it the seat of parliament of the federal state has begun, turning the centre into a building site.

The *Nikolaikirche or Church of St Nicholas dates back to a hall church built between 1721 and 1724 by Philipp Gerlach, although that church burned down in 1795. In 1830 a new church was built on the site, adopting Karl Friedrich Schinkel's suggestion of having a dome, but when the church was dedicated in 1837, it only had a flat roof. The 78m/256ft dome was only added after Schinkel's death in a subsequent phase of building that took place from 1843 to 1849 at the behest of Friedrich Wilhelm IV. he obelisk in the square is from an original design by von Knobelsdorff that was destroyed during the Second World War. It was reconstructed in 1979, although the original depictions of Prussian rulers were replaced by statues of Prussian architects.

The **Altes Rathaus** or Old Town Hall was built from 1753 to 1755 by Johann Boumann the Elder in Palladian style. The gilded Atlas carrying the globe of the world on the tower is visible from far and wide. In 2012 the **Potsdam Museum** moved into the Altes Rathaus and an adjoining new building, thus returning to its original place on Alter Markt after more than 100 years. It presents the early modern period, recent history, older and contemporary art.

Potsdam Museum: Tue–Fri 10am–5pm, Thu until 7pm, Sat and Sun 10am–6pm; admission €5

Marstall   Opposite Alter Markt the Marstall or stables can be seen stretching into the distance. This is all that remains of the original palace complex. It was originally built as an orangery in 1685 to plans by Johann Arnold Nehring but converted to stables in 1714. It gained its present form in 1746 at the hands of Georg Wenzeslaus von Knobelsdorff.

The **Filmmuseum** in the Marstall building is not as pepped up with high technology as its rival on Potsdamer Platz in Berlin, it can still show off eight decades of Babelsberg's film history with no less impressive original items once owned by such figures as Zarah Leander, Lilian Harvey and, in particular, Hans Albers. The main theme is the GDR era, including the topic of state censorship.

● Tue–Sun 10am–6pm; admission €5, www.filmmuseum-potsdam.de

Breite Strasse   The Marstall lies on Breite Strasse, which was laid out under Elector Friedrich Wilhelm in 1668 as a showpiece boulevard. Little survived the Second World War, and the road is being diverted for reconstruction of the palace.

Pass the computer centre (1969–72). Until 1968 this was the site of the **Garnisonkirche** (military church) built between 1732 and 1735 by Philipp Gerlach, in which the sarcophaguses of Friedrich Wilhelm I and Friedrich II were placed until 1943. History was made here on 21 March 1933, the »Day of Potsdam«, when Hitler opened the Reichstag in the presence of Reich President von Hindenburg. Behind the computer centre is a replica of the famous glockenspiel; a surviving gate grille can be seen at the Predigerwitwenhaus (see below). A society promoting reconstruction has constructed a temporary »chapel of reconciliation« for an exhibition next to the excavated historic foundations. It is planned to rebuild the Garnisonkirche by 2017.

The late Baroque/Neoclassical façade a few paces further on is what survives of the so-called *Langer Stall, which was built in 1734 as a space for military exercises in winter.

At the corner of Dortustrasse stands the four-storey **former military orphanage**, founded in 1722 by Friedrich Wilhelm I, in which more than 2000 soldiers' orphans were accommodated during the Seven Years' War.

The building opposite (nos. 8 –12), known as the **Hiller-Brandtsche houses** – was constructed in 1769 and based on Whitehall Palace in London; next to it is the **Predigerwitwenhaus** (preacher's widow's house, 1664) the oldest residential building in Potsdam.

Two memorial exhibitions are close by: »**Potsdam and 20 July 1944**« in the Ministry of Infrastructure and Agriculture (Henning-von-Tresckow-Str. 2-8) and the place of memorial at Lindenstrasse 54–55 for victims of political violence in the 20th century, in the Grosses Holländisches Haus, built in 1737. It was used as a remand prison by the Nazis, Soviets and from 1952 by the Stasi, and nicknamed »Lindenhotel«.

Going out of town on Breite Strasse you reach the »**mosque**« on Neustädter Havel Bay. This is in fact a steam-engine house, built in 1842 to designs by Persius to power the fountains at Sanssouci. Water was pumped from here up to the Ruinenberg for the fountains in the gardens.

Potsdam and 20 July 1944: Mon–Fri 9am–4pm, free admission
Memorial Lindenstrasse: March–Oct Tue–Sun 10am–6pm, Nov–Feb untl 5pm; admission €1.50; www.gedenkstaette-lindenstrasse.de
Mosque/steam-engine house: May–Oct Sat and Sun 10am–6pm, only as part of a tour, admission €3 ; www.spsg.de

Luisenplatz is a good place to start a visit of the park and palace of Sanssouci, as a short avenue leads from its north-west corner to Sanssouci. It is dominated by the MBrandenburg Gater, erected in 1770 to commemorate the Seven Years' War. Mars and Hercules adorn the attic storey.   **Luisenplatz**

From the square the pedestrian street Brandenburger Strasse leads back to the city centre. The writer Theodor Storm lived in while working as a lawyer at no. 70 the Potsdam district court (1853–56).   **Brandenbur-ger Strasse**

Dortustrasse leads to Yorckstrasse, originally called Am Kanal, as it was the course of a canal that was filled in during the 1960s, but restored in this section.

Yorckstrasse and *Neuer Markt

Go right from here along Siefertstrasse to reach Neuer Markt, site of the coach house, built in 1671 and embellished with a fine gateway between 1787 and 1789; it is home to the **Haus der Brandenburgisch-Preussischen Geschichte** (museum of Brandenburg and Prussian history). The house called Neuer Markt 1 (1753) was supposedly the birthplace of Wilhelm von Humboldt; until 1786 the later King Friedrich Wilhelm II lived here.
Haus der Brandenburgisch-Preussischen Geschichte: Tue–Thu 10am–5pm, Fri–Sun until 6pm; admission €4.50; www.hbpg.de

Bassinplatz

Go left into Friedrich-Ebert-Strasse and right to Bassinplatz, which was constructed at the same time as the Dutch quarter. Its name derives from a basin constructed between 1737 and 1739, which was linked with the Heiliger See by a canal. It was filled in during 1863. Nowadays it is the site of a daily market, which takes place in the shadow of the **Peter-und-Pauls-Kirche** (Church of Saints Peter and Paul) built in 1870. The French Church or **Französische Kirche** at the southeastern corner is reminiscent of the Pantheon in Rome and was probably designed by von Knobelsdorff and built in 1752–53.

**Dutch Quarter

Not far from Bassinplatz is the Dutch Quarter, 134 truly exquisite houses built between 1732 and 1742 for Dutch immigrants. Johann Boumann the Elder's plans mainly featured five-storey buildings with eaves or brick gabled houses with a triple axis. They have now been lovingly restored and are occupied by all kinds of shops (many of them craft shops), bars and cafés. Only the front gardens once possessed by each of the houses are no longer in existence. In the **Jan-Bouman-Haus** in Mittelstrasse is an exhibition about the history of this quarter.
Jan-Bouman-Haus: Mon–Fri 1–6pm, Sat and Sun from 11am admission €2; www.jan-bouman-haus.de

Tiefer See

To the east of the Dutch Quarter, at Tiefer See (the name means »deep lake«), a lively cultural scene and high-tech companies have taken over an area formerly used for military and industrial purposes. Above all the new waterside Hans-Otto-Theater designed by Gottfried Böhm pulls in crowds (tram 93 from Potsdam Hauptbahnhof). At Schiffbauergasse the Museum Fluxus presents works by Fluxus artists, especially Wolf Vostell.
❶ Wed–Sun 1–6pm, admission €7.50; www.fluxus-plus.de

Just looking at this gable makes it clear where the Durch quarter got its name

✴ Neuer Garten (New Garden)

✦ A/B 4/5

Location: Northeast of the town centre
Bus: 692

**The Neuer Garten is a wonderful example of a »sentimental«
landscape park.**

The Neuer Garten (New Garden) extends over 74ha/183 acres on the
west bank of the Heilige See as far as the Jungfernsee. The land is mentioned as early as the 18th century when it is described as the king's
vineyard. In 1783 the crown prince, who was later to become King
Friedrich Wilhelm II, built a vineyard here with its own pleasure house.
Between 1787 and 1791, inspired by Wörlitzer Park near Dessau, the
prince had Johann August Eyserbeck the Younger, son of the Wörlitzer
garden's architect, lay out a »sentimental« landscape garden.

A WALK THROUGH THE NEUER GARTEN

**Holländisches
Etablisse-
ment**

From the main avenue the southern end of the Heiliger See can be
seen with the Gothic Library, completed in 1794 by Langhans. On the
left-hand side of the avenue is the Holländisches Etablissement
(Dutch establishment) with its ladies' quarters, stables and carriage
house, built in 1789–90 to plans by von Carl Gotthard Gontard and
Andreas L. Krüger.

Orangery

Two years later Langhans' Orangery between the Holländisches Etablissement and the Marble Palace was completed. Its sphinx, two black
guards by Gottfried Schadow and the statue of Isis near the lake all
took up its Egyptian theme. Here Friedrich Wilhelm III received the
message about the Convention of Tauroggen, which started the process of wresting Prussia from Napoleon's hands in 1812.

***Marmor-
palais
(Marble
Palace)**

The main building in the Neuer Garten was built between 1787 and
1791 as a summer residence for King Friedrich Wilhelm II and goes by
the name of the Marmorpalais or Marble Palace. This early classical
palace with a red-brick façade decorated by grey Silesian granite was
started by Karl von Gontard and completed by Langhans. Guided tours
take in the concert hall and the Gesellschaftszimmer (parlour) on the
upper floor with some lovely views of the lakes and gardens, just as
Langhans conceived it. The pyramid north of the marble palace, also
by Langhans, was used as an ice cellar and for refrigerating food.

❶ Tours: May–Oct Tue– Sun 10am – 6pm, April Sat/Sun only 10am–6pm,
Nov–March Sat/Sun only 10am–4pm; admission €5; www.spsg.de

Right behind the northern entrance to the Neuer Garten is the Goth-ic-looking Meierei, built in 1791 by Langhans and modified by Persius in 1844 with the addition of a pumping house in the style of a Norman castle.

Meierei

At the northern edge of the Neuer Garten stands Schloss Cecilienhof, the last palace to be built for the Hohenzollern dynasty in Prussia. It was built from 1913 to 1917 at the instigation of Crown Prince Wilhelm by Paul Schultze-Naumburg and takes the form of an English country mansion. After the return of the Crown Prince from exile in Holland in 1923, he was given the right of abode in Schloss Cecilienhof. In February 1945, two months before Potsdam was bombed, the family fled the town and their right of abode was abandoned. Between 17 July and 2 August 1945 the heads of the allied forces met together at Schloss Cecilienhof – Stalin for the USSR, Truman for the USA and Churchill representing Britain until he was replaced by his successor Clement Attlee. The conference led to the **Potsdam Agreement**, which was to cement the political regime in Europe after the end of the Second World War. For the conference 36 rooms plus the audience chamber were furnished with items from various Potsdam palaces. Those rooms have been left in their 1945 condition. One major attraction is the audience chamber with its table, around which the conference negotiations took place. Most of the other parts of the palace now belong to an expensive hotel.

*Schloss Cecilienhof

? Did you know

MARCO POLO INSIGHT

The national leaders Truman, Stalin and Attlee did not stay at the Cecilienhof palace during the Potsdam conference, but in various villas around Babelsberg. The US president had the Villa Müller-Grote, which he called the »Little White House« in his memoirs. It was from here that he gave the order to drop the atomic bomb on Hiroshima.

❶ April–Oct Tue–Sun 10am–5pm, Nov–Mar closes 4pm; admission €6

★★ Sanssouci

✦ **B – D 1 – 3**

Bus: 606, 695
Entrances: Obelisk Portal (Schopen-hauerstrasse), Grünes Portal (avenue to Sanssouci), historic windmill
Visitor centre: An der Orangerie 1, April-Oct daily 8.30am–6pm,

Nov–March 8.30am–5pm
Admission: premium day ticket sanssouci+ for all palaces €19; or combined, family and individual tickets; https://tickets.spsg.de/
www.spsg.de

The area once known as the »Desolate Hill« is now an incomparable landscape of palaces and gardens, which was declared a World Heritage site by UNESCO in 1990.

The fabulous assemblage of palaces and gardens at Sanssouci was born on 5 April 1744, when Friedrich II decreed that the barren hill north-west of the town, where Friedrich Wilhelm I had already laid out a kitchen garden in 1725, was now to be redeployed as a hillside vineyard. The building of the summer palace was started as early as 1745, with the orangery following in 1747 followed by the Neptune Grotto in 1751 and the picture gallery in 1753. All the buildings were designed by Georg Wenzeslaus von Knobelsdorff, who was prob-ably also responsible for laying out the gardens. In the 19th century Friedrich Wilhelm IV had large areas of the grounds redesigned or newly laid out in the form of a landscape park by Pe-ter Joseph Lenné. On the northern side of the east-west avenue that runs for 2.3km/1.5mi lies the Lustgarten or pleasure park. To the south (as far as Ökonomieweg) is the Rehgarten or deer park and Charlottenhof Park. Some 60km/37mi of paths run through the park.

Insider Tip

! *Navigation in Sanssouci*

MARCO ⊕ POLO TIP

The visitor centre hires out satellite-supported multimedia guides for tours of Sanssouci Park (€7.50, with two headsets €9.50) and the city of Potsdam (€10).

✶✶ SCHLOSS SANSSOUCI

➊ April–Oct Tue–Sun 10am–6pm, Nov–March until 5pm; admission €12
Ladies' wing: May–Oct Sat, Sun, holidays 10am–6pm, admission €2
Kitchen and wine cellar: only April–Oct Tue–Sun 10am–6pm; admission €3

Georg Wenzeslaus von Knobelsdorff incorporated into his plans umerous sketches that had been made by the king himself. The palace was ready for its inauguration as early as May 1747. The palace is considered to be the architect's masterpiece and the epitome of Prus-sian Rococo. The name »sans souci« is French for »no cares« and indicates the fact that Friedrich II wished to use it as a retreat, which explains why it has just twelve rooms, a remarkably small number for a royal palace. Persius added some short and slightly set-back wings in 1841–42. The frontage looks out over the park, to which an out-door staircase leads down, taking in six curving vineyard terraces. The decoration of the façade – herm pilasters with bacchantes – stems from Friedrich Christian Glume. On the eastern side of the terrace is the grave of ✶**Grave of Frederick the Great** Frederick the Great: as early as 1744 he had requested that he be buried in Sans-souci next to his wind chimes. On the 205th anniversary of his death, 17 August 1991, his well-travelled mortal remains were finally laid to rest here under a modest gravestone.

Interior The **design of the rooms** inside the palace is considered to be among the most successful examples of the Rococo style. Apart from von Knobelsdorff, the main participants in the achievement were Johann August Nahl and Johann Hoppenhaupt the Elder. Above the vestibule is the Kleine Galerie (Small Gallery), which displays antiques from the collection of Cardinal Polignac, purchased in 1742, along with paintings by Watteau. The royal chambers start with the audience chamber. Its ceiling painting of Zephyr Crowning Flora was created by Antoine Pesne. The most important room in terms of art history is also the most intimate room in the building, the cedar-panelled circular library with its four wall cupboards containing 2000 of the king's books. After Frederick died, the adjoining study, bedroom and living room were redecorated in classical style in 1786 by his nephew and successor, Friedrich Wilhelm II. The chair in which Frederick died and his work desk are display here. The concert room is a symphony of playful Rococo. The artistically minded king, himself a talented flute player and composer, gave many a concert in this room. The pictures on the walls hark back to Ovid's Metamorphoses and were also painted by Pesne. The centrepiece of the palace is the oval Marmorsaal (Marble Hall), which among other things was the site of Frederick's famous round table meetings. The west wing contains some uniform guest rooms. A bust in the fourth of them is a reminder of one of the Prussian court's most distinguished guests – although he never actually slept in these chambers – the French philosopher Voltaire.

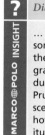

MARCO POLO INSIGHT

? Did you know

… why there are always some potatoes along with the flowers on Friedrich II's grave? Friedrich introduced the humble tuber to Prussia in spite of all the scepticism about it: this is how many show their gratitude.

Two similar buildings flank the palace. The Neue Kammern to the west were built as of 1747 in the form of an orangery. In 1771 they were reconfigured for use as a guest house with four richly decorated banqueting halls and seven smaller apartments four courtiers. Among the finest are the Jaspissaal (Jasper Hall) and the Ovid Gallery. The *Bildergalerie (Picture Gallery) on the eastern side was built between 1755 and 1764 to plans by Johann Gottfried Büring in order to accommodate Friedrich II's art collection. It is the oldest surviving museum building in Germany. Even if the collection as displayed today is not as extensive as in former times, its paintings by Rubens, van Dyck, Vasari, Reni, Tintoretto and Caravaggio clearly reflect Friedrich's excellent taste.

Neue Kammern (New Chambers)

In the Holländischer Garten (Dutch Garden) in front of the gallery there are eight massive busts representing rulers of the House of Orange.

Neue Kammern: April–Oct Tue–Sun 10am–6pm, admission €4
Bildergalerie: May–Oct Tue–Sun 10am–6pm; admission €6

Schloss Sanssouci

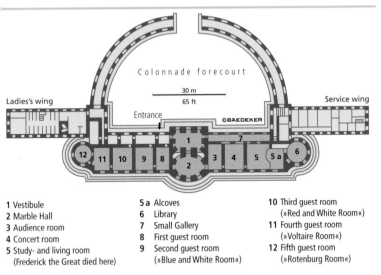

1 Vestibule
2 Marble Hall
3 Audience room
4 Concert room
5 Study- and living room
 (Frederick the Great died here)

5 a Alcoves
6 Library
7 Small Gallery
8 First guest room
9 Second guest room
 (»Blue and White Room«)

10 Third guest room
 (»Red and White Room«)
11 Fourth guest room
 (»Voltaire Room«)
12 Fifth guest room
 (»Rotenburg Room«)

Sanssouci windmill

The historic windmill behind the palace is a reconstruction of an original that was obliterated down to its base in 1945. This mill was itself built in 1790 to succeed a post mill that had been in operation since 1739. Legend has it that Friedrich II was irritated by the rattling of the windmill, but the miller managed to plead against its demolition. However it has been shown that this story really is no more than hearsay.

❶ April–Oct 10am–6pm daily, Nov, and Jan–March only Sat/Sun till 4pm; admission €3

✶✶ SANSSOUCI PARK

Obeliskportal

An obelisk and the Obeliskportal, both by von Knobelsdorff, mark the eastern end of the Hauptallee. The hieroglyphics on the obelisk are just simple decoration and make no sense, while the busts on the portal and alongside it represent Roman gods and emperors.

✶Marlygarten

To the south of the Obeliskportal Friedrich Wilhelm I commissioned the construction of the Marlygarten, originally a kitchen garden that would later be laid out as a magical landscape garden by Lenné in 1850. The garden **✶Friedenskirche** encircles the Friedenskirche or

Peace Church, which was built between 1845 and 1848 by the combined efforts of Persius, Hesse and Stüler. It is modelled on the basilica of San Clemente in Rome. Its most valuable feature is the late 12th-century mosaic from the Church of San Cypriano on the island of Murano near Venice that has been incorporated into the apse. It was purchased by Friedrich IV in 1834 and is one of only two original Italo-Byzantine mosaics to be found north of the Alps. Underneath the altar is the grave of Friedrich Wilhelm IV and his wife Elisabeth. To the north of the atriums is the mausoleum of Emperor Friedrich III and his wife Victoria, where the sarcophagus of Friedrich Wilhelm I was also kept until 1991.

The Neptune Grotto north of the Obeliskportal (1751–54) contains a giant clam made from a huge number of real shells.

Neptungrotte

At the foot of the Weinberg is a roundel that includes the Grosse Fontäne with its depiction of the four elements and figures from ancient mythology. Passing the Glockenfontäne (Bell Fountain) from 1750 and the Musenrondell (Roundel of the Muses) with its eight marble statues sculpted in around 1752, you reach the Entführungsrondell (Abduction Roundel), which has four groups of marble figures (from about 1750) representing »abductions« in ancient mythology. These include the Romans' abduction of the Sabine women, Paris' seduction of Helen, Pluto and Persephone, Bacchus and Ariadne.

Grosse Fontäne (Great Fountain)

Southwards from here is the Chinese House, emblematic of the playfulness of Rococo and the fashion for China at that time. The house was constructed between 1754 and 1756 to plans by Johann Gottfried Bühring using the Turkish trèfle from the palace gardens at Lunéville as his model. It imitates a sweeping tent supported by posts in the form of palm trees, beneath which three cabinets are clustered around a central hall. Life-size gilded Chinese figures made of sandstone by Johann Peter Benckert and Johann Gottlieb Heymüller bring the scene to life. Also to be admired here are porcelain exhibits from the 18th century.
❶ May–Oct Tue–Sun 10am–6pm; admission €2

**Chinesisches Haus (Chinese House)

Friedrich Wilhelm IV had planned a major »Höhenstrassenprojekt« (»main road« project), but between 1851 and 1860 all that came to pass of this idea was the Orangery Palace. 300m/330yd long and linking motifs from the later part of the Italian Renaissance and Baroque periods, the building was constructed by Stüler using the king's own sketches and a design put together by Persius. In the Raffaelsaal (Raphael Hall) in the middle, which is modelled on the Sala Regia in the Vatican, there are copies of paintings by Raphael and sculptures of the Deutschrömer school. Both towers offer a fabulous view. The

*Orangerie

** *Sanssouci Park and Palace*

Frederick the Great ordered construction of a positively modest palace as a place to withdraw to. Yet Sanssouci is more than just the palace: in and around the park many more delights are to be found.

Hauptallee
The main avenue of the park, 2.3km/1.5mi long, runs straight as a die between the Obelisk Gate and the Neues Palais.

❶ Neues Palais
Right at the western end of the park, the Neues Palais seems a little out of place with its gigantic dimensions. Friedrich II (Frederick the Great) seldom stayed there.

❷ Temple of Friendship

❸ Temple of Antiquities

❹ Belvedere
The last building at Sanssouci dating from the 18th century

❺ Dragon House
Ideal for taking a break at the café

❻ Orangery
A beautiful backdrop for summer concerts. From the towers there is a wonderful view of Sanssouci and Potsdam.

❼ Hill of Ruins
Though outside the park, the Ruinenberg was intended to provide water for the palace and park, but it only worked once – on Good Friday 1754.

❽ Historic windmill
A legend tells that the miller of the mill behind the palace defied the king, who was annoyed by its rattling.

❾ Neue Kammern
They accommodate the Picture Gallery.

❿ Chinese House
An architectural expression of the mode for chinoiserie in the Rococo period

⓫ Bell Fountain
Near the Neues Palais is the Roundel of the Muses, near the Obelisk Gate the Roundel of Abduction.

⓬ Great Fountain

⓭ Vineyard Terrace
The Weinbergterrasse consists of six levels planted with cherry, apricot and plum trees.

⓮ Sanssouci Palace

⓯ Tomb of Frederick the Great
Lying on the grave there are always a few potatoes, which the king introduced to Prussia. The wind chimes were buried with him.

⓰ Courtiers' accommodation

⓱ Small Fountain

⓲ Friedenskirche
The Church of Peace contains the mausoleums of Friedrich Wilhelm I and Friedrich II, as well as the crypt of Friedrich Wilhelm IV.

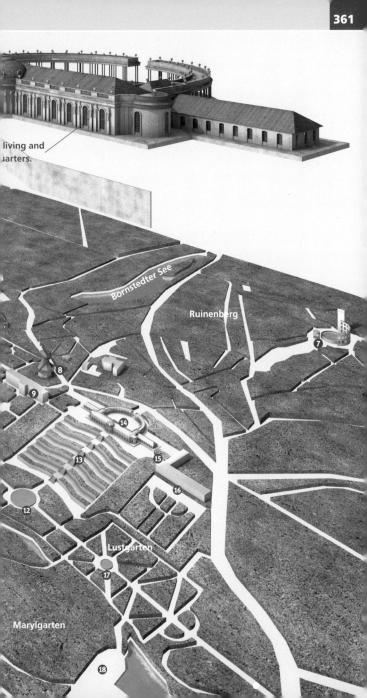

living and
uarters.

Bornstedter See

Ruinenberg

7

8

9

14

13

15

16

12

Lustgarten

17

Marylgarten

18

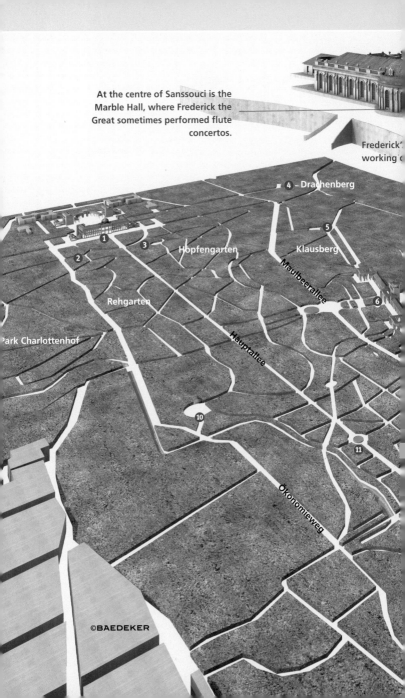

At the centre of Sanssouci is the Marble Hall, where Frederick the Great sometimes performed flute concertos.

Frederick'
working

4 – Drachenberg

5

Klausberg

Hopfengarten

1

3

2

Maulbeerallee

Rehgarten

6

Park Charlottenhof

Hauptallee

10

11

Ökonomieweg

©BAEDEKER

equestrian statue of Friedrich II is a copy of the bronze statue by Rauch on Unter den Linden (▶p.337).

ⓘ April Sat/Sun only, May–Oct Tue–Sun 10am–6pm; admission €4

Drachenhaus

From the Orangerie it is not far to the Drachenhaus (Dragon House), built in 1770 by von Gontard for storing wine and modelled on London's Kew Gardens pagoda. Here visitors can have a rest and refreshments.

Belvedere on Klausberg hill

Belvedere, built atop Klausberg hill between 1770 and 1772, is the last of Sanssouci's 18th-century buildings. Unger patterned the building on a painting by Francesco Biarchini that was in Friedrich II's collection and depicted Nero's macellum or meat market in Rome.

★★ NEUES PALAIS

ⓘ April–Oct and Jan–March daily except Tue 10am– 6pm, Nov and Dec till 5pm; admission €8
Royal apartment: April–Oct daily except Tue only with guided tour at 10am, 12 noon, 2pm, 4pm; admission €5
Pesne-Galerie: Sat, Sun, holidays 10am–6pm; admission €2

The Neue Palais or New Palace was built at the western end of the Hauptallee. It is the most recent and most magnificent of the palace buildings in the park. It was conceived as a »fanfaronade« or ostentatious boast after the end of the Seven Years' War to express the might and glory of Prussia and to realize Friedrich II's notion of a prestigious summer residence. Building work began in 1763 under Büring and he was succeeded by von Gontard in 1765. After just seven years, a three-storey palace covering some 240m/260yd with single-storey pavilions at the corners had come into existence. The façades are decorated with an allegorical and mythological set of figures, there are 292 sandstone sculptures in front of the pilasters and parapet alone. The king stubbornly insisted on using forms of the late Baroque period, making the Neues Palais the last important late Baroque palace building in Prussia; it is considered the epitome of Prussian Baroque architecture. The New Palace was mainly used as a court guest house although members of the royal family also lived there.

Interior

The design for the rooms inside is by von Gontard. One conspicuous feature is the large number of motifs taken from other Prussian palaces. About 60 rooms are open to visitors and contain furniture and porcelain by local craftsmen and artists that mainly came from the demolished Stadtschloss. The original furniture is kept in the palace of Doorn in the Netherlands, where Kaiser Wilhelm II fled into exile in 1918. The highlights include the rooms of Friedrich II, the cabinet of paintings in the lower nobles' quarters, the oval cabinet, the concert room in the upper nobles' quarters, the Marmorsaal (Marble Hall), which extends across two storeys and the Schlosstheater or Palace Theatre, which opened in 1768 and still stages plays.

The splendid pair of buildings opposite the Neues Palais are not another set of palaces but service buildings known by the name Communs. They were built between 1766 and 1769. The southern one contained a kitchen and service rooms that were connected to the Neues Palais by means of an underground tunnel. The northern building contained the servants' quarters.

Communs

North of the Hauptallee is the Antikentempel or Temple of Antiquities, built in 1768 by von Gontard using sketches by Friedrich II. It once contained statues from Friedrich II's collection, most of which were passed on to the Altes Museum in Berlin in 1829. The grave of Auguste Victoria, wife of the last German emperor, Wilhelm II, is here. The **Freundschaftstempel** or Friendship Temple south of the Hauptallee is also the work of von Gontard in 1768 with a major contribution to the design from Friedrich II himself. The building is dedicated to the memory of the king's sister Countess Wilhelmine von Bayreuth, who died in 1758.

**Antiken-
tempel
(Temple of
Antiquities)**

✱ SCHLOSS CHARLOTTENHOF AND PARK

The area to the south of the Freundschaftstempel was added to Sanssouci park in 1826. In 1825 Friedrich Wilhelm III obtained lands belonging to Charlotte von Gentzkow and gifted them to his son Crown Prince Friedrich Wilhelm. Schinkel and Lenné realized his ideas for a palace and gardens between 1826 and 1829 and created in the process one of the most consummate ensembles of romantic classicism.

The palace of Schloss Charlottenhof has a projecting central section. In front of the entrance there is a fountain with a statue of Neptune (1850) and a poets' arbour created in 1851. At the rear there is a Doric gabled portico leading to an artificially raised terrace. The interior of the miniature palace was abundantly furnished by Schinkel in the style of unprepossessing bourgeois classicism. One of the most comfortable rooms is the living room, coloured uniformly in light blue and featuring landscape water colours from Italy and Switzerland. The most surprising room, though, is the tent room with its striped wallpaper and tent-like ceiling. It was originally a bedroom for ladies-in-waiting and later the apartment of Alexander von Humboldt when he stayed at Sanssouci .

**Schloss
Charlotten-
hof**

❶ May–Oct Tue–Sun 10am–6pm; €4, combined ticket with Roman Baths €5.

Charlotten-hof Park

In the gardens Lenné, along with Schinkel and Persius, was able to realize his concept of an English landscape garden. To the west of the palace he added a Hippodrome in 1836, a garden in the shape of an ancient horse racing circuit. The pheasant compound was built between 1841 and 1844. Next to the machine pond east of the palace, Persius spent from 1829 to 1840 realizing Schinkel's plans for **Roman baths**. Its eight buildings are modelled on Italian country houses. They comprise the Hofgärtnerhaus (1829), built as a guest-house, a tea pavilion in the style of a Roman podium temple (1830), various apartment buildings, and the Roman bath itself (1834–40), with its large jasper basin, a gift from Tsar Nicholas I. The bath is now used as a venue for art exhibitions.

❶ **Roman baths:** as above; admission €5

Suburbs

For visitors who have a little more time in Potsdam, it is well worth taking a look at the suburbs.

Alexand-rowka · Russian Colony

✦ B 4

The 13 houses in the colony of Alexandrowka with their wooden balconies and carved gables remain unique to this day in western Europe as an example of Russian architecture outside the Russian homeland. They were built to the north of the town centre as the result of a »most high cabinet order« decreed by Friedrich Wilhelm III on 10 April 1826 on behalf of twelve Russian singers, who had been brought to Potsdam as prisoners of war in 1812 by General Yorck, who had captured them while they were fighting for Napoleon. They later sang in the local choir and remained in Potsdam after the defeat of Napoleon, officially designated as a »gift from Tsar Alexander«. The royal decree that the colony should be designed in the form of the Russian saltire of St Andrew was implemented by Peter Joseph Lenné: he populated the two lines of the cross with four opposing pairs of houses, each of which was aligned to four other houses built on the arcs of the oval site. The foreman's house (no. 8) was

---

! Insider Tip

Truly wonderful

MARCO ⊕ POLO TIP

This is how the painter Carl Ludwig Häberlin described the view of the palaces and gardens of Potsdam from the Belvedere on the Pfingstberg (reached from Puschkinallee; daily 10am–6pm, in summer until 8pm). The Belvedere was built between 1847 and 1863, based on sketches by Friedrich Wilhelm IV. Don't be so distracted by the view that you miss the small Pomonatempel by Schinkel (1801), located north of the Kapellenberg (opening times: mid-April–Oct Sat, Sun and holidays 3–6pm).

built at the intersection of the cross. The homes were not to be sold. Instead, they were passed on to the next generation as long as the oldest child was a boy, and the name plates thus describe the history of the families to this day. White writing on a black background denotes the deceased family heads, while the names of the present-day descendants of the original Russian singers are written black on white. At house no. 2, originally built in 1826, the lower floor has been converted into the Museum Alexandrowka.

The orthodox Church of **St Alexander Nevski** on the chapel hill was dedicated in 1829 in the presence of Tsar Nicholas I. Karl Friedrich Schinkel designed the chapel using the Desiatin Church in Kiev as his model. To the north of the Russian colony, in the area of fine villas between the Pfingstberg and Neuer Garten, the Soviet secret service made itself a home in the so-called Forbidden City until 1994. The wall that closed it off still stands at the corner of Langhansstrasse. In the imperial period aristocrats, army officers and bankers lived here, well out of sight of proletarian Berlin. Some of these villas are dilapidated, but others, such as Villa Lepsius, built on the Grosse Weinmeisterstrasse for Frederick the Great's chamberlain, have been carefully restored. It takes its name from the theologian Johannes Lepsius (1858–1926), who lived their until his death. A Lepsius archive was established here in 2011. Villa Quandt next door houses an archive relating to the writer Fontane.

Museum Alexandrowka: tram 92, 96 to Puschkinallee; March–Oct Tue–Sun 10am–6pm, Nov–Dec only Fri–Sun till 5pm; admission €3.50; www.alexandrowka.de

Babelsberg, which lies to the east and is Potsdam's largest suburb in terms of area, has gained renown as a centre for film and the media. Schloss Babelsberg, on the Babelsberg hill to the north of the present-day town centre, was built on land leased in 1833 by Friedrich Wilhelm III to his son, the future Emperor Wilhelm I, who commissioned Schinkel to design a palace for him and his wife Augusta von Sachsen-Weimar, an admirer of the English Tudor style. The decidedly modest building was finished by the end of 1835. Schinkel was soon commissioned again for extension work, which would be carried on after his death by Persius, Strack and Gottgetreu. Schinkel's original plan, based on Windsor Castle, was partially realized by Persius in the east wing. Between 1844 and 1849 Strack completed the western section in the form of a neo-Roman fort. Little of Schinkel's initial interior design can be seen today. The palace provides a magnificent view over the bowling green that descends down to the Havel and as far as Glienicker Brücke bridge and Glienicker Park itself (opening hours: March – Oct Tue – Sun 9am – 5pm). MBabelsberg Park 130ha/321ac of parkland stretch away to the west of the palace between Tiefer See and Glienicker Lake. The Babelsberg Park was laid out by Lenné and

Babelsberg

later by Fürst Pückler-Muskau. Take a stroll to Glienicker Lake where there is a steam engine shed built by Persius between 1843 and 1845. The walk leads further west, past the Kleines Schloss, built for the court ladies in waiting in 1841/42, all the way to the Matrosenhaus, which was erected in 1842 for the crews of the boats and gondolas belonging to the palace. On the hill is the landmark of the Babelsberg Park, the 46m/150ft Flatowturm or Flatow Tower, built between 1853 and 1856 and modelled on the tower of the Eschenheimer Tor in Frankfurt am Main. The Bismarck Bridge beneath it is said to be where Wilhelm I named Bismarck as Prussian prime minister. Northeast of the Flatow Tower is the medieval Gerichtslaube or Court Arbour, which was moved here from Berlin in 1872 to make way for the building of the Rotes Rathaus. The lower floor dates from about 1280 and includes the Schöffenstuhl or seat of the lay judges. Above it is the Ratsstube or council hall, added in 1485.

German film history was made from 1912 on the 45ha/111 acres of studio grounds belonging to the former UFA production company. Nowadays it is home to the Medienstadt Babelsberg estate, where countless film companies and TV broadcasters produce movies and TV series. **Filmpark Babelsberg** is a key highlight for tourists. It offers a look behind the scenes at many famous productions.

Schloss Babelsberg: bus 694 from Potsdam main station, www.spsg.de
Flatowturm: Sat and Sun 10am–6pm, admission €2
Filmpark: bus 690 from Potsdam main station, April–June and Sept Tue–Sun 10am–6pm, July and Aug daily; admission €21 (children €14); www.filmpark-babelsberg.de

Telegrafen-
berg

Telegrafenberg hill, 94m/308ft above sea level, gets its name from the optical telegraph system that was installed there in 1832. It was the fourth of 61 stations forming a route from Berlin to Koblenz. After the establishment of the German Empire in 1871 the hill was made the site of various scientific institutes: the Astrophysics Institute from 1879, the Meteorological Observatory in 1890 and the Geodetic Institute in 1892. Nowadays it is the site of the Albert Einstein Science Park. The Astrophysics Institute remains the principal buildin,g with the fourth largest lens in the world. The main attraction among the buildings is the extraordinary 18m/59ft-high **Einsteinturm** (Einstein Tower). An example of organic architecture, it was built between 1919 and 1924 to designs by Erich Mendelsohn for research into Einstein's prediction that light might be bent by the gravitational field of the sun. Einstein himself never actually worked here.

❶ Bus: 691 to Telegrafenberg

Royal Manor
of Bornstedt
✦ B 2

The royal manor of Bornstedt north of the orangerie of Sanssouci on the Bornstedter See was rebuilt in 1846 by Johann Heinrich Haeberlin in the Italian style after a fire as a model farm for Crown Prince

Friedrich Wilhelm and Princess Victoria. Lenné designed the garden. Apart from allowing a visit to the royal chambers, it also provides a glimpse into a cross section of Brandenburg's tradition of crafts with attractions such as a brewery and beer garden, a schnaps distillery, a glass-blowing workshop, a pottery, etc.

In Bornstedt cemetery west of the royal manor are the graves of Ludwig Persius (1803 –45), the family of court gardener Johann Samuel Sello (1715 – 87) and Peter Joseph Lenné (1789 – 1866). Memorial stones recall the conspirators of the attempt to assassinate Hitler on 20 July 1944, Henning von Tresckow and Ulrich Freiherr von Sell.

Krongut Bornstedt: tram 92 to final stop, daily from 11am, www.krongut-bornstedt.de

The 74m/243ft-high Ruinenberg east of the Bornstedter See really is crowned by ruins. Friedrich II had a reservoir built there to supply water to the fountains and hothouses of Sanssouci Park, and Knobelsdorff adorned it with architectural ruins. He and the scene painter at the Berlin Italian opera, Innocente Bellavita, arranged fragments of an amphitheatre, a round temple with a collapsed roof, three Ionic columns and a fourth, toppled column. The watchtower that was added in 1845, destroyed in 1945, has been restored to give a sweeping view from a height of 23m/75ft. The installations did not serve their purpose: the sluice gates of the reservoir were opened only once, on Good Friday 1754, but the fountain in front of the picture gallery only briefly spurted water. The reservoir did not come into use until the Mosque Pumphouse on the Havel was built in 1842 (▶p.352).

Ruinenberg
✢ **B 2**

❶ Bus 692 to Ruinenbergstrasse; watchtower: Sat, Sun, holidays 10am–6pm; admission €2

Bornstedter Field was an army training ground in Prussian days and remained so until Soviet troops left at the end of the last century. The site was reanimated as a leisure park for the 2001 German national garden show and is now called the Volkspark. Its broad meadows and ancient trees have been supplemented by lines of roses, kitchens, a giant slide, playgrounds, a skating rink and the Potsdam Biosphere (**Biosphäre Potsdam**), which at the time of the garden show was a hyper-modern, 200m/220yd-long greenhouse but has now been made into a »Naturerlebniswelt« or nature experience, a mixture of high-tech museum and tropical greenhouse (opening hours:).

Volkspark

❶ Tram 96 to Volkspark; Mon – Fri 9am – 6pm; Sat, Sun and holidays 10am – 7pm; admission €11.50; www.biosphaere-potsdam.de

PRACTICAL INFORMATION

Hints and facts for planning your journey, using public transport in Berlin, getting the information you need and finding background reading.

Arrival · Before the Journey

By car Berlin is nearly 1100km / 700mi from London, but most of the journey can be made on motorways and the German autobahn. The journey takes over twelve hours. Those coming from northern France having taken the ferry from Dover will pass through Belgium and then Holland, entering Germany near Venlo. Taking the A 40 towards Cologne, join the A 3 close to Duisburg, and then the A 2 near Oberhausen. The A 2 now leads most of the remaining 500km / 300mi to Berlin. **Environmental zone** The part of the city within the inner S-Bahn (local rail) circle has been declared an environmental zone, which only vehicles that have a yellow or green sticker certifying their emission level may enter.

Crossing the Channel There are car ferry services from Dover or Folkestone to Calais. Alternatively, those wishing to take their car through the tunnel can travel on the Eurotunnel Shuttle Service, a rail link between Folkstone and Calais.

By bus or coach Eurolines operate a daily service from London Victoria to Berlin. The trip takes 19 hours. Coaches run regularly from many towns and cities in Germany to Berlin's central bus station, Zentrale Omnibusbahnhof (ZOB), located near the International Congress Centre (ICC) in Charlottenburg. Within Germany and elsewhere, travel agents offer cheap coach trips, weekend breaks and fixed-price deals.

By train It is possible to travel from London St Pancras to Berlin quite comfortably. The Eurostar from London reaches Brussels in 2.5 hours; the high-speed Thalys train continues to Cologne in a little more than 2 hours. From Cologne there is a regular ICE (inter-city express) service to Berlin, taking 4.5 hours. Travellers can also take an early evening Eurostar from London to Paris or Brussels and then the overnight sleeper train to Berlin.

Rail connections The main inter-city stations are the **Hauptbahnhof** in Berlin-Mitte, Gesundbrunnenstation in the north and a southerly interchange now called Südkreuz, which connect to the local S-Bahn stations on the ring that encircles the city centre. Zoologischer Garten station is only frequented by night trains to Munich and Zurich nowadays, but there are new regional stations at Jungfernheide, Gesundbrunnen, Potsdamer Platz, Südkreuz and Lichterfelde Ost.

By air Plenty of airlines fly to the two airports in Berlin. Direct flights are available from all the most important towns in Germany as well as cities in the rest of Europe, though with many airlines there is a change of planes when flying out of London. Those offering direct

RAIL TRAVEL
In UK
Rail Europe: tel. 0844 8 48 58 48
www.raileurope.co.uk
Eurostar: www.eurostar.com

In Berlin
Deutsche Bahn information:
tel. (0 18 0) 5 99 66 33 (24 hours)
Rail information for Berlin:
tel. (0 800) 1 50 70 90
www.bahn.de

BUS
Eurolines
Bookings online and in UK through
Eurolines: tel. 08717 81 81 78
www.eurolines.co.uk

RAILWAY STATIONS
Hauptbahnhof
S/U-Bahn: S 5, S 7, S 75, S 9, U 55

Bahnhof Zoologischer Garten
Hardenbergplatz
S/U-Bahn: S 5, S 7, S 75, U 2, U 9

Ostbahnhof
Friedrichshain
S-Bahn: S 5, S 7, S 75

Bahnhof Gesundbrunnen
Wedding
S/U-Bahn: S 1, S 2, S 25, S 41, S 42, U 8

Bahnhof Südkreuz
Schöneberg
S-Bahn: S 2, S 25, S 41, S 42

AIRPORTS
Berlin Tegel (TXL)
Location: 10 km / 6 mi northwest of the
centre
Bus: TXL via Hauptbahnhof to Alexanderplatz; X 9 and 109 (stopping at Ja-

kob-Kaiser-Platz U-Bahn station for U 7)
to Zoologischer Garten station; 128 to
Osloer Str. U-Bahn station .

Berlin-Schönefeld (SXF)
Location: 20 km / 12 mi south-east of the
centre von Mitte
Train: Airport to Hauptbahnhof in 30
min. Flughafenexpress. Hourly regional
trains to Potsdam.
S-Bahn local train: S 9 and S 45.

Airport information
For both airports: tel. (0 18 05) 00 01 86

AIRLINES
Air Berlin
Tel. Germany (030) 34 34 34 34
Tel. UK (0871) 5000 737
www.airberlin.com

British Airways
Tel. Germany (0421) 5575 758
Tel. UK (0844) 493 0787
www.britishairways.com

easyJet
Tel. (0 18 0) 321 2610
Tel. (US) 800 231 0856
www.easyjet.com

Germanwings
Tel. Germany (0 18 0) 320 320
Tel. UK (0330) 365 1918
www.germanwings.com

Lufthansa
Tel. (Germany) 069 86 799 799
Tel. (UK) 0871 945 9747
www.lufthansa.com

Ryanair
Tel. Germany (0 18 0) 060 606
Tel. UK (0330) 365 5000
www.ryanair.com

flights from the UK include British Airways and Air Berlin (Stansted to Tegel) and Ryanair (Stansted to Schönefeld). Berlin has two major airports: Berlin Tegel (Flughafen Otto Lilienthal) in the north-west and Berlin-Schönefeld in the south of the city. Tegel is set for closure when the long-delayed expansion of Schönefeld to Berlin Brandenburg International has been completed.

IMMIGRATION AND CUSTOMS REGULATIONS

Travel documents

The identity cards and passports of EU citizens from countries which have signed up to the Schengen agreement are often no longer checked. However, the UK is not party to this agreement, to passport checks on flights from the UK to Germany are carried out at the border. In general identification is required at airports, so all visitors should be able to show their **passport** or an ID card when they enter the country. Children under 16 years of age must carry a children's passport or be entered in the parent's passport. Always carry your driving licence, the motor vehicle registration and the international green insurance card when driving in Germany. Motor vehicles must have the oval sticker showing nationality unless they have a Euro licence plate. **Loss or theft** If your travel papers are lost or stolen, contact your diplomatic representation in Germany, but first go to the police to obtain a **report of theft**. It is easier to obtain replacement documents if you have **photocopies of the originals** or can download them from your electronic mailbox.

Car documents

Pets and travel

Those who wish to bring pets (dogs, cats) to Germany from the UK require a **pet pass**. It contains an official veterinary statement of health (no more than 30 days old), a rabies vaccination certificate that is at least 20 days and no more than eleven months old, and a passport photo. In addition, the animal must have a microchip or tattoo. A muzzle and leash are required at all times for dogs.

Customs regulations for EU citizens

The European Union member states (including Germany) form a common economic area within which the movement of goods for private purposes is largely duty-free. There are merely certain maximum quantities which apply (for example 800 cigarettes, 10 litres of spirits and 90 litres of wine per person). During random inspections customs officers must be convinced that the wares are actually intended for private use.

Customs regulations for non-EU citizens

For travellers from outside the EU, the following duty-free quantities apply: 200 cigarettes or 100 cigarillos or 50 cigars or 250g of tobacco; also 2 litres of wine and 2 litres of sparkling wine or 1 litre of spirits with an alcohol content of more than 22% vol.; 500g of coffee or 200g of coffee extract, 100g of tea or 40g of tea extract, 50ml of perfume or 0.25 litres of eau de toilette. Gifts up to a value of €175 are also duty-free.

TRAVEL INSURANCE

Citizens of EU countries are entitled to treatment in Germany under the local regulations in case of illness on production of their **European health insurance card**. Even with this card, in most cases some of the costs for medical care and prescribed medication must be paid by the patient. Upon presentation of receipts the health insurance at home covers the costs – but not for all treatments. Citizens of non-EU countries must pay for medical treatment and medicine them-selves and should take out private health insurance.

Health insurance

Since some of the costs for medical treatment and medication typically have to be covered by the patient, and the costs for return transportation may not be covered by the normal health insurance, additional travel insurance is recommended.

Private travel insurance

Electricity

The German mains grid generally supplies 230-volt electricity at 50Hz. Due to the variety of sockets all visitors, especially who are not from mainland Europe, are advised to take an **adapter**.

Emergency

Fire brigade, paramedics
Tel. 112

Police
Tel. 110

Emergency medical service
Tel. 31 00 31

Emergency dental service
Tel. 89 00 4333

Child emergency service
Tel. 61 00 61

Drugs emergency service
Tel. 1 92 37

Poison emergency service
Tel. 1 92 40

Counselling hotline
Tel. 08 00–1 11 01 11
Tel. 08 00–1 11 02 22

Etiquette and Customs

Berliner Schnauze

Germans in general favour straightforwardness, and will be direct to the point of bluntness. Accordingly, Berliners tend not to waste time with unnecessary niceties when it comes to expressing an opinion or making a request. There is a temptation for outsiders to interpret this as rudeness, but Berlin bluntness (known in Germany as the »Berliner Schnauze«) is better viewed as an endearing local quirk. In Berlin, as in Yorkshire, there is no need to beat about the bush.

Discussing Berlin's history

Many Germans do not feel comfortable discussing the events of the Second World War: while the period is fascinating it is for obvious reasons regarded as a subject for serious discussion and private thought only, and the somewhat gung ho, flag-waving approach taken in the UK and other places is anathema in Germany. Unless you intend to engage in learned discourse, it is best to follow the famous advice – and not mention the war. In contrast the communist era is viewed with affectionate nostalgia and even romanticized by many, and is celebrated in films and shops selling Eastern bloc memorabilia.

Rules and regulations

Germany is heavily regulated and extremely bureaucratic, and Germans tend to follow rules to the letter and often display more deference to those in authority than other nationalities. It is an offence (albeit a minor one) for example to step out into the road at a crossing if the pedestrian signal shows red, even if there is no vehicle in sight – visitors may be surprised to see large groups of people patiently waiting for the figure of the green »Ampelmännchen« to illuminate and indicate that they may now cross the empty road. Moreover, there will be disapproving looks – and possibly verbal reprimands – for those who break this rule (not to mention a fine should a police officer spot the guilty party). It is arguable however that Berlin, less conservative than other German cities and with its diverse influences, does not quite fit this German cliché: in Berlin, perhaps, the rulebook is still being written.

Efficiency versus bureaucracy

German efficiency is of course world renowned, and though it will be regularly encountered in banks, hotels, and even government offices, the visitor may at times also come across instances of clanking bureaucracy. Here, Berlin is no exception. Those who lock horns with the city's bureaucratic machinery should prepare to have their patience well tested.

No smoking

Smoking is prohibited in all public buildings in Germany, including cafés, bars, restaurants and nightclubs. A smoking area is permitted, but smokers are only served in non-smoking areas (in order to protect staff from the effects of passive smoking). Individuals breaking this law are liable to a fine of €100; a €2000 penalty applies to the proprietor of the offending establishment.

Tipping

In restaurants and cafés it is usual to tip about 10% of the amount on the bill. If you pay cash, tell the waiter the amount you wish to pay (normally a rounded up figure) as you hand over the money, or say »Stimmt so« if you don't expect any change at all. If you pay by cheque or credit card, leave the tip in cash on the table or on the plate provided. Taxi drivers, city guides, toilet attendants and room service personnel are also pleased to receive a tip.

Greeting Berliners

The accepted way to greet somebody in Berlin is to shake hands; men and women who know each other better will kiss each other on both cheeks, like in France; established friends, men included, will even hug one another.

Health

Medical help

Germany's healthcare system is excellent. Berlin's doctors and dentists are listed in the »Gelbe Seiten« (Yellow Pages) under »Ärzte« and »Zahnärzte« respectively. The US and UK consulates can point you in the direction of medical practitioners who speak English.

Pharmacies

Pharmacies (Apotheken) are generally open Mon–Sat 9.30am–8pm. They are closed on Sundays. Every pharmacy displays in the window or door a list of pharmacies which are open at night and on holidays.

Medical emergency service
Tel. 112

Medical emergencies for Berlin visitors
Tel. 01804 / 22 55 23 62

Information

FOR BERLIN
Berlin-Tourismus
Am Karlsbad 11
D-10785 Berlin

Tel. (030) 25 00 25
www.visitberlin.de
From abroad:
Tel. 00 49 (30) 2500 23 33

Berlin Infostores:
Hauptbahnhof (main station)
North entrance, Europaplatz 1
Daily 8am–10pm

Neues Kranzlereck
Kurfürstendamm 21, Passage
Mon–Sat 10am–8pm, Sun 10am–6pm

Brandenburg Gate (south wing)
April–Oct 9.30am–6pm daily, 10am–
6pm at other times

FOR POTSDAM
Potsdam Tourist Service
Am Neuen Markt 1
D-14467 Potsdam
Tel. 0331 27 55 88 99
Tel. (03 31) 275 580

Tourist Information Centres
Brandenburger Tor
Brandenburger Str. 3
April–Oct Mon–Fri 9.30am–6pm, Sat
and Sun until 4pm; Nov– March Mon–Fri
10am–6pm, Sat and Sun 9.30am–2pm
Potsdam Main Station
Mon–Fri 9.30am–8pm, Sat 9am–8pm,
Sun 10am–4pm
www.potsdam-tourism.com

EMBASSIES IN BERLIN
Australian embassy
Wallstrasse 76–79, Mitte
Tel. 880 0880
www.australian-embassy.de

British embassy
Wilhelmstrasse 70, Mitte
Tel. 204 570

Canadian embassy
Leipziger Platz 17, Tiergarten
Tel. 203 120
www.kanada-info.de

Embassy of the Republic of Ireland
Jägerstr. 51, Mitte
Tel. 220 720
www.embassyofireland.de

New Zealand embassy
Friedrichstrasse 60, Mitte
Tel. 206 210, www.nzembassy.com

United States embassy
Clayallee 170
Tel. 832 9233, www.us-botschaft.de

INTERNET
www.berlin.de
Official page for the Berlin federal state:
a well-structured, fast and extensive
source of information, with pages in
English.

www.berlin-info.de
Private and commercial information
from and about Berlin, also covering
sightseeing, hotels and leisure options.
English version of the site.

www.berlinonline.de
Practical information on everything from
cinema and theatre programmes to
pharmacy hours, cultural venues and
cash machines. German only.

www.visitberlin.de
Home page of Berlin Tourismus Marketing, a good place to start amid the flood
of information. Able to handle bookings, and in English.

www.bundestag.de
Parliament and its activities; good English version.

www.friedrichstrasse.de
All you need to know about the shopping street of Friedrichstrasse, in a vari-

ety of languages. Also available for the shopping centres in the west of Berlin: www.kurfuerstendamm.de.

www.art-in-berlin.de
Online magazine with up-to-date information on exhibitions, art, literature and architecture, in German only.

www.berlin-hidden-places.de
Featuring hidden places, parks, back yards and many other spots in Berlin that you might never find if it were not

for this website, which is in both German and English.

www.smb.museum/en/home.html
English version of the website for museums belonging to the Prussian Cultural Heritage Trust, in comprehensive and well-presented fashion.

www.spsg.de
Information about Potsdam's palaces and gardens; much of it also in English.

Language

German Phrases

General

Yes/No	Ja/Nein
Perhaps./Maybe.	Vielleicht.
Please.	Bitte.
Thank you./Thank you very much.	Danke./Vielen Dank!
You're welcome.	Gern geschehen.
Excuse me!	Entschuldigung!
Pardon?	Wie bitte?
I don't understand.	Ich verstehe Sie/Dich nicht.
I only speak a bit of ...	Ich spreche nur wenig ...
Can you help me, please?	Können Sie mir bitte helfen?
I'd like ...	Ich möchte ...
I (don't) like this.	Das gefällt mir (nicht).
Do you have ...?	Haben Sie ...?
How much is this?	Wieviel kostet es?
What time is it?	Wieviel Uhr ist es?
What is this called?	Wie heißt dies hier?

Getting acquainted

Good morning!	Guten Morgen!
Good afternoon!	Guten Tag!
Good evening!	Guten Abend!

Hello!/Hi!	Hallo! Grüß Dich!
My name is ...	Mein Name ist ...
What's your name?	Wie ist Ihr/Dein Name?
How are you?	Wie geht es Ihnen/Dir?
Fine thanks. And you?	Danke. Und Ihnen/Dir?
Goodbye!/Bye-bye!	Auf Wiedersehen!
Good night!	Gute Nacht!
See you!/Bye!	Tschüss!

Travelling

left/right	links/rechts
straight ahead	geradeaus
near/far	nah/weit
Excuse me, where's ..., please?	Bitte, wo ist ...?
... the train station	... der Bahnhof
... the bus stop	... die Bushaltestelle
... the harbour	... der Hafen
... the airport	... der Flughafen
How far is it?	Wie weit ist das?
I'd like to rent a car.	Ich möchte ein Auto mieten.
How long?	Wie lange?

Traffic

My car's broken down.	Ich habe eine Panne.
Is there a service station nearby?	Gibt es hier in der Nähe eine Werkstatt?
Where's the nearest gas station?	Wo ist die nächste Tankstelle?
I want	Ich möchte ...
... liters/gallons of ...	Liter/Gallonen (3.8 l) ...
... regular./premium.	.... Normalbenzin./Super.
... diesel.	... Diesel.
... unleaded	... bleifrei.
Full, please.	Volltanken, bitte.
Help!	Hilfe!
Attention!/Look out!	Achtung!/Vorsicht!
Please call ...	Rufen Sie bitte ...
... an ambulance.	... einen Krankenwagen.
... the police.	... die Polizei.
It was my fault.	Es war meine Schuld.
It was your fault.	Es war Ihre Schuld.
Please give me your name and address.	Geben Sie mir bitte Namen und Anschrift.
Beware of ...	Vorsicht vor ...

Bypass (with road number)	Ortsumgehung (mit Straßennummer)
Bypass (Byp)	Umgehungsstraße
Causeway	Brücke, Pontonbrücke
Construction	Bauarbeiten
Crossing (Xing)	Kreuzung, Überweg
Dead end	Sackgasse
Detour	Umleitung
Divided highway	Straße mit Mittelstreifen
Do not enter	Einfahrt verboten
Exit	Ausfahrt
Hill	Steigung/Gefälle/unübersichtlich (Überholverbot)
Handicapped parking	Behindertenparkplatz
Junction (Jct)	Kreuzung, Abzweigung, Einmündung
Keep off ...	Abstand halten ...
Loading zone	Ladezone
Merge (merging traffic)	Einmündender Verkehr
Narrow bridge	Schmale Brücke
No parking	Parken verboten
No passing	Überholen verboten
No turn on red	Rechtsabbiegen bei Rot verboten
U Turn	Wenden erlaubt
No U turn	Wenden verboten
One Way	Einbahnstraße
Passenger loading zone	Ein- und Aussteigen erlaubt
Ped Xing	Fußgängerüberweg
Restricted parking zone	Zeitlich begrenztes Parken erlaubt
Right of way	Vorfahrt
Road construction	Straßenbauarbeiten
Slippery when wet	Schleudergefahr bei Nässe
Slow	Langsam fahren
Soft choulders	Straßenbankette nicht befestigt
Speed limit	Geschwindigkeitsbegrenzung
Toll	Benutzungsgebühr, Maut
Tow away zone	Absolutes Parkverbot, Abschleppzone
Xing (crossing)	Kreuzung, Überweg
Yield	Vorfahrt beachten

Shopping

Where can I find a ...?	Wo finde ich ... eine/ein ..?
... pharmacy	... Apotheke
... bakery	... Bäckerei

... department store	... Kaufhaus
... food store	... Lebensmittelgeschäft
... supermarket	... Supermarkt

Accommodation

Could you recommend ... ?	Können Sie mir ... empfehlen?
... a hotel/motel	... ein Hotel/Motel
... a bed & breakfast	... eine Frühstückspension
Do you have ...?	Haben Sie noch ...?
... a room for one	... ein Einzelzimmer
... a room for two	... ein Doppelzimmer
... with a shower/bath	... mit Dusche/Bad
... for one night	... für eine Nacht
... for a week	... für eine Woche
I've reserved a room.	Ich habe ein Zimmer reserviert.
How much is the room...?	Was kostet das Zimmer...?
... with breakfast	... mit Frühstück

Doctor

Can you recommend a good doctor?	Können Sie mir einen guten Arzt empfehlen?
I need a dentist.	Ich brauche einen Zahnarzt.
I feel some pain here.	Ich habe hier Schmerzen.
I've got a temperature.	Ich habe Fieber.
Prescription	Rezept
Injection/shot	Spritze

Bank/Post

Where's the nearest bank?	Wo ist hier bitte eine Bank?
ATM (Automated Teller Machine)	Geldautomat
I'd like to change dollars/pounds into euros.	Ich möchte Dollars/Pfund in Euro wechseln.
How much is ...	Was kostet ...
... a letter ...	... ein Brief ...
... a postcard ...	... eine Postkarte ...
to Europe?	nach Europa?

Numbers

1	eins	2	zwei
3	drei	4	vier
5	fünf	6	sechs

7	sieben	8	acht
9	neun	10	zehn
11	elf	12	zwölf
13	dreizehn	14	vierzehn
15	fünfzehn	16	sechzehn
17	siebzehn	18	achtzehn
19	neunzehn	20	zwanzig
21	einundzwanzig	30	dreißig
40	vierzig	50	fünfzig
60	sechzig	70	siebzig
80	achtzig	90	neunzig
100	(ein-)hundert	1000	(ein-)tausend
1/2	ein Halb	1/3	ein Drittel
1/4	ein Viertel		

Restaurant

Is there a good restaurant here?	Gibt es hier ein gutes Restaurant?
Would you reserve us a table for this evening, please?	Reservieren Sie uns bitte für heute Abend einen Tisch!
The menu please!	Die Speisekarte bitte!
Cheers!	Auf Ihr Wohl!
Could I have the check, please?	Bezahlen, bitte.
Where is the restroom, please?	Wo ist bitte die Toilette?

Frühstück/Breakfast

Kaffee (mit Sahne/Milch)	coffee (with cream/milk)
koffeinfreier Kaffee	decaffeinated coffee
heiße Schokolade	hot chocolate
Tee (mit Milch/Zitrone)	tea (with milk/lemon)
Rühreier	scrambled eggs
pochierte Eier	poached eggs
Eier mit Speck	bacon and eggs
Spiegeleier	eggs sunny side up
harte/weiche Eier	hard-boiled/soft-boiled eggs
(Käse-/Champignon-)Omelett	(cheese/mushroom) omelette
Pfannkuchen	pancake
Brot/Brötchen/Toast	bread/rolls/toast
Butter	butter
Zucker	sugar
Honig	honey
Marmelade/Orangenmarmelade	jam/marmelade
Joghurt	yoghurt
Obst	fruit

Vorspeisen und Suppen/Starters and Soups

Fleischbrühe	broth/consommé
Hühnercremesuppe	cream of chicken soup
Tomatensuppe	cream of tomato soup
gemischter Salat	mixed salad
grüner Salat	green salad
frittierte Zwiebelringe	onion rings
Meeresfrüchtesalat	seafood salad
Garnelen-/Krabbencocktail	shrimp/prawn cocktail
Räucherlachs	smoked salmon
Gemüsesuppe	vegetable soup

Fisch und Meeresfrüchte/Fish and Seafood

Kabeljau	cod
Krebs	crab
Aal	eel
Schellfisch	haddock
Hering	herring
Hummer	lobster
Muscheln/Austern	mussels/oysters
Barsch	perch
Scholle	plaice
Lachs	salmon
Jakobsmuscheln	scallops
Seezunge	sole
Tintenfisch	squid
Forelle	trout
Tunfisch	tuna

Fleisch und Geflügel/Meat and Poultry

gegrillte Schweinerippchen	barbecued spare ribs
Rindfleisch	beef
Hähnchen	chicken
Geflügel	poultry
Kotelett	chop/cutlet
Filetsteak	fillet
(junge) Ente	duck(ling)
Schinkensteak	gammon
Fleischsoße	gravy
Hackfleisch vom Rind	ground beef
gekochter Schinken	ham
Nieren	kidneys
Lamm	lamb

Leber	liver
Schweinefleisch	pork
Würstchen	sausages
Lendenstück vom Rind, Steak	sirloin steak
Truthahn	turkey
Kalbfleisch	veal
Reh oder Hirsch	venison

Nachspeise und Käse/Dessert and Cheese

gedeckter Apfelkuchen	apple pie
Schokoladenplätzchen	brownies
Hüttenkäse	cottage cheese
Sahne	cream
Vanillesoße	custard
Obstsalat	fruit salad
Ziegenkäse	goat's cheese
Eiscreme	ice cream
Gebäck	pastries

Gemüse und Salat/Vegetables and Salad

gebackene Kartoffeln in der Schale	baked potatoes
Pommes frites	french fries
Bratkartoffeln	hash browns
Kartoffelpüree	mashed potatoes
gebackene Bohnen in Tomatensoße	baked beans
Kohl	cabbage
Karotten	carrots
Blumenkohl	cauliflower
Tomaten	tomatoes
Gurke	cucumber
Knoblauch	garlic
Lauch	leek
Kopfsalat	lettuce
Pilze	mushrooms
Zwiebeln	onions
Erbsen	peas
Paprika	peppers
Kürbis	pumpkin
Spinat	spinach
Mais	sweet corn
Maiskolben	corn-on-the-cob

Obst/Fruit

Äpfel	apples	Birnen	pears
Aprikosen	apricots	Orange	orange
Brombeeren	blackberries	Pfirsiche	peaches
Kirschen	cherries	Ananas	pineapple
Weintrauben	grapes	Pflaumen	plums
Grapefruit	grapefruit	Himbeeren	raspberries
Zitrone	lemon	Erdbeeren	strawberries
Preiselbeeren	cranberries		

Getränke/Beverages

Bier (vom Fass)	beer (on tap)
Apfelwein	cider
Rotwein/Weißwein	red wine/white wine
trocken/lieblich	dry/sweet
Sekt, Schaumwein	sparkling wine
alkoholfreie Getränke	soft drinks
Fruchtsaft	fruit juice
gesüßter Zitronensaft	lemonade
Milch	milk
Mineralwasser	mineral water/spring water

Literature

Novels and journalism

Alfred Döblin: Berlin Alexanderplatz: The Story of Franz Biberkopf. Continuum International Publishing Group Ltd. (2004). In the Berlin of the 1920s Franz Biberkopf tries to re-enter normal life after a spell in gaol and fails, not least because of the city itself.

Joseph Roth: What I Saw: Reports from Berlin 1920-33. Granta Books (2004). Novelist Roth (The Radetzky March) describes both the exciting cosmopolitanism and the sinister cruelty of Berlin in the early years of the Weimar republic.

Theodor Fontane: Delusions, Confusions and the Poggenpuhl Family. Continuum International Publishing Group Ltd. (1997). Story of an illicit and doomed love affair in imperial Berlin.

Anna Funder: Stasiland: Stories from Behind the Berlin Wall. Granta Books 2004. A brilliant and sometimes amusing account of life under a dictatorship. London's Evening Standard made it a book of the year.

Judith Hermann: The Summer House, Latery. Flamingo 2002. Set principally in Germany's modern capital, Hermann's short stories revolve around the contemporary concerns of thirty-something Berliners.

Antony Beevor: Berlin: The Downfall 1945. Penguin 2007. Antony Beevor's brilliant account of the fall of the Third Reich.

Helga Schneider: The Bonfire of Berlin: A Lost Childhood in Wartime Germany. Vintage 2006. Schneider gives a shocking account of the horrors of wartime Berlin, which she experienced as a child abandoned by her parents.

History

Anonymous; Philip Boehm (Translator): A Woman in Berlin: Diary 20 April 1945 to 22 June 1945. Virago Press Ltd 2006. First-hand account of the events in Berlin immediately after the end of the War, when the Russians moved in, written from a woman's point of view. Sometimes harrowing, very popular with the critics.

Paul Kohl: 111 Places in Berlin on the Trails of the Nazis. Emons Verlag 2014. An easy-to-read and informative guide to what happened where in the Nazi years, with modern and historical photos.

Peter Millar: The Berlin Wall: My Part in Its Downfall. Arcadia Books 2009. A light-hearted but well-informed account by a British journalist who was stationed in East Berlin.

Frederick Taylor: The Berlin Wall: 13 August 1961 - 9 November 1989. Bloomsbury Publishing PLC 2007. The story of the post-war political conflict which was symbolized by the Wall; a mix of history, archive research and personal accounts.

Michael S. Cullen: The Reichstag: German parliament between monarchy and federalism. Bebra/VAH, Berlin 1999. The most detailed book about the building by far, including its varied history, the spectacular art project that wrapped it up in 1995 and its rebuilding for the new German parliament.

Lost Property

Zentrales Fundbüro
(central lost property office)
Platz der Luftbrücke 6
D-12101 Berlin
Tel. 030 902 773101

Berliner Verkehrsbetriebe
(public transport authority)
Potsdamer Str. 182, tel. 030 25 62 30 40

Deutsche Bahn AG
Enquire about lost property at the »ServicePoints« in the stations or call the Lost Property hotline: tel. (0900) 199 05 99

Media

Newspapers Several major newspapers are published in Berlin. The range covers taz and Neues Deutschland on the alternative or left wing to the tabloid BZ. Between the two poles are papers like Tagesspiegel, Berliner Zeitung, the Welt and the Berliner Morgenpost.

City magazines The two city and events magazines zitty and tip both appear fortnightly while Berlin-Programm comes out once a month.

English-language newspapers British and American newspapers can be purchased at any of the main stations or the International Presse newsagents. Kiosks in areas especially frequented by tourists, such as Checkpoint Charlie and the Europa Center, are also good places to find English language press. The British Bookshop is excellent for British and London newspapers while bookshops like Hugendubel and Dussman also stock international titles.

Berlin-based monthly in English The Exberliner (www.exberliner.com) is an English-language monthly magazine with articles, commentaries, reviews and a what's-on guide, as well as classified ads.

WiFi WiFi is available in many places, for example in the Sony-Center on Potsdamer Platz, Café St. Oberholz on Rosenthaler Platz (Mitte), the Espressolounge at Bergmannstr. 92 in Kreuzberg and Café Tasso at Frankfurter Allee 11 (Friedrichshain).
At the numerous Bluespot terminals at transport stops and advertising hoardings (e.g. Unter den Linden, Ernst-Reuter-Platz, Potsdamer Platz, Friedrichstrasse, Brandenburger Tor, Alexanderplatz) it is possible to surf and read emails.

Money

Since 2002 the euro has been the official currency of Germany.

Euro

Citizens of EU members countries may import to and export from Germany unlimited amounts in euros.

Currency regulations

At Schönefeld Airport (in Terminal A) and Tegel (on the main concourse) there are various banks and bureaux de change with long opening hours.
Cash dispensers operated by various banks are dotted all over the city and money can be obtained without problems round the clock by using credit and debit cards with a PIN. **Loss of a card** must be reported immediately.

Bureaux de change and cash dispensers

Most international credit cards are accepted by hotels, restaurants, car rentals and many shops. Credit cards have limits.

Credit cards

CONTACT DETAILS FOR CREDIT CARDS

In the event of lost bank or credit cards you can contact the following numbers in UK and USA (phone numbers when dialling from Germany):

Eurocard/MasterCard
Tel. 001/636 7227 111

Visa
Tel. 001/410 581 336

American Express UK
Tel. 0044/1273 696 933

American Express USA
Tel. 001/800 528 4800

Diners Club UK
Tel. 0044/1252 513 500

Diners Club USA
Tel. 001/303 799 9000

Have the bank sort code, account number and card number as well as the expiry date ready.

The following numbers of UK banks (dialling from Germany) can be used to report and stop lost or stolen bank and credit cards issued by those banks:

HSBC
Tel. 0044/1442 422 929

Barclaycard
Tel. 0044/1604 230 230

NatWest
Tel. 0044/142 370 0545

Lloyds TSB
Tel. 0044/1702 278 270

EXCHANGE RATES
1 € = 1.24 US$
1 US$ = 0.81 €
1 £ = 1.28 €
1 € = 0.78 £

Loss of bank cards and credit cards

If bank cards or cheque and credit cards should get lost, you should call your own bank or credit card organization to make sure they are immediately stopped. It is a good idea to make a note of the telephone number on the back of the card.

Post and Communications

Post

Post offices tend to be open 9am – 6pm Mon – Fri, 9am – 1pm Sat (closed Sun). **Postage stamps** for letters up to 20g / 0.7oz within Germany cost €0.62, to other countries €0.75. Postcards are cheaper only within Germany (€0.45), the same price as letters internationally.

Telephone

Public telephones accept coins (€0.10, 0.20, 0.50), credit cards and/ or Deutsche Telekom phonecards, available from post offices and newsagents. International calling cards offer more competitive rates (www.comfi.com). A large number of call shops or »Telefon-Cafés« offer cheap rates for calls abroad. The German **mobile networks** function with providers such as T-Mobile, Vodafone, E-Plus, Base and O2. It is worth checking on roaming tariffs before you leave.

DIALLING CODES
Dialling codes to Berlin
from Germany: tel. 030
from the UK and Republic of Ireland: tel. 00 49 30
from the USA, Canada and Australia: tel. 00 11 49 30
It is not necessary to dial the 030 area code for local calls within Berlin.

Dialling codes from Berlin
to the UK: tel. 00 44
to the Rep. of Ireland: tel. 00 353
to the USA and Canada: tel. 00 1

to Australia: tel. 00 61
The 0 that precedes the subsequent local area code is omitted.

DIRECTORY ENQUIRIES
National
Tel. 11 833

International
Tel. 11 834

Enquiries in English
Tel. 11 837

Prices and Discounts

WelcomeCard

A WelcomeCard allows you to travel free on all buses and trains as well as offering discounts of up to 50% at more than 200 places of interest for tourists, such as museums, theatres, city tours, bars, pubs,

restaurants, and sights. Cards are valid for either 48 hours (18.50 €
for one person), 72 hours (25.50 €) or five days (32.50 €) and apply to
the inner Berlin fare zone (zones AB). Other tickets are valid for one
person with up to three children, or for Berlin and Potsdam (zones
ABC). Cards are available online (www.visitberlin.de/welcomecard)
at Infostores, in hotels, at airports, service counters of public transport concerns (►Public Transport) and their ticket machines or from
Potsdam Information (►In-formation).

This is a card valid for for three days costing 24 € and allowing entry   Museums-
to about 50 museums, including those run by the Staatliche Museen   pass Berlin
Berlin. They are available only from tourist offices or online (►Infor-
mation).

Time

Berlin is in the central European time zone (CET), one hour ahead
of Greenwich Mean Time. For the summer months from the end of
March to the end of October European summer time is used
(CEST = CET+1 hour).

Transport

The various transport companies serving Berlin and its environs have   See back flap
been merged into the Verkehrsgemeinschaft Berlin-Brandenburg   for network
(VBB). The main carriers of passengers are the S-Bahn, U-Bahn,
trams and buses.

There are three fare zones: A is the innermost part of Berlin, en-   Fare zones
closed by the S-Bahn (local train) ring of tracks. Zone B ends at the
city limits of Berlin, while zone C includes the regions thereabouts.
Normally an AB ticket will suffice for visitors to Berlin; but Schönefeld Airport is in zone C.

Individual tickets and period tickets are available from most U-Bahn   Ticket sales
and S-Bahn stations, from ticket machines, on buses and trams, in
tobacconists and drug stores.

Ordinary tickets are valid for two hours and only in one direction of   Tickets
travel (i.e. not valid for the return journey). Anyone making a journey of 3 stations or less on the S-Bahn or up to six stations on the U-
Bahn or stops on the bus can buy a short journey ticket or »Kur-

BVG
VBB
Hardenbergplatz 2
Tel. 25 41 4141
www.vbbonline.de

Price and route information
Tel. 030 1 94 49 (24-hour service))
www.bvg.de
Pavilion at Bahnhof Zoo
Hardenbergplatz
6am – 10pm

Customer centres
at Alexanderplatz: Mon–Fri
6.30am – 9.30pm, Sat and Sun
11am – 6.30 pm

S-Bahn Berlin
Tel. 030 29 74 33 33
www.s-bahn-berlin.de

CYCLE HIRE
ADFC (German cycle club)
Brunnenstr. 28
D-10119 Berlin
Tel. 4 48 47 24
www.adfc-berlin.de

DB Callabike
Available at many places in the city, to
register tel. 07000 5 22 55 22 or
www.callabike-interaktiv.de

Fahrradstation
(www.fahrradstation.de)
Leipziger Str. 56 (Mitte)
Tel. 030 66 64 91 80
Branches: Auguststr. 29 (Mitte)
Tel. 030 22 50 80 70
Bergmannstr. 9 (Kreuzberg)
Tel. 030 2 15 15 66
Dorotheenstr. 30 (Mitte)
Tel. 030 28 38 48 48

The S-Bahn trains must be something special if even the Queen uses them

Goethestr. 46 (Charlottenburg)
Tel. 030 93 95 27 57
Kollwitzstr. 56 (Prenzl. Berg)
Tel. 030 93 95 81 30

AUTOMOBILE CLUBS/ BREAKDOWN SERVICE
ADAC
Bundesallee 29/30
D-10717 Berlin
Tel. 030 86 86-0
Taubenstr. 20–22
Tel. 030 20 39 37 0
ADAC Information Service
Tel. (0 18 05) 10 11 12
Breakdown service:
Tel. *0180 2 22 22 22
www.adac.de

ACE
Märkisches Ufer 28
Tel. 030 27 87 25-0
Breakdown service: tel. *01802 34 35 36
www.ace-online.de

AvD
Friedrichstr. 204
D-10117 Berlin
Tel. 030 22 48 73 73
Breakdown service:
Tel. *0800 9 90 99 09
www.avd.de

VCD
Rudi-Dutschke-Straße 9
Tel. 030 28 03 51-0
www.vcd.org/berlin

TAXI SERVICES
Cityfunk
Tel. 030 21 02 02

QualityTaxi
Tel. 030 26 0 00

Taxi Berlin
Tel. 030 20 20 20

Taxi Funk
Tel. 030 44 33 32

WBT
Tel. 030 26 10 26

Würfelfunk
Tel. 030 21 01 01

---

zstreckenkarte«. Children travel free until their 7th birthday while between the ages of 7 and 14 they travel at a discount rate. **Period tickets** There are tickets valid for 1 day, tourist offers for 48 and 72 hours as well as a transferrable ticket called an »Umweltkarte« (environment ticket), which is valid for one month.

R-Bahn A total of 26 lines are operated by the DB as R-Bahn services along with 8 RegionalExpress lines that connect Berlin with outlying towns in Brandenburg.

S-Bahn 15 S-Bahn (local train) lines serve the city, some of them running 24 hours.

U-Bahn Ten U-Bahn (underground train) lines operate on working days between 4am in the morning and 2am at night. At the weekends (Fri–

Sun) they run around the clock (except for the U 4 service where there is a night bus replacement). Some U-Bahn stations have been beautifully restored. Among the nicest are the Art Nouveau stop at Wittenbergplatz (U 1, U 2, U 15) and the stations at Hausvogteiplatz, Märkisches Museum (U 2) and Brandenburger Tor (U 55).

Buses and trams

Trams run almost exclusively in the eastern part of Berlin. Countless bus services serve areas where no rail or tram access is available. The Zentrale Omnibusbahnhof, the central bus station for long-distance coaches, is located near the Funkturm, Messedamm 19. **Metro lines** Most of the major routes with no U-bahn or S-Bahn link are served by trams and buses under the Metro banner that run for 20 hours a day, seven days a week at regular intervals. Metro line services are indicated by an **»M« in front of the service number**.

Cycle hire

Berlin offers no particular hindrance to cyclists and there are cycle paths alongside all the main roads. There are many cycle hire companies. A list of places from which bikes can be rented is available from the Allgemeiner Deutscher Fahrrad-Club (ADFC) of Berlin. 1700 so-called **Call Bikes** belonging to the Deutsche Bahn railway company are available in the city. They can be rented by telephone (phone number on the wheels). Payment is made by means of a credit card – no cash is needed.

Car rental

Branches of the major car rental companies are mostly found at the airports (▶Airports) and there are some at the Hauptbahnhof and Ostbahnhof. Apart from the major firms, there is of course a wide range of smaller rental companies.

Travellers with Disabilities

SUPPORT SERVICES IN BERLIN
Berliner Behindertenverband (disa-bled society)
Jägerstr. 63 D, D-10117 Berlin
Tel. 030 2 04 38 47
www.bbv-ev.de

Mobidat
Tel. 030 74 77 71 15, www.mobidat.net
Information about assistance on public transport and details of accessibility of restaurants, shopping centres, theatres, cinemas and many other venues; rescue service for broken wheelchairs.

Museums
Many Berlin museums organize tours for wheelchair users, the blind and visually impaired, the deaf and hard of hearing. For information see www.museumspor-tal-berlin.de/besucherinfo

Weights and Measures

The metric system is used in Germany. Visitors should keep in mind that a comma is used for decimals (2,5 not 2.5) and a point indicates thousands (2.500 instead of 2,500).

IMPERIAL/ METRIC MEASURES

1 inch = 2.54 centimetres	1 centimetre = 0.39 inches
1 foot = 0.3 metres	1 metre = 3.3 feet
1 mile = 1.61 kilometres	1 kilometre = 0.62 miles
1 kilogram = 2.2 pounds	1 pound = 0.45 kilograms
1 gallon = 4.54 litres	1 litre = 0.22 gallons

When to Go

There is always something going on in a city like Berlin. Those who choose to visit in winter should be aware that temperatures are likely to hover just above or below freezing. In spring it is worth planning a trip to the Baumblüte (tree blossom festival) festival in Werder, 12km/8mi west of Potsdam: Erich Kästner once wrote that »Berlin's spring took place in Werder«. Summer is of course the season of open-air festivals and drinking in beer gardens, for which there are plenty of opportunities in Berlin.

Index

9 November 1985 **37**
17 June 1953 **31**

A

Abgusssammlung antiker Plastik **124**
accommodation **64**
Adass Jisroel **304**
Admiralspalast **197**
Ägyptisches Museum **259**
airlines **371**
Akademie der Künste **47, 171**
Alexanderhaus **163**
Alexanderplatz **162**
Alliierten-Museum **163**
Alte Bibliothek **336**
Alte Nationalgalerie **260**
Alter Jüdischer Friedhof **178**
Alter Markt **347**
Alter St. Matthäus-Kirchhof **177**
Altes Palais **336**
Altes Rathaus **350**
Altes Stadthaus **270**
Alt-Köpenick **164**
Alt-Marzahn **247**
Anhalter Bahnhof **326**
Anna-Seghers-Gedenkstätte **126**
Anne Frank Zentrum **119**
Antikensammlung **258, 261**
Anti-Kriegs-Museum **119**
Aquadom **167**
Arboretum at the Humboldt University in Berlin **128**
Archenhold Sternenwarte **329**
arrival **370**

art history **41**
Ascanians **23**
assistance for the disabled **392**
ATM machines **387**
Auswärtiges Amt **296**
automobile clubs **391**
Avus **21**
Axel-Springer Tower **201**

B

Badeschiff **195**
Baeck, Leo **304**
Bahnhof Friedrichstrasse **197**
Bahnhof Grunewald **214**
Bahnhof Zoo **237**
ballet **85**
baroque **42**
bars **80**
Base Flyer **163**
basketball **91**
Bauakademie **334**
Bauhaus Archive Berlin **118**
Bear pit **246**
beer **94**
before the journey **370**
Bendlerblock **206**
Bergmannstraße **224**
Berlin Airlift monument **309**
Berliner Abgeordnetenhaus **326**
Berliner Dom **166**
Berliner Ensemble **198**
Berliner Gruselkabinett **327**
Berliner Medizinhistorisches Museum **199**
Berliner Rathaus **293**
Berliner Ring **21**

Berliner S-Bahn Museum **128**
Berliner Stadtschloss **294**
Berliner U-Bahn Museum **128**
Berliner Unterwelten-Museum **130**
Berlinische Galerie **219**
Berlin Museum of Medical History **199**
Berlin state **14**
Bernauer Strasse **201**
Berolina **162**
Berolinahaus **163**
Bikini Berlin **238**
Bildergalerie **357**
Blindenmuseum **130**
Bode-Museum **263**
Bode, Wilhelm von **254**
Böhmisches Dorf (Bohemian village) **265**
Bölschestrasse **249**
Botanischer Garten (Botanical gardens) **184**
Botanisches Museum (Botanical Museum) **185**
Boulevard der Stars **287**
Brandenburger Tor **168**
Brandt, Willy **51**
breakdown service **391**
breakfast **94**
Brecht, Bertolt **52**
Brecht-Weigel-Gedenkstätte **127**
British embassy **171**
Britz **265**
Britzer Dorfkirche **265**
Britzer Garten **266**
Britzer Mühle **266**
Britz, Schloss **265**
Bröhan Museum **252**

Brücke Museum **215**
Brunnen der Völker-
  freundschaft **163**
Buchstabenmuseum **130**
Buckower Dorfkirche **266**
Bundeskanzleramt **280**
Bundespresseamt **281**
Bundespressekonferenz
  281
Bundesrat **240**
Bundestag **274**
buses **392**
by bus to Berlin **370**
by car to Berlin **370**
by train to Berlin **370**

C
cabaret **86**
Café Kranzler **238**
calendar of events **89**
call shops **388**
Captain of Köpenick **164**
car documents **372**
car rental **392**
cash dispensers **387**
cemeteries **172**
Centrum Judaicum **304**
Charité **199**
Charlottenburg, Schloss
  180
Checkpoint Charlie **200**
children in Berlin **72**
Christo **275**
cinema **78**
city history **22**
city magazines **386**
Clärchens Ballhaus **306**
classicism **43**
comedy **86**
Comenius Garten **265**
communications **388**
Communs **363**
Computerspielemuseum
  128
concerts **82, 85**
credit cards **387**

cross-Channel ferry ser-
  vice **370**
currency regulations **387**
Currywurst **96**
Currywurstmuseum **200**
customs **374**
customs regulations **372**
cycle hire **390, 392**

D
Dahlem **184**
Dahlem-Dorf U-Bahn
  station **185**
Dahlem museums **186**
Daimler Contemporary
  287
Dali – Die Ausstellung
  240
dancing **78**
Das Stille Museum **126**
Das Verborgene Museum
  126
DDR-Motorradmuseum
  127
Deutsch-Deutsches
  Museum **212**
Deutscher Dom **211**
Deutsches Fußballmuse-
  um **131**
Deutsches Historisches
  Museum **333**
Deutsche Staatsoper
  Unter den Linden **335**
Deutsches Technikmu-
  seum **188**
Deutsches Theater **199**
dialling codes **388**
Dietrich, Marlene **52**
discounts **388**
Distel cabaret **197**
districts **14**
Domäne Dahlem **185**
Dom Aquarée **167**
Dreifaltigkeitskirchhof
  174, 175
drinks **92**

Dunckerstrasse **291**
Dutschke, Rudi **53**
DZ Bank **171**

E
East Side Gallery **194**
economy **13**
Eierkühlhaus **195**
electricity **373**
emergency numbers
  373
English-language news-
  papers **386**
entertainment **76**
Ephraim Palais **269**
Equestrian statue of
  Frederick the Great
  337
Erinnerungsstätte Not-
  aufnahmelager Ma-
  rienfelde **119**
Ermelerhaus **244**
Ernst-Thälmann-Park
  292
Erotik-Museum Beate
  Uhse **131**
Ethnologisches Museum
  187
etiquette **374**
euro **387**
Europa-Center **237**
events **88**
exchange rates **387**
exhibition grounds **189**

F
fare zones **389**
Fasanenstrasse **238**
Fernsehturm **190**
festivals **88**
Feuerwehrmuseum **128**
film **48**
Filmmuseum Berlin **288**
Fischerinsel **246**
Fischerkietz **165**
Flick Collection **217**

Flughafen Otto Lilienthal
 307
Flugplatz Gatow **299**
Fontane, Theodor **53**
food **92**
football **91**
Former Staatsrat build-
 ing **296**
Forschungs- und
 Gedenkstätte Norman-
 nenstrasse **241**
Fort Hahneberg **301**
Forum Willy Brandt **122**
Franziskanerkloster-
 kirche (Franciscan mon-
 astery church) **271**
Französische Kirche **352**
Französischer Dom **210**
Französischer Friedhof
 (Hugenottenfriedhof)
 173
Frederician Rococo **42**
Freiheits- und Einheits-
 denkmal **295**
Friedhof der Doro-
 theenstädtischen und
 Friedrichswerderschen
 Gemeinde **172**
Friedhof der März-
 gefallenen **195**
Friedhof Heerstrasse **176**
Friedhof Nikolassee **178**
Friedhof Stubenrauch-
 strasse **177**
Friedrich I **25**
Friedrich II **25, 54, 166**
Friedrich III **27**
Friedrichsfelde zoo **316**
Friedrichshagen **249**
Friedrichshagen water-
 works **250**
Friedrichshain **191**
Friedrichstadtpalast **198**
Friedrichstrasse **196**
Friedrichstrasse station
 197

Friedrichswerdersche
 Kirche **334**
Friedrich Wilhelm **24**
Friedrich Wilhelm I **25**
Funkturm **189, 190**

G

Galeries Lafayette **200**
Galgenhaus **296**
galleries **116, 118**
Gärten der Welt **247**
Garten des wiedergewon-
 nenen Mondes **248**
Gas Lamp Museum **311**
Gedenkstätte Berlin-Ho-
 henschönhausen **122**
Gedenkstätte Deutscher
 Widerstand **206**
Gedenkstätte Köpe-
 nicker Blutwoche Juni
 1933 **122**
Gedenkstätte Plötzen-
 see **207**
Gemäldegalerie **228,
 264**
Gendarmenmarkt **208**
Georg Kolbe Museum
 125
Gerichtslaube **269**
Gertraudenbrücke **241**
Gethsemane-Kirche **291**
Glienicke, Jagdschloss
 213
Glienicker Brücke **211**
Glienicke, Schloss **211**
Goebbels, Joseph **29**
Goethe Monument **311**
Gotisches Haus **298**
Grave of Frederick the
 Great **356**
Gropius, Walter **44**
Grosse Hamburger
 Strasse **304**
Grosser Stern **311**
Grünauer Wassersport-
 museum **131**

Gründerzeitmuseum
 Mahlsdorf **249**
Grunewaldturm **216**
guides **140**
Gutshaus Dahlem **186**
Gutshaus Steglitz **125**

H

Hackesche Höfe **305**
Hain der Kosmonauten
 329
Hamburger Bahnhof
 217
Hanfmuseum **269**
Hauptbahnhof **21, 281,
 370**
Haus am Waldsee **125**
Haus der Demokratie
 199
Haus der Kulturen der
 Welt **315**
Haus der Schweiz **338**
Haus des Rundfunks **190**
Haus Liebermann **171**
Haus Sommer **171**
health **375**
health insurance **373**
Heckmann-Höfe **304**
Heinrich-Zille Museum
 268
Hellersdorf **247**
Helmut Newton
 Foundation **238**
Hippodrome **364**
Historicism **43**
Historischer Hafen Berlin
 245
Hitler, Adolf **29**
Hoffmann collection **305**
Hoffmann, E.T.A. **54**
Hofgärtnermuseum **213**
Hohenzollern crypt **167**
Holocaust Memorial
 171
Hotel Adlon **171**
hotels **65**

Hufeisensiedlung **265**
Hugenottenmuseum **210**
Humboldt, Alexander von **55**
Humboldt, Wilhelm von **55**
Humboldt Forum **295**
Humboldtschlösschen **307**
Humboldt University **337**
Hungerkralle **309**
Husemannstrasse **291**

I
ICC **189, 190**
ice hockey **91**
Iduna-Haus **236**
immigrants **13**
industry **15**
information **375**
Insel der Jugend **328**
International Congress Centre **190**
internet **376**
Invalidenfriedhof **174**

J
Jagdschloss Grunewald **214**
Jagdzeugmagazin **215**
Jahn, Friedrich Ludwig **56, 265**
Jakob-Kaiser-Haus **281**
Jüdischer Friedhof Heerstrasse **180**
Jüdischer Friedhof Schönhauser Allee **179**
Jüdischer Friedhof Weissensee **180**
Jüdisches Gemeindehaus **238**
Jüdisches Museum **218**
Jungfernbrücke **246, 296**

K
KaDeWe **220**
Kaisersaal **288**
Kaiser-Wilhelm-Gedächtniskirche **237**
Kantdreieck **239**
Kantstrasse **239**
Kapelle der Versöhnung **206**
Karl-Marx-Allee **194**
Kastanienalle **290**
Kastanienwäldchen **334**
Käthe-Kollwitz Museum **238**
Katte, Hans Hermann von **166**
Kaufhaus des Westens **220**
Kennedy, John F. **36, 294**
Keramik-Museum Berlin **125**
Kleist's grave **341**
Knef, Hildegard **56**
Knobelsdorff, Georg Wenzeslaus von **42**
Knoblauchhaus **269**
Kollegienhaus **219**
Köllnischer Park **246**
Kollwitz, Käthe **57, 291**
Kollwitzplatz **291**
Kommandantenhaus **334**
Kongresshalle **315**
Königliche Porzellan-Manufaktur **315**
Konnopke **290**
Konzerthaus Berlin **209**
Köpenick **164**
Köpenicker Heimat- und Fischereimuseum **165**
Köpenick, Schloss **165**
KPM **315**
Kreuzberg **220**
Kronprinzenpalais **334**
Kulturforum **227**
Kulturzentrum Pfefferberg **289**

Kunckel, Johann **282**
Kunstbibliothek **231**
Kunstgewerbemuseum **166, 231**
Kunst-Werke Berlin **306**
Kupferstichkabinett **231**
Kurfürstendamm **235**
Kurfürstendamm-Karree **239**

L
Landwehrkanal **225**
Langhans, Carl Gotthard **43**
language **377**
Lasalle, Ferdinand **27**
Lessinghaus **268**
Lichtenberg **241**
Liebermann, Max **46, 57**
Liebermann Villa **340**
Liebknecht, Karl **28, 311**
Lincke, Paul **57**
Lindencorso **199, 338**
literature **49, 384**
Literaturhaus Berlin **238**
lost property **386**
Ludwig-Erhard-Haus **239**
Lübars **159**
Luftwaffenmuseum **299**
Lustgarten **167**
Luther statue **244**
Lutter & Wegner **209**
Luxemburg, Rosa **28, 311**

M
Madame Tussaud's **339**
magazines **386**
Maifeld **272**
mains grid **373**
Märchenbrunnen **195**
March Revolution **26**
Mariannenplatz **226**
Maria Regina Martyrum **208**
Marie-Elisabeth-Lüders-Haus **281**

Marienkirche 243
Märkisches Museum 244, 245
Märkisches Ufer 244
Marlene-Dietrich-Platz 287
Martin-Gropius-Bau 322
Marx-Engels Forum 293
Marzahn 247
Mauerpark 290
Maxim-Gorki Theater 334
measures 393
media 386
medical help 375
Mehringplatz 226
Memorial to the burning of books 336
Mendelssohn, Moses 304
Mendelssohn-Remise 123
Menzel, Adolph 44, 58
Metropol theatre 197
Mies van der Rohe, Ludwig 44
Miniature world of Loxx 163
centre Museum am Gesundbrunnen 130
Molkenmarkt 270
money 387
Monument to Friedrich Wilhelm III 311
Monument to Queen Luise 311
Mori-Ogai-Gedenkstätte 127
Mounted statue of the Great Elector 182
Müggelberge 250
Müggelsee 249
Müggelturm 250
Münzkabinett 264
Museum Berggruen 251

Museum Berlin-Karlshorst 242
Museum Charlottenburg- Wilmersdorf 129
Museum der Dinge 118
Museum der unerhörten Dinge (Museum of Unheard-of Things) 130
Museum Europäischer Kulturen 186
Museum for Marzahn-Hellersdorf 247
Museum für Asiatische Kunst 186
Museum für Byzantinische Kunst 264
Museum für Fotografie 238
Museum für Gegenwart 217
Museum für Islamische Kunst 263
Museum für Kommunikation Berlin 240
Museum für Naturkunde 252
Museum Haus am Checkpoint Charlie 200
Museum im Wasserwerk 250
Museum Island 254
museums 116
Museumsdorf Düppel 123
Museumsinsel 254
Museum Spandovia Sacra 298
Museumspass Berlin 389
music 48, 78, 82
Musikinstrumenten Museum 234

N
Nefertiti 259
Neptunbrunnen 293

Neue Nationalgalerie 234
Neues Kranzler Eck 238
Neues Museum 258
Neue Synagoge 304
Neue Wache 333
Neukölln 264
Neuss, Wolfgang 58
Newspaper district 201
newspapers 386
Nikolaikirche 267, 350
Nikolaiviertel 266
Nikolskoe 213
Nolde Stiftung Seebüll 126
Nordbahnhof 201

O
Oberbaumbrücke 226
Oberbaum City 195
Ökowerk Berlin 129
Old Fritz 25
Old National Gallery 260
Olympiagelände 271
Olympiastadion 272
opera 85
operetta 85
Oranienburger Strasse 303
Ostbahnhof 194
Otto Weidt's blind workshop 306

P
Palais am Festungsgraben 334
Palast der Republik 294
Pariser Platz 171, 337
Park Kolonnaden 285
Parochialkirche 270
Paul-Lincke-Ufer 225
Paul-Löbe-Haus 281
Pergamonmuseum 261
Peter Behrens building 164

pets **372**
Pfaueninsel **282**
pharmacies **375**
Philharmonie **233**
phonecards **388**
politics **13**
Polizeihistorische
  Sammlung **123**
population **13**
post **388**
postage **388**
Postfuhramt **303**
Poststrasse **269**
Potsdam 344
 -Alexandrowka **364**
 -Alter Markt **347**
 -Altes Rathaus **350**
 -Antikentempel **363**
 -Babelsberg **365**
 -Babelsberg Park **365**
 -Bassinplatz **352**
 -Belvedere on
   Klausberg Hill **362**
 -Bildergalerie **357**
 -Biosphäre Potsdam
   367
 -Brandenburger Strasse
   351
 -Breite Strasse **350**
 -Charlottenhof Park
   364
 -Chinesisches Haus **359**
 -Drachenhaus **362**
 -Einsteinturm **366**
 -Entführungsrondell
   359
 -Filmmuseum **350**
 -Flatowturm **366**
 -Französische Kirche
   352
 -Freundschaftstempel
   363
 -Friedenskirche **358**
 -Garnisonkirche **350**
 -Glockenfontäne **359**
 -Grosse Fontäne **359**

 -Haus der Branden-
   burgisch-Preussischen
   Geschichte **352**
 -Hiller-Brandtsche
   houses **351**
 -Holländischer Garten
   357
 -Holländisches Viertel
   352
 -Jan-Bouman-Haus **352**
 -Klausberg hill **362**
 -Krongut Bornstedt **367**
 -Langer Stall **351**
 -Luisenplatz **351**
 -Marlygarten **358**
 -Marstall **350**
 -mosque **351**
 -Musenrondell **359**
 -Museum Alexan-
   drowka **365**
 -Neptungrotte **359**
 -Neue Kammern **357**
 -Neuer Garten **354**
 -Neuer Markt **352**
 -Neues Gouverneurs-
   haus **338**
 -Neues Palais **362**
 -Nikolaikirche **350**
 -Obeliskportal **358**
 -Orangerie **359**
 -Peter-und-Pauls-Kirche
   352
 -Potsdam and 20 July
   1944 **351**
 -Potsdam conference
   355
 -Potsdam Museum **350**
 -Predigerwitwenhaus
   351
 -Römische Bäder **364**
 -Ruinenberg **367**
 -Sanssouci **355**, **356**
 -Sanssouci Windmühle
   358
 -Schloss Babelsberg **365**
 -Schloss Cecilienhof **355**

 -Schloss Charlottenhof
   363
 -Schloss Sanssouci **356**
 -St Alexander Nevski
   365
 -Telegrafenberg **366**
 -Tiefer See **352**
 -Volkspark **367**
 -Yorckstrasse **352**
Potsdamer Platz **284**
Prenzlauer Berg **289**
Preussisches Herrenhaus
  240
prices **388**
Prinz Albrecht area **322**
Prinzessinnengarten **335**
Prinzessinnenpalais **335**
public telephones **388**
pubs **80**
puppet theatre **86**

Q
Quartier 205 **200**
Quartier 206 **200**
Quartier Daimler **287**
Quasimodo **239**

R
railway stations **371**
Ranke, Leopold von **305**
Rathaus **292**
Rathaus Schöneberg **294**
Rauch, Christian Dan-
  iel **43**
R-Bahn **391**
Reichsluftfahrtministe-
  rium **240**
Reichsmünze **270**
Reichstag building **274**
Reichstag fire **274**
remnants of city wall
  270
renaissance **41**
restaurants **101**
Reuter, Ernst **59**
Ribbeckhaus **296**

Riehmers Hofgarten 224
Romanticism 43
Rosenthal, Hans 59
Rotes Rathaus 293
Rotkreuz-Museum Berlin 123
Royal Porcelain Factory 315
Russian embassy 339
Russisches Haus 199

S
Sankt-Hedwigs-Kathedrale 336
Savignyplatz 239
S-Bahn 391
Schadow, Gottfried 43
Scharoun, Hans 44
Schauspielhaus 209
Scheidemann, Philipp 28
Scheringianum 129
Scheunenviertel 302
Schiffbauerdamm 198
Schillerdenkmal (Schiller memorial) 209
Schinkel, Karl Friedrich 43
Schinkelmuseum 334
Schinkel Pavillon 183
Schinkelplatz 334
Schleuse Spandau 301
Schlossbrücke 330
Schloss Friedrichsfelde 321
Schloss Köpenick 165
Schlossplatz 294
Schlüter, Andreas 42
Schöneberg City Hall 294
Schönhausen, Schloss 297
Schönhauser Allee 289
Schwules Museum 131
sculpture boulevard 236
Sealife 167
Segenskirche 289

Senefelder, Alois 289
shopping 132
shows 86
Siegessäule 311
Socialist Memorial 176
Sophie-Gips-Höfe 305
Sophienfriedhof 206
Sophienkirche 305
Sophiensäle 305
Sophienstrasse 305
Soviet memorial (Tiergarten) 315
Soviet monument (Treptow) 328
Spandau 297
Spandauer Vorstadt 302
spectator sport 91
Spielbank Berlin 287
Spittelkolonnaden 241
Spittelmarkt 241
Sportmuseum Berlin 131
Spreedreieck 197
Staatsbibliothek zu Berlin 234, 337
Staatsoper Unter den Linden 335
Stadtbibliothek 296
Stadtgeschichte 23
Stadtschloss 295
Stalinallee 194
Stasi headquarters 241
Stasi Museum 242
Stasi – The Exhibition 122
St. Annenkirche 186
St.-Matthäus-Kirche 228
Strandbad Müggelsee 250
Südwestfriedhof 178
sweet factory 304
Swiss embassy 280

T
Tacheles 303
Taut, Bruno 265
taxi services 391

Tegel 307
Tegel Airport 307
Tegel, Schloss 307
telephone 388
Tempelhof Airport 308
Tempodrom 327
Teufelsberg 215
Teufelssee 250
Theater des Westens 239
theatre 82
The Kennedys 124
tickets 82, 389
Tiergarten 310
Tierpark Friedrichsfelde 316
time 389
tipping advice 375
tours 140, 145
trams 392
Tränenpalast 197
transport 21, 389
travel documents 372
travel insurance 373
travellers with disabilities 392
Treptower Park 327
Tucholsky, Kurt 60
Tucholskystrasse 303
typical dishes 98

U
U-Bahn 391
ufa-Fabrik 308
Ulbricht, Walter 32
Ullsteinhaus 308
Unter den Linden 329

V
venues 85
Viktoriapark 224
Villa Grisebach 238
Villa Schöningen 212
Voigt, Wilhelm 60
Volkspark Friedrichshain 195

Volkspark Hasenheide
  264
von Stauffenberg, Claus
  207
Vorderasiatisches
  Museum **263**

W

Wagner, Martin **265**
Waldbühne **272**
Waldfriedhof Dahlem
  177
Waldfriedhof Zehlendorf
  177
Waldmuseum **214**
Waldoff, Claire **61**
Wallot, Paul **43**
Wannsee **339**
Wannsee Conference
  341

Weidendammbrücke
  198
weights **393**
WelcomeCard **388**
Weltzeituhr **163**
Wendenschloss **298**
when to go **393**
Wilhelm-Foerster-Stern-
  warte **129**
Wilhelm I **27**
Wilhelm II **27**
Willy Brandt Founda-
  tion **339**
Willy-Brandt-Haus **226**

Z

Zeiss-Grossplanetarium
  291
Zelter, Carl Friedrich **305**
Zenner **328**

Zentralfriedhof Frie-
  drichsfelde **175**
Zentrum für Berlin-
  Studien **296**
Zeughaus **331**
Zille, Heinrich **46**, **61**
Zitadelle Spandau **299**
Zoologischer Garten **341**
Zoologischer Garten
  station **237**
Zucker-Museum im
  Institut für Lebensmit-
  teltechnologie **129**
Zum Nussbaum **268**
Zur letzten Instanz **270**

List of Maps and Illustrations

Berlin at a glance (Infographic) **16/17**
Four Sectors **33**
Hotels, Cafés, Restaurants & Entertainment in Berlin East **104/105**
Hotels, Cafés, Restaurants & Entertainment in Berlin West **106/107**
Tour 1 and Tour 2 **152/153**
Tour 3 and Tour 4 **154/155**
Tour 5 **157**
Highlights in the Outer Boroughs **159**
Charlottenburg Castle **181**
Fernsehturm **190**
Berlin – From Above and Below (Infographic) **192/193**
The Wall has Gone! (Infographic) **202/203**
The Wall (3D) **204/205**
Multicultural Berlin (Infographic) **222/223**

Kulturforum **227**
Gemäldegalerie **229**
Marienkirche **243**
Museumsinsel (3D) **256/257**
Pergamonmuseum **262**
Nikolai Quarter **268**
More Deputies = More Democracy? (Infographic) **276/277**
Reichstag Building (3D) **278/279**
Pfaueninsel **283**
Zitadelle Spandau **299**
Green Berlin (Infographic) **312/313**
Tierpark Friedrichsfelde **320/321**
Wilhelmstrasse **325**
Zoological Garden **342/343**
Potsdam **348/349**
Schloss Sanssouci **358**
Sanssouci Park and Palace (3D) **362/363**

Photo Credits

Publisher's Information

1st Edition 2015
Worldwide Distribution: Marco Polo
Travel Publishing Ltd
Pinewood, Chineham Business Park
Crockford Lane, Chineham
Basingstoke, Hampshire RG24 8AL,
United Kingdom.

Photos, illlustrations, maps:
142 photos, 31 maps and and
illustrations, one large map
Text:
Rainer Eisenschmid, Gisela Buddée
Editing:
John Sykes
Translation: John Sykes
Cartography:
Franz Huber, Munich; MAIRDUMONT
Ostfildern (large map)
3D illustrations:
jangled nerves, Stuttgart
Infographics:
Golden Section Graphics GmbH, Berlin
Design:
independent Medien-Design, Munich
Editor-in-chief:
Rainer Eisenschmid, Mairdumont
Ostfildern

Printed in China

Despite all of our authors' thorough
research, errors can creep in. The publishers do not accept any liability for thi
Whether you want to praise, alert us to
errors or give us a personal tip Please
contact us by email or post:

MARCO POLO Travel Publishing Ltd
Pinewood, Chineham Business Park
Crockford Lane, Chineham
Basingstoke, Hampshire RG24 8AL
United Kingdom
Email: sales@marcopolouk.com

FSC
www.fsc.org
MIX
Paper from
responsible sources
FSC® C011918

MARCO POLO

HANDBOOKS

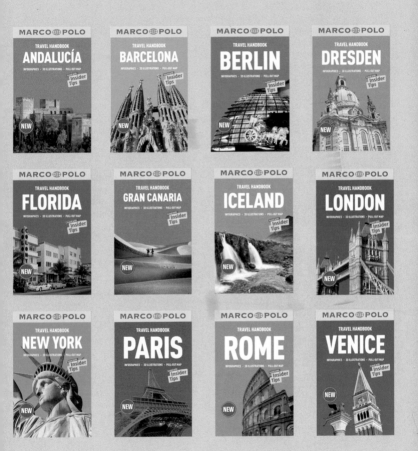

www.marco-polo.com

Berlin Curiosities

Watch your step on the pavement, a wrongly named district, a heavy burden from dark days: strange aspects of Berlin.

►Shit happens
There are thought to be 108,508 dogs in Berlin, producing 55 tons of excrement daily. 2.4 tons are vacuumed up by purpose-built machines on the streets. Where the rest goes is a secret only to those who don't watch where they walk.

►Assassination
An attack by a resident of Kreuzberg brought welcome publicity to Madame Tussaud's in 2008: he ripped the head off the waxwork figure of Hitler. It is now behind glass.

►TV sport
The first-ever TV broadcasts of Olympic Games were aired in 1936. Public TV rooms were installed for the purpose – but only in Berlin, as the transmission signals were weak.

►All or nothing
Following years of curfew during and after the war, in 1949 the head of the hotels and catering association successfully appealed to the Allies to end the restrictions. Since then Berlin has been open for entertainment round the clock.

►Heavy
In order to test whether the ground in Berlin would bear the weight of the gigantic structures of Hitler's planned capital, Germania, Albert Speer ordered construction of a 40,000-ton block of concrete, which now stands on General-Pape-Strasse. It is thought to have sunk by 20cm/8 inches.

►centre is not the middle
The geographical centre of Berlin is on Alexandrinenstrasse in Kreuzberg: 52° 30' 10" north, 13° 24' 15" east.

►Rue de Duosan
The plan was to build residential palaces for workers on Karl-Marx-Allee in the years when it was still called Stalinallee. They had columns, cornices and balustrades, and were clad with tiles made in Meissen. It was not long before the large numbers of tiles fell off, and the avenue got its nickname from a popular East German glue: Duosan.

►Golden Twenties
Billy Wilder earned his money as a dancer in top hat and tails: »I only had one shirt. I didn't wash it, I rubbed it clean with an eraser.«

MARCO ⬤ POLO INSIGHT